Real-World Media Ethics

Real-World Media Ethics
Inside the Broadcast and Entertainment Industries

Philippe Perebinossoff

AMSTERDAM • BOSTON • HEIDELBERG • LONDON
NEW YORK • OXFORD • PARIS • SAN DIEGO
SAN FRANCISCO • SINGAPORE • SYDNEY • TOKYO

Focal Press is an imprint of Elsevier

Acquisitions Editor: Elinor Actipis
Publishing Services Manager: George Morrison
Project Manager: Lianne Hong
Associate Acquisitions Editor: Michele Cronin
Assistant Editor: Robin Weston
Marketing Manager: Christine Degon, Marcel Koppes
Design Direction: Joanne Blank
Cover Design: Riezebos Holzbaur Design Group
Cover Image: Philip Dvorak/Getty Images

Focal Press is an imprint of Elsevier
30 Corporate Drive, Suite 400, Burlington, MA 01803, USA
Linacre House, Jordan Hill, Oxford OX2 8DP, UK

Library of Congress Cataloging-in-Publication Data
Perebinossoff, Philippe.
   Real-world media ethics : inside the broadcast and entertainment industries / by
Philippe Perebinossoff.
      p.   cm.
   Includes bibliographical references and index.
   ISBN-13: 978-0-240-80921-2 (pbk. : alk. paper)   1. Mass media—Moral and ethical
aspects.   I. Title.
   P94.P3825 2008
   174—dc22

                                                                2007043042

British Library Cataloguing-in-Publication Data
A catalogue record for this book is available from the British Library.

ISBN: 978-0-240-809212

For information on all Focal Press publications
visit our website at www.books.elsevier.com

08 09 10 11 12   5 4 3 2 1

Printed in the United States of America

Working together to grow
libraries in developing countries

www.elsevier.com | www.bookaid.org | www.sabre.org

ELSEVIER   BOOK AID International   Sabre Foundation

About the Website

When I undertook to write this text, I wanted to complement it with something that would help illustrate the issues discussed. It was important for me that the book provide something that students and professionals alike could refer to if they wanted to explore a topic more fully. One of the reasons I asked specialists to contribute chapters is because I very much want the text to provide a variety of perspectives. Throughout the text, I refer to available DVDs, websites, and the like, but I also wanted the book itself to provide some additional resources.

I thought about what to do for a long time, and then was lucky enough to speak with Professor Edward J. Fink, chair of the Radio-TV-Film Department at California State University, Fullerton, and he offered to put together some clips that would accompany the text. In essence, these clips would be part of the text itself. Some of the clips we wanted to include were not available or were too expensive to license, even for educational purposes. Nevertheless, we were able to gather key elements for the website. All the elements were selected because of their relevance to the text and because we felt they provided valuable real-life perspectives.

We are very grateful to the individuals who gave of their time to be filmed and who gave us permission to include clips of their work. Professor Fink and I and all the *Focal* editors hope you agree and hope that you find the website additions useful, relevant, and informative.

Website Contents

Deni Elliott, the Poynter Jamison chair in Media Ethics and Press Policy at the University of South Florida on the importance of studying media ethics, (4 minutes)

Producer Ken Kaufman on the ethical issues that confront a producer, (9 minutes, 20 seconds)

California State University student Mike Kroll on *If I Did It*, discussing why people sometimes crave stories with dubious ethical pedigrees, (3 minutes, 48 seconds)

California State University Fullerton Professor Paul Lester on visual and global ethics, (8 minutes, 23 seconds)

Star of *The Donna Reed Show* and founder of A Minor Consideration, Paul Petersen on consequences that result from ethical violations (9 minutes, 16 seconds)

Brett Meyer's six-minute film, *Picture Perfect*, which addresses misplaced values in our society, (8 minutes)

Clips from the telefilm *In the Line of Duty: Ambush in Waco*, executive-produced by Kaufman, that illustrate some of the issues Kaufman raised in his interview, (6 minutes, 26 seconds)

Graduate student Adair Cole's film, *Number 87*, which explores the issue of torture, (9 minutes, 19 seconds)

Contents

ix

CONTENTS

x

xi

CONTENTS

CONTENTS

xv

Acknowledgments

When undertaking the multifaceted task of writing a text on media ethics from a variety of different perspectives, including an emphasis on an industry point of view, it really helps if you have a large number of people willing to assist. I have been particularly fortunate in this regard.

Specifically, four specialists agreed to write key chapters: Carol Ames, who wrote Chapter 12 on ethical issues connected with work in public relations; Jeff Brody, who wrote Chapter 8 about journalistic ethics; Martin P. Carlson, who analyzed some ethical issues that arise in business affairs negotiations in Chapter 2; and Brian Gross who wrote about ethical issues in new media in Chapter 9.

I am also particularly grateful to Mary Ann Watson for the detailed sidebar she wrote for Chapter 4 from a unique perspective as an expert witness about ethical issues related to an episode of *The Jenny Jones Show*. The episode never aired, though parts of it were played in the lawsuit. After the episode was filmed, a male guest who was ambushed by a "secret crush" who turned out to be male resorted to murder in a misguided attempt to ease the pain and humiliation he experienced on the program.

I also thank Bob Saget for his thoughtful foreword to the text. It is a personal pleasure for me to have Bob, who I worked with when I was an executive at ABC Television, be a part of my book.

Very thankful am I also to the large numbers of people who took the time to provide invaluable assistance and support. Had I not been able to meet with and interview these individuals, my book would have a much more limited focus. I am a firm believer that one learns from people practicing in the field, and I am particularly pleased that so many industry professionals were willing to share their views with me. These individuals include Norma Bains, Neil Baldwin, Ilene Amy Berg, Steven M. Blacher, Lin Bolen, David Brownfield, Paul Brownfield, Patricia Bosworth, Olivia Cohen-Cutler, Adair Cole, Dave Collins, Jane Collins, Jon Cowan, David Craig, Vickie Curlis, Lisa Demberg, Deni Eliott, Edward Fink, Tom Fortuna, Allison Fox, John Fox, Paul Gadd, Tom Grasty, Lynne Gross, Linda Haskell, Gary Hoffman, Rick Jones, Ken Kaufman, Mike

ACKNOWLEDGMENTS

Kroll, Phillip Krupp, Paul Lester, Ron McFarland, Paul McGuire, Mitch Metcalf, Brett L. Meyer, Mia Moody, John Morrone, Bill Norton, Michael O'Hara, Michael Ontkean, Judd Parkin: Kathryn Paulsen, Paul Petersen, Judy Pies, Roberta Plutzik, Jonathan Rintels, Rob Rovner, Jeff Sagansky, Howard Schneider, Jule Selbo, George Sher, Wade Sherman, Michael Sluchan, Don Spetner, Ron Taylor, Bill Unger, Larry Ward, and Louis Wiley.

I am also grateful to iStockphoto.com for the use of their stock photos.

I would also like to thank my editors at Focal, Michele Cronin, Lianne Hong, and Elinor Actipis, for their much-appreciated steady support and encouragement. I also want to thank Doug Shults, who has since left Focal, for his help, specifically with clearances. I also wish to thank my previous editor at Focal, Amy Jollymore, who started me on the incredible journey of examining the complex issues associated with media ethics.

I am sure I am omitting some people who also helped, for which I apologize in advance.

Note: Websites and URLs frequently change. We tested the websites that were active when we did our research. We apologize in advance if the websites cited are no longer active and we hope that the information provided will enable you to find any additional research you are seeking.

Foreword

I shoplifted a toy gun when I was younger. Five years ago. No, actually, I was nine years old, which would make the year 1965. I had not made a young career out of stealing, and I knew it was wrong, yet, I didn't have the seven dollars to buy this incredible object of my desire. It was a product of my favorite television show, *The Wild Wild West*—a simulated gold, tiny metal gun that popped out of its fitted belt buckle to fire caps. I hadn't yet started mowing lawns during my summers in Norfolk, Virginia, so I had no cash, and I didn't want to ask my mom for it, as I was certain she wouldn't think it was worth the money. I walked from my house through the back of the neighborhood to King's Department Store, went directly to the toy aisle, grabbed the gun in its plastic-sealed factory casing, shoved it under my jacket, and walked briskly out of the store. This entire exercise was done alone, no accomplice. When I got home, I ripped it out of its packaging, slipped it onto my belt over the existing belt buckle, and started flexing my stomach like James West, making the gun pop out, to shoot any foe that crossed my path. A couple hours later my mom saw me playing in the yard.

"Where'd you get that, Bobby?"

"Uh, I found it." I think subliminally she knew what I'd done but wanted to believe that I was always the good boy that I'd pretended to be.

Truth be known, I was a thief. Small time stuff, but still, ethically, no different than an embezzler. I knew it was wrong. But that didn't stop me from pursuing a few more childhood crimes before I put that part of my career to rest. My last theft had instant karma attached. I stole a fancy retractable pencil off the desk of the third grader next to me. He saw me do it.

"Where'd you get that pencil?"

"It's mine," I told him.

He grabbed it out of my hand and stabbed me in the finger with it. The lead is still visible to this day—my Scarlet Letter of thievery, right there in my right-hand middle finger.

xix

When my friend, Philippe Perebinossoff, asked me to write a foreword to this book and told me it was about ethics, I was honored and frightened. Shoplifting, which I gave up when I was about nine, is probably a lighter crime than other things I've done. But those things don't seem to haunt me to this day. Who among us has not done something unethical? I've always been fascinated by where we draw the line on ethics—"Well, if this is going help this situation, then even though I have to do something a bit unorthodox, it's all for the positive result." "It's just a white lie." "What they don't know won't hurt them."

I am in a business where the passion people put into their work often causes them to act with blinders—to only see their vision and purpose—hence, all the lying, cheating, and backstabbing that goes on in show business. When I met Philippe, he was my ABC network executive on a made-for-television movie I was directing and executive-producing, titled *For Hope*, starring Dana Delany. It was based loosely on how my family dealt with the death of my sister, Gay, of the disease scleroderma. As a result of our accomplishment, I continued to get more involved and today I am on the board of the Scleroderma Research Foundation. I have been to Washington, perhaps the capital of ethics on the earth. It's amazing to me how all of the groups in different not-for-profits—whether related to disease, the environment, politics, or education—will all stop at nothing to move their causes forward. There's only so much funding to go around, so the competition grows, the need for attention and differences of opinion run rampant, and ethics are often a façade. It's the higher plane we'd all like to operate on but unfortunately do not. And as soon as we judge others for their "unethical" approach, are we not exercising our own ethics upon them?

The campaign on television when I was young was something that stayed with me: "Shoplifting is stealing." The purpose was to educate the nine year old. I would hope that message helped many people. But the world is full of people who may have never stolen a "thing" in their lives, yet they will know, as soon as they read this, the crimes they have committed.

I'd like to take this time to apologize to King's Department Store and the kid sitting next to me in third grade. Oh, yeah, and to my mom, for lying to her. If I listed everything I feel I may have done wrong so far in my life, Philippe would be writing the foreword and I'd be confessing my sins and probably owe some people money or letters of apology.

I'd also like to thank Philippe for being such an ethical man. Working with him on such a poignant project in my life was a true pleasure and brought everyone involved with *For Hope* to a higher self. Attempting to do "higher work" is a great start to demonstrating pure ethical behavior. That would mean that this book has already accomplished what it has set out to do—spark thought, reflection, and perhaps more honest behavior. I hope you enjoy reading it as much as I did.

To my knowledge, I did not plagiarize this foreword.

—Bob Saget

CHAPTER 1

Ethical Issues

A Starting Framework

When journalists or media practitioners boast about being ethical, people tend to run in the opposite direction. This is because many individuals who pride themselves on having a strong ethical pedigree don't, even as they pontificate about being more ethical than thou. Thus, there's often a mass exodus whenever anyone proclaims too loudly and too vehemently about being ethical. So often are ethics found to be lacking that many observers maintain that talking about ethics in the media doesn't compute; for them, it's an oxymoron.

Many insist that media players (and who doesn't want to be viewed as a player?) pay homage to their egos and their need to succeed, ignoring pesky ethical considerations as they aggressively compete with anyone who dares to get in their way. For example, Bill Carter in *Desperate Networks* reports that ABC Entertainment president Steve McPherson underestimated the unethical and desperate behavior of his competitors, specifically Fox for *Trading Spouses*, perceived by ABC to be a rip-off of its show, *Wife Swap*.[1] In truth, ethical issues faced in Hollywood (Figure 1-1), where much entertainment like *Trading Spouses* or *Wife Swap* originates, are the issues faced by media everywhere.

Supporting, possibly even embracing, the lack of ethics in Hollywood, writer Adam Clay, in an article called "That's a Rep: If You Want to Get Your Script Read in Hollywood, Dishonesty Might Be the Best Policy," boasts of masquerading as his own manager to sell his scripts. When someone accuses him of being unethical, he retorts, "I'm not sure what town this guy thinks he's working in,

---

[1] Bill Carter, *Desperate Networks* (New York: Doubleday, 2006), p. 303.

FIGURE 1-1
Ethical issues faced in Hollywood, California, are confronted by the media globally. (iStockphoto.com #000003299043, Dmitrig Rashap.)

but if this sort of behavior puts him off, he might want to rethink his career path. After all, the wheels of this town have always been greased by an endless supply of Grade-A bullshit."[2]

Similarly, many journalists reportedly value "getting a story" over how a story is gotten; it's more important to land a story than it is to acquire the necessary ingredients to build a story properly. With shorter and shorter deadlines and with the competition from other outlets looming, along with the rush to get the story before anyone else does, it becomes harder and harder to maintain journalistic ethics. Also, with lines between journalism and entertainment constantly blurring, journalistic ethics often fall by the wayside. As budgets for research in news divisions are cut, shortcuts become standard operating procedures and ethics often get the short end of the stick.

As discussed in Chapter 8, if journalists such as Janet Cook at *The Washington Post*, Justin Blair at *The New York Times*, or Stephen Glass at *The New Republic* write fictional pieces presenting them as fact, ethical norms are being violated and more scrutiny is needed.

A NEED FOR STUDYING ETHICS

The situation may be changing, however. For one thing, students are increasingly demanding that ethics courses be added to the curriculum to prepare them to function responsibly in the real world. According to a study by the Aspen Institute, a nonprofit organization that researches business issues, students at MBA programs want courses that teach values-based decision making, as they feel that too few courses teach them about ethics in the workplace. According to the Aspen study, only 22% of the survey participants said their schools were doing "a lot" to prepare them to meet ethical conflicts in the workplace.[3]

[2]Adam Clay, "That's a Rep: If You Want to Get Your Script Read in Hollywood, Dishonesty Just Might Be the Best Policy," *Los Angeles Magazine*, February, 2006, pp. 292–293.
[3]Lynnley Browning, "Ethics Lacking in Business School Curriculum, Students Say in Survey," *The New York Times*, May 30, 2003, www.fosterwinans.com/EthicsBusinessSchools.html, accessed October 31, 2005.

For another, the word "integrity" was 2005's most looked-up word on Merriam-Webster's online dictionary.[4] And at my school, California State University Fullerton, notepads proclaim that the school is "making integrity count," a further indication of the importance attached to the concept of integrity (Figure 1-2).

Responding to this perceived need, many schools, such as Arizona State University, are creating special professorships in media ethics, some of which are funded by grant organizations such as the Ethics in Journalism Foundation.

FIGURE 1-2
The concept of integrity features prominently on the California State University notepads.

Organizations such as the Accrediting Council on Education in Journalism and Mass Media Communications (ACEJMC) are also doing their part to put ethics in the foreground. At the World Journalism Education Congress in Singapore in June 2007, attended by representatives from 45 different countries from around the world, Susanne Shaw, executive director of the ACEJMC, presented her organization's mission statement, which includes a section on core values requiring students of the media to be able "to demonstrate an understanding of professional ethical principles and work ethically in pursuit of truth, accuracy, fairness and diversity."

Ethics scandals and allegations abound in many areas, reinforcing the need for ethics to be studied seriously. Athletes in baseball and cycling are charged with taking performance-enhancing drugs, thus violating the premise that sports constitute a fair fight where skill and talent prevail; basketball referees are charged with fixing games; athletes like NFL player Michael Vick of the Atlanta Falcons are charged with sponsoring illegal dog fights.

Outside of the world of sports, there's Enron and accounting misdeeds; Tom DeLay and lobbying and strong arm influence peddling; the leaking of the name of Valerie Plame, a CIA operative; charges that the Federal Communications Commission (FCC) buried or destroyed a report that questioned the advisability of loosening media ownership rules because increased concentration would hurt local television news coverage; rumors about which Hollywood movers and shakers used the services of private investigator Anthony Pellicano, who used intimidation tactics and questionable wiretaps to get all the dirt he needed to win cases. The list goes on. Some are entertaining or amusing gossip. Others are very troubling.

3

[4]Wendy Solomon, "'Integrity' Often Questioned in '05," *The Los Angeles Times*, December 25, 2005, A-37.

The large number of ethical scandals caused the creation of the Corporate Corruption Bill of 2002, which requires corporate officers to function with integrity and honesty, though, significantly, in 2006, the Senate rejected a bill designed to investigate ethics abuses in Congress. In early 2007, however, a Democratic-controlled legislature passed an ethics bill designed to curtail abuses.

In March 2006, Andrew Cuomo, a candidate for New York State attorney general, sought to tighten ethics rules in state government as well as to ban elected officials and other state executives from lobbying the government for three years after leaving office. In this way, Cuomo sought to end what he termed "a culture of corruption."[5]

In the world of finance, Pax World, an investment company, trumpeted "ethical investing" to drum up business. Is this a clever way to gain business, or is this a sincere effort to address a pervasive lack of ethics? In the business world, are strip clubs the norm? Should executives meet in private rooms at strip clubs? A March 23, 2006, cover story in *USA Today* raised these and other questions, noting, "Adult entertainment is enjoyed by men—and some women—in most every industry in the USA, and it's a tax-deductible business expense allowed by the IRS."[6]

4

Of course, ethical questions have been around for a long time, all over the world, not just in the United States. For a list of links, many of which deal with ethics in different parts of the world, I recommend an excellent website created by Cal State Fullerton professor Paul Lester, http://commfaculty.fullerton.edu/lester. See also the text's website for a conversation with Lester and Deni Elliott, the Poynter Jamison chair in Media Ethics and Press Policy at the University of South Florida where they talk about media ethics from a global perspective.

Ethical issues are clearly not new. In the 1920s, Thomas A. Edison, the genius behind electricity, asked potential scholarship recipients if and when they would consider a lie to be permissible.[7] But these issues need to be reviewed and updated on a regular basis. The ethical landscape is constantly changing, creating a need for careful scrutiny of the ethical issues that confront media practitioners.

[5]Johnathan P. Hicks, "Candidate Urges New Ethics Rules," *The New York Times*, March 31, 2006, A-19.

[6]Jayne O'Donnell, "Should Business Execs Meet at Strip Clubs," *USA Today*, March 23, 2006, a1–2.

[7]John Schwartz, "Wilbur Huston, 93, Dies; 'Brightest Boy' in 1929," *The New York Times*, June 10, 2006, A-28.

A number of media ethics books exist, but most focus primarily on journalistic ethics. This text does include a chapter on journalism (Chapter 8); but there are also chapters on new media (Chapter 9) and on public relations (Chapter 12), all very much a part of the changing media landscape. The primary focus of the book, however, is on ethics and visual communications, with a particular emphasis on television, my particular area of expertise, as I was a television executive at ABC for 20 years.

All four of the major broadcasters, ABC, CBS, Fox, and NBC, as well as other media companies, for example, administer ethics surveys/questionnaires tests to key employees to ensure that ethical behavior is maintained. Media companies have guidelines outlining what is ethically permissible and what is not. PBS's Channel 13 in New York City, for example, has a 13-page booklet describing the gift acceptance procedures of the Educational Broadcasting Corporation (EBC), stating, "The Policy delineates EBC policy regarding such matters as a code of ethics, avoiding conflicts of interest, types of assets EBC will accept as gifts as well as acceptable gift methods."[8]

There exists a significant back and forth when it comes to ethical issues in the media: often one step to address the problems and then several steps back to maintain the status quo. On the one hand, various ethical codes—some of which are referred to or reprinted in this text—are instituted to strengthen media ethics. Yet the ethical scandals and loopholes remain.

According to the survey "How Employees View Ethics in Their Organizations 1993–2005," conducted by the Ethics Resource Center, "Where top management displays certain ethics-related actions, employees are 50 percentage points less likely to observe misconduct." This finding supports the belief that it's the boss who sets the tone. It follows that if the boss or top management sets high ethical standards, fewer ethical infractions are likely to occur. The survey also found that "When employees perceive that others are held accountable for their actions, their overall satisfaction increases by 32 percentage points."[9]

Students are very aware of the ethical dilemmas that exist and want them to be discussed, examined, and dissected in the classroom. And for good reason. Ethics *do* indeed matter as students envision the next 50 or so years of their lives. For an earlier generation, the question at the end of the road might have been whether or not enough time was spent with one's family. Today's question

[8]Educational Broadcasting Corporation, Gift Acceptance Procedures, October 2006, p. 1.
[9]For a copy of the survey, contact the Ethics Resource Center at 202-737-2227 or though its website at www.ethics.org.

might be whether or not one has lived an ethical life, in the workplace as well as at home.

Tom Fortuna, a member of the faculty at the Los Angeles branch of Emerson College, Boston, asks his students in his internship class exactly how much they want to be a part of the world of entertainment. If they really want it, he asks, what are they willing to do to succeed? What will they not do? Will they back-stab? Will they bad-mouth? What will they do or not do to show their passion? He feels it's important for students to define their own ethical rules as they make their way in the business. Students need to be prepared for the real world; they need to know what kinds of ethical issues they will be facing. They need to know what is expected of them.

New media has created a whole new set of ethical issues, presenting students with many challenges their parents did not experience, as discussed in Chapter 9. Ethics are not simply about doing what's morally correct. They are also about behaving the right way and displaying good manners. Often, students about to start their media careers don't know what is expected of them as new media and the Internet assume greater and greater significance. For example, is an e-mail thank you after a meeting or a job interview good enough? Most media professionals will tell you that an e-mail thank you after a business interview does not do the trick. It may be easier, but it's inadequate. A handwritten note should be used instead.

Students need to know how management and colleagues define good manners in an age of new and ever-expanding media: how much importance *is* attached to *how* people are treated and *how* ethical issues are resolved. The bottom line is that students need to know how management and colleagues handle ethical issues, which is what this text explores.

THE RESPONSIBILITIES OF THE MEDIA

The media has great responsibilities. Sometimes the media rises to the occasion; sometimes it doesn't, as was charged when the media failed to report defects in Firestone tires in 1996, resulting in many lost lives that could have been saved if the major media outlets had acted quickly.[10] Often, the public only seeks out one version of events, necessitating that the media exercise utmost responsibility. Indeed, people don't always seek double or triple sources; people don't

---

[10]Jim Edwards, "Wrong Turns," *Brill's Content*, December 2000–January 2001, pp. 113–115, 168–169.

FIGURE 1-3
When legendary newsman Edward R.
Murrow addressed the Radio Television
News Directors Association in 1958, he laid
out some lofty aspirations for the media,
goals that many would say have not been
met. (Globe Photos, Inc.)

FIGURE 1-4
As newspapers continue to lose
readership, many stress sensationalism
and negativity in what some say is a
misguided attempt to cling to as many
readers as possible. (iStockphoto.com
#3265233, Nicholas Belton.)

7

always check or have access to multiple sources, and thus that single version
needs to be accurate and complete.

If the media's role is to enlighten or educate, as Edward R. Murrow (Figure 1-3)
stated when he addressed the Radio Television News Directors Association in
1958 complaining about the dumbing down of news, it follows that an ethical
framework is needed in order for the media to realize its potential.

If the media is to keep the corridors of power in check by breaking important
stories, it also follows that these breaking stories must have a sound basis and
not simply be someone's calculated version of spin. As newspapers (Figure 1-4)
continue to lose readership, should writers and editors abandon ethical guidelines to sensationalize news items and possibly titillate readers to return?

The responsibility of the media extends beyond the importance attached to
news coverage. It extends to entertainment as well. As box office receipts and
television ratings suffer, do ethics take a back seat to embrace gross humor and
a further coarsening of the culture?

A lively debate took place about the Fox television show *24* in 2007. Some saw the program about the superheroic actions of counterterrorist agent Jack Bauer as advocating torture as a way to win the war on terror. They complained that it's well-known that torture does not work—that people will say anything when tortured and that information gathered using torture is invalid. They also charged that the show instructed people in the military how to use torture and, in the process, served to diminish America's standing around the world. These media observers feared that a show where the characters employ torture to achieve results would mislead viewers into condoning torture. Others saw *24* as simply entertainment, devoid of any political messages about torture and America's reputation abroad.

The debate about *24* involved the responsibility that a mass-market television program faces when tackling a topic that has serious repercussions all over the world (i.e., the use of torture). All media practitioners, not just the ones covering news, confront the question of responsibility because of the media's vast power to influence audiences. How this responsibility is handled in a number of different situations is a primary focus of this book.

AN ETHICAL APPROACH

The purpose of this book is not to provide students, as well as current and future media practitioners, with unequivocal solutions to ethical questions but rather to illustrate the various kinds of real-world ethical situations that arise in various divisions of the media. The intent is not to offer solutions to all possible or probable ethical dilemmas but rather to enable students, as well as media professionals, to anticipate ethical issues and to provide them with tools to utilize as they find their personal interpretations and solutions. There are, in fact, no always-to-be-applied rules in the world of media ethics, and it would not be useful to try to create such rules. It makes more sense to understand the kinds of issues that arise and to be able to evaluate situations on a case-by-case basis.

In keeping with the book's industry perspective, a number of key executives from different parts of the media will be interviewed about the kinds of ethical issues they face on a regular basis to ascertain how they approach these issues. What factors do they consider? How do they define ethics? How do real-world concerns affect their sense of ethics? How quickly do they have to make these ethical decisions? And how do they explain or rationalize their actions?

One cannot and should not forget the business aspects of the media. Among the creators of entertainment are many committed artists; our entertainment would be sorely lacking if only out-to-make-a-dollar entrepreneurs were involved. But entertainment is a business.

Journalists can similarly raise the bar for reporters regardless of corporate and other pressures, particularly if one agrees with some media observers that journalism and news reporting should be held to a higher standard than entertainment programming. But like entertainment, journalism is a business. If there's no revenue (Figure 1-5), if there's no return for investors, if there's no audience, then it doesn't much matter if ethical standards were or were not maintained. If artists are so pure that they won't dare venture outside the cubicle where they create for themselves and themselves alone, their art, if it is indeed art, won't make it to the marketplace during their lifetimes.

FIGURE 1-5
If there's no revenue, investors aren't happy, even if ethical norms are maintained. (iStockphoto.com #1950771, Kativ.)

9

It would thus be inappropriate and unrealistic to approach the topic of media ethics in isolation. Ignoring the realities of the marketplace and focusing solely on isolated ethical issues devoid of any real-world situations is a serious mistake and, sadly, one that has been made too often. As John M. Higgins, who passed away unexpectedly in 2006, observed in *Broadcasting & Cable*, media companies "are forced to dance to impress Wall Street."[11] Ethics do not have to fall victim to the bottom line to please Wall Street, but financial realities nevertheless do have an impact.

In this text, we will approach ethics in the context of the real world. This, of course, is not to say that perceived ethical violations will be justified and upheld because "that's just the way it is and that's just the way it's been done." This is not what today's students want or need, but real-world circumstances similarly cannot be ignored in the serious study of contemporary media ethics.

DEFINING THE TERMS

There is a tendency in our society to be vague about defining key concepts. The often-used phrase "words cannot express" is usually meant as a compliment, suggesting that a complex idea or emotion simply cannot be defined. These ideas or emotions are simply too deep. It's an easy way out, a short cut.

[11]John M. Higgins, "Money Talks: In the Hot Seat," *Broadcasting & Cable*, September 25, 2006, p. 14.

Thus, we have Supreme Court Justice Potter Stewart's comment about obscenity, that he can't define it, but that he knows it when he sees it. Or we have Rule 14 from former Operation Desert Storm Commander Schwarzkopf in his 1992 statements to the Academy of Achievement, which states that Rule 14 is doing what's right, what's moral, what's ethical, and what's the correct thing to do. Commander Schwarzkopf claims we all know this—we all know deep down what is right and what is wrong without having to define the terms.

When it comes to the media, however, we don't always know what's right. There's also the confusing distinction between ethics and the law, making our understanding of ethics all that much more complicated. Law and ethics may be related, but they are not the same thing. Sometimes something that is perfectly legal is not ethical or something that is ethical may not be legal.

For our purposes, ethics, based on the Greek word *ethos*, is defined in terms of what is morally right or wrong in terms of the self in relation to others—simply put, doing the right thing from a moral point of view when decision making is required. This is particularly hard to do when actions have to be taken quickly, as is often the case in the media. Instant analysis has become the norm almost since 1969 when Vice President Spiro Agnew criticized the instant analysis that accompanied the coverage of the Vietnam War by what he termed an "effete corps of impudent snobs." Despite the faulty instant analysis that declared presidential candidate Al Gore the winner over George W. Bush in Florida in the 2000 election, instant analysis is here to stay, necessitating that media practitioners be able to think and act quickly, correctly, and ethically.

A great many philosophical tenets have provided ethical guidelines (and many, many debates and controversies) over the years, though no single ethical theory stands at the ready for each and every situation. Also, as Seth Ashley observed in his article, "Please Keep Telling Me What I Want to Hear: Perhaps Timeless Ethical Principles Have Lost Relevancy," too great an emphasis on philosophical theories, what he terms "prefabricated absolutes," confuses rather than helps students determine what makes a decision ethical, as many of the established theories can be manipulated any number of ways to justify behavior.[12]

---

[12]Seth Ashley, "Please Keep Telling Me What I Want to Hear: Perhaps Timeless Ethical Principles Have Lost Relevancy," *Media Ethics*, Fall 2003, vol. 15, no. 1, pp. 19–20.

The focus of this book thus remains on ethical questions and issues that come up in real-life situations. For our purposes, ethical decision making in the media is based on critical analysis and evaluation, not on a preponderance of theory.

INDUSTRY STANDARDS

Many have wondered if there are industry standards that apply to the entertainment industry. Granted, codes of behavior exist and different companies have ethical guidelines they want

FIGURE 1-6
Today's hard-working, smiling assistant may be promoted to be the person in charge, one more reason to treat everyone with respect. (iStockphoto.com #307667, Jeffrey Smith.)

their employees to uphold, but one would be hard put to say that an accepted ethical industry standard exists. It would make things easier if there were clearly defined ethical standards, but no clear-cut rules apply.

Of course, players can claim to treat every single person they encounter with respect, particularly as the assistant (Figure 1-6) you encounter today may be in a position of power next week, but this doesn't really constitute an industry standard.

If there is anything that passes as a general industry standard, it's one based on trust and experience. The industry professionals interviewed for this book approach the topic of ethics in the following way: They want to associate with people they know and have previously worked with. Known quantities—these are the people they can trust; these are the people their experience tells them will not cross ethical lines.

In a business where everyone knows everybody else, where Steve McPherson, head of ABC, and Kevin Reilly, former NBC programming chief now at Fox, are "best friends and competitors,"[13] where having key information can make or break a career, and where executives and creators repeatedly encounter one another at various social and business events, it becomes increasingly important to know who can and who cannot be trusted. This is why industry professionals like to work with people they have worked with before, making it difficult for newcomers to break into the club. Several people I interviewed specifically said they hire people they have worked with, or, as one executive put it, "someone

11

[13]Carter, *Desperate Networks*, p. 367.

I've been in the trenches with." Industry practitioners are reluctant to give recommendations for people they have not worked with. The reason is that unless they've worked with a person, they won't know how that individual reacts under pressure.

David Brownfield is the senior vice president of current programs, in charge of the CBS lineup. For him, determining who can be trusted not to cross ethical lines depends on the history he's had with the person in question. For example, if a sense of trust has been established, Brownfield will not worry that a confidence has been betrayed. The more experience Brownfield has had with the person, the more comfortable he will be about exchanging information.

It's almost as if there's an unwritten ritual that works like this: an agent who you don't know tells you that a particular writer has gotten sole writing credit on a project. As you don't know the agent well, you exercise due diligence to check if the information is correct. As your relationship with the agent develops and she continues to give you accurate information, the need to verify information is eliminated and trust is established. Should the agent subsequently betray the trust that's being established, your experience tells you to exercise extreme caution about sharing any sensitive information.

12

FIGURE 1-7
Information is a valuable commodity in the world of media. How much gossiping and backstabbing exists, however, is a matter of opinion. (iStockphoto.com #2991594, Charity Myers.)

For Brownfield, it's all based on experience, knowing whom you can trust to trade information with and whom you can't. Of course, there's some corporate information about company policies, such as schedule changes, airdates, or contractual details, that Brownfield simply will not share, even with someone who has gained his trust. Per Brownfield, it's people who are too full of themselves who cross ethical lines. If someone who is dishonest burns him, Brownfield won't let that individual burn him again. Instead, he will seek out those individuals he's worked with in the past who have proven themselves to be trustworthy.

For Mitch Metcalf, executive vice president of planning and scheduling at NBC, experience and training also matter. In addition, Metcalf feels that industry standards are maintained, in part, as a result of antitrust concerns. True, everyone does know everyone else, and what he terms "a network of gossiping" (Figure 1-7) exists, but he points out that competitors will avoid talking about key issues because antitrust regulations are structured to keep broadcasters from carving up nights in the way that airlines carve up routes. For Metcalf, the antitrust concerns are one more reason why executives might not share confidential information, avoiding the appearance of collusion.

Metcalf also makes a distinction between what can be said in-house and outside NBC. He works on the assumption that what is said inside the halls of NBC stays at NBC. If someone goes outside, say to the press, he feels that an ethical line has been crossed, a bond of trust has been broken. Like Brownfield, Metcalf feels that sensitive corporate information should not be revealed. Keeping corporate machinations private is an accepted standard of behavior.

Metcalf defines the scheduling of programs as "a full contact sport" where few fouls are called. It's accepted practice to go after the premieres of the competition or to schedule a new episode as soon as one finds out that the opposition is planning a repeat. This is simply seen as doing one's job. Metcalf says that one might question the ethics behind calling a marginally successful show a hit. It might be ethically questionable to define a show that simply manages to survive a hit, but that too is simply part of doing one's job.

DATING

Dating (Figure 1-8) is never really easy, but it may be even more difficult in the world of media, where accepted standards are hard to discern and where, as noted earlier, everyone tends to know everyone else. Truly, the ethical quandaries that accompany dating and entertainment abound. Everyone has heard rumors about how some people climbed the entertainment ladder by having sex with powerful people who could help their careers. No doubt, some people have benefited or been victimized as a result of whom they slept with, but it's my perception that casting couch incidents are far less frequent than the public at large believes.

The focus of this section is more on issues surrounding dating than it is on how the casting couch is used or abused. Clearly, if a person in power lures an aspiring actor to the casting couch, ethical norms are being violated. Persons in power should not use their positions to trade sexual favors for jobs, nor should supplicants at the entertainment altar offer sexual favors to trump other candidates.

FIGURE 1-8
The television program *The Bachelor* popularized the "rose ceremony," during which roses are awarded to those remaining in contention for the bachelor's affection, but dating in the world of media is even more complicated than beating out other contestants for the affection of that special someone, and it is filled with complications that test ethical boundaries. (iStockphoto.com #1787342, Pavel Pospisil.)

13

It is important to define exactly what is meant by "working together." Most people in the media work long hours, and it's a given that they are going to come into contact with people while working. Chances are also good that their friends will also be in similar fields and that any potential fix ups will be with people who work in the same general environments.

Years ago, the conventional wisdom was that people who worked in entertainment should marry schoolteachers who could provide a much-needed perspective as well as distance, but this seemingly sound piece of advice has taken a beating as one of the individuals who espoused the theory recently left his schoolteacher wife to take up with a movie star. So if you aren't on a vigilant lookout for a schoolteacher or someone who toils anywhere but within the entertainment industry, chances are that you will be meeting people who work in your field, if not directly in your office or on projects you are involved with. The often-repeated advice that parents used to give their children that one shouldn't date anyone he or she works with is increasingly difficult to adhere to, because work hours are longer than they used to be, leaving little free time to cultivate outside relationships. Also, the rigid rule may be broken because people may be more attracted to those who have similar career interests. Livelier conversations and more direct connections may result if two people share a passion for the same field.

It makes sense, does it not, that you might want to spend time with someone who has the same interests as you do and whose work dovetails with yours? As lifestyles change and become more flexible, it seems harder to say with authority, "I simply will not go out with someone I work with or might someday work with should our paths ever cross."

But from an ethical point of view, is it too easy to maintain that dating people you work with is simply an acceptable fact of life? Are there instances when dating a work colleague crosses ethical lines? Does it, for example, depend on how closely you work together or who reports to whom?

Throughout the text, you will be presented with "You Decide" boxes, sections in which a number of situations are offered for your analysis. These sections are designed to raise ethical issues that you may or may not have considered previously. They are included in the text to encourage you to think about ethical considerations and to develop your own ethical standards. The first "You Decide" box poses questions about dating relationships within the entertainment business.

You Decide

All relationships or dating situations are different, necessitating individual consideration and analysis. In general terms, however, take a look at the following real-life dating scenarios tied to the world of entertainment and see if and when ethical lines are crossed. The scenarios are randomly sequenced, not scaled in terms of possible increasing or decreasing ethical infractions. If you feel that extenuating circumstances exist in the following brief descriptions, be ready to define what those circumstances might be.

- A journalist finds the subject of a story he is covering to his liking and asks her out after the interview appears in print.
- A journalist finds the subject of a story he is covering to his liking, but waits until a third party arranges for them to meet "by chance."
- A journalist finds the subject of a story he is covering to his liking and asks her out at the conclusion of the interview.
- The supervising producer of a television program finds herself attracted to a junior writer on staff. She invites him to be her escort at an industry function. He accepts, knowing it will help his career if he attends the event.
- The supervising producer of a television program finds herself attracted to a junior writer on staff. She asks him to stay late one night to go over the script.
- The supervising producer of a television program finds herself attracted to a junior writer on staff. She invites him to her house to have a drink and go over the script.
- The director of a feature film asks a grip to drive her home. In the car, she tells him she finds him attractive.
- Before starting to date, a television executive asks a colleague at his level to keep any relationship they might have a secret, as he would not want anyone to know about a possible office romance.
- A supporting player arranges to be alone with the director of a film, suggesting he drive her home as she is without a ride.
- An entertainment executive invites his assistant of three years for a holiday drink. She accepts, hoping that he will finally express some interest in dating her.

- An entertainment executive invites a group of junior executives as well as his assistant of three months for an after-work drink. He arranges for everyone except his assistant to leave early.
- An entertainment executive who finds his assistant to his liking invites her for an after-work drink, which he charges to his corporate expense account.
- A 34-year-old journalist invites her 24-year-old assistant to share a ski weekend (Figure 1-9) with her in Vail as she doesn't want to ski alone and none of her friends are free.
- The head of an Internet company finds himself alone with an executive in his company and asks her if she is a lesbian or if she enjoys sex with men such as himself.
- The head of an Internet company gets drunk at an industry event and gets up the courage to ask the assistant he's been interested in if she would like to go out with him.
- A director asks the star of his movie for a date after the film has finished shooting.

And what about when industry guest speakers come to campus?

FIGURE 1-9
Inviting a subordinate to share a ski weekend can test ethical boundaries. (iStockphoto.com #1429319, aka Plummer.)

- An industry guest speaker spots an attractive male student in the classroom during his presentation and after class arranges to get his phone number and offers to help jump-start his career. The student senses the guest speaker's interest in him, debating what his response should be.
- An industry speaker is impressed by a student who asks a lot of good questions and after class gives him his card to see if he has any further questions.
- A student eager to break into the business goes up to an industry guest speaker after his presentation and gives him her business card, telling him she will call him to discuss what steps she should follow to meet her career objectives.
- A student eager to break into the business goes up to an industry guest speaker after his presentation and gives him her business card, telling him she will call him as she'd like to meet him for coffee.

How many of these scenarios do you feel cross ethical lines? One? Two? Six? All of them? None of them? Do you feel any of these scenarios approach or constitute sexual harassment, here defined as a superior taking sexual advantage of a subordinate? Lastly, what, for example, is the difference between the last two scenarios about the student and the industry guest speaker? The first one is

exactly what an ambitious, aggressive student *should* do, whereas many would say the second one is inappropriate because the student has not specified *why* she wants to meet for coffee (Figure 1-10).

FIGURE 1-10
Following up a meeting with a phone call is often very much the right thing to do in terms of furthering one's career, but if the phone message is unclear or misleading, ethical boundaries may be violated. (iStockphoto.com #88565, Sandra O'Claire.)

A STARTING FRAMEWORK

Defining limits is never easy. A few guidelines or theories do, however, provide a beginning context for our study:

- The Greek philosopher Aristotle (384–322 BC) believed in the Golden Mean. For him, avoiding extremes and excesses prevented an individual from being swept away in torrents of passion or despair. These extremes would prevent a person from following a virtuous, measured path. For Aristotle, all things in moderation made for reasoned, sound ethical judgments.

- For Immanuel Kant (1724–1804), it's strong sense of duty determined by reason that defines a moral or ethical action. Doing the right thing for the wrong reasons does not make for a morally praiseworthy act. Self-interest is not part of what Kant would refer to as moral law. For him, moral or ethical behavior exists independently of individual goals and desires, apart from personal gain. Kant created a set of moral maxims or categorical imperatives that are universal in application. Based on his schematic, you should not use people exclusively as a means to get what you yourself desire.

- Utilitarian theories, espoused by John Stuart Mill (1806–1873), stress making ethical decisions based on what would bring about the greatest amount of good for the greatest number of individuals. For Mill, it's the consequences of actions that matter. In his book, *Utilitarianism* (1863), he defines actions as being right if they promote happiness, but wrong if they produce the absence of happiness (i.e., pain). For Mill, happiness, or pleasure, for the greatest numbers is what is intrinsically good. His ethical framework rejects egoism, which seeks consequences that benefit a single person. Instead, Mill seeks the greatest balance of good for the greatest numbers.

- In sharp contrast to Mill's utilitarianism and to Kant's view of duty as a moral action is the objectivism advocated by Ayn Rand (1905–1982). A rationalist, Rand based her ethics on self-interest, not the needs of others. She believed a person had to take responsibility for his or her own life. The needs of others might be considered, but self comes first, as opposed to a commitment to the greatest good for all. Rand's philosophy is clearly laid out in her writings, specifically *The Fountainhead* (1943) and *Atlas Shrugged* (1957).

There are many additional ethical theories that seek to define what's right or wrong, including ethical principles based on religious teachings, that offer a basis for decision making. The Bible, for example, has provided many with interpretations of ethical guidelines.

PLAYER WANNABE: BILL SILVER'S STORY

Before looking at this book's suggested approach to ethical issues in the media, let's, as an exercise, create a would-be-player and analyze him using a combination of the theories of Aristotle, Kant, Mill, Rand, and religious teachings.

Bill is 22, a junior at a Midwestern college, eager to become a writer/producer, and willing to pay his dues. Not afraid of hard work, he is committed to becoming a professional writer. He has written several scripts that he feels show his range. He wrote some of the scripts in his scriptwriting class where he received positive feedback. The others he wrote on his own. He hears from a family friend that a Hollywood agent who attended his college will be in town to revisit her old stomping ground. Bill arranges to be invited to a party, given by a friend of his mother, where he hopes he will be able to interest the visiting agent in his career. He has done his research—he looked up the agent in the *Hollywood Creative Directory's Agents & Managers* and on the www.imdb.com website and discovered she has brokered a number of big deals. Bill's goal is to get her to read one or more of his scripts and maybe even sign him to her agency. He tells his girlfriend that he has to work that night and can't take her with him. The script he is most interested in pitching is about a male stripper who is murdered at a bachelorette party. He wrote it as a guilty pleasure, a kind of low-budget fun, entertaining film. He has described it to his friends as *Girls Gone Wild* with a story, though he has modified his pitch to make the story more of a caution-ary tale about the pitfalls of exploiting one's body for money.

At the dinner party, Bill essentially bypasses the hostess, his mother's friend, ignoring her suggested seating arrangement. He has applied twice to be a vol-unteer at the Sundance Film Festival, and though he wasn't selected he knows that one of the festival's rules is that volunteers are prohibited from pitching their stories to power brokers in attendance. He knows the rule about not pitch-ing one's projects to buyers like Harvey Weinstein when they are having lunch, walking down the street, or heading to the restroom, but he nevertheless latches on to the powerful agent and tells her how passionate he is about this story. The agent tries to change the subject by suggesting a dinner party is not the place to do a formal pitch, but a charged up Bill keeps telling her that this is a story that could better people's lives.

Because he has heard that in order to get anywhere, one has to be totally pas-sionate about things, Bill repeats that this is a project he is truly passionate about. The agent tries to change the subject again, but Bill keeps talking about his passion project. Desperate to find an angle the agent will respond to, he switches tactics and challenges her to read the script, thinking that as an agent it is her duty to find new talent, and *he* is new talent in need of a chance. Someone interrupts Bill's pitch to say that he followed the real story about the male stripper who was killed and thought the story was sleazy, though he's heard that some of the tabloids picked it up. Bill pointedly ignores this intru-sion, and then decides to switch tactics.

Bill starts to flirt with the agent by complimenting her on what she's wearing. He plans to ask the agent out for coffee and decides that if she wants to see it as a date, that's okay with him. After all, he's a good-looking guy (maybe he could perform his own striptease for her!), and she might find him to her liking. She was checking him out earlier, wasn't she, and he's heard rumors that some agents select their clients by how they perform in the bedroom. The agent turns him down for the coffee date, saying she is heading back to Los Angeles in a couple of days and can't spare the time. She then gets up and places her chair at the other end of the table. After the dinner party, Bill calls his girlfriend and tells her he missed her and wished she had accepted his invite to come to the party with him.

> Golden Mean: What is the basis of Bill's passion for his script? Does he have any perspective about the project?
>
> Self-interest: What is Bill's sense of what he wants?
>
> Duty: What is Bill's sense of duty?
>
> Greatest good for the greatest numbers: Bill's view of his script as helping people?
>
> Moral behavior: If the verbal pitch doesn't work, how about the casting couch routine?
>
> Concern for others: What is Bill's concern for the girlfriend he lied to and puts on the defensive by telling her that she turned down his invitation to attend the party when he told her she couldn't come with him? What is his concern for the other guests at the party and the hostess?

At the core of this fictional story is an important question: How does someone break into the entertainment industry without violating a number of ethical norms, specifically an obsessive concern with oneself, an obsession that makes it difficult if not impossible to consider the feelings of others as you charge ahead to get what you want? If you have few or no contacts and nevertheless want to succeed, how can you avoid being overly concerned with yourself? Was Ayn Rand correct? Does charity really begin at home? Although it is not easy to work in the media and have ethics, this text seeks to provide helpful guidelines.

THE E*T*H*I*C*S RUBRIC

Here's how we are going to explore and analyze ethics in the media. We're going to apply an E*T*H*I*C*S rubric to different situations. Using E*T*H*I*C*S is a comprehensive way to analyze what is ethically at stake in a number of situations. Periodically, we'll refer back to this rubric to keep the methodology fresh. This rubric does not cover every possible aspect of a situation, but it does provide a clear way to approach a wide range of ethical dilemmas. How exactly does it work?

E
T
H
I
C
S

E stands for *E*valuate. The ethical situation needs to be examined a number of different ways, not just from a single perspective. Study the issue from a number of different viewpoints. Though it's important to consider a creator's intentions and goals, do not simply buy into one person's point of view. Take time to analyze. Even under deadlines and the rush to get there first, take the time to evaluate.

T stands for *T*ruth. What is the objective truth of the situation? Make sure you have a clear definition of the facts as well as a definition that can be agreed upon by others. The truth is not always black and white; the truth is not always easy to ascertain, particularly when the stakes are high and a lot of players are involved. Though not always easy to do in the heat of a meeting or under pressure, stop for a moment to grasp the truth of the situation. In a world where exaggeration seems to be the norm, it's often difficult to get to the essential truth. If someone says it's so, does that make it so, even if the person making the assertion commands respect?

H stands for *H*arm. What harm is likely to ensue from a given action? It's important here to consider that real-world situations are involved. Media rumors can ruin lives. Pranks can similarly backfire. Stop to evaluate negative outcomes that can ensue, even from seemingly ethical decisions. Of course, intentional harm should similarly be evaluated.

I stands for *I*nvestigating, going beyond a cursory review. Investigating requires digging deep to gather the necessary information. Thorough investigations are needed in order for the media to take ethical action, even if research staffs are reduced while news heads still want to get the story first. The trend of instant analysis often does not allow for a thorough investigation, particularly if too few people are doing the investigating. Do not fall into the trap of getting there first and getting it wrong. This holds especially true for news, but it's applicable elsewhere. Avoid the rush to incorrectly call Florida for Gore in 2000 without pausing to make sure you've got your ducks in a row.

C stands for *C*odes of ethics. Codes provide valuable guidelines that can facilitate ethical decision making, though, as Jeffrey L. Seglin pointed out in his

20

article, "Codes of Ethics: Why Writing Them Is Not Enough," "Crafting a strong code of ethics is a start. But for it to work, there needs to be some mechanism to ensure that employees from the top of the organization on down have internalized the code." Seglin also observed that there can be a "disconnect" between what a code stipulates and what is done in actuality,[14] but this doesn't mean that codes don't provide strong guidance. Before you make a final determination about a course of action, it's wise to pause to check if there's a code of ethics that addresses the case in question. Codes can at times be an after-the-fact public relations means to present an organization under a favorable light, but this overly cynical view of codes undermines the care and thought that has gone into the creation of codes designed to curtail ethical abuses.

S is for *S*ituational ethics. Starting with on open mind and approaching issues on a case-by-case basis allows one to adjust ethical theories or beliefs to meet a particular situation. Here the situation comes first, not the imposition of a rule. Using situational ethics creates a sensitivity to a set of particular circumstances and avoids the tendency to rush to judgment based on other, possibly very different cases.

Armed with this E*T*H*I*C*S rubric, let's examine some ethical situations associated with today's media. Chapter 2, written by Martin P. Carlson, a senior vice president in business affairs at Fox, focuses on issues related to business ethics.

21

---

[14]Jeffrey L. Seglin, "Codes of Ethics: Why Writing Them Is Not Enough," *Media Ethics*, Spring 2002, vol. 13, no. 2, pp. 1, 24–25.

CHAPTER 2

Business Ethics in Mass Media

By Martin P. Carlson

Because financial considerations underlie many media activities—after all, they don't call it show *business* for nothing—let's first take a look at how business is conducted and then examine how ethical issues come into play, with a particular focus on television, an area of the entertainment industry where I have worked for more than 15 years.

Studio executives looking for the next big hit turn to a variety of sources as ideas for new television programs. As an example of the breadth of potential sources, take a look at these recognizable television series, grouped according to their origins.

- Writer's original idea: *Cheers, The Wonder Years, The X-Files, ER, Malcolm in the Middle*
- Preexisting scripted series: *The Office* (from the UK series), *Ugly Betty* (from the Colombian Spanish-language telenovela *Yo soy Betty la fea*)
- Preexisting unscripted series: *Big Brother* (American version of a popular Dutch series), *Survivor* (based on a Swedish television format originally known as *Expedition Robinson*)
- Developed for an actor/comedian: *The Cosby Show, Roseanne, Home Improvement, Seinfeld, The Drew Carey Show, Everybody Loves Raymond, The Bernie Mac Show*
- Underlying literary material: *Sex and the City* (based on Candace Bushnell's book of the same title), *Lois & Clark* and *Smallville* (from the Superman comic books), *Sabrina: The Teenage Witch* (also comic books), *Friday Night Lights* (also produced as a feature film)

- Feature film: *Mash, Buffy the Vampire Slayer, In the Heat of the Night*
- "Spin-off" of existing series: *A Different World* (from *The Cosby Show*), *Frasier* (from *Cheers*), *The Parkers* (from *Moesha*), *Star Trek: Voyager* (from the original *Star Trek*), *Law & Order: SVU* (again, from the original *Law & Order*)

FIGURE 2-1
Trying to find the next entertainment hit is a complicated process, one that involves establishing the legal parameter. (iStockphoto.com #380233, Joseph Jean and Rolland Dube.)

The threshold issue for the studio (Figure 2-1) seeking to find the next hit is identifying the source and determining what legal rights the studio needs to acquire to develop a particular project. The studio's creative executive wishing to develop a particular project typically will turn to the studio business affairs executive to make the determination and to decide which deals the business affairs executive needs to negotiate to acquire such rights.

For television series, the most common source is an original idea created by a writer, in which case the business affairs executive negotiates with the writer's representative, usually a Los Angeles agent who may work in conjunction with the writer's attorney. Feature films and television movies often rely on underlying source material (such as books or life stories); in this case, the business affairs executive needs to track down the owner of such rights (such as the book publisher, the author, or the person with the particular life story) before commissioning a script from a writer based on these underlying rights.

Once the script is written, the studio or the network determines whether to produce a film or television program based on the script. At this point, the studio hires other personnel to work on the production. Usually minimal individual negotiation is involved for above-the-line personnel (writers, directors, producers, and actors) with limited bargaining power ("leverage") and many below-the-line personnel. These are "scale" engagements for which the talent will be paid the minimum fee and have the minimum level of protections of the applicable collective bargaining agreement. However, as with the original scriptwriter deal, agreements for many above-the-line artists often require more extensive negotiations. See the accompanying box for definitions of key terms used during the development and negotiation process.

KEY TERMS USED IN BUSINESS AFFAIRS NEGOTIATIONS

Above-the-line. Writers, directors, producers, and actors working on a film or television production.

Agency package. Sometimes granted by a studio to an agency in exchange for the agency delivery of key talent to a studio project; if granted, the studio will pay the agency a fee and a percentage of the profits from the project.

Below-the-line. People other than above-the-line personnel working on a film or television production.

Deficit. Difference between the cost of production paid by the studio for a particular television program and the license fee paid by the network to the studio for the right to broadcast the program. The studio pays off the deficit and earns a profit primarily through international sales and off-network syndication sales (both cable and broadcast).

Favored nations. Guarantee with regard to a certain contractual provision that no other party will receive a better provision.

Guild. Union representing above-the-line personnel (namely, the Screen Actors Guild or American Federation of Television and Radio Artists, Directors Guild of America, Writers Guild of America). The federal government does not recognize the Producers Guild as a bargaining unit.

Leverage. Bargaining power.

Pilot. Prototype first episode of a television series.

Quote. What a studio was willing to pay particular talent for a particular job; a person's salary history. A quote can be "earned" or "unearned." *Earned quote*: The studio hired the person and the person performed the job. *Unearned quote*: Applied to actors who audition for a part, negotiate an agreement with the studio in the event they get the part, but ultimately do not get the part. *Recognize the quote*: To acknowledge the quote as valid and agree to pay the quote (or an increase on the quote).

Scale. Minimum wage required by the applicable collective bargaining agreement (the contract between the studios and the union).

Showrunner. The writer/producer in charge of running a television series.

Vertical integration. Control by one company of the means of production and exploitation of a product, such as control over the production, distribution, and exhibition of a television program.

As an example of the volume of negotiation involved in hiring personnel for film and television development and production, take a look at the typical television series production cycle. For each new television series that makes it to the fall schedule, during the preceding spring, the network orders production of several pilots, or prototype first series episodes, most of which are never ordered to series. Each pilot typically contains at least a few series regular actors—that is, actors with long-term contracts that appear in all or most of the series episodes and are prohibited by contract from working on other television series. Most series regular actors audition for a part in the pilot, but before they audition, the studio business affairs executive and the talent representative must fully negotiate a contract, which the actor must sign before the audition and which will govern the actor's employment on the pilot and series if the actor gets the part. So for series regular actors alone, the studio is engaged in volume negotiation. Then, on top of the series regular actors come guest cast members (those hired for the pilot and each separate episode) and noncast members (often in excess of 100 behind-the-camera personnel) hired by a studio to work on a television series.

ETHICS IN NEGOTIATIONS

Like any job application process, personnel seeking employment on a film or television production will provide the studio with information about past work experience ("credits") and a salary history ("quotes"), and like any diligent prospective employer, the studio will confirm credits and quotes, as they are factors in determining how much the studio will pay for the particular talent. For example, suppose an actor recently auditioned for a co-lead role in a single-camera, half-hour, prime-time network comedy series with a budget of $1.5 million per episode. After Studio A agreed to pay the actor $30,000 per episode, the actor did not get the part and moved shortly thereafter to audition for Studio B for a similar part in a similar production. Studio B likely would "recognize the quote" and agree to pay the actor the same fee.

In hiring personnel for film and television production, Internet services such as FilmTracker or the Internet Movie Data Base are good supplemental sources for examining and verifying credits, but the studio negotiator typically must call the talent's previous employers to "check quotes." Is this an issue of the studio negotiator not trusting the talent representative? Yes and no. This is a routine studio business practice—part of a company's "due diligence"—whether or not the studio negotiator and the talent representative have a working relationship. Maybe the quote is not accurate, but maybe the representative doesn't paint the entire picture that the studio needs to see to negotiate the deal—the quote may be considered low, the client may be pressuring the representative to "raise the quote," and the representative may be reluctant to fess up. The novice studio negotiator may get upset with a fuzzy misrepresentation ("They're lying!") or may accept at face value the quote representation (without verification)—after all, as George Constanza observed on *Seinfeld*, "It's not a lie if you believe it."

Other factors enter negotiations in determining how much the studio will pay talent, including such an abstract factor as the "heat" on the talent. The talent representative will typically engage in "puffing" in an attempt to get the studio to think the client has "heat" and is worthy of a higher fee. This is the typical exaggeration of any salesperson, hardly an ethical lapse. In response to the puffery, the negotiator must research the talent's credits and discuss with the studio creative executives to gauge the proper "heat" on the talent (and make a business decision of the studio's willingness to pay the fee requested by the talent representative). For example, a young actor with a few, recent, high-profile credits could be deemed "hot" and demand more aggressive studio bidding than an actor with numerous credits in the distant past but few recent credits.

What about the "bluff"? It's common for an agent to tell the studio that the client has "other opportunities" or that "it's a competitive situation" with other studios bidding on the same talent. These statements may or may not be true. Again, the novice might treat bluffs as personal affronts or accept the bluff as true. However, the seasoned negotiator must try to verify bluffs wherever possible or simply ignore them when immaterial to the negotiation.

A talent representative will often ask the studio negotiator to give a "favored nations" representation—a guarantee with regard to a certain contractual provision that no other party will get a better provision. An actor's representative might hear an earful if the actor shows up on the first day of shooting and sees that his trailer is smaller than any other trailer on the production, or if the client attends his movie premiere and sees that his onscreen credit is smaller than that for any other actor. Studios will routinely give some sort of written protection for these sorts of contractual provisions; in this instance, the issue of ethics and verbal representations does not come into play. But sometimes the studio negotiator cannot give a written assurance—only a verbal assurance during the negotiation. For example, the studio negotiator may refuse to give a "favored nations" back-end definition to a profit participant on a show, but in an effort to move the deal along, the negotiator will verbally tell the talent representative that the client currently has the same definition as other participants. Here, the concept of ethics enters the picture with one party relying on the truth of the other party's statement. The reputation of the negotiator and the past dealings of the parties are factors; as discussed in Chapter 1, previous interactions play a significant role in these types of negotiations. If you know the negotiator for the opposing party and have developed a relationship based on trust, the negotiations tend to proceed more smoothly.

27

Lying is part of the game in business negotiations and the bluffing and puffery examples outlined here typically would not constitute ethical lapses. But the participants must recognize boundaries. If a negotiator consistently makes bold-faced lies during a negotiation, the lie—if discovered—might come back to haunt her in subsequent negotiations with the same parties. After all, Hollywood is a small town. The ethical issue of lying during negotiations can overlap the business issue of how to carry on an efficient and effective negotiation.

You Decide

- When do you think that bluffing could become lying?
- What role do you think ethics play when it comes to both written and verbal agreements?

- How would you define ethical boundaries involved in a negotiation?

28

ETHICS AND CONFLICTS OF INTEREST

As mentioned previously, the talent/artists working in the entertainment industry often are represented by agents, managers, or attorneys who negotiate deals on behalf of their clients. Ethical issues arise when the talent representative assumes a position that conflicts with the best interests of the client. In recent years, the lines that traditionally have distinguished various representatives from each other—and representatives from studios—have become so blurred that the potential for conflict has increased.

ATTORNEYS AND ETHICS

Attorneys face potential conflicts of interest by representing adverse parties in a transaction or in litigation. At issue is whether an attorney can simultaneously represent the interests of competing parties.

Attorneys are licensed by the state in which they practice, and conflicts of interest are regulated in varying degrees by state code and civil case law. In California, the Rules of Professional Conduct regulate the professional conduct of members and provide ethical guidelines governing conflicts of interest. Some applicable rules include the following:

- An attorney must provide written disclosure to a client if the attorney has a "legal, business, financial, professional, or personal relationship" with a party in the same matter.[1]
- An attorney must obtain the client's "informed written consent" before the attorney can represent more than one client in a matter in which the interests of the clients might conflict.[2]
- An attorney cannot represent a client in a matter in which another party's lawyer is related without informing the client of the relationship.[3]

According to some observers, consolidation among law firms and their business clients has created a conflicts nightmare.[4] However, for a client in the entertainment industry, an attorney entanglement that would be considered a conflict in other industries is often viewed as an asset, a sign that the lawyer is well connected.[5] For a law firm, the risk of an ethics violation might be deemed a cost of doing business—if an attorney has a substantial client base, hiring firms have an economic incentive to ignore potential problems.[6] As an example, suppose a studio executive wants to hire talent represented by an attorney who happens to be the studio executive's wife. Is this a conflict of interest for the attorney? Is this "smart business" for the talent? Would the law firm look favorably or unfavorably at the attorney's connections?

Despite the potential benefits of being well connected, violations of the ethics guidelines can and do result in disciplinary action by the state bar, court sanctions, or malpractice lawsuits. Several entertainment law firms have been sued for alleged conflicts of interest. For example, three such lawsuits were filed in 1992 against the prominent Los Angeles entertainment law firm of Ziffren, Brittenham, Branca, Fischer, Gilbert-Lurie, Stiffelman & Cook. One of those suits was filed by a former partner, Gregg Homer, after the firm fired him for cause, alleging that Homer "did not measure up."[7] Homer claimed that the firm made deals that benefited the more important clients without disclosing the effect of those deals to its other clients. In so doing, Homer said, founding partners Skip Brittenham and Ken Ziffren "were placing their own interests

---

[1]California Rules of Professional Conduct, Rule 3-310 (B).

[2]Id., Rule 3-310 (C).

[3]Id., Rule 3-320.

[4]Thomas Brom, "Full Disclosure: Taint So," *California Lawyer*, June 2006, pp. 17–18.

[5]Claudia Eller, "Entertainment Lawyer Reels in the Big Deals," September 15, 2005, latimes.com, accessed June 28, 2006.

[6]Brom, "Full Disclosure," pp. 17–18.

[7]Eller, "Entertainment Lawyer Reels in the Big Deals."

ahead of those of their clients." Because the law firm settled the case out of court—and a jury never made a fact determination[8]—it's difficult to have a definitive legal precedent to follow. However, the threat of a lawsuit is substantial and serious when there is a potential conflict of interest.

AGENTS AND ETHICS

The traditional role of the talent agent is to procure employment for clients in exchange for a commission of the client's earnings. Like attorneys, talent agents are regulated by the state in which they work. In California, the Labor Code specifies that, among many guidelines, a talent agent:

- Must immediately deposit client salaries in a trust fund account and the funds, less commission, must be disbursed within 30 days
- May not divide fees with an employer
- May not refer an artist to any business in which the talent agency has a financial interest[9]

In addition to state regulation, talent guilds—the Screen Actors Guild (SAG), Writers Guild of America (WGA), and Directors Guild of America (DGA)—have sought to establish appropriate standards for agents who represent guild members in individual negotiations. For example, the SAG franchise agreement limits an agent's commission to 10% (even if the state may approve a higher commission rate), requires a shorter period for disbursing client funds than required by the state, prohibits agents from producing or owning pieces of their clients' work, and limits agency contracts to three years (even though California permits a contract with a term up to seven years).[10]

Unlike attorneys, agents are not specifically prohibited from representing multiple sides in a negotiation; but talent/artists nonetheless have made claims for perceived conflicts. A recent example involved Doris Roberts—"Marie Barone" on the television series *Everybody Loves Raymond*—who alleged that her talent agency had a conflict of interest involving a law firm representing both the agency and the agency's owner.

The law firm had renegotiated a contract for Roberts as well as for her *Raymond* costars Peter Boyle and Patricia Heaton. When Roberts didn't get some provisions that the other actors received, she sued.

[8]Eller, "Entertainment Lawyer Reels in the Big Deals."
[9]California Labor Code, Sections 1700-1700.47.
[10]David Zelenski, "Talent Agents, Personal Managers, and Their Conflicts in the New Hollywood," *Southern California Law Review*, 2003, vol. 76, p. 979.

Another area rife with potential conflict is agency packages (Figure 2-2). Basically, an agency will demand a "package" from a studio in exchange for delivering key talent to a project; if the studio agrees to recognize a package, the studio will pay directly to the agency a fee and a percentage of the profits from the project. Packages are prominent and profitable in television series, where a studio might agree to recognize an agency package if the agency delivers, for example, an experienced show runner or a bona fide star who will garner a production commitment from the licensing network. The agency will receive a percentage of the license fee paid by the network to the studio (typically 3% of the network "base" license fee, i.e., without add-ons for extraordinary production or cast costs). This upfront fee becomes a line item in the studio's series production budget and is included in the negative cost of the series. In addition, the agency will receive a percentage of the network license fee that is deferred and payable out of a portion of the series net profits. Finally, the agency will receive a percentage of the profits derived from the series (typically 10% of the series profits using the same back-end definition as the agency's client). Although agents are prohibited by guild franchise agreements from acting as producers, they are not prohibited from assembling packages. Nonetheless, some argue that agency packaging is a "blurring of legal lines" that is "opposite to California law."[11]

FIGURE 2-2
As discussed in this chapter, agency packages are different from what most people associate with packages. (iStockphoto #2944682, Ed Hidden.)

The benefit to the client is that the agency typically waives the client's commission payment if the agency is granted a package. Clearly, the agency will make more money from a package than from commissioning 10% of the client's income, and the studio—not the client—will make the package payment. However, it's not entirely clear that the client is better off with the studio paying a package to the agency in lieu of the client paying a commission to the agency.

[11]Rick Siegle, "Art vs. Commerce: Big Boys Play Dirty," posted March 1, 2006, Monstersandcritics.com, accessed June 22, 2006. The tension surrounding agencies serving as producers is not recent. The first Hollywood mogul to build a production company off the strength of talent representation was the late Lew Wasserman, who won a special exemption from SAG in the 1950s and transformed his talent agency, Music Corp. of America (MCA), into a major studio. Brett Pulley, "The Celebrity 100: Hollywood Hit Man," posted July 8, 2002, Forbes.com, accessed June 20, 2006. Federal antitrust investigation of MCA led to divestiture of the agency division. Siegle, "Art vs. Commerce."

Let's consider four examples of how a package might be seen as an ethical conflict. In the first situation, we'll walk through the analysis using the E*T*H*I*C*S
rubric. Situations 2 through 4 will be part of a "You Decide" box.

1. In a studio negotiation with an agency for an actor to star in a potential
   network comedy series loosely based on the actor's life, the agency also
   represented a writer with whom the studio had worked in the past (and
   was not particularly keen on working with in the future).

- *E*valuate. Examine situation from the point of view of each party involved
  in the project: the studio, network, actor, writer, and agency.
- *T*ruth. Here are some important facts underlying the negotiation:
  - The studio would have been willing to grant the agency a package
    based solely on delivery of the actor to the studio, but such package
    would be subject to splitting with another agency in the event another
    agency delivered the writer to work with the actor to create and execu-
    tive produce the series.
  - The agency refused to deliver the actor to the studio without the
    agency's writer in an effort to "protect its package" (that is, preclude
    sharing the package with another agency).
  - The writer turned in a lifeless script, and the network quickly passed
    on the project.
- *H*arm. Did the "bundling" of the writer and the actor harm any party?
  The agency that wanted to protect its package never collected fees because
  the project did not proceed. The studio and the network paid money for
  both the writer and the actor, but they did not receive a strong project in
  return. You could hardly say the writer was harmed—the writer received
  payment in full for a weak script. Possibly the actor was most harmed:
  The actor received payment from the studio and the network but didn't
  get to move forward with a pet project.
- *I*nvestigating. Examine who knew what and when they knew it. The
  studio had a working relationship with the writer going into the project,
  and the agency had represented the writer for some time. The network
  would have (or easily could have) uncovered information about the
  writer—Hollywood is a small town, and a good network executive can
  get people to talk. But what about the actor? Did the actor or the
  actor's managers have access to information to make a judgment about
  the writer? Did the actor realize the agency was pushing to "protect its
  package"?
- *C*odes of ethics. As mentioned previously, the SAG franchise agreement
  prohibits an agent from producing or owning a piece of a client's work,

but there is no explicit prohibition on packages. Unlike the California Rules of Professional Conduct for attorneys, the Labor Code governing agents does not explicitly delineate prohibitions on conflicts.

- *S*ituational ethics. Because there are no defined rules drawn from an applicable code of ethics, you must look at the ethics of the situation. Was there an unethical conflict of interest in this situation?

You Decide

How would you use the E*T*H*I*C*S rubric to evaluate these remaining three situations?

33

2. If an agency is granted a package, the package fee paid by the studio to the agency is included in the series production costs, which are recouped before the client receives any profits from the series. Payment of the package fee could delay and reduce the client's profits from the series. In addition, under certain studio contingent compensation definitions, profit participants reduce each other ("everybody reduces everybody") such that the agency's back end would reduce the client's back end. What ethical obligation does the agency have to its client in such a situation?

3. The writer/creator/executive producer of a television series is typically engaged for a maximum of the first two years on a series. If the series lives past two seasons and the studio wants to retain the writer/producer, the studio must negotiate a new deal with the artist's representative. If the series is successful, the studio often engages the writer/producer for additional years for a guaranteed sum significantly greater than the original deal (especially if the writer/producer was a relative "unknown" at the time of the original deal). The cost for the new deal will be charged to the production cost of the series, which will be recouped before the studio pays profit participation. The packaging agency does not commission the new deal but is a profit participant on the series. Does the packaging agency have a conflict of interest by being a profit participant on the series while handling the client's renegotiation?

4. Earlier in the chapter, we talked about bluffing as a negotiation tactic. Consider this bluff: In a negotiation for a writer/producer, the agent and attorney scheduled a conference call with the studio negotiator to discuss deal terms. After the agent's assistant announced to the agent and attorney (already on the call) that the studio negotiator had joined the call, the agent and attorney, both of whom didn't hear the assistant, continued their conversation, unaware that the studio negotiator was listening, and outlined their plan to bluff about a competing bid from another studio in an effort to garner a better deal for their client. Was it unethical for the studio negotiator to listen to the conversation? Do you think it was unethical for the agent and attorney to lie about a competing bid?

MANAGERS AND ETHICS

Managers traditionally have performed a strictly advisory function for their clients. Compared to agents, they tend to represent fewer clients with more personalized service, and, since they are regulated by neither the state nor the talent guilds, they are permitted to charge higher commissions—15% is common. Managers for high-profile talent often attached themselves as producers to their clients' projects; in such cases, the studio typically pays producing fees and any profit participation directly to the manager, and the manager won't charge the client a commission.

Some agents and studio executives balk at managers who attach themselves as producers, arguing that they are not legitimate producers and merely serve to drive up production costs. Managers argue that it is no different than when an agency packages a television series—it gets a fee and back end in exchange for providing key talent.[12] Like packaging agents, managers who function as producers may face a conflict: because they will not receive any of the series profits until the studio recoups production costs, they have an incentive to keep production costs (including client salaries) down.[13] Whether or not a manager acts in a manner that harms the client—there is often no clear legal guideline—the potential for conflict exists and the manager may face legal action from a disgruntled client.

[12]Maria Mondavi, "Agent vs. Manager," *The Script Journal*, scriptshark.com, accessed June 23, 2006.
[13]Zelenski, "Talent Agents, Personal Managers, and Their Conflicts in the New Hollywood."

To illustrate the type of ethical conflicts a manager may face, let's look at Brad Grey. Before joining the studio ranks as a film executive at Paramount, Grey was a high-profile example of the manager/producer, a role that was rife with potential conflicts. In an attempt to avoid conflict (and potential legal claims), Grey's policy was to inform clients that he was also in business as a producer and to require clients to hire an outside attorney and agent to negotiate separately on their behalf. David Chase, creator of *The Sopranos* (produced by Grey for HBO), opted for different management to avoid conflict.[14]

Despite precautions, Grey's potential conflicts came to light in a 1998 lawsuit filed by his former client Garry Shandling (Figure 2-3). Grey served both as Shandling's manager and as executive producer of *The Larry Sanders Show* starring Shandling on HBO. Shandling disputed Grey's earning from the series: 10% manager fee on Shandling's earnings, plus an executive producing fee in the neighborhood of $45,000 per episode, plus 50% of the series net profits. Following an audit of the series, Grey returned $1.2 million, but Shandling claimed he was owed additional amounts. Grey dropped Shandling as a client in 1997, and in early 1998 Shandling sued for $100 million in damages. The lawsuit ultimately settled out of court for $10 million.[15]

FIGURE 2-3
Entertainer Garry Shandling felt that Brad Grey, now head of Paramount, had a conflict of interest while functioning as both his manager and the executive producer of *The Larry Sanders Show*. (Globe Photos, Inc.)

35

You Decide

Could the lawsuit between Brad Grey and Garry Shandling have been avoided? Or was this relationship inherently an unethical conflict of interest? Do you think it is ethically acceptable for a manager to serve as a producer on a client's project?

[14]Pulley, "The Celebrity 100."

[15]David M. Halbfinger and Allison Hope Weiner, "A Studio Boss and a Private Eye Star in a Bitter Hollywood Tale," March 13, 2006, NYTimes.com, accessed June 20, 2006.

CORPORATE SELF-DEALING

Relaxed government regulation of the mass media since the early 1990s has lead to increased concentration of ownership in certain areas, a topic we will discuss in depth in Chapter 11. Here, we will approach consolidation in relation to corporate self-dealing. Transactions that at one point were between competing companies are now between divisions of the same company. As a result, are there business ethics issues that arise? If so, can these be distinguished from broader public policy issues relating to media ownership?

GOVERNMENT REGULATION

Before examining issues surrounding corporate self-dealing, let's examine key developments leading up to the current situation. Government and media companies have long been at odds over who controls access to the American public. In the area of theatrical motion pictures, the U.S. Justice Department initiated the Paramount antitrust litigation against the major Hollywood studios in 1938, and the U.S. Supreme Court held in 1948 that there had been a conspiracy that "had monopoly in exhibition for one of its goals" and endorsed a host of restrictions and divestitures.[16] The studios subsequently entered into consent decrees, which limited exhibition activities and required some defendants to divest themselves of some theater chains.[17]

In radio, the Federal Communications Commission (FCC) launched an investigation in 1938 of NBC, CBS, and the Mutual Broadcasting System amid concerns of the increasing dominance of the three major radio networks. The investigation culminated three years later with the issuance of the *Report on Chain Broadcasting* and the Chain Broadcasting Rules, which were upheld by the U.S. Supreme Court in 1943 and later applied to television networks.[18]

The FCC continued to examine network practices relating to the acquisition, ownership, production, distribution, sales, and licensing of television programming, which culminated in the FCC adoption of the Financial Interest and Syndication Rules in 1970. Basically, "Fin-Syn," as the rules were called, prohibited the networks from having a financial interest in the production or syn-

---

[16]*United States v. Paramount Pictures, Inc.*, 334 U.S. 131 (1948).

[17]Id.

[18]*NBC v. United States*, 319 U.S. 190 (1943). See also, Christopher S. Yoo, "Vertical Integration and Media Regulation in the New Economy," *Yale Journal on Regulation*, 2002, vol. 19, pp. 171, 186.

dication of many of the programs the networks broadcast. The principal rationale for Fin-Syn was that vertical integration unfairly increased the power of the networks. By separating production from distribution, the FCC would foster diversity of programming by fostering diversity of program ownership.[19]

Fin-Syn was controversial from the beginning. Some argued that independent producers per se would not produce more diverse or higher quality programming. In fact, because only large studio production companies are financially capable of paying television series deficits, independent producers largely produced made-for-television movies, talk shows, or game shows. Consent decrees executed by the Justice Department in 1977 solidified Fin-Syn and limited the amount of prime-time programming the networks could produce.

When Fin-Syn was enacted, the networks' combined share of the television audience was around 90%. By the early 1990s, however, this share had dropped to roughly 65% as a result of the new forms of competition (e.g., cable, Fox Broadcasting Company), and large media companies were pressuring the FCC and Congress to relax government ownership restrictions.

By November 1995, all traces of Fin-Syn had been eliminated. Further deregulation of media ownership came with the Telecommunications Act of 1996, which accomplished, among other things, the following:

- Removed all limitations on the number of radio stations one company can own nationally and allowed up to eight per company locally (instead of only four)
- Relaxed the rules about how many television stations one company can operate
- Ordered the FCC to consider easing the rule limiting ownership to one television station per market, as well as the bar to ownership of a newspaper and a broadcast outlet in the same city
- Permitted common ownership of cable systems and broadcast networks
- Ended all rate regulation of smaller cable television systems and promised the same for large ones later on
- Extended the license term of television and radio stations to eight years from four years
- Allowed television networks to start and own another broadcast network if they choose

[19]James N. Talbott, "Will Mega-Media Mergers Destroy Hollywood & Democracy?" 2000, *The Legal Interface*, http://www.legalinterface.com, accessed March 31, 2006.

RESULTS OF RELAXATION OF GOVERNMENT REGULATION

Research indicates that in the area of prime-time broadcast network television, the number of production companies has decreased and the market share of the top studio production companies has increased since the repeal of the Fin-Syn rules and the Telecommunications Act of 1996. Consider the following highlights of the prime-time network television schedules for the following four seasons:[20]

1991–1992 Season

- The top six production companies produced about 66% of the series programming.
- About 20 production companies produced prime-time broadcast network television series.
- Made-for-television movies were staples of the prime-time network schedule.
- Numerous production companies that were not affiliated with networks or major studios produced series for the broadcast networks (e.g., Cannell, Spelling, Cosgrove-Meurer).

1995–1996 Season

- The top six production companies produced about 69% of the series programming.
- About 15 production companies produced prime-time broadcast network television series.
- Made-for-television movies continued to be a staple of the broadcast networks.
- Fewer small productions companies produced series for the broadcast networks.

1999–2000 Season

- The top six production companies increased their market share to 76% of the series programming.
- About 18 production companies produced prime-time broadcast network television series.

---

[20]Neil Hickey, "So Big," *Columbia Journalism Review*, January/February 1997. Unrelated to media ownership, the Telecommunications Act of 1996 also required that all television sets come equipped with a V-chip to help screen out violent and sexually explicit shows and imposed prison terms and fines on anybody who transmits pornography over the Internet. Id.

- Made-for-television movies continued to be a staple of the broadcast networks.
- Small productions companies continued to produce series for the broadcast networks.

2006–2007 Season

- The top six production companies produced about 91% of the series programming and produced primarily for networks owned by common parent companies (such as 20th Century Fox Television producing for Fox Broadcasting and Touchstone Television producing for ABC). Increased vertical integration was noticeable.
- About 15 production companies produced prime-time broadcast network television series.
- Made-for-television movies had for the most part disappeared from the broadcast networks.
- Fewer small productions companies produced television series for the broadcast networks. The increased number of broadcast television series in both the 1995–1996 and 1999–2000 seasons reflected the addition of the WB and UPN networks. The reduced number of broadcast series in the 2006–2007 season reflected the merger of the WB and UPN to form the new CW network.

To some observers, such as producer Len Hill, the elimination of Fin-Syn caused a tectonic shift in the organization of national media that permitted "vertically integrated media empires" increasingly engaging in anticompetitive practices.[21] Profit participants on television series soon made such allegations in lawsuits against the series production companies. The essence of these claims was that the vertically integrated companies engaged in self-dealing by artificially decreasing license fees paid by one affiliated company to another, thereby decreasing the amount of profit paid by the studio to the profit participant.[22]

A simplified version of profit participation goes something like this: The series television production company typically earns revenue from the initial network license fees, international sales, off-network broadcast license fees, off-network cable sales, home video/DVD, merchandising, and other revenue streams. From all these revenue sources, the production company first recoups the following

---

[21]Leonard Hill, "The Axis of Access," Weidenbaum Center Forum, "Entertainment Economics: The Movie Industry," Washington University in St. Louis, April 3, 2003.

[22]Stanton L. Stein and Marcia J. Harris, "Vertically Challenged," *Los Angeles Lawyer*, May 2003, vol. 26, no. 3, pp. 30.

costs and expenses before paying profits: production costs, distribution costs and expenses, distribution fees, overhead, and interest. Reduction in any of the revenue streams will translate into a reduction in the profits paid by the studio.

The studios countered that they had strict contractual business relationships with the profit participants but no fiduciary duties toward the profit participants—in other words, they had no *ethical* obligations to maximize the profits paid to the participants.

FIGURE 2-4
David Duchovny, star of *The X-Files*, accused 20th Century Fox of "self-dealing" by licensing the series at below-market rates to 20th Century Fox subsidiaries. (Globe Photos, Inc.)

A high-profile example of a lawsuit alleging "self-dealing" was *The X-Files* star David Duchovny's (Figure 2-4) claim against 20th Century Fox Film Corporation, alleging that 20th Century Fox Television—the production company for *The X-Files* and a subsidiary of 20th Century Fox Film Corporation—licensed the series at below-market prices to other subsidiaries of 20th Century Fox Film Corporation, to Fox Broadcasting Company for initial network broadcast, to FX for off-network cable syndication rights, and to the Fox Stations Groups for off-network broadcast syndication rights.[23] Although this case settled out of court, it illustrates the opposing viewpoints of a fiduciary relationship with ethical obligations versus a strictly contractual business relationship.[24]

At the time of the first lawsuits alleging "self-dealing," many of the contracts between the studios and the profit participants did not contain language governing the dealings with affiliated companies. Following the appearance of such lawsuits, studios included prophylactic contractual provisions such as the one shown in the accompanying box, which govern dealings with affiliates, mandatory arbitration, and a limitation of awards from a lawsuit to actual damages (i.e., a breach of contract claim only).

Still, lawsuits continue. A more recent case that "strikes at the heart of the modern vertically integrated media company"[25] involves Peter Jackson's claim against New Line Cinema, the subsidiary of Time Warner that financed and distributed the Oscar-winning *Lord*

[23]Janet Shprintz, "Duchovny Sues Fox over TV Rights Sales," posted August 13, 1999, Variety.com, accessed March 31, 2006.
[24]Ross Johnson, "The Lawsuit of the Rings," published June 27, 2005, NYTimes.com, accessed March 31, 2006. "Since no studio head or corporate executive wants to be subpoenaed in a lawsuit over accounting, vertical integration lawsuits are almost always settled before reaching open court." Id.
[25]Johnson, "The Lawsuit of the Rings."

SAMPLE STUDIO CONTRACTUAL PROVISION FOR PROFIT PARTICIPANTS

Distribution Controls:

General: Studio shall have complete, exclusive and unqualified discretion and control as to the time, manner, and terms of its distribution, exhibition and exploitation of each Series episode (including the Pilot), separately or in connection with other programs, in accordance with such policies, terms and conditions and through such parties as Studio in its business judgment may in good faith determine are consistent with business policy and proper or expedient and the decision of Studio in all such matters shall be binding and conclusive upon Artist. Notwithstanding the foregoing, Studio shall accord good faith (meaningful) consultation to Artist with respect to the initial domestic off-network sales plan, subject to the reasonable availability and reasonable response time of Artist. Studio makes no express or implied warranty or representation as to the manner or extent of any distribution or exploitation of each Series episode (including the Pilot) nor the amount of money to be derived from the distribution, exhibition and exploitation of each Series episode (including the Pilot), nor as to any maximum or minimum amount of such monies to be expended in connection therewith. Studio does not guarantee the performance by any Subdistributor, licensee or exhibitor, of any contract regarding the distribution and exploitation of each Series episode (including the Pilot).

Dealings with Affiliates:

Artist acknowledges that Studio is part of a diversified, multi-faceted, international company, whose affiliates include, or may in the future include, among others, exhibitors, television "platforms," networks, stations and programming services, video device distributors, record companies, internet companies, so called "E.Commerce companies," publishers (literary and electronic) and wholesale and retail outlets (individually or collectively, "Affiliated Company or Companies"). Artist further acknowledges that Studio has informed Artist that Studio intends to make use of Affiliated Companies in connection with its distribution and exploitation of the Series episodes (including the Pilot), as, when and where Studio deems it appropriate to do so. Artist expressly waives any right to object to such distribution and exploitation of any Series episode (including the Pilot) (or aspects thereof) or assert any claim that Studio should have offered the applicable distribution/exploitation rights to unaffiliated third parties (in lieu of, or in addition to, offering the same to Affiliated Companies). In consideration thereof, Studio agrees that Studio's transactions with Affiliated Companies will be on monetary terms comparable to the terms on which the Affiliated Company enters into similar transactions with unrelated third party distributors for comparable programs. Artist agrees that Artist's sole remedy against Studio for any alleged failure by Studio to comply with the terms of this paragraph shall be actual damages, and Artist hereby waives any right to seek or obtain preliminary or permanent equitable relief or punitive relief in connection with any such alleged failure.

> **Arbitration:**
> Any dispute arising under the provisions of this paragraph shall be arbitrated by, and under the rules of, J.A.M.S. ("JAMS") in binding arbitration in Los Angeles, California, and before a mutually selected arbitrator experienced in the United States television industry. Although each side shall advance one-half of the fee of the arbitrator and for JAMS' services, the prevailing party in such arbitration shall be entitled to recover all costs of arbitration, including reasonable outside attorneys' fees and costs.

of the Rings film trilogy. Jackson alleged that the company used "preemptive bidding" (a process closed to external parties) rather than open bidding for subsidiary rights to such things as *Lord of the Rings* books, DVDs, and merchandise. As a result, Jackson claimed, "New Line received far less than market value for these rights, the suit says."[26]

PAYOLA

The Communications Act and longstanding FCC rules and policies provide serious penalties for broadcasters and others who engage in payola or plugola or otherwise fail to satisfy sponsorship identification requirements. Payola is the unreported payment to, or acceptance by, employees of broadcast stations, program producers, or program suppliers of any money, service, or valuable consideration in return for the broadcast of any programming material. Plugola is the use or promotion on the air of goods or services in which the individual responsible for including that promotion material has an undisclosed financial interest. Section 507 of the Communications Act of 1934 requires that if an employee receives money or anything else of value in exchange for broadcasting any material, both the person making the payment and the employee must disclose the payment to the stations. The law does not prohibit an employee from taking money; it is the failure to report the payment to station management that constitutes a violation. Section 317 of the Communications Act of 1934 requires a station to make an on-air disclosure whenever it is advised, pursuant to Section 507, that an employee has received payment for putting material (Figure 2-5) on the air. Also, the station must use reasonable diligence to obtain from employees and others involved in

FIGURE 2-5
According to Section 317 of the Communications Act, on-air disclosures are required if payment has been made to air material. For example, it must be disclosed if payment has been made on behalf of a song being listened to by an appreciative fan. (iStockphotos.com #2136934, Tyler Stalman.)

[26]Ibid.

program production or selection the information necessary to make any required announcements.[27]

Despite the payola scandals of the 1950s, the practice has once again jumped to the headlines primarily as a result of investigations by Elliot Spitzer while he served as New York State attorney general and ensuing out-of-court settlements with major record labels.

As an example of the recent, updated payola practices, *Billboard* magazine reported that on April 23, 2005, radio station WQZQ in Nashville played "Don't Tell Me," a single by Avril Lavigne, three times an hour over a six-hour time period. An independent promoter working for Lavigne's record label had paid the station to play the song (a "spot buy"). "Don't Tell Me" had been lingering just outside the *Billboard* list of the country's 10 most frequently played songs, a list radio programmers use to decide what singles get airtime. The additional spins the promoter bought were meant to push "Don't Tell Me" up the list. By early June, Lavigne had a Top 10 hit.[28]

You Decide

How might you apply the E*T*H*I*C*S rubric to analyze the new, updated payola practice as exemplified by the "Don't Tell Me" situation?

- *E*valuate. Look at the situation from the point-of-view of all parties involved. What about the radio listener? Other recording artists? Other record labels?
- *T*ruth. The radio station played the song so often because it was paid to do so, not because the audience requested it or because the DJ thought the song had special merit.
- *H*arm. Who was harmed? Again, think about the radio listener, other artists, and other record labels.
- *I*nvestigating. Think about analogies in other businesses, such as supermarkets and drugstores that accept money to position products at the end of an aisle or at eye level, or book chains that sell space on the tables at the front of their stores. But also think about the

differences: whereas the old form of payola would buy exposure, spot buys like the one that propelled Avril Lavigne into the Top 10 aren't meant to introduce listeners to songs; they're meant to game the playlist system. It's a salient feature of modern media that being thought to be popular can make you more popular. Best-selling books and records are discounted more than slow-selling ones and are positioned more prominently. Songs in *Billboard*'s Top 10 automatically end up being spun more. And if you invest lots of money in creating an illusion of popularity—by, say, buying hours of airplay on the radio—you may end up making yourself more popular.[29]

- *C*odes of ethics. In this case, we're dealing with specific laws.
- *S*ituational ethics. Because we have specific laws governing the facts of the case, should we take a special examination of the situation?

43

[27] "Safeguarding Against Payola and Plugola Problems," Wiley Rein & Fielding LLP, 2006. Note that payola and plugola are not issues in theatrical motion pictures because the distribution is not licensed and governed by the FCC.

[28] James Surowiecki, "Paying to Play," *The New Yorker*, Issues 2004-07-12 and 19, www. newyorker.com, accessed June 1, 2006.

[29] Id.

In describing Sony BMG's practice following his 2005 settlement, Spitzer said that, "contrary to listener expectations that songs are selected for airplay based on artistic merit and popularity, air time is often determined by undisclosed payoffs to radio stations and their employees."[30] According to Spitzer, the payola took several forms:

- Bribes to radio programmers, including expensive vacation packages, electronics, and other valuable items
- Contest giveaways for stations' listening audiences
- Payments to radio stations to cover operational expenses
- Retention of middlemen, known as independent promoters, as conduits for illegal payments to radio stations
- Payments for "spin programs," airplay under the guise of advertising[31]

As part of the settlement, Sony BMG agreed to stop making payoffs in return for airplay and to disclose in full all items of value provided to radio stations in the future; Sony BMG also agreed to hire a compliance officer and to implement an internal accounting system. In addition, the company agreed to make a $10 million charitable contribution for music education and appreciation for New York State.[32] Spitzer continued the payola probes of the music industry and subsequently reached out-of-court settlements with other record labels, including Universal Music Group Recordings Inc., Warner Music Group, and EMI Music America.[33]

The following guidelines can be used to navigate the ethical and legal dilemmas of payola/plugola:

- Broadcasters must air sponsorship identification announcements if the station or any person involved in the selection or production of a program has received or has been promised payment or other valuable consideration in return for the inclusion of programming material in a broadcast.
- All sponsored material must be explicitly identified at the time of broadcast as paid for, and the party who paid for the broadcast must be identified as well.

---

[30]"Sony Settles Payola Investigation" July 25, 2005, press release from the office of New York State attorney general Elliot Spitzer.
[31]Id.
[32]Id.
[33]"EMI Settles Payola Probe for $3.75 Million," posted June 16, 2006, www.hollywoodreporter.com, accessed June 16, 2006.

- Sponsorship identification may not be necessary if products or services are furnished without or at a nominal charge and any product mention is incidental to its reasonable use in the broadcast. Additionally, the receipt of small gifts ($25 or less) usually is exempt from payola/plugola restrictions.
- The law does not directly prohibit an individual or station from receiving or making a payment or gift (Figure 2-6); rather, the law prohibits the failure to disclose the receipt of the payment or gift.
- A station should require employees to sign affidavits (1) affirming that they have not received or been offered money or other valuable consideration in return for airing any programming material; (2) disclosing, or agreeing not to engage in, any outside business activities that could create a conflict of interest in the selection of program material; and (3) agreeing not to promote any outside business activities or interests on the air without an appropriate commercial announcement.[34]

FIGURE 2-6
Gifts are allowed as long as they are disclosed, according to the legal guidelines of payola and plugola. (iStockphotos.com #2565703, blackred.)

45

Networks that license programs from production companies require representations and warranties from suppliers; in turn, studios should require talent representations and warranties in contracts directly with talent. Here is an example of a provision from a contract between talent and a television production company:

FCC Compliance. Artist warrants and represents that Artist will neither pay nor agree to pay any money, service, or other valuable consideration as defined in Section 507 of the Communications Act of 1934 as amended, for the inclusion of any matter in any motion picture, and that Artist has not accepted nor will knowingly accept nor agree to accept any money, service, or other valuable consideration (other than payment to Artist hereunder) for the inclusion of any matter in any motion picture. Artist will, during or after the term of Artist's services hereunder, promptly on request, complete Studio's standard Section 507 report form.

---

[34]"Safeguarding Against Payola and Plugola Problems."

You Decide

Here are some examples of potential payola and plugola issues. Given the restrictions and guidelines outlined earlier and following the E*T*H*I*C*S rubric, how do you think these issues should or could be resolved?

■ A director of a prime-time network television pilot asks the production crew to place a bottle of beer with a visible label in a scene because her friend owns the beer manufacturing company.

■ An over-the-counter antacid manufacturer offers to pay a studio $75,000 to include mention of its product in a scene featuring the lead actor of a television series.

■ A restaurant chain that advertises significantly on the television network that broadcasts a series produced by a third-party studio offers to buy advertising time on the network in exchange for having the network require that the studio include the company's product in the program that the studio produces for broadcast on the network.

■ A large national retail chain approaches the producers of a prime-time network television series about tying a sweepstakes contest with the series, with one of the series' characters carrying a shopping bag with the retail chain's logo.

■ A cable network requires a studio to place a bottle of wine (Figure 2-7) with the label clearly visible as a prop in one of the scenes in an episode of a television series produced by the studio for the cable network.

■ A studio approaches a car dealer about supplying cars to use as "picture vehicles" in the production of a television series. The car dealer offers to supply a picture vehicle for the entire series. If the studio had to rent the car on the open market, the studio would have to pay a considerable fee.

■ A vendor offers a favor to a production executive in exchange for repeat business in the future.

■ A television station manager receives a packaged news story about an advance in medicine produced by a pharmaceutical company using an actor portraying a reporter who is paid by a pharmaceutical company.

FIGURE 2-7
Asking a set designer to feature a wine bottle as a prop can lead to potential payola/plugola ethical violations. (iStockphotos. com #244714, Diane Diederich.)

46

In this chapter, we have explored some of the ethical issues involved in entertainment business negotiations. In the next chapter, let's look at ethical issues that regularly confront producers, writers, actors, and directors.

CHAPTER 3

Ethics and the Role of Producers, Writers, Actors, and Directors

Writers, directors, actors, and producers all have to decide what part ethics will play in their work. The creative team may chose to ignore, embrace, or co-opt ethical issues, but they can't readily deny their existence; sometimes the ethical quandaries lurk below the surface before imploding and creating a crisis situation. Sometimes the quandaries are readily apparent at the start. In this chapter, we will examine some of the ethical issues that creative individuals face on a daily basis.

FINDING MATERIAL: THE SEARCH FOR A GOOD STORY

We've all been taught that stealing is wrong. And we've also heard Fred Allen's famous line that imitation is the sincerest form of television. Some also claim that there are only seven or eight different stories to tell. Variations abound, but original stories are not easy to come by. So how does a writer, producer, director, or hyphenate come up with an original idea that will sell without violating one's moral code?

Students and professionals alike live in great fear that their ideas are going to be stolen, that the sharks will gather around and abscond with the goods. Some people are so protective of their ideas, in fact, that they keep them well hidden, refusing to share them with anyone who might be in a position to make the idea reach fruition, thus guaranteeing that their idea will never see the light of day.

Many writers protect themselves by registering a story concept with the Writers Guild (www.wga.org) before taking it out. This is a good idea and highly recommended, but beginning writers, specifically, should not be afraid of having their ideas stolen. This is not to say that ideas aren't ever stolen. They are, but beginning writers and producers should have a supply of material at the ready at all times instead of clinging to a single concept that they refuse to share for fear of being ripped off.

One never knows when a person with power might say, "What are you working on?" You tell her the concept. She says, "Interesting, but that is not what I am looking for right now." For many, that would be the end of the conversation and a missed opportunity. If you are working on a number of ideas and are willing to share, you can continue describing some of your other ideas. Maybe one of them will hit. If one thing doesn't work, try others.

FIGURE 3-1
As discussed in the text, developing a story about someone raised as a flower child can raise some serious ethical questions, particularly if the person is a friend. (iStockphoto.com #2877944, Sang Nguyem.)

48

Step 1 is being ready to expose your ideas without excessive fear of having them stolen. As writer Ian Gurvitz observed, "So to anyone who feels their idea has been ripped off, chances are it hasn't. If you think Hollywood stole your idea, maybe what you need to think about is having another idea."[1] He noted, sarcastically, "Hollywood does not steal. Hollywood copies, imitates, panders and plagiarizes, rips off and robs, but Hollywood does not steal ideas for one reason and one reason only—it's not ethical."[2]

Step 2 is confronting the ethical situations that are likely to occur in acquiring and creating material. Here are a few situations where getting started can raise ethical concerns:

A friend tells you how she was raised in a cult with a charismatic leader who seduced her sister and mother before she escaped to San Francisco at 17 where she became a flower child (Figure 3-1) who panhandled on the street outside the famed Mark Hopkins Hotel. You see some real possibilities for a fictionalized version of the story. What next? Let's look at several possibilities.

■ You go home and start writing without telling your friend what you are doing.

[1] Ian Gurvitz, "The Rules of Hollywood: If You Think Your Idea Was Stolen, Think Again," *The Los Angeles Times, West*, October 1, 2006, 14.
[2] Gurvitz, "The Rules of Hollywood."

- After several days when the writing is not going as well as you hoped, you decide to tell your friend you are going to use her story as a basis for your story. Perhaps your friend can be of some help.
- Your friend objects, saying what you are doing is a violation of her life.
- You tell her you are only taking the idea of her life story and that no one will be able to know the film started with her life experiences.
- She rejects this argument.
- You stand firm and tell her that you're only using her story as a blueprint and that you'd like her cooperation though, you tell her, legally you don't need it.
- She rejects this argument as well.
- You tell her your friendship is more important to you than this story and that you have abandoned the idea, but you continue to write a script clandestinely.
- You decide you really need her for key details and you offer to give her 10% of whatever you earn writing the script.
- She says she wants more than that. She wants to be a producer. You tell her she is being greedy and unrealistic about the way things work in the entertainment industry.
- You come back to her and ask her to write the script with you.
- She agrees, but ups the ante by saying she wants her name to be first on the credits.
- You agree to this demand, though you know that it's not up to you to determine credits; you realize that you are making an empty promise, though you are pleased that you are able to go ahead with what you see as a promising story.

Clearly, a number of ethical issues are raised along the way, much like the story about Bill Silver in Chapter 1.

You Decide

Do you feel ethical lines have been crossed at any point in the scenario about the writer and friend? Where specifically? If you feel that ethical lines have been crossed, be prepared to analyze why.

Here are other situations for your evaluation:

The student film you directed is criticized by the judges at a film festival for being too derivative. The four judges cite four sequences that, in their view, are exact copies of scenes in Roman Polanski's classic film *Repulsion* (1965).

- Are you guilty of stealing shots?
- Are you simply learning your craft and paying homage to a master, or are you stealing and justifying it by quoting those in Hollywood who proudly proclaim that they only steal from the best?
- Do you blame your teacher for not pointing out that you might be accused of copying shots?
- Do you picket the film festival?
- Do you give up your dream of becoming a filmmaker?

Or consider this situation: As a producer, you read a magazine article that you feel has the right elements in terms of today's marketplace. You know, however, that optioning that particular article will be costly. So you go on the Internet to find other articles about that particular story to avoid optioning the initial story that peaked your interest.

- Are you simply exercising good business judgment?
- Do you owe the initial story a debt of gratitude, a debt that has to be acknowledged in some way before you proceed?
- Are you simply doing what everybody else does, in the process calling everyone you know to reassure yourself that others have done the same?

To answer these and other ethical questions in terms of acquiring material, you might employ the E*T*H*I*C*S rubric, particularly the *T* element, by asking yourself, what, for example, is the *T*ruth of the situation in terms of how much you are taking from another source. Industry standards suggest that it's best to give credit where credit is due, but it's not always clear where influences come from, and there are also times when the impulse for self-preservation or self-aggrandizement makes it hard to give others credit when it would be so much easier to claim the credit for yourself.

PRODUCING A STUDENT FILM

Brett Meyer is a recent college graduate who seeks a career as a filmmaker. His film *Picture Perfect* (see the text's website to view the six-minute film with a score by Robert Litton) has won awards at various film festivals, including the

Newport Beach Festival (where *Crash* [2005] premiered before going on to win an Academy Award for Best Picture), the California State University Media Arts Festival, and the International Student Film Festival of Hollywood.

Meyer described *Picture Perfect* as "a story of struggle with the unachievable expectations placed on women in American society." A filmmaker who wants to use film as a vehicle to influence and change people's minds, Meyer said that the genesis for *Picture Perfect* took place on a night when he was clubbing in Los Angeles. He realized that he was being looked at by a gauntlet of women as if he were a piece of meat to be consumed with relish or spit out in disgust.

Raised in a small town outside of Detroit, Michigan, Meyer found his experience at the club unnerving. Examined from head to toe, he felt uncomfortable about the scrutiny and empathized with women who are similarly judged on their appearance. Indeed, many women have been conditioned to accept that men are going to be judging them on their looks. Perish the thought that these women don't live up to the expectations that society has placed on them. The more analysis Meyer did, the more he realized that the media steadfastly reinforces the expectations for women to look good. This issue motivated him to make *Picture Perfect*.

For Meyer, television is primarily responsible for defining who is or is not beautiful. For this reason, a television set features prominently in his film. The film takes the position that if a person does not meet society's concept of beauty, that person will be marginalized, much in the way that under Hitler, Josef Mengele, the Angel of Death, sent undesirables to the gas chamber. *Picture Perfect* also uses religious imagery (Figure 3-2) throughout to add texture to the ethical issues the film is exploring.

As a young filmmaker, Meyer had many things to consider when making his film. He had to secure funding. To economize, he went digital (Panasonic 24 P) and spent a lot of time in postproduction color correcting to make the film look good, an approach he recommends to student filmmakers working on a tight budget. He had to cast the film and found the woman he cast as the lead in a Religion and the Media class he was taking. He had to select and clear locations, making sure that he had the requisite permissions. He had to select the color pallet he would use, deciding on dark colors for

FIGURE 3-2   **51**

The film *Picture Perfect* found in the text's website contains religious imagery, which may not be as readily identifiable as the cross in this picture. (iStockphoto. com #1516900, creacart.)

the people society deems beautiful and light (innocent) colors for those society finds undesirable. He shot the film during three weekends. He had to edit the hours of footage. He had to find the right music for the film, and had to cut the film to the music once he made his selection.

In short, he had a great many things to do, many more than are listed here to illustrate his tasks, but it is important to note the significant role ethics played in the development of the film. Meyer observed how society creates unrealistic, *H*armful definitions of physical attractiveness and he created a film to address the issue.

Asked about any ethical issues he faced during filming, Meyer discussed the scene where a woman who does not meet standard, media-reinforced definitions of beauty walks by a group of beautiful people who look down upon her. As a director, Meyer had to get the actress to respond to the denigration she received without saying something as harsh as "You are fat and they are laughing at you." Meyer did not want to insult his actress or to embarrass her, yet he needed to make sure the scene played the way he had conceived it. Treating the actress with respect, he told her that the people she walked by were judging her and they were the ones with a warped sensibility, not her character and not her as a person.

Later in this chapter, we'll discuss some additional ethical issues directors face, many of which are equally complex to handle, though they must be addressed if one wants to be in the game.

A late addition to the text at press time is Adair Cole's work-in-progress film, *Number 87*, which focuses on ethical issues involving brutality from a popular culture perspective. We will discuss ratings in Chapter 7 of the text but, before viewing the film, which is on the website, please know that it contains strong language and violence.

PARTNERING

A producer most often needs to partner with another producer or studio to get a project off the ground. Finding the right partner becomes key, particularly at a time when so few people have the power to say yes, thereby green-lighting a project and allowing it to go forward.

Partnering is so crucial, in fact, that some have waited sometimes too long to find just the right partner. One acquaintance who refused to compromise his standards turned down partnership after partnership until the offers stopped coming. Some have also said that they would partner with Hitler himself if that helped get a project made. So much for selling one's soul to the devil for success in Hollywood!

CREATING A PARTNERSHIP

For our study, let's focus on when a partnership is coalesced or formalized and the accompanying ethical issues. In considering the following situations, ask yourself, does a partnership exist?

- When someone says he would like to work with you
- When together you explore how an idea might be developed
- When the two of you have several meetings to flesh out the concept
- When one of you writes up the concept
- When the two of you prepare "leave behind" pages to give to a development executive
- When the two of you pitch the concept of the script to a development executive and leave the pages behind
- When the development executive asks you to prepare one or more of the following: a director's list, a casting list, a writer's list
- When a development executive passes on a project
- When a development executive puts the project into development
- When a contract is dawn up
- When all parties sign a contract

As an exercise, check off the places in the above list where you feel that a moral commitment to a partnership has taken place. Different people will define the moral obligations of a partnership differently. Each situation may be different, depending in large part on how the ethical boundaries are defined.

For experienced writer/producer Judd Parkin (*Nicholas' Gift*, 1998; *Jesus*, 2000; *Have No Fear: The Life of John Paul II*, 2005), a viable partnership exists when there is a perfect balance between players, when both partners need each other equally and both bring valuable assets to the party (e.g., access, contacts, production facilities). Parkin feels strongly that both partners have to need the other for a partnership to be viable, avoiding a one-sided coupling where one of the partners is likely to feel taken advantage of. For Parkin, one-sided partnerships tend to fail, creating bad feelings and often leading to lawsuits.

Can even a balanced partnership fail? Sometimes a new player enters the picture, ostensibly offering a better deal, causing one of the partners to be forced out because the new player does not want too many cooks in the kitchen. Is this ethical? Is it the cost of doing business? If you are the partner who is squeezed out, do you sue, or hang your head lamenting the lack of ethics that permeate the business? How the money is distributed to the new players as well as to the old ones can really stir the pot, leading to all sorts of publicized claims and counterclaims that abound with many ethical dilemmas.

PRODUCING ON A TIGHT SCHEDULE

The raid on the Branch Davidian compound in Waco, Texas, which began on February 28, 1993, resulted in many deaths and many charges and counter-charges about what went wrong. The standoff at Mount Carmel, where the Branch Davidians lived, lasted 51 days until April 19, 1993, after Attorney General Janet Reno authorized a final assault on the compound. David Koresh, the charismatic leader of the Branch Davidians defined himself as a religious prophet, one who controlled all aspects of the lives of his followers, but the Bureau of Alcohol, Tobacco and Firearms (ATF) defined him as a dangerous cult leader who had hoarded an arsenal of firearms.

The raid on Waco was a big story in l993, and it remains a controversial episode in American history. The day after the raid, Ken Kaufman, the experienced pro-ducer of the *In the Line of Duty* telefilms, received a call from a programming executive at NBC. The executive wanted Kaufman to produce a film about Waco to air during the May sweeps period of May 1993. Kaufman's initial response was, "But it just happened yesterday."

Kaufman asked for two days to *E*valuate the feasibility of the assignment, an assignment which would have only 10 weeks from start to finish: 10 weeks to prep, shoot, edit, score, and turn in a finished film. He was given 24 hours to think it over.

Kaufman was concerned about the lack of perspective he faced in making the film on such a tight schedule. His primary concern was that the film would give viewers the wrong information, but NBC convinced him that if he didn't do it, someone else would. Kaufman took this information seriously. Already everyone in the business was saying that he or she had a Waco project in development. He was well aware that a rushed schedule might make it difficult to consider all of the relevant issues, but for him, a producer produces. He decided to undertake the assignment and to do the most responsible job that he could.

Kaufman makes his living as a producer, and his concerns became secondary as he undertook the task of making a movie about a current topic. Because the siege at Waco was not over (in fact, it had just begun when NBC called him), Kaufman said he wanted to end the movie with the raid on the compound that occurred on February 28, 1993.

Kaufman made this decision because he didn't know how the situation would end and he didn't want to speculate on the outcome. He decided on a two-prong structure to address the question of how the situation at

Waco happened: (1) how the religious cult functioned under Koresh and (2) how the law enforcement perspective developed. He went into a 24/7 research mode to be able to document and combine these two story lines into dramatic form.

Questions Kaufman faced beyond the tight production schedule included the following, many of which address key ethical concerns:

- Which version of why law enforcement acted the way it did would he select?
- If you accept that Koresh was tipped off that a raid was going to take place, who do you portray tipping Koresh off?
- Do you depict the raid on Waco as a betrayal? As a screwup?
- How do you determine the validity of the documentation that your research provides?
- How do you determine which confidential sources can be trusted and which ones cannot?
- Whose rights, if any, do you acquire?
- Who do you depict as firing the first shot during the raid?
- What do you show in the movie about how the religious cult functioned?
- How young should the girls be that Koresh selects to receive "his seed"?
- Which questions about the raid should you raise or not raise in the film? A few possibilities that required attention include why did ATF go after Koresh at the compound instead of in town, as he was known to go into town on occasion? Or, if the raid was undertaken to protect the children at the compound, why didn't Child Protective Services do more to get the children out before the raid?
- Do you film in Texas for authenticity, or do you stay out of Texas where the standoff is ongoing?
- Because this is a movie and not reality, do you "juice it up" to create dramatic moments that may not actually have happened?

Kaufman faced a number of ethical issues throughout the development and production of *In the Line of Duty: Ambush at Waco* (Figure 3-3), as the finished film was called. He knew that people were killed during the raid. He repeatedly asked himself if he had made the right decision to go ahead and produce the movie. Kaufman also repeatedly asked himself if he had tampered with the truth in order to tell a story. He also wondered if he knew the *T*ruth about what happened and why.

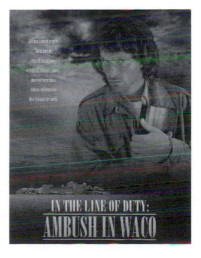

FIGURE 3-3
The television film *In the Line of Duty: Ambush at Waco* raised a number of issues, many of which are still debated years later. The poster copy reads, "Self-proclaimed prophet David Koresh seduced his followers with his charismatic power—then led them into a violent confrontation that shocked the world." (Courtesy of Patchett Kaufman Entertainment.)

55

In retrospect, Kaufman has said that the lack of perspective would prevent him from undertaking the assignment if he were asked to do the movie today. Though he feels he did a responsible job and that the movie is 98% accurate (he provided NBC with a fully annotated script detailing the sources for individual scenes), he feels strongly that films should not be started unless a trial has been completed. For Kaufman, perspective is very much needed before setting out to make a movie.

Kaufman also feels that telefilms have lost all credibility and that ripped-from-the-headlines stories no longer resonate, whether or not they are responsibly done. Had he known how fragile it would be to conduct the research, he would have turned down the assignment. He had to circumvent a news blackout after the raid on the Branch Davidian compound, as key people were instructed not to talk to anyone. When he was prepping the movie, Kaufman made the decision not to acquire any rights to avoid being beholden to any one point of view, though he paid $500 to individuals who were willing to come forward and to provide usable, verifiable information.

Back in 1993, during the promotion of the film, Kaufman did not share his doubts and concerns about doing the film. Possibly because commerce was involved, he felt no compulsion to share his reservations with the press. He had made the movie, and it was now his job to promote it.

Before *In the Line of Duty: Ambush at Waco* aired on NBC, a promo was broadcast. This promo aired at a time when Washington was expressing concern about violence on television. Kaufman was able to reassure NBC that the promo was made from footage from dailies and that the images in the promo that raised concerns were not in the finished film. This, of course, is a side effect of producing a work on a rushed schedule; promos have to be made from dailies, sometimes including material not found in the film that airs. One may ask if this practice is unethical or represents false advertising? In Chapter 13, we'll discuss misleading advertising from an ethical point of view, but suffice it here to say that for some, misleading promos are simply a part of how business is done.

In the Line of Duty: Ambush at Waco, starring Tim Daly as David Koresh and directed by Dick Lowry, contained the following audio/visual disclaimer at the top of the film: "This dramatization is based on extensive research and personal interviews. The events of this film are still being investigated by law enforcement agencies." At the end of the film, an audio/visual crawl stated, "The raid on Mt. Carmel was the bloodiest day in the history of the AFT. Fifteen agents were wounded and four—Steve Willis, 32, Todd McKehan, 28, Conway Lebleu, 30,

Robert Williams, 26—were killed in the line of duty. On April 19, 1993, after 51 days of standoff with federal agents, the tragedy of Mt. Carmel continued. David Koresh and at least 71 of his followers died by fire, as he had willed. The confirmed dead included 17 children."

The credits also included this statement: "The producers gratefully acknowledge the assistance of the Department of Defense and the Oklahoma National Guard in the making of this motion picture." The film was shot in Oklahoma where Kaufman's team built an exact replica of the Branch Davidian compound. Because the siege had been such a big story in the media, Kaufman felt viewers would be familiar with how the compound looked, and he wanted his movie to be accurate.

Incidentally, Kaufman would have been willing to do a sequel to *In the Line of Duty: Ambush at Waco*, NBC's highest rated movie of the 1992–1993 season, precisely because enough information would have been known, but after considering it, NBC decided not to do a sequel.

To see selected clips from *In the Line of Duty: Ambush at Waco* and to access an interview with Ken Kaufman about ethics, please see the text's website. First, Kaufman will address key ethical issues related to the production of the film and then there will be clips from the film itself.

57

You Decide

Do you think that Kaufman should have agreed to make *In the Line of Duty: Ambush at Waco* on a rushed schedule? Using the E*T*H*I*C*S rubric, examine the various issues involved in producing this story on a rushed basis.

Put yourself in Kaufman's place. There's commerce on one side and ethics on the other. Would you make the movie? What ethical considerations do you think should factor into your decision?

Do you think the disclaimer at the top of the film and the crawl at the end of the film provide audiences with the right kind of information?

In an article about Waco written six years after the Waco movie aired, then–*Los Angeles Times* media columnist Howard Rosenberg wrote, "Seen in retrospect, *Ambush at Waco* is a powerful argument against quickie movies about complex topics ripped from the headlines, those written, filmed and presented as fact before the smoke has cleared."[3] Do you agree or disagree with this position? Are there a number of different ways to *E*valuate the responsible handling of timely stories?

[3]Howard Rosenberg, "Waco and the Perils of Instant History," *The Los Angeles Times*, September 6, 1999, F-1, 15.

SELLING

Here's a variation on an oft-told anecdote about show business: Feeling dejected because he can't find a project anyone wants to make, a producer walks out of a convenience store. The devil comes up to him as he makes his way to his car and makes him an offer. Two of his projects will be sold. The producer nods his head in agreement, barely able to contain his excitement. But, the devil adds, there are a few conditions. The producer listens. The devil wants the producer's soul. He also wants the soul of the producer's wife, that of his first-born, as well as that of his grandmother. For good measure, the devil adds that he wants the soul of the convenience store clerk who sold him the producer's purchases. The producer looks at the devil long and hard and says, "Okay, what's the catch?"

Indeed, one has to be aggressive when trying to sell a project, but when does a hard-sell approach cross the line? Producer-director Tony Bill (*The Sting*, 1973; *Five Corners*, 1987; *Flyboys*, 2006) once said that someone could throw a script out a car window on the highway and that if the script were any good, it would find a way to get made. In reality, it's not that easy. Selling is a full-time job, even if what you've got is really great.

So how does one become a super salesperson? How aggressive do you have to be? How ethical do you have to be to excel at making a sale with just the right amount of hype, not too much and not too little?

It's not enough to be passionate, though passion is definitely required. It's not enough to insist that a project is timely or that it teaches a valuable lesson. Take the case of Joseph Medavar, a producer who had a full-throttle sales pitch but not much else. Medavar allegedly masterminded a selling campaign that, according to the charges against him, included conning investors out of some $5 million dollars.[4]

Medavar's project involved turning the Department of Homeland Security into a television series. To accomplish his goal, Medavar recruited approximately 70 well-heeled and powerful investors from Los Angeles and Orange County. He claimed to have governmental support, including the permission to use the Homeland Security name in the show. According to the charges, he used the

[4]"TV Producer Facing Fraud Charges Is Subject of 2nd Criminal Probe," SFGate.com, September 27, 2005, http://sfgate.com/cgi-bin/article.cgi?file=/n/a/2005/09/27/state/n055720D27.DTL&type=pr, accessed June 21, 2006.

money he had raised to maintain a lavish lifestyle, which, to some anyway, made him appear credible by giving him the requisite producer image.

He even had his picture taken with President George W. Bush, and he was introduced to California Governor Arnold Schwarzenegger at the Staples Center in Los Angeles, after he had donated $21,200 to Schwarzenegger.[5]

Medavar was thus able to be seen with power players and by association to become one himself, gaining some sort of chutzpah credentials as a super sales-man in the process. Lawsuits and FBI probes revealed his Homeland Security project to be a sham, the work of an ambitious con artist. Medavar may have had the necessary aggressiveness for selling, but what about his ethics, not to mention the law?

Medavar was sentenced to a year and a day in prison for his actions, plus "9 months' home detention after his prison sentence and 3,000 hours of commu-nity service, and he was ordered to pay at least $2.6 million in restitution,"[6] a ruling that many investors felt was inadequate. He may have been punished for his fraudulent behavior, but the punishment was considerably less than what the prosecution had requested, specifically a sentence of no less than nearly six years.[7]

In Medavar's case, high-powered salesmanship didn't work, though many pro-ducers continue to find new ways to make a sale. Rumor has it that Tom Rickman (*Coal Miner's Daughter*, 1980; *Oprah Winfrey Presents: Tuesdays with Morrie*, 1999) got his first movie made (*Kansas City Bomber*, 1972) by surrepti-tiously dropping off the script at the home of Raquel Welch, a performer who could make the movie happen if she agreed to star. Aggressive salesmanship? Yes. Unethical? No. But all producers have to decide how far they are willing to go for a sale and what ethical lines they are willing to cross in the pursuit of getting a project made.

PRODUCERS AND THE COARSENING OF THE CULTURE

Media entrepreneur and former head programmer at CBS Jeff Sagansky feels that the culture has coarsened. He is not alone in describing the culture in

[5]Greg Krikorian and Christine Hanley, "Screening of TV Producer Was Lax," *The Los Angeles Times*, October 13, 2005, B-1, 6.

[6]Christine Hanley and Greg Krikorian, "Producer Gets Short Sentence in TV Scam," *The Los Angeles Times*, December 5, 2006, B-1.

[7]Ibid., B-7.

this way. When during the 1990–1991 season, six-year-old Maizy in the 8 p.m. comedy *Uncle Buck* said, "You suck" to her brother, the country as a whole found the utterance in poor taste. Today, despite its original meaning referring to oral sex, "suck" is universally accepted to mean that something is less than perfect. "It sucks" means that something is disappointing or no good. It has lost its sexual connotation. At one point in the past, "suck" may even have been a derogatory comment addressed to gays who did not engage in traditional male-female sexual intercourse. This interpretation clearly no longer applies, as "suck" has become acceptable. For some, the embracing of terms like "suck" in contemporary speech reveals the coarsening of the culture.

Other examples of this coarsening involve films such as *George of the Jungle* (1997), a family film ostensibly aimed at children who enjoyed the book series, which prominently features hits and kicks to the groin; or the *Jackass* television series and movies that revel in bad boy behavior; or the imported-from-England television series *Bad Girls*. Another example is the question of whether Oxygen is branding itself as the network where girls behave badly, as Professor Heather Osborne-Thompson discussed in a lecture to California State University Fullerton students in 2007. Bad behavior is funny, universally funny, in fact, as displays of rude behavior travel well to different parts of the world. Not all parts, of course, but many.

Thus, many producers seek to exploit rudeness and coarseness in an attempt to get on a bandwagon that thrives on bad behavior. All producers have to ask themselves how far they are willing to go to outgross the competition. What ethical lines will they or won't they cross? If *Borat* (2007) starring Sasha Baron Cohen succeeded at the box office by having a nude wrestling match involving Cohen and an overweight man, what's next? *Borat* may be a culturally relevant film that contained serious social and cultural commentary, in the process destroying some misconceptions and stereotypes, but will cash-hungry producers imitate the gross-out humor and forget about the social commentary?

These questions extend to other genres as well. For instance, how extreme does a horror film have to be to titillate a jaded public? As the coarsening of the culture continues, it's likely that producers will keep trying to find new ways to gross out the public. "You suck" will be tame indeed. How producers deal with the coarsening of the culture has become an important ethical issue, one that deserves mention in this text.

PRODUCER LOYALTY

When I started in the television business a number of years ago, the first thing that struck me was how poorly writers were treated, specifically how quickly writers were replaced if anything went wrong. Even if the problems were not a writer's fault, the writer would be blamed and replaced. But how far should a producer's loyalty to a writer go, particularly if a project risks banishment if a writer is not replaced? The following real-life example provides a complex and sobering road map:

1. A producer with a good reputation but a limited track record puts up his own money to option a book.
2. The producer attaches a writer to the project following an extensive search to find the writer best suited to the material.
3. The producer receives a lukewarm response to the writer from a number of studio executives.
4. The producer perseveres.
5. The optioned book becomes a hot property.
6. A studio head asks the producer to come in and lay out an approach to the story.
7. The producer's agent strongly suggests that she replace the writer before going in for the meeting at the studio. The producer sticks with the writer.
8. The producer works with the writer to come up with an approach.
9. The writer accompanies the producer to the studio meeting, but his pitch is underdeveloped and lacks a clear approach.
10. The producer again works with the writer to fine-tune the pitch.
11. At a subsequent pitch, the writer appears tired as well as bored, making a poor showing.
12. A studio executive tells the producer he'll put the project into development, but with a different writer. The producer continues to stick with the writer.
13. The producer renews the option on the book.
14. The agent calls the producer to tell her that he can't set up any more meetings with the same writer attached.
15. The producer explores independent financing with the same writer attached.
16. The producer asks the writer to split the option cost with her. The writer refuses.

You Decide

From an ethical as well as a business point of view, at what point in the producer-writer scenario might the producer's loyalty to her writer be reevaluated? Ask yourself if and when you would feel ethically comfortable replacing the writer in question. Would you replace the writer at stage 3? Would you stick with the writer at stage 16? Does the producer's financial situation make a difference in determining if and when you would replace the writer? What about the writer's financial situation?

PRODUCER FEUDS: MOTIVATED BY ETHICAL CONSIDERATIONS—OR NOT?

In the world of the media, where egos are fragile and real or imagined slights are often magnified tenfold, it's hard to know when to hold a grudge and come out fighting and when to air-kiss and make nice.

Oftentimes one feels pressured to assume a fighting stance to avoid seeming like a lightweight. You can't be any good, conventional wisdom has it, if you don't have any enemies. One junior executive was told by an old hand that she had to pick a fight, lest a producer roll all over her. It didn't matter if there was any reason for the attack. It was simply for show. When the executive said she didn't feel it was right to do this, she was told to grow up and get real. Either she wanted to be a player in the game or she didn't.

Some feuds may be real, however. According to Kim Masters, DreamWorks' Jeffrey Katzenberg's feud with Gail Berman, one-time head of Fox Television, may be an actual feud. He was angered over Fox's "alleged rip-off of the Dream-Works boxing reality show, *The Contender*."[8]

Fake feuds are often calculated to make things interesting, as they provide entertainment for producers and entertainment reporters who thrive on bits of gossip. For example, at the ABC press tour in 2007, weary reporters were thrilled when ABC Entertainment president Steve McPherson attacked newly appointed NBC programming head Ben Silverman, challenging him to "be a man" by admitting that former NBC head Kevin Reilly had been fired instead of beating around the bush refusing to call a spade a spade. Here was juicy gossip to reward tired journalists and give them something to write about!

[8]Kim Masters, "Experience Required," *Los Angeles Magazine*, July 2006, p. 54.

Sometimes even the littlest bit of gossip can fascinate. One executive, for example, appeared to be enthralled when a rival agent told him that a highly placed agent at another agency had left a messy desk when he quit. According to another producer who might herself have benefited from repeating the story, one television producer was regularly employed because he provided the bored executives who hired him with juicy stories about feuds and sexual liaisons on the set. Whether the gossip from the set was true or false, it kept the producer employed, at least according to the producer who enjoyed repeating the story.

Real or imagined feuds, the subject of much speculation in Hollywood, can be analyzed in terms of the E*T*H*I*C*S rubric, particularly the *T* and the *H.* What's the truth of the situation and what is the harm that can come from the feud? If the feud escalates to name calling, rumor spreading, allegations of misconduct on the set, leaks to the press, and so on, who gets hurt? Who gets ahead?

VIDEO GAME PRODUCERS AND CREATORS

The video game explosion (Figure 3-4) at one time generated more yearly income than theatrical films, but the video game market has suffered a number of setbacks. So what is a video game producer to do to capture new gamers and to hold on to the old ones, and what role does ethics play in the mix?

FIGURE 3-4
Some people feel that many video games handle controversial topics irresponsibly. (iStockphoto.com #2651949, slobo mitic.)

Interactivity is key. Gamers want to be inter-actively involved, and conventional wisdom has it that gamers want edgier material that they can't get elsewhere. They also want things to happen a lot faster than they do, for example, on a conventional afternoon soap opera where the action takes one step backward for every two steps forward.

A program like *24* on Fox may capture a number of viewers who seek nonstop action, but most action-seeking viewers and gamers tend to look elsewhere. Movies such as *The Matrix* series with its philosophical overtones connect with action seekers (Figure 3-5), but for the most part it's video games that have provided the desired excitement that people

FIGURE 3-5
Martial arts action finds a responsive audience in video games. Game sales are down, however, causing some game makers to increase the amount of action, thus contributing to the coarsening of the culture. This increased action could lead to more violent content. (iStockphoto.com #1717316, Mark Stay.)

crave, although not so much now as before. Game sales are down, and the gaming industry is at a crossroad.

So how does the industry get gamers back? How do producers and creators make games that are edgy enough to capture players while avoiding the scrutiny of watchdog groups that could lead to governmental regulation? Let's take a look at some of the ethical questions that might arise as the gaming industry seeks to reclaim its hold on those it's left behind:

- On the assumption that gamers like to discover hidden things on their own, do producers and creators hide content in a game like *Grand Theft Auto*?
- Do producers and creators insist that violent action in video games is fantasy play with no causal relation to violent action in real life?
- Do producers and creators stand with the First Amendment whenever there is a legislative push to regulate video games?
- Do producers, creators, and distributors swear by studies that say that playing video games increases the visual skills of players, thus making video games educational?
- Do distributors advertise "M" (for Mature) games to minors?
- Do producers and creators assert that video game makers are no more obsessed with sexual violence than are the makers of most films and television shows?

In an article titled "Ethics of Game Design," Dean Takahashi, the author of *The Xbox 360 Uncloaked: The Real Story Behind Microsoft's Next-Generation Video Game Console*, raises some timely questions about using real-life events such as the death of Saddam Hussein or John Kerry's Swift Boat experiences, but he concludes, "The ethics of game design has entered a new era in which the developers offer the players ethical choices of their own."[9] These ethical choices enable players to confront the results of their choices. Consequences matter, indicating that some video games seek to address ethical issues.

ETHICS AND A WRITER'S CREATIVE PROCESS

Writers deal with ethical issues in a number of ways. Do they, for example, sell out by taking on a script they aren't interested in? Do they stab someone in the back to get an assignment? Or do they write a scene that they find distasteful because it's what the market or the producer demands?

[9]Dean Takahashi, "Ethics of Game Design," *Game Developer*, December 2004, pp. 14–19.

How does a writer handle male rape in prison? As a joke? As a cliché that requires no comment and no development or explanation on the writer's part, making the job easier? How does a writer handle terrorism? How about creating a villain? If the writer shows the villain's childhood years, does that mean the writer has made the villain too sympathetic because the childhood years might justify his later villainous actions, as was the objection when CBS aired a mini-series about Hitler in 2003, *Hitler: The Rise of Evil*?

The list of ethical issues writers face is a long one filled with many bumps along the road. For our purposes, however, we are going to approach ethics as part of character development during the writer's creative process.

For Jule Selbo (Figure 3-6), a professor and screenwriter whose credits include *Hard Promises* (1991) and *The Young Indiana Jones Chronicles* (1992–1993), conflict is the essence of drama, and a character's conflicts over ethical issues set the stage for compelling stories. Selbo has suggested examining the ethical conflicts in a number of works to understand how ethics influence dramatic conflict. Consider the following examples:

- In *Sophie's Choice* (1982), which child does Sophie select to save during the Holocaust, if she can only save one?
- In *Gladiator* (2000), is dedicating one's life to seeking revenge what makes a hero?
- In *Munich* (2005), does planning to kill others to gain revenge become heroic?
- In Ibsen's plays, does maintaining a "life lie" preserve the illusion of well-being?
- In *Mrs. Doubtfire* (1993), does a person pretend to be someone other than who he is to get what he feels is rightfully his?
- In *Disclosure* (1994), does one lie about sexual harassment in order to get revenge?
- In the *Law & Order* television series, does Jack McCoy, played by Sam Waterson, push his own agenda no matter what?
- In AMC's television show *Hustle* or in FX's *The Shield*, do the ends justify the means?

FIGURE 3-6   **65**
Screenwriter Jule Selbo finds that the ethical conflicts characters experience help create powerful drama. (Courtesy of Jule Selbo.)

The list goes on. You can create your own and, I think, you'll agree with Selbo that many works have an ethical dilemma at their center.

For Selbo, the bigger the ethical conflict, the more evenly sided the conflict, the better. If the bad guy is 100% morally evil, the good guy's position becomes marginalized. Making the ethical conflict more complex and less clear cut creates stronger drama.

A film where the main character's actions are all based on self-interest doesn't carry as much weight as films like *The Bourne Identity* (2002), with Matt Damon as Bourne, or HBO's *Live from Baghdad* (2002), where both sides have valid moral positions. In *The Bourne Identity*, Alexander Conklin, played by Chris Cooper, has valid reasons why Bourne must be killed, and Bourne himself has valid reasons to support his desire to survive. In *Live from Baghdad*, both sides want peace and both sides lie to achieve their goals.

For Selbo, a writer needs to argue both sides of the ethical issue in a script. The writer first needs to know what her position is and then needs to make the opposing position as strongly as possible. Some writers start with characters they find compelling and present them with an ethical conflict, whereas others create a believable ethical situation and then create the characters to suit the conflict. Either way, in Selbo's analysis of the writing process, the ethical conflict is at the heart of the drama.

THE DEBATE OVER CREDITS

Getting credit (i.e., being visible, and recognized for your contribution) is a big deal in Hollywood. Not getting credit means you are a nobody, a wannabe without clout. Thus, disputes over credits for writers and producers in particular can become quite contentious.

The number of producers on theatrical films has increased significantly, causing the Producers Guild under former president Thom Mount to limit the title of producer to individuals who have fulfilled actual producer functions. Before the 2006 Academy Award presentation, producer Bob Yari waged a fierce legal and public relations campaign when he was denied a producer credit in arbitration by the Producers Guild of America and also denied recognition as a producer by the Academy of Motion Picture Arts and Sciences for the film *Crash*. Yari raised money for the independently financed film, but according to the academy and to the Producers Code of Credit (www.producersguild.org) developed by the Producers Guild of America, he did not perform enough of the duties of a producer to claim the title. Yari disagreed vehemently.

The *Crash* credit controversy did not end with the Academy Awards, however. When Lifetime promoted its series *Angela's Eyes* as coming from "the producers of the Academy Award–winning movie *Crash*," as Cathy Schulman and Tom Nunan from *Crash* were executive producers on the series, other producers of *Crash* vehemently objected, filing a lawsuit against Lifetime to have this tagline removed, causing some to question the pettiness of such a lawsuit. For Lifetime, Schulman and Nunan were indeed producers of *Crash* and thus the tagline was correct,[10] illustrating once again how contentious credit debates can become and how much importance and prestige is attached to a producer credit.

For the 2007 Academy Awards, there were other credit debates, involving *The Departed* and *Little Miss Sunshine*. Brad Grey, head of Paramount Pictures, felt he deserved a producer credit for *The Departed* because he had helped gather the elements to make the film, but the academy disagreed, saying he could not accept the Oscar if the film won. The academy also ruled that only three of *Little Miss Sunshine's* five producers could legitimately claim to be producers of that film; three producers, not five, would be eligible to accept the Oscar if that film won.

A reported feud developed over credits in connection with *Babel*, a 2006 film with an international scope, also up for Best Picture along with *The Departed* and *Little Miss Sunshine*. According to an article in *The New York Times* by Terrence Rafferty, the feud between the writer, Guillermo Arriaga, and the director, Alejandro Gonzalez Inarritu, had to do with who is more important to a film, the writer or the director, with Arriaga stressing the importance of the writer over the contribution of the director.[11] Even artists who have collaborated well together, as Arriaga and Inarritu had on *Amores Perros* (2000) and *21 Grams* (2003), can get testy when the topic of credits comes up.

Similarly, when a number of writers work on a project, determining who gets a writing credit becomes a complicated process, often resulting in lengthy arbitrations that many feel are clouded in secrecy and capricious decision making. Others, like Frank Pierson, past president of the Writers Guild, insist that the arbitration system is sound and that writer credits are fairly administered.[12]

[10]Greg Braxton, "*Crash* Fight Moves to the Small Screen," *The Los Angeles Times*, July 14, 2006, E-1, 23.
[11]Terrence Rafferty, "Now Playing: Auteur vs. Auteur," *The New York Times*, October 22, 2006, AR-13.
[12]Frank Pierson, "Who Did What to Whom and When Did They Write It?" *Written By*, www.Wga/writtenby/writtenbysub.aspx?id = 1340, accessed January 18, 2006.

You Decide

Using the E*T*H*I*C*S rubric, where applicable, how do you think the following hotly debated credit situations should be resolved.

- Many people feel that arbitrations favor the first writer, even if the script has been completely changed. Do you think the first writer on a project should be given special consideration in a credit dispute?
- Should a writer who has been replaced refuse to cooperate with the new writer to maintain his hold on the writing credit?
- Should a replaced writer monitor what changes the new writer has made to see if the new writer has significantly altered the original structure, thereby making it harder for the first writer to get more than "Story By" (a lesser designation, to most people meaning you only provided the general concept behind a story) credit instead of "Written By" credit?
- Should a writer with clout insist on getting a producer credit as well before committing to writing a project?
- Should a producer give a writer a producer credit to entice her to commit to a project?

- Should the manager of a sought-after star insist on a producer credit before allowing his star to commit to a project and to sign a contract?
- How much actual producing do you think a producer should do to receive a producer credit?
- How many days on the set should a producer spend to fulfill a producer function?
- Is a producer who has raised the funding, supervised the writing of the script, attended all notes meetings, created a budget, selected the cast, hired the crew, selected the location, viewed all the dailies, and supervised the wardrobe qualified to call himself a producer, even if he never sets foot on a set?
- When should a director request a producer credit?
- Should writer/producer arbitrations take place behind closed doors, as Marshall Herskovitz, vice president of the Producers Guild, maintains is standard procedure?[13]
- How many people (costumers, gaffers, cinematographers, editors, etc.) should be consulted to determine if a producer credit is warranted?

There are industry standards about credits that guilds and organizations strive to maintain, as indicated by the rulings about who can legitimately claim to be a producer on a project, but many of the debates presented here depend on ethical considerations. All of these questions are faced on all productions. Different people have different answers, answers that reveal a great deal about one's ethical framework.

[13]Marshall Herskovitz in a letter to the editor, *The Los Angeles Times*, March 11, 2006, E-15.

ACTORS AND ETHICS

Actors like to work. Actors need to work. Unless an actor is a major A-list player, role choices don't always present themselves as options. Julia Roberts may be selective about the roles she accepts, but most working actors, even those who manage to support themselves through their craft without having to wait tables or drive cabs, aren't so lucky (Figures 3-7 and 3-8).

If actors manage to get a "general" meeting with a casting director, they will probably be asked what kinds of roles they are interested in playing. This is a standard part of meet-and-greet meetings. Rather than screaming, "I want to work! I'll do anything, particularly if it means traveling to Paris!" an actor will probably say something innocuous like "I'm looking for roles that challenge me, ones where my character is allowed to grow, to expand horizons." Or the actor can do a variation on Charlotte Rampling's "I choose the parts that challenge me to break through my own barriers."[14] Such answers are sage in that they don't exclude any roles that the casting director might need to fill and they also indicate that the actor is a serious thespian who wants challenging roles.

Ethics can, and often do, enter the picture very early. For example, are there certain things an actor will not do? Are there certain roles or films that an actor will veto?

69

FIGURES 3-7 and 3-8
Actors often have to wait on tables or drive cabs before they become successful performers and are in positions to select their roles, though some actors would prefer to continue to wait on tables or drive cabs if the roles they are offered conflict with their ethics. (iStockphoto.com #2469664, Juan Monimo; iStockphoto.com #536074, Bart Sadowski.)

[14]Judith Thurman, "The Pictures: Ready, Set, Rample," *The New Yorker*, July 10 and 17, 2006, p. 37.

Exploitation can mean different things depending on who is doing the talking. A maker of low budget action/sex exploitation films might see himself as a maker of fun entertainment, an auteur like Russ Meyer who made low-budget films like *Lorna* (1964), *Faster, Pussycat! Kill! Kill* (1965), and *Supervixens* (1975), all of which featured well-endowed women in sexual situations. An actor, on the other hand, might refuse to appear in a film that smacks of exploitation, ones that are headed straight to video.

Some actors refuse to play roles or appear in films that include violence against women. Some actors refuse to do nudity, even if the producer insists that the nudity is integral to the story and that it will be handled in the most tasteful way. Rumor has it, for example, that John Travolta refused to do a nude scene in *Saturday Night Fever* (1977), agreeing instead to some crotch adjusting while dressed. Kate Bosworth, who played Lois Lane in *Superman Returns* (2006), said in an interview with Susan King of *The Los Angeles Times* that she has turned down parts because she won't do nudity, this in spite of her stated claim that she's not yet in a position to pick and choose her roles.[15]

Ethics thus play a part in making career decisions for actors. Michael Ontkean skated in a jock strap in *Slapshot* (1977) and took on a role as a gay man in *Making Love* (1982) when it was not fashionable to play homosexuals. In fact, some might say playing a gay man at that time was akin to career suicide. He also played a cherry pie–eating sheriff in the quirky *Twin Peaks* (1990–1991) television series. Ontkean is thus not afraid of challenging, controversial roles, but he has said that he refuses roles that involve harming children.

Other actors draw ethical lines elsewhere. Even if they are starving or haven't paid the rent, some actors simply will not take on roles in projects they find ethically unacceptable.

At the 2006 California State University Media Arts Festival, held at the California State University campus of Channel Islands, the creator of the television show *Rescue Me*, Peter Tolan, talked about a woman who refused to play someone having an affair and an actor playing a priest who refused to play a pedophile. Both quit rather than assuming parts that conflicted with their

[15]Susan King, "Brief Encounter: To Greater Heights," *The Los Angeles Times*, July 2, 2006, E-3.

morals. Though he respected the commitment to their position, Tolan seemed surprised by the refusals, questioning what had happened to the concept of "acting." He wondered if Jack Nicholson felt he had to have killed people in order to portray a killer in *The Departed*. Tolan feels that the emphasis should be on acting (i.e., assuming a different persona). Nevertheless, many actors do not want to assume a persona that feels ethically wrong to them, even if these actors want to work and need to work.

Interestingly enough, if there comes a time that the Federal Communications Commission fines performers for violating FCC indecency and obscenity rules, many more performers may not want to risk fines by taking on roles that could result in serious penalties.

DIRECTOR CHOICES

Directors have a lot on their plates. On the set, they're the quarterbacks, making the decisions. Directors see the total picture. They rely strongly on the cast and crew, but they are the ones calling the shots. Off the set, however, there are often other, more powerful forces directing the plays. Oftentimes a director has to answer to these outside forces, resulting in a number of different conflicts. Included in these conflicts are ethical questions about where the director's loyalties lie. To himself? To the producer? To the cast and crew? To the network or studio? To the investors?

Experienced director Bill Norton, whose credits as a director-writer include the classic *Cisco Pike* (1972) and *More American Graffiti* (1979) as well as director credits on numerous episodes and television movies, has said that a director is constantly faced with having to make compromises. Norton has noted that directors have to walk a fine line between doing the best job possible to remain employable while facing budget pressures as well as demands from actors and crew members, producers, development executives, and financiers.

According to Norton, directors also find themselves at a loss in terms of knowing exactly where the power lies. Sometimes it's the actor who has the power; at other times it's the producer. On episodic television, the director is a guest and has very little power. As a visitor to an often smoothly functioning set, a director has to ingratiate himself all around, no easy task and one that can surely test one's ethical stamina.

You Decide

Here then are some real-life situations a director faces that raise specific ethical questions. How do you think these situations could or should be handled? As needed, refer to the E*T*H*I*C*S rubric.

- The casting director, a friend, asks you, as a favor, to cast his girlfriend in the movie you are directing because if he doesn't get the girlfriend an assignment, she is going to leave him. Does it make a difference if instead of simply asking, the casting director pressures or begs or implores or threatens? Or is this just the price of having friends in the business? After all, aren't people always asking for help, often phrasing the request as a favor?

- You're working with a difficult actress on a television show. The producer says you've got to control her outbursts because you must stick to the schedule. The producer threatens that if you don't rein in the actress you're going to be fired. "She stays, you go," he says. First of all, do you believe the producer's threat? Is the threat coming from the producer or from the network? Isn't the producer's job at risk as well? Second, how do you fight back in this situation to protect yourself, particularly if the actress raises the stakes by charging that you made sexual advances toward her?

- The producer is running behind schedule. She has devised a way to get around the unions by claiming that the workday was 12 hours instead of the actual 14 in order to save money. What do you do? Your loyalties are to the producer who hired you, but do you have an obligation to take a stand against what she is doing?

- Similarly, a producer of a television movie tells the network that the shooting schedule will be 20 days, which the network is paying for, though the producer has another schedule that calls for a 17-day shoot, much like the fake log a truck driver might have claiming he only drove a certain number of hour when in actuality he drove many more. Should you as the director take a stand on this bit of subterfuge?

- Do you praise an actor for a performance that is merely adequate because your experience tells you that additional takes will not improve the performance and additional takes will put you behind schedule? The more the actor begs for a reshoot, the more you praise the performance. Is this an ethical response?

- A newly converted actor who is the star and possibly the real power behind a production insists that a Bible be included in a scene. In your opinion, the Bible does not make sense dramatically. As the director, you view this as forcing religion into a scene where it does not belong. How do you handle the situation?

- Budgets are tight. The producer makes a deal for product integration. She comes to you and says that a story line containing four verbal references and two visual references needs to be included in the one-hour television show you are directing. You feel that such an integration will dilute the integrity of the story, but the writer, who was alerted earlier by the producer, is already on board, having found a way to make the integration work. What is your position?

- Do you convince yourself that the actors and the script are better than they are so you can take an assignment without feeling that you have sold out?

- Do you fake a rapport with an actor to find common ground that will enable you to get the job done more easily than if you had no connection to the actor?

- Do you copy shots from master directors, claiming that you are paying homage to the greats?

- You are up for a directing assignment. You are one of three candidates. Do you bad-mouth your competition directly, targeting your comments to hit home with a budget-conscious producer ("Her last film was a bomb, poorly directed, and way over budget") or indirectly, almost innocently ("Has she done action before?")?

- You've often admired how nonactors can elevate projects, bringing a palpable reality to a part; however, with so many talented actors unemployed, should you hire professionals first?

- Do you turn down directing assignments because they conflict with your politics? Just as actors refuse certain roles, directors can make choices based on their personal convictions. Norton, for example, will not commit to works that glorify war or advocate sadism, among others.

In this chapter, we have explored issues confronting producers, writers, actors, and directors. In the next chapter, let's look at ethical issues surrounding controversy.

CHAPTER 4
Controversy and Ethics

A producer, writer, actor, or director may decide to tackle controversial material for a variety of reasons. Some of these reasons might be to address a timely issue, to find a good story, to undertake a challenging part, to get ratings or to be a box office winner, to be true to one's personal convictions, or simply to make some noise and garner some attention.

Before analyzing the ethical issues associated with controversy, let's consider what constitutes controversy. One artist's controversy may be another's pabulum. Would the public find the material controversial? Would advertisers? After all, advertisers are a generally conservative group, well aware that a negative campaign launched by the Parents Television Council (PTC), for example, can hurt sales. There are, however, a few so-called heat-seeking advertisers who go after controversy, embracing edgy shows like FX's *Nip Tuck* despite PTC criticism.

Gay subject matter may seem like business as usual, as most every television sitcom has requisite gay characters, but gays and gay marriage are controversial to many advertisers and to large segments of the population. In my classes, for example, well over 50% of the students feel that television condones and glorifies alternate or gay lifestyles. Not to mention how gay material plays around the globe. In China, the South Korean film *King and the Clown* was banned in 2006 because of its homosexual overtones. The film may have been a big success in South Korea, but the homosexual theme kept it out of China.[1]

---

[1] "China Wary of S. Korean Film," *The Los Angeles Times*, July 5, 2006, E-3.

Suppose that a producer, writer, actor, or director decides in favor of controversy, however the term is defined. How should controversy be approached, and what ethical issues are likely to arise? What guidelines, if any, should be developed? For example, talk show host Geraldo Rivera created a "Bill of Rights and Responsibility," which included the commitment to "tackle tough social issues in a responsible, nonsensational manner."[2] One needs to decide on a clear approach when tackling a controversial topic. Let's take a look at some hot topics and see what questions and issues come up.

FATAL CONTACT: BIRD FLU IN AMERICA

During the 2006 May sweeps, ABC aired a television movie called *Fatal Contact: Bird Flu in America*. The film, which is available on DVD, dealt with the hot-button topic of bird flu, the H5N1 virus (see www.pandemicflu.gov for detailed information about bird flu). *Fatal Contact* created a great deal of controversy, which centered around the charge that the film exploited people's fears. Disaster films are expected to exploit fears, the more the better, in fact, but was *Fatal Contact* a disaster film designed to scare people, or was it designed to be a serious exploration of a possible pandemic?

Marc Siegel, M.D., claimed in *The Nation* that there is a vast overreaction worldwide to a bird flu invasion, because there are many more pressing health issues, such as malaria, malnutrition, the acquisition of clean water, and proper sewage. For Siegel, *Fatal Contact* exploited people's fears by overreacting to the threat of a pandemic.[3] Similarly, the technical consultant, John M. Barry, who worked on the film, found it unrealistic and much "overdone."[4]

For others, including spokespeople for the film, *Fatal Contact* handled a controversial topic responsibly. They saw the film as a much needed and medically accurate wake-up call to a very real problem.[5]

---

[2]"As Daytime Talk Gets Religion: Geraldo Rivera's Bill of Rights," *Electronic Media*, January 18, 1996, p. 10.

[3]Marc Siegel, "The False Bird Flu Scare," *The Nation*, June 5, 2006, pp. 5–6.

[4]Donald G. McNeil Jr., "Two Experts Criticize Film as Unrealistic," *The New York Times*, May 9, 2006, B-8.

[5]McNeil, "Two Experts Criticize Film as Unrealistic."

You Decide

Let's explore some ethical considerations about *Fatal Contact*. You do not have to have seen the film in order to answer these general questions that deal with a controversial topic, in this case bird flu. Suppose that you are the producer, writer, actor, or director making the decisions about the script and the production of the movie.

- How many times do you mention the threat that bird flu presents?
- Do you include lines that suggest a bird flu pandemic is imminent?
- How do you address the controversial topic of human-to-human contamination? Is it medically possible? Should it be depicted, even if many scientists claim human-to-human infection is unlikely?

- As an actor, how do you react to the bird flu outbreak? Do you panic? Are you calm and in charge of the situation?
- What kinds of juxtapositions do you include to maximize the drama?
- Who do you blame? Most movies need villains and a movie about the flu is no exception. Do you, for example, show government officials keeping a flu mutation quiet? Reports do, in fact, suggest that the Chinese government withheld information about Chinese flu outbreaks.[6] But are you on ethically solid ground if you present the Chinese or any other government as negligent? Are you on sound medical ground if you do this?

Fatal Contact carried a telling disclaimer at the end of the film. It read: "The characters and incidents used in this motion picture are entirely fictitious and any similarity to actual names, character or history of any persons, living or dead, or actual events or locales, is entirely coincidental and unintentional." Do you think such a disclaimer takes care of any ethical concerns about the film? Or is such a disclaimer merely standard, general legal protection?

A great many questions can arise when dealing with controversy, and, not surprisingly, *Fatal Contact* raised quite a few of them, warranting inclusion in this section of the book. When you mix a timely medical issue with a disaster movie format, you as the producer are going to encounter a number of difficult issues.

For another look at controversy and ethics, see the accompanying sidebar by Mary Ann Watson, a professor of media and film studies at Eastern Michigan University, about the *Jenny Jones Show*. The sidebar is set up as a series of questions that Watson addresses based on her thorough review of the program as an expert witness in the negligence lawsuit against the show.

[6]"China Had Bird Flu Case in '03, Letter Says," *The New York Times*, June 23, 2006, A-20; Donald G. McNeil Jr., "Mystery Deepens on Possible Avian Flu Cases in China in 2003," *The New York Times*, June 24, 2006, A-8.

THE JURY AND JENNY JONES

What Led to the So-Called Jenny Jones Murder?

In March 1995, Scott Amedure, a 32-year-old bartender, from Oakland County, Michigan, responded to a solicitation he saw on the *Jenny Jones Show* for possible participants on a "Same-Sex Secret Crush" episode. That set in motion a horrible chain of events that ultimately led to his death.

Amedure's "crush" was Jonathan Schmitz, a 24-year-old waiter and neighbor of a friend. Schmitz was contacted by the *Jenny Jones Show*, a program he'd never seen, and told that he had a secret admirer who would be revealed at the taping of the broadcast. After initial reservations, Schmitz ultimately agreed to appear with the hope his secret admirer would be a lovely young woman he didn't suspect or, perhaps even better, his ex-fiancée.

But that's not how it worked out. It was Scott Amedure waiting on the stage for him. Instead of a joyful reunion or a new chance for romance, Schmitz learned that Amedure had vivid sexual fantasies about him. Jenny Jones encouraged graphic details. Amedure seemed a bit embarrassed, but he obliged. "I thought about tying him up in my hammock," he said.

"And . . ." Jones prodded.

"It entails like whipped cream and champagne and stuff like that."

Three days after the taping, on March 9, 1995, Schmitz found an anonymous sexually suggestive note on his doorstep. He assumed Amedure was the author. Schmitz then purchased a 12-gauge shotgun, drove to Amedure's mobile home, and fired two shots at close range into Amedure's chest. Just minutes later, a distraught Schmitz called 911 from a nearby gas station to turn himself in.

"I just shot this guy," he told the dispatcher amid inaudible sobs.

"Okay. Why did you do that?" she asked.

"The guy was on national TV," he told her.

The dispatcher continued to try to get as much information as she could, ascertaining that the weapon was still in the car with one shell left. "Just try to relax," she told Schmitz. "You did the right thing by calling me, okay, and we will help you. Okay. Catch your breath a little. Okay. Can you tell me again why you shot the man?" She could only make out two words in his answer to that question: "Jenny Jones."

Was Jonathan Schmitz Homophobic?

No one could testify that Schmitz ever indicated one jot of malice toward homosexuals. But there was voluminous documentation of his fragile psyche. Schmitz was bipolar, had suicidal tendencies, and suffered occasional psychotic episodes. His Graves' disease, a thyroid condition, may have contributed to his instability.

The statements of mental health professionals, family, friends, and coworkers added up to a portrait of a troubled, struggling, hard-working, and engaging young man. An incident from childhood—a spanking by his father with a belt in front of his sixth-grade class—might have contributed to his aversion to being made into a public spectacle.

Didn't the *Jenny Jones Show* Tell Him That the Secret Admirer Could Be a Man?

Schmitz was told the person could be a man or a woman. There was convincing testimony, however, from four of his female coworkers that the *Jenny Jones Show* falsely assured him his secret crush would be a woman. One overheard him talking to a representative of the show on the phone at work: "If it's a guy, tell me it's a guy; if it is, I'm not coming." Another woman took him shopping for clothes because he thought there was good chance the crush would be his former girlfriend—and he was certain it was going to be a woman. Another overheard him on the phone in another conversation with someone from the show indicating he would not come if it were a man. Yet another who had watched the *Jenny Jones Show* the day the "Same-Sex Secret Crush" solicitation aired tried to warn him of what might happen. "No, it's a woman," he told her. "Don't worry."

Was Schmitz Convicted of Murder?

Yes, but instead of first-degree, with which he was charged, Schmitz was convicted of second-degree murder because the jury believed the slaying wouldn't have occurred if the *Jenny Jones Show* had been honest with him and not led him to believe his secret crush was a woman. "We saw the show as a catalyst in a young man's life who had a lot of problems," one juror offered. "It sent his life back into an emotional tailspin."

What Was His Sentence?

Jonathan Schmitz is serving 25 to 50 years in prison. His first chance for parole will be in 2017.

Following the Criminal Trial, There Was a Civil Trial. What Was That About?

In 1999, the family of the murdered man sued the *Jenny Jones Show*, its parent company Warner Bros., and the production company Telepictures for negligence that led to the death of Scott Amedure.

What Was the Evidence of Negligence?

Part of my task was to read all the production materials that were subpoenaed. When producers or producers' assistants made their initial contact with potential guests, they filled out a "plug sheet" with comments on each person. All of the plug sheets for this particular program indicated it was a same-sex show. The name John Schmidt, rather than Jon Schmitz, appeared on the sheet dated 3/2/95. An arrow went from his name to the margin of the page where a note read, "Don't want a guy saying this to me on the air." And then "Thinking about it."

It seemed logical to conclude that if he had been told the truth about the show—that it was definitely going to be a man with the secret crush—Schmitz would have declined the offer. He agreed to "think about it" because the false possibility that it might be a woman was held out to him.

This theory was confirmed to me when I read the "Dear Jenny" letter included in the packet. The day before each show, the producer provided Jenny Jones with a rundown of the guests and circumstances in each segment. "John is nervous about this and is hoping that his crush is a woman," the letter read. "I think John is going to die when he sees it's Scott." A fair-minded person would have to surmise that Jonathan's discomfort was of no concern to the *Jenny Jones Show* and, clearly, the more discomfort he felt, the better it would be for the broadcast.

How Did the *Jenny Jones Show* Defend Itself?

I waded through thousands of pages of depositions and transcripts from the criminal trial. It was astonishing to me that time and again Jenny Jones, the executive producers, the show producer, and the associate producer all denied the true and obviously sordid nature of the show. They called it "lighthearted" and "fun." One of the executive producers had the audacity to call the Amedure-Schmitz segment "cute" and "romantic"— a "love story."

In her 1995 deposition, Jones was asked about Jonathan Schmitz's appearance on the program, "Did it ever occur to you that it could be embarrassing?" Under oath she said, "No."

Individuals connected with the production of the *Jenny Jones Show* denied that they ever strove for sensationalism in their work—they just wanted to tell good human-interest stories, a claim that is incredible on its face.

What Were Your Conclusions?

Based on my review of the material and the videotape of the show, I believe the *Jenny Jones Show* acted unethically, and negligently, by lying to Jonathan Schmitz. It was intentional deceit with a reckless disregard for the consequences. A responsible producer, realizing Schmitz did not want to be put in that situation, would have thanked him for his time and told him he was not a good candidate for the program. And had that simple act of human decency happened, two families would have been spared unrelenting grief.

The Amedure Family's High-Profile Attorney Geoffrey Fieger Gave an Impassioned Closing Argument, Didn't He?

I thought he was eloquent. "This is a case about exploitation, and ultimately responsibility," he said in asking the jury to award the Amedure family more than $70 million. The deceit of the *Jenny Jones Show* led to Jonathan Schmitz's "descent into madness" and there was no doubt, he said, that the ambush led to the shooting. The First Amendment gives talk show producers the right to put on this type of episode, Fieger conceded, but if they have to lie to their guests to do it, they must be held accountable.

What Did the Jury Decide in the Civil Case?

The five-woman, four-man jury deliberated for six-and-a-half hours over two days and decided 8-1 in favor of the Amedures. There was little disagreement among the panel members on the liability of the *Jenny Jones Show*. Most of the time was spent arriving at the amount of the $25 million award.

Did Jenny Jones Show Any Contrition after the Verdict?

No, quite the opposite. She continued to claim "this is about homophobia" and promised no changes would be made in the production practices of her program. Jonathan Schmitz "knew what he was in for" by coming on her show, Jones told Jane Pauley on *Dateline*. Charging her detractors with "elitist snobbery," she took on the mantle of a populist crusader. On *Today*, she insisted to Katie Couric, "We have a right to give a venue to real people—gay, straight, tall, short, fat, thin—we don't discriminate."

But the Jury Is Supposed to Discriminate, Isn't It?

Yes, between truth and lies, right and wrong. Average people, not elitist snobs, sat in judgment of the *Jenny Jones Show*. And they decided that in exchange for the great American freedom to make a huge amount of money on a tawdry television show, a modicum of responsibility and respect for guests is not too much to ask.

The Legal Team Representing the *Jenny Jones Show* Vowed the Verdict Would Be Overturned on Appeal. Were They Right?

They were. In October 2002, in a 2-1 decision, the Michigan Court of Appeals described the show as "the epitome of bad taste and sensationalism" but concluded the case should never have been brought to trial. The evidence, two judges believed, failed to establish if it was "reasonably foreseeable" that Schmitz would murder Amedure as a "natural and probable result of the events of the show."

The Michigan Supreme Court and the U.S. Supreme Court both refused to hear an appeal of the case, eliminating any further legal recourse. The infamous "Same-Sex Secret Crush" episode was never broadcast. The *Jenny Jones Show* went off the air in 2003.

What Lesson Should We Take from This Case?

Just because something is allowable does not mean it's ethical. And, if a job in the entertainment industry requires that you check your conscience and integrity at the elevator, it's not likely that in the big picture it'll be worth it.

More recently, a similar, though nevertheless different, situation to the one on the *Jenny Jones Show* occurred when *CNN Headline News* host Nancy Grace interviewed Melinda Duckett on September 7, 2006. Duckett was a 21-year-old South Korean whose two-year-old son had disappeared. In her interview, Grace challenged Duckett with some tough questions, including "Where were you? Why aren't you telling us where you were that day?"

Twenty-four hours after the interview, Duckett committed suicide by shooting herself in the head. Grace refused to shoulder any blame for her interview or to draw connections between her in-your-face, you-must-be-guilty interview and the subsequent suicide. CNN even aired the interview a few hours after Duckett's suicide. Though some felt that Grace became a prosecutor instead of a journalist[7] and may have waged a jihad against Duckett,[8] this particular suicide did not result in the kind of furor caused by the Jenny Jones case. It nevertheless serves as a reminder to question if and when producers or reporters should cross ethical lines in the pursuit of a hot story.

CATCHING A PREDATOR

Another program, NBC's series "To Catch a Predator" on *Dateline*, raises a number of additional ethical questions, specifically, is the show designed to alert the public about a growing problem or does it exist to exploit controversy to get ratings during sweeps? An in-depth report on *20/20* which aired on September 7, 2007 examined the tactics and ethics of the program.

Here's the setup. The *Dateline* team works with local police and a watchdog group called Perverted Justice, an organization dedicated to apprehending sexual predators who troll the Internet searching for sex with minors. In Florida, where a 2006 episode took place, it is a felony to use the Internet to have sex with a minor. *Dateline* pays Perverted Justice a consultant fee of between $70,000 and $100,000.[9,10] An actor then poses as a decoy to lure the predators to a house *Dateline*'s host, Chris Hansen, refers to as "our house." When the predator who had been chatting online with the decoy shows up at the house, the decoy, off-camera, invites him in, suggesting he sit down while she gets ready. She then encourages him to have some of the cookies she's left on the table. All of this is videotaped as part of the *Dateline* series.

---

[7]"Cheers & Jeers," *TV Guide*, October 2–8, 2006, p. 20.

[8]David Bauder, "CNN's Nancy Grace: Passion for Justice, or 'Personal Jihad'?" *The Seattle Times*, September 25, 2006, http://seattletimes.nwsource.com/cgi-bin, accessed September 29, 2006.

[9]Allen Salkin, "Web Site Hunting Pedophiles Racks Up Arrests," *The New York Times*, December 13, 2006, A-26.

[10]Transcript of the April 30, 2006, CNN program *Reliable Sources with Howard Kurtz*, http://transcripts.cnn.com?TRANSCRIPTS/0604/30/rs.01.html, accessed May 7, 2006.

At this point, Hansen enters the room and confronts the predator, grilling him about his expectations of sexual activity and asking him why he feels that what he is doing is okay. Hansen seeks to get inside the mind of the predator and he often succeeds in getting a mea culpa, though some of the predators claim that what goes on in a chat room is fantasy, not tied to any real expectations or intentions. Some have even seen previous *Dateline* "To Catch a Predator" episodes and know what is coming. One even suspected he was being set up, but he took the bait anyway.

After his interview with the predator, Hansen tells him he is free to leave. As he leaves the *Dateline* house, the police seize and arrest him. In the Internet chats preceding the predator's arrival at the house, the representative from Perverted Justice asks the predator to bring something specific to the presumed assignation. Perverted Justice does this because bringing something shows intent, making a conviction easier.

According to a December 13, 2006, front-page article in *The New York Times*, Perverted Justice said it has been responsible for 113 convictions, fueled by a "nationwide force of cyberspace vigilantes, financed by a network television program hungry for ratings."[11] This, despite the report on *20/20* that said that none of the 23 men who were arrested in the *Dateline* stings were prosecuted because of the way the evidence was obtained.

Some of the ethical questions raised by the "To Catch a Predator" series include the following:

- Are the *Dateline* producers guilty of checkbook journalism by paying Perverted Justice $70,000 to 100,000?
- Is the program a glorification of the vigilante justice that occurs when one takes the law into one's own hands?
- Is *Dateline* guilty of using entrapment techniques?
- Is this type of program "ambush journalism"? Ambush journalism here is defined as setting up an individual, much like the unsuspecting crush in the Jenny Jones case, to be attacked or surprised. The ambushes are usually carefully orchestrated in a green room situation where a producer will goad a participant to come out swinging at another guest who has similarly been geared up to expect one thing, finding out too late that something entirely different is in the offing.
- Should *Dateline* be working so closely with the police?

[11]Salkin, "Web Site Hunting Pedophiles Racks Up Arrests," A-1.

83

■ Are the on-camera interviews with the predators exploitation, designed to titillate under the guise of serving the public good by revealing how predators operate? Do the statistics that support the good that the show does in catching predators ignore that the majority of online sexual solicitations are between teenagers, not between a teenager and an adult sexual predator, as on the *Dateline* program?

Most would agree that sexual predators deserve to be caught, particularly because the rate of recidivism among sexual predators of children is very high, but do the ends justify the means? A website, www.Corrupted-Justice.com, questions what it terms the vigilante actions of Perverted Justice.

Dateline clearly stipulates that it is working with the police and with Perverted Justice. The show does not hide this fact from viewers, but does this absolve the producers from their ethical responsibilities as investigative journalists?

You Decide

Many investigative programs like "To Catch a Predator" are on the air. Are such shows serving up cautionary tales designed to inform viewers, or are they simply attempts to get ratings? Using the E*T*H*I*C*S rubric, examine some of these investigative reports to see if you think ethical lines are being crossed. Do such shows do more harm than good or more good than harm? Do they titillate instead of helping? Do the ends justify the means, even if some ethical violations occur?

84

O.J. SIMPSON REDUX

FIGURE 4-1
Few people are more controversial than O. J. Simpson, as the book *If I Did It*, a hypothetical account of the murders of Simpson's wife and Ron Goldman, demonstrated. (Globe Photos, Inc.)

How controversial is O. J. Simpson (Figure 4-1)? Very controversial, very controversial indeed. When Simpson was found not guilty of the murder of his ex-wife, Nicole Brown, and her friend Ron Goldman in a criminal trial in 1995, many people were outraged, though he was subsequently found liable in a civil court.

Some 10 years later, in November of 2006, when News Corp. announced Fox's sweeps strategy to air a two-part interview with Simpson based on a book titled *If I Did It*, a book that speculates on how Simpson would have committed the murders, had he done them, the controversy about O. J. Simpson was reignited. The interview was called "O. J. Simpson: If I Did It, Here's How It Happened."

The response to this announcement was swift. People objected both to the Fox interview and to the publication of the book, an imprint of Regan Books, a subsidiary of HarperCollins, which is a part of News Corp. Many felt that *If I Did It* established a new low in terms of appealing to the lowest possible common denominator. Would it be possible to find anything that stooped lower than this, people asked? An editorial in the influential trade paper *Broadcasting & Cable* did not mince words. Titled "Immoral Convictions" it said,

> The point is that there has to be a line that doesn't get crossed, even when you are trying to set ad rates for the next quarter. Fox's decision to air a sweeps special featuring O. J. Simpson detailing how he would have killed his wife and waiter Ron Goldman, *if he had killed them*, is so far over that line that it's hard to understand how the programmers involved justified it to themselves or others.[12]

Commentators such as Fox's own Bill O'Reilly, stations owners such as Pappas Telecasting, owner of four Fox stations, and Lin Broadcasting, owner of five Fox stations, victims' right groups, as well as the families of Nicole Brown and Ron Goldman questioned the ethics behind the two-part interview.

The outcry against the interview was such that not only was the television special pulled, but the book, which had already been sent to bookstores, was recalled. According to Steve Zeitchik in *Daily Variety*, "Retailers are being asked to ship boxes back unopened and the publisher said it would destroy all copies."[13] Shortly after the television special and the book were canceled, publisher Judith Regan herself was fired. She may not have been the only person who okayed the book and special, but she was deemed to be too hot and too controversial for News Corp. head Rupert Murdoch.[14] Being a moneymaker with a keen eye toward what the public craves was not enough to protect Regan, particularly if she was rude or offensive to a Harper Collins attorney, as widely reported.[15]

85

[12]"Immoral Convictions," *Broadcasting & Cable*, November 20, 2006, p. 26.
[13]Steve Zeitchik, "Regan Turns a Page," *Daily Variety*, November 21, 2006, pp. 1–19.
[14]Julie Bosman and Richard Siklos, "Murdoch Is Said to Have Ordered Editor's Dismissal," *The New York Times*, December 18, 2006, A-18.
[15]Josh Getlin and Sallie Hofmeister, "'Offensive' Phone Call by Publisher Preceded Her Firing," *The Los Angeles Times*, December 17, 2006, B-1.

Fox's quest for sweeps ratings using controversy over Simpson backfired, as people questioned the use of the public airwaves for the two-part interview. Controversy may sometimes generate ratings or book sales, but not this time. The premise behind *If I Did It* was too controversial, too objectionable. NBC's Mitch Metcalf said that his network was offered the *If I Did It* interview and that NBC turned it down for two reasons: first, the network felt it was unethical to do the program, and, second, it didn't make sense from a business point of view because advertisers would stay away.

Indeed, Fox and News Corp. did not look good. It was a full-blown public relations nightmare, causing many to question how far or low Fox, the network that unleashed *When Animals Attack* or *Who Wants to Marry a Multi-Millionaire*, would go to get ratings. On the other hand, networks like NBC who refused the project looked mighty good. For an additional take on controversy and ethics, see Chapter 13.

But from a business point of view, Fox may not have been hit too hard, as advertisers would not have wanted to be part of the special.[16] The special would never have had any advertisers, so Fox didn't lose out on advertiser dollars. In one respect, the decision to pull the Simpson interview and book validates the process, suggesting that the misuse of controversy can be rectified. In other words, ethical behavior can triumph. On the other hand, that the special and book almost aired and landed in bookstores, respectively, makes one question the ethics behind the initial decisions to go forward. Afterwards, almost a year following the initial outcry, the book was ultimately published by Beaufort Books with an amended title, *If I Did It: Confessions of the Killer*.

You Decide

Before the television special was canceled, one Cal State Fullerton student, Michael Kroll, told a class that he was appalled by the ethics behind the broadcast but that he would certainly watch it, much in the way that people cannot keep from watching an accident or a train wreck (or, for that matter, Simpson's white Bronco on the freeway). Be honest. You decide: Would you have watched *If I Did It* had it aired? For a recent grad's discussion of why he might watch *If I Did It*, please see the text's website.

Regardless of any ethical questions raised by the proposed programming of the Simpson interview or the publication of *If I Did It*, do you think that News Corp. should have looked at the potential ratings bonanza and not caved to the outcry? Also, do you think that Judith Regan should have been fired?

[16]Jill Goldsmith and Josef Adalian, "Rupe Doesn't Stoop," *Daily Variety*, November 21, 2006, pp. 1–19.

CROSSING JORDAN AND CONTROVERSY

Jon Cowan and Rob Rovner have been writers and supervising producers on NBC's *Crossing Jordan* since season 4; in season 6, 2006–2007, they became showrunners along with Kathy McCormick. In order for the show to be topical, it tackles some serious, controversial topics, frequently employing story lines that allude to the events of 9/11 and to terrorism.

Sometimes controversy makes news, as with *If I Did It*. Sometimes, however, controversy slips below the radar. Many programs that are not readily associated with controversy touch on some hot topics. For example, the long-running *Murder She Wrote* (1984–1996) with Angela Lansbury as Jessica Fletcher, a mystery writer who lived in a small town (Figures 4-2 and 4-3) and solved crimes was such a show. It was much more hard-edged than most people thought. For some, *Crossing Jordan* is a more contemporary example of a below-the-radar show.

When Cowan and Rovner address controversial topics, such as in the "Thin Ice" episode aired on April 16, 2006, about rape, they strive to balance entertain-

FIGURES 4-2 and 4-3
Small towns with their quaint Main Streets generally represent solid, traditional American values, but not all small towns are free of controversies. According to much entertainment fare, many small towns are filled with secrets and mysteries. For example, think of *Twin Peaks* on ABC or the long-running *Murder, She Wrote* on CBS. (iStockphoto.com # 2345407, Christine Balderas; iStockphoto.com #3086656, Grant Dougall.)

ment programming with a sense of veracity. In "Thin Ice," the rape victim was flawed. She was drunk at the time of the rape, for example. The episode also contained some graphic, controversial details, such as finding semen in a person's mouth. Rovner and Cowan tried to stress the issue of victim responsibility along with the idea that no one deserves to be raped.

I was unable to get permission to include clips from *Crossing Jordan* for the text's website. You may, however, catch episodes in syndication to see how the show handled controversial topics.

SEX SLAVES

The writer, producer, and director of *Sex Slaves*, Ric Esther Bienstock, faced an interesting ethical dilemma while working on a *Frontline* documentary about global sex trafficking that mostly originates in Eastern Europe and Russia, an ethical conflict she was willing to discuss on camera, as opposed to Chris Hanson (introduced earlier), who never seemed to question the ethics of what he was doing to catch predators on *Dateline*.

In her desire to expose how sex trafficking operates, Bienstock joined forces with a man named Viorel who was searching for Katia, his wife who had been abducted into the sex trade. Bienstock and her team had made a tape of Viorel talking to the wife of the pimp, Apo, who claimed to "own" Katia. Viorel wanted to confront the pimp's wife by showing her this tape, hoping that this would prompt some action that would lead to the release of his wife. Bienstock worried on camera that Viorel's using the tape in this way might be crossing ethical lines, because Viorel could be hurt, or worse, and she and her team would be responsible because they had provided the tape. Katia was eventually reunited with Viorel, and Bienstock, whose director's notes (www.pbs.org/wgbh/pages/frontline/slaves) reveal her emotional involvement in the story, set up a trust fund to assist sex trade victims.

What if a filmmaker or photojournalist shoots something of political or cultural significance, say, a sequence or a photo of someone being attacked. The picture may be important in terms of allowing people to know and understand what is going on, but should the filmmaker or journalist forget about the shot and rush to the aid of the victim instead of shooting? This is a constant concern, one that Bienstock was willing to address as she went deeper and deeper into the world of sex trafficking. For more information about the growing field of visual ethics, please refer to the text's website and Paul Lester's discussion of this topic.

CONTROVERSY OR ADVOCACY?

What's the difference between controversy and advocacy? When does controversy become advocacy, advocacy occurring when a particular point of view is taken without seeking to present a balanced portrait? If a controversial topic is handled from an advocacy point of view, has an ethical line been crossed? Does the balanced portrait have to be contained in an individual show, or can the balance be in a network's overall schedule? In other words, does the balanced portrayal need to be in a given program, or can another program, perhaps on another day, reflect the balancing point of view? A lot of media watchers take these questions very seriously and worry that writers, producers, and directors often find it hard to avoid tackling controversial material without taking an advocacy position, thus creating advocacy entertainment.

Going back to Aristotle, is it always possible or even advisable to take a balanced, middle-of-the-road position, never going too far toward one extreme or another? Opinion pieces are clearly labeled as such in journalism, and writers like Maureen Dowd and David Brooks in *The New York Times* reflect advocacy positions, so why not have advocacy positions in entertainment? Again, I suggest looking at the E*T*H*I*C*S rubric as you analyze the following situations.

89

You Decide

In the May 25, 2005, episode of NBC's *Law & Order: Criminal Intent*, a detective searching for a white supremacist says, "Maybe we should put out an APB for somebody in a Tom DeLay T-shirt." The comment infuriated then House Majority leader DeLay (Figure 4-4). Did the producers and writers allow entertainment to become advocacy? Did they cross an ethical line?

Ryan Murphy and the producers of the controversial television show *Nip/Tuck* included an episode in the first season, episode 10, 2003, where plastic surgeon Sean McNamarra helps the terminally ill woman he is having an affair with

FIGURE 4-4
Former House majority leader Tom DeLay found a line in *Law & Order: Criminal Intent* about him offensive. (Globe Photos, Inc.)

to commit suicide. Did the episode become an advocacy piece romanticizing assisted suicide? Does it, perhaps, depend on the number of steps depicted in the assisted suicide? Does it depend on how long the scene is and what kind of music is played during the process?

Does the following dialogue from the show between Sean and his partner, Christian, help you firm up your position?

Sean: Suicide. Do you believe in that?
Christian: (pauses) I think that if a person is in a great deal of pain, physical or spiritual, and they've exhausted all their options, I wouldn't judge them for it. I'd say a silent prayer and hope death brought them the peace of mind life never could give them.

In *Million Dollar Baby*, Clint Eastwood's 2005 Academy Award–winning film, Maggie, played by Hillary Swank, suffers from a catastrophic spinal cord injury. She asks her trainer, Frankie, played by Clint Eastwood, to perform euthanasia. In your opinion, did the film become an advocacy piece on the part of Eastwood, as the National Spinal Cord Injury Association maintains in the *Electronic Magazine for People with Spinal Cord Injury*?[17]

90

In 2001, a number of organizations including the Centers for Disease Control, the National Institute of Mental Health, and the Office of the Surgeon General, among others, got together to produce a document that provided guidelines for the responsible coverage of suicide in the media. These guidelines included avoiding mentioning the method of the suicide, minimizing the prominence of stories about suicide, and making sure that the psychiatric disorders that accompany up to 90% of suicides are included.[18]

If these or similar guidelines on the proper handling of controversial subjects like suicide are not adhered to, does it follow that the filmmaker or other media practitioner has taken an advocacy position? Or is the controversial topic simply not being responsibly handled? As an exercise, create your own questions about the handling of controversy to determine if it comes down to individual situations (the *S* in our rubric) or if one should base his or her decision on the possible harm (the *H* in our rubric) that can come from an irresponsible handling of controversy.

ABORTION

Abortion remains one of the most controversial subjects, for advertisers and for the population as a whole. Thus, most works that tackle abortion end with the individual who had been considering abortion opting not to have the procedure.

If a television show like *Degrassi: The Next Generation* has an episode where a girl decides to go through with an abortion, does this mean that the makers of the show have taken an advocacy position in favor of abortion? The N, Noggin, a cable channel owned by Viacom that is geared to teen viewers, postponed the

---

[17]www.paralinks.net/eastwoodsci.html, accessed June 24, 2006.
[18]Patrick E. Jamieson and Kathleen Hall Jamieson, "Covering Suicide Responsibly in Print Journalism," *Media Ethics*, Spring 2003, vol. 14, no. 2, p. 6.

airing of an episode of this Canadian-made series, causing *Degrassi* creator Linda Schuyler to say that if kids are talking about abortion in schoolyards, television should be able to address the topic.[19]

Because abortion is such a hot-button topic, both sides—those who favor abortion rights and a woman's right to chose and those who oppose abortion on religious and other grounds—are likely to charge that an advocacy position has been adopted whenever abortion appears in a story line. It's thus increasingly important for producers, writers, actors, and directors to exercise responsibility when dealing with abortion.

CHILDREN AND CONTROVERSY

Ever since the mother and stepfather of child actor Jackie Coogan (*The Kid*, 1921) took his earnings, which resulted in the passage in 1938 of a bill to protect a child's earnings, the California Child Actor's Bill, much attention has been paid to the rights of child actors, including limiting the number of hours a child can work per day.

As entertainment becomes edgier, roles that children portray increasingly explore the dark side of life. As a result, the roles child actors are given often raise a variety of ethical questions. Paul Petersen, who was an original member of *The Mouseketeers* and the son on *The Donna Reed Show* (1958–1966), formed an organization called A Minor Consideration to combat what he sees as the abuse of child actors. He formed the advocacy group in 1990, the day after child star Rusty Hamer from *The Danny Thomas Show* (1953–1971) committed suicide. Petersen was distraught over the number of child stars whose lives ended in disappointment and tragedy. His organization, www.minorcon.org, has 600 former child stars as members and includes numerous professional volunteers. Petersen and his volunteers make impromptu visits to sets where he has been alerted to problems involving child actors.

Believing our culture uses up children and then disposes of them, Petersen is convinced that child actors who speak other people's words and pretend that they have feelings that they themselves don't have are in danger of not being able to adjust to the real world. Acting is pretending, after all. Child actors who "lie" about feelings may face repercussions many years afterward, even if they are confident at the time that, as children, they can handle the pretense.

91

---

[19] "'Degrassi' Abortion Episode Sparks Fan Outcry in U.S.," www.cbc.ca/story/art/national/2004/07/20/Arts/degrassi040720.html?print, accessed June 23, 2006.

If you want to embarrass someone, say a boyfriend or girlfriend, pull out a baby picture and pass it around. Think about how you'd feel if your mother pulled out your baby photos and showed them to your friends. In Petersen's view, child actors have constant reminders of what they were like as children. DVDs, classic television shows, countless channels that show old films, and so on keep their childhoods alive, in a sense, freezing the child actor in a time warp.

These reminders of past glory, if the child actor was successful, can have a damaging impact, according to Petersen. Sometimes it's hard to tell if the child who was successful as a child actor has an easier or harder adjustment than the child who did not succeed. Just as Gloria Swanson in the classic film *Sunset Boulevard* (1950), directed by Billy Wilder, repeatedly watched her old movies in her isolated mansion, child actors whose childhoods are plastered all over the media can have trouble breaking with the past.

All child actors may have a difficult time, but Peterson has noted that some things child actors are asked to do can cause more *H*arm than others. He is particularly troubled by the increasing sexualization of children, which he finds ethically deplorable. For him, child pornography is not limited to sites on the Internet. It's everywhere and readily available.

HOUNDDOG

In 2006, A Minor Consideration focused its attention on *Hounddog*, a film in which then 12-year-old Dakota Fanning was sexually abused and raped. In an article titled "Fanning's Role Stirs Controversy," Scott Martelle wrote, "Early reports of the film's contents have stirred a minor Internet storm over whether Fanning's mother, Joy, and her agent, Cindy Osbrink, are exploiting the girl in hopes of an Oscar nomination."[20] Hard-hitting performances that transition a child into adult roles have been known to garner awards, providing some insight into why children are often encouraged to take on such parts.

The director of *Hounddog*, Deborah Kampmeier, has vehemently defended herself against charges that she is exploiting Fanning. She stated, "I think to some extent what they're accusing me of is putting Dakota through some ordeal or a simulation of rape, but that's not the case."[21] She said the rape scene in

[20]Scott Martelle, "Fanning's Role Stirs Controversy," *The Los Angeles Times*, January 11, 2007, E-14.
[21]Henry Cabot Beck, "In the Works: No More Kid Stuff," *Premiere*, January/February 2007, p. 55.

question was carefully rehearsed, that Fanning was not naked (as charged), that no boy was on top of her (as also charged), and that Fanning's mother, her agent, and her teacher/well-fare worker were all present during the filming of the rape scene. Fanning's agent, Cindy Osbrink, also asserted that making *Hounddog* was a great experience for Fanning.[22] In her interviews, Kampmeier has stressed how hard she worked to raise money to finance this passion project of hers, and the end result of all the furor may be that the film finds a distributor after screening at the Sundance Film Festival in January of 2007, though as of this writing no distributor has stepped forward. For Petersen, finding a distributor would not be the desired result, but controversy can mean money, and a distributor might equate the controversy with box office success. Go to the text's website for clips of Paul Petersen addressing a class at Cal State Fullerton where he talks about *Hounddog* and A Minor Consideration.

BASTARD OUT OF CAROLINA

In 1996, *Bastard Out of Carolina*, based on the ground-breaking novel by Dorothy Allison, caused a similar furor over the portrayal of the sexual abuse of a child. The film, written by Anne Meredith, executive produced by Gary Hoffman, and directed by Angelica Huston, made news when Ted Turner refused to allow the film to air on TNT because he found the child abuse scenes personally disturbing. Known to be against violence on television, Turner found the film objectionable and not suitable for his network. Rejected by TNT, the film then found a home at Showtime, where it was acclaimed as a critical, commercial, and artistic success. It became the highest rated film on Showtime that year and won the Television Critics Award for best movie and miniseries.

In *Bastard Out of Carolina*, the sexually abused child, Bone, is played by 11-year-old Jena Malone. There are two scenes in the film that feature the sexual abuse Bone experienced, one in a car and one inside a house. While talking about the film and the controversy it caused, Hoffman made the following observations:

- He felt a strong sense of obligation to Allison to be true to her book, a serious examination of abuse, as well as to protect Malone. Though the book was labeled a novel, it was inspired by Allison's own experiences. He wanted viewers of the film to feel the emotional impact of the novel.
- Portraying the abuse with the emotional intensity felt by readers of the book was important to him, as was the need to ensure Malone's safety and well-being.

[22]Ibid.

- In the casting session for Bone, Jena Malone was asked if she could handle the content of the script (which she had read with her mother). She said she could, and after reading an intense scene for the audition, she again became a carefree child, proving to Hoffman that she understood the difference between acting and real life.
- During filming, he spent a lot of time with Malone's mother, making sure she and her daughter were comfortable with the film. Jena's mother was on the set at all times and she had no objections.
- His son, who was the same age as Malone, played with her on the set in between scenes.
- Ron Eldard, who played the abuser, rehearsed the abuse scenes with Malone and developed a close working relationship with her.
- When asked about any long term effects the role might have had on Malone, Hoffman said there is no way of predicting how someone will react years later.
- Lastly, and most importantly for him perhaps, Hoffman stressed that the reality of what viewers see on the screen is not the reality experienced by the actors during filming. For example, Malone repeatedly told him how much "fun" she had rehearsing and filming the scene in the house. On screen, it looks as if Eldard is lifting her up by her head, but in reality she is holding on to his arms, which is what they had rehearsed.

Hoffman's last point is in keeping with what director Deborah Kampmeier had to say in connection with Dakota Fanning and *Hounddog*. The actor may not have experienced during filming what the viewer experiences, movies being make-believe, after all.

Addressing the controversy over the film, director Huston said that Malone was "very grown-up" about handling the horror of some of the scenes and that she wanted to do them.[23]

EDGES OF THE LORD

The feature film *Edges of the Lord* (2001) stars Haley Joel Osment and Willem Dafoe and was written and directed by Yurek Bogayevicz. The film was never released theatrically in the United States, though it is available on DVD. A holocaust movie (Figure 4-5) about a Jewish child (Osment) who is sent to live with a Catholic family to save him from the Nazis, it's a controversial film about

---

[23]Harper Barnes, "'Bastard' Finds Home: Project Dumped by TNT Goes to Showtime," *St. Louis Post Dispatch*, December 15, 1996, www.Ron-Eldard.com, accessed January 12, 2007.

children during wartime. For Phillip Krupp, a producer on the film, a paramount concern in terms of the child actors was to ensure their safety during filming. The parents were present during the shoot and Bogayevicz spoke to the children about their scenes, as the movie contains some

FIGURE 4-5
Auschwitz is the largest concentration camp established by the Nazis. Projects about the Holocaust require careful handling, as producer Phillip Krupp demonstrated when making *Edges of the Lord.* (iStockphoto.com #1166571, Jason Walton.)

rough scenes for child actors, including being threatened, a rape, shootings, delusional behavior, witnessing Nazi executions, and boys having to pull down their pants to see if they were circumcised. Throughout the shooting of these intense scenes, Krupp had to make sure that the child actors felt safe.

You Decide

Using our E*T*H*I*C*S rubric, analyze the roles some child actors undertake to see if you feel any ethical lines are being crossed and if children are being asked to act in scenes that they should not be in. Refer to specific shows or movies. What kinds of roles do you feel are inappropriate for child actors?

Times change, of course, and what at one time may have been considered inappropriate for a child no longer is, but even if children are more sophisticated these days, should child actors appear in increasingly controversial scenes?

Do you think that children have the ability to decide what's right or wrong for them or what could cause them *H*arm? At what age do you think a child is no longer a child? 16?

18? 21? Quoted in *The New York Times* about *Hounddog*, Petersen said that if the character had been 15 in the film and a 19-year-old played the part, he would not have complained.[24] At what age do you think it is appropriate for a child actor to be in a rape scene?

How important do you think it is for a parent to be involved in the projects their children undertake? If a parent is on the set, does that suggest that what the child is asked to do is okay? What type of *C*ode, if any, do you think should exist for child actors? Or do you think it depends on the individual *S*ituation? Do you agree or disagree with Paul Petersen that there can be delayed reactions to having been a child actor? How important do you think it is for a child actor to feel safe on a set?

95

In this chapter, we have examined how producers, writers, actors, and directors tackle controversy and the ethical issues involved. In the next chapter, let's look at ethics from the perspective of programmers.

[24]David M. Halbfinger, "Furor over 12-Year-Old Actress's Rape Scene," *The New York Times*, January 20, 2007, A-1, 22.

CHAPTER 5
Ethics and Programmers

Programmers/creative executives select what projects they are going to develop or produce based on a number of factors, such as does the project appeal to the target audience? Or does it fit the network schedule or the studio release time table, as described in a *New York Times* article by Carol Ames, who wrote Chapter 12 on public relations and ethics? She noted that studios jockey hard to select domestic and international release dates. If they pick a wrong release date, box office results will suffer. She wrote, "A film shown on more than 3,000 screens earns an average of 31.6 percent of its total domestic box office during its first weekend."[1] The studio thus needs to find the right release date, one that also works globally because more and more films open all over the world on the same date. Programmers and creative executives also need to question if other divisions at the network or studio will support a given project, or if the financials make sense, not to mention, if it is any good?

In the previous chapter, we examined how producers, writers, actors, and directors interact with studio or network executives from an ethical perspective. In this chapter, let's look at possible pressures that impact programming decisions, again focusing on ethics.

[1]Carol Ames, "Box Office Battles, Begun Long Ago and Far Away," *The New York Times*, May 8, 2005, MT-13, 29.

PROGRAMMING DECISIONS AND POLITICS
Stolen Honor: Wounds That Never Heal

Programmers or station group owners decide what to program, usually based on what they think audiences or advertisers want. Sometimes, however, the decisions about what to program are based on other factors. The other factor we're going to talk about here is politics. We will also talk more about politics in terms of programming later in this chapter when we take a look at the television movie, *Flight 93*.

Programming based on political decisions raises complex ethical questions because (1) the reasons provided for the programming decisions often are not the real ones (even if possibly more compelling, understandable reasons are given—poor execution, for example—the real reasons are political), (2) programming decisions based on politics often conflict with the public's right to know, and (3) the fear of offending can cause self-censorship, as programmers, producers, and writers avoid controversial topics.

For example, here is a timeline for Sinclair Broadcasting and the anti–John Kerry documentary *Stolen Honor: Wounds That Never Heal*:

- Sinclair Broadcasting began in 1971 with a single UHF station.
- In 2004, Sinclair had 62 television stations, making it the nation's largest owner of television stations.
- Sinclair executives are major Republican donors who support George W. Bush.
- Mark Hyman, Sinclair's vice president for corporate relations, provides a centralized conservative commentary for the stations.[2]
- According to Bill Carter in *The New York Times*, after 9/11, Sinclair orders its Baltimore station "to read patriotic statements praising President Bush."[3]
- In 2004, Hyman goes to Iraq to report some positive stories because he feels that the media is ignoring positive developments.[4]
- In April 2004, Sinclair's ABC affiliated stations refuse to carry a *Nightline* program in which Ted Koppel reads the names of American war dead in

[2]Bill Carter, "Risks Seen for TV Chains Showing Film about Kerry," *The New York Times*, October 18, 2004, C-1, 11.
[3]Carter, "Risks Seen for TV Chains Showing Film about Kerry," C-11.
[4]Elizabeth Jensen, "Sinclair Fires Journalist after Critical Comments," *The Los Angeles Times*, October 19, 2004, A-13.

Iraq, because the program is deemed unpatriotic and harmful to the war effort.

- In October 2004, Sinclair announces its plan to air as news, not commentary, *Stolen Honor: Wounds That Never Heal*, a film by Carlton Sherwood that alleges that John Kerry's comments about American soldiers committing atrocities in Vietnam prolonged the war. The film charged that Kerry endangered the lives of American prisoners of war, because the North Vietnamese would use Kerry's comments as an excuse to engage in torture.[5]

- Sinclair stations are ordered to carry *Stolen Honor* a week before the 2004 presidential election.

- Advertisers, commissioner of the Federal Communications Commission (FCC) Michael Copps, media watchdog groups, and consumer advocates complain about Sinclair's partisan action in scheduling *Stolen Hours*.

- Sinclair's stock drops.

- Sinclair fires Jon Lieberman, its Washington bureau chief, after he makes statements denouncing Sinclair's use of *Stolen Honor* as political propaganda.[6]

- Sinclair changes its mind about airing *Stolen Honor*, substituting a news special, *A POW Story: Politics, Pressure and the Media*, which includes approximately five minutes from *Stolen Hours*.

- News website NewsMax.com buys time on Pax for a reported $294,500 to air *Stolen Honor* in its entirety[7] (Figure 5-1).

FIGURE 5-1

Political campaigning can raise all sorts of ethical issues as candidates and supporters seek support, as illustrated by the film *Stolen Honor: Wounds That Never Heal*. (iStockphoto.com 3010448, Jim Jurica.)

Sinclair said Jon Lieberman was fired because he violated company policy by speaking to the media without prior approval.[8] If you go to the Sinclair Broadcast Group website (www.sbgi.net) and click "About Sinclair" and then "Ethics," you will find Sinclair's code of ethics for directors and Sinclair employees. Copyrighted in 2007, the code includes "It is the policy of the Corporation to prohibit its directors and employees from engaging in any activity or practice in conflict with the interests of the corporation."

[5]John Dempsey, "Copps Blasts Sinclair," *Daily Variety*, October 13, 2004, p. 8.
[6]Jensen, "Sinclair Fires Journalist after Critical Comments," A-13.
[7]Walter J. Roche Jr., "Group Challenges Sinclair Licenses," *The Los Angeles Times*, November 2, 2004, A-22.
[8]Jensen, "Sinclair Fires Journalist after Critical Comments," A-13.

You Decide

Should business decisions come first? Should the interests of the corporation come first? The essential question is should ethics or politics come first?

Do you think that Sinclair has the right to air what it wants when it wants, based on First Amendment protections? Take a look at Sinclair's entire code of ethics and *E*valuate it in light of the previous discussion. Do you think Sinclair backed off from showing the entire film because it realized that some ethical violations might be involved, or did it back off for business reasons, because its stock was dropping? Or do you think Sinclair backed off because if Kerry got elected, he might have supported legislation that would restrict media consolidation, hurting Sinclair's expansion by making it increasingly difficult for Sinclair's stations to renew their licenses?

What about using the public airwaves to advance a personal or corporate agenda? Was Sinclair's initial intention with *Stolen Honor* the equivalent of a large campaign donation under the guise of a news program? Lastly, consider doing your own study of Sinclair and *Stolen Honor* using the E*T*H*I*C*S rubric as a guide.

PUBLIC BROADCASTING AND POLITICS

A battle has long raged about public broadcasting. On one side, critics complain that public broadcasting has a clear left-wing bias with *Now* with Bill Moyers as the rallying point for this position; on the other side, supporters of public broadcasting claim that it is indeed fair and balanced with full representations from the right as well as from the left. At times, the battle over the politics of public broadcasting becomes fierce as both sides engage in loaded rhetoric.

Conservative distaste for public broadcasting is not new, almost going back to the creation of the Public Broadcasting Act of 1967. In 1972, the Nixon administration vetoed the budget of PBS, the Public Broadcasting Service. In the l990s, House Speaker Newt Gingrich referred to PBS as "a sandbox for the elite."

As the head of the Corporation for Public Broadcasting (CPB), which allocates government funds for public broadcasting, Kenneth J. Tomlinson stood in a long line of conservative individuals concerned about a perceived liberal bias in PBS programming. As a member of the board of CPB, Tomlinson sought to make PBS carry more conservative programming.

To accomplish his goals, Tomlinson, without CPB board approval, hired a researcher to monitor the political stances of PBS programs in 2004. This researcher, Fred Mann, tabulated the political positions of people on PBS shows, labeling them as "anti-Bush," "anti-business," "anti–Tom DeLay," or "liberal."[9]

Though board-approved studies had already been assigned, Tomlinson wanted his own study to prove that PBS wore a liberal mantle. For his zealotry in serving his political agenda, Tomlinson was removed from the CPB board in 2005 for a number of ethical violations, breaking public broadcasting guidelines, and using corporate funds to promote a conservative agenda. Tomlinson's decision to hire two lobbyists to help defeat a proposal to require more broadcasters to be on CPB's board also contributed to his being removed.

Whether you agree or disagree with Tomlinson and his methods, any pressure on the media to program particular points of view has significant ethical implications. If "other" reasons are used on behalf of a partisan, political agenda, most people would agree that the public is being misled. If one uses "fairness and balance" as a means to silence opposition, the media may eventually be intimidated into practicing self-censorship, which is our next topic.

SELF-CENSORSHIP AND PROGRAMMING DECISIONS

According to Frank Rich in an opinion piece in *The New York Times*, December 12, 2004, self-censorship blossomed after the November 2004 election.[10] Fear of FCC indecency fines and other reprisals can definitely intimidate programmers into self-censorship. Self-censorship thus has become a major factor in how programming decisions are made.

At the Broadcast Educator's Association meeting in 2006, Louis Wiley, executive director of *Frontline*, discussed repercussions that are taking place as a result of self-censorship. He said, "What should be editorial decisions made by filmmakers, producers and station managers with due regard to standards and their local communities are more and more being shaped by the fear of a government agency."

---

[9]Eric Boehlert, "Trying to Turn PBS to the Right," *Television Week*, June 5, 2006, p. 32.

[10]Frank Rich, "The Plot Against Sex in America," *The New York Times*, December 12, 2004, reprinted by Fox Searchlight Pictures, 2004.

WGBH Boston, which produces *Frontline*, is concerned that PBS stations scheduled to air *Frontline* reports might decide not to air the reports at all or they might select to air a piece later at a different time (for example, after 10 p.m., the so-called safe harbor time zone reserved for times when children are not expected to be watching) for fear of FCC fines.

Frontline made the difficult decision to prepare edited versions of some of its programs to accommodate stations afraid of FCC reprisals (Figure 5-2). Wiley stressed that the fear of FCC fines is palpable and that programmers will select to air on the side of caution, more frequently engaging in self- or prior censorship.

FIGURE 5-2
In February 2005, *Frontline* broadcast *A Company of Soldiers* and did not bleep the f-word used by soldiers in the heat of battle. Stations that aired the program before 10 p. m. put themselves at legal risk. (Photograph Courtesy of WGBH.)

Self-censorship is likely to extend beyond PBS, of course, as broadcast network programmers elect to take fewer risks to protect affiliates from increased fines, resulting in more programming decisions being based on self-censorship rather than on strong ethical principles and thereby limiting audience's access to material and to different points of view, according to many media observers.

PROGRAMMERS AND THE CREATIVE TEAM

Programming executives at studios and networks have many responsibilities, not the least of which is how to handle the creative team. The manner in which the team is treated can have wide ranging repercussions. If the programmer is too tough, feathers and egos can get ruffled, particularly as creative individuals often display thin skins. If the executive is too easygoing, projects can falter and budgets can escalate dramatically. It's thus necessary for programmers to make the right decisions.

The "You Decide" box lists a number of representative situations that programmers frequently face when dealing with the creative team. All of these examples have ethical implications, particularly if you agree with former VH1 programming executive Tom Grasty that a programmer's job is frequently defined as doing what benefits the studio or network.

You Decide

Take a look at the following real-life scenarios. How do you think the following situations should be handled?

■ The studio head has said she wants a particular high-end writer attached to an upcoming project, *Hearts in Turmoil*. It then becomes the creative executive's responsibility to convince that writer to come on board. The writer in question usually does bigger projects than *Hearts in Turmoil*, a traditional story about a family coming together after a long absence, not unlike the script that is satirized in Christopher Guest's *For Your Consideration*: *Home for Purim* (2006). The writer, no novice he, says he has a passion project *The Last Albino* that he has been developing for a number of years that he would very much like to do. Set in 1400, it's the story of one man's search for the parrot (Figure 5-3) he had as a child. The creative executive understands immediately what the writer is driving at and says that the studio would be very interested in *The Last Albino* after *Hearts in Turmoil*. Here, the executive is making no promises, simply saying the studio would be interested, even though he knows that *The Last Albino* doesn't have a snowball's chance in hell. But the writer

FIGURE 5-3
A project about a writer's childhood search for a parrot doesn't stand much of a chance of getting made, unless the writer is wanted for another project. (iStockphoto.com #2112396, Jeremy Edwards.)

presses, seeking a commitment for *The Last Albino*. How should the executive respond?

■ A writer comes in to see a programmer with a pitch that seems right for the network in question. It's close, but it's not quite there. Knowing that according to the Writers Guild rules, she cannot specifically ask the writer to prepare some pages without payment, the programmer carefully suggests that she has to take some pages to her boss to move the project along. She waits for the writer to volunteer. The writer does, in fact, take the hint and offers to write up some pages. When the pages come in, they don't do the trick. The programmer feels that more work is needed. She schedules a notes meeting and suggests some tweaks here and there. The writer again complies. That afternoon, the programmer gets a call from the writer's agent complaining that she is asking the writer to do too much free work. The programmer knows that this is a powerful agent who would be able to help her land her next job when she is ready to leave the network (read, fired). What should the programmer's response be?

■ A creative executive has read a number of scripts by a gifted writer. This writer pitched the executive a project that the executive feels is wrong for the studio, but he feels the writer could be right for some projects down the road. The executive goes to his boss telling her that he has arranged for said writer to pitch his story to her. The executive tells the boss that he does not want her to go into development on the project. He wants her to pass on the project. He simply wants her to have a face-to-face meeting with a talented writer. Is the writer being exploited in this situation, or is the writer being given a chance to enhance his visibility by getting a meeting with a powerful executive?

■ A programmer gets a call from a director saying that a particular crowd scene in which the film's star watches as a group of terrorists are searched in a busy airport (Figure 5-4) is not working in rehearsals and that, as a courtesy, he is requesting permission to cut the scene. A number of thoughts quickly run through the programmer's mind.

103

FIGURE 5-4
A crowd scene at a busy airport, such as O'Hare Airport in Chicago, can be costly to film, causing producers and directors to scramble to try to find ways to cut back on expenses. (iStockphoto.com #3335477, Terraxplorer.)

First, though the request is coming from the director, it's probably the star who is feeling that she doesn't have enough to do in the scene. Second, the request could be coming from the producer who wants to save money by dropping an expensive scene. The programmer wants to make this decision on his own in order to cement his hold on the film. Given this information, you decide what additional information might be needed and on what basis the decision might be made. What role do you think ethics should play in the deliberation?

■ An actor with a solid track record is somehow not delivering the goods in dailies. It would be exorbitantly expensive to replace him after he's already filmed for five days. Nevertheless, something needs to be done; the producer has already spoken to the actor, but there's been no change in the performance. Unsure of how best to handle the situation, the programmer ponders (1) calling the actor directly, (2) calling the casting director, (3) showing his boss the dailies without saying anything to see if she has a similar reaction, or (4) checking with the legal department to see if there is a way to get out of the contract with the actor. Do ethics factor into the programmer's decision, or is this primarily a business call with no ethical ramifications?

■ Several producers have pitched the same project to a creative executive who wants the project steered to a particular producer, a producer with a string of successes who the boss really likes. The creative executive wants to protect herself from angry calls from those producers who don't get the assignment. Here's what the executive does: She carefully lays out exactly what it would take for each of the producers to be chosen. Thus, a level playing field has been established, and the producer who delivers the goods first will win the development prize. But the executive gives the favored producer a way to get the necessary life rights, something that is not shared with the others. Has the creative executive done something unethical? Apply the *S* from our rubric as you ponder this particular situation. What additional factors in this representative scenario might change your position?

■ There's a lot of internal turmoil about the status of a particular project. Should it go forward to production, should it be abandoned, or should it remain in development, possibly with a new writer? Some divisions at the studio are in favor of the project, others are not. The creative executive sees himself as the producers' ally, but he also feels strongly that it is not a creative executive's job to tell a producer about a studio's internal affairs, even if knowing the inside scoop might help a project make it to the finish line. Is the executive making the right decision here? What is the basis for your evaluation?

■ The creative executive tells a producer whose project is in fast-track development at a network to "jack it up" in terms of pushing the envelope, for example, including an opening sex scene designed to capture viewers' attention. She tells the producer that it's always best to include more edgy material than what the censors will approve. Better to have to pull back a bit later than to bow to the censor's authority at the start. The producer questions this tactic, but the creative executive says she'll support the producer and fight with him to get the censors to back off. Subsequently, she tells the in-house censors that she doesn't understand why the producer is taking a hard-line position. Is the creative executive playing fair and simply doing things the way things are done?

Programmers and studio creative executives face many such situations regularly. It's a constant juggling act to determine what's right: Right ethically? Right in terms of one's career? Right in terms of the studio or network? Right in terms of someone else's career? It's important for individuals who want to work in media to understand what's at stake in these types of situations. It's also important for media practitioners and observers alike to know what ethical principles apply.

You Decide, Round 2

The previous scenarios involved programming decisions that confront executives in terms of the projects they are supervising or in terms of their relationships with their bosses or other executives in the company. In round 2, let's look at offers (some might call them bribes) that programmers often receive from producers. If a producer offers and a programmer accepts, where might the programmer become beholden to the producer? At what points, if any, might the programmer owe the producer something in return? If you feel there are places where ethical lines are crossed, circle the corresponding numbers and be prepared to discuss your reasoning.

1. The producer pays for a breakfast meeting.
2. After a meeting, the producer sends the programmer some travel books to help in the planning of the programmer's upcoming vacation.
3. The producer pays for a lunch meeting.
4. The producer pays for a dinner meeting. The cost for two people is $100.
5. The producer pays for a dinner meeting. The cost for two people is $450 (Figure 5-5).
6. The producer invites the programmer to a private screening for 15 power players in Malibu.
7. The producer invites the programmer to sit at her table at a Hollywood function.
8. The producer gives the programmer a $100 gift certificate as a Christmas gift.
9. The producer invites the programmer to join her in her box at a Laker game.
10. The producer gives the programmer four courtside seats to a Laker game.
11. The producer gives the programmer a weekend stay at a Santa Barbara resort.
12. The producer offers the programmer's spouse a job, "no strings attached."

How many have you circled as ethically problematical?

Every situation is different, so each of these offers can have shades of meanings for different people. Nevertheless, the scale raises important questions about the role of ethics and about how business is conducted in the media. Offer 8, for example, is tricky because a $100 gift certificate exceeds the limit most programmers are allowed to accept. Offers 10 and 11 are similarly problematical because the producer is not present. And most would find the "no strings attached" proposal in offer 12 hard to accept, but greasing the wheels has been an accepted practice in politics and entertainment for many years, regardless of the ethics involved.

FIGURE 5-5
Are dinners at nice restaurants simply the cost of doing business, or are high-priced expense account meals suspect from an ethical point of view? (iStockphoto.com #3253892, Nilgun Bostanci.)

BUYER ENTHUSIASM AND ETHICAL BEHAVIOR

It's a given that sellers must be passionate about their projects. If the enthusiasm is lacking, a project's chances are slim to nonexistent. One may wonder why enthusiasm and passion are such prerequisites, almost as if a buyer can't tell what might work without them, even if the seller didn't preface his remarks with "This is something I really care about. It's a particular passion of mine."

Nevertheless, sellers have to convey passion in order to succeed. But what about the buyers of material who determine what television shows get on the air, what radio programs make the cut, what films are made, and what countries around the world might buy a particular product? How much enthusiasm and passion must they display?

No one likes to pitch to a dead presence. Buyers who don't respond to a pitch, who don't indicate they want to know what happens next, make the pitching process that much more difficult. Significantly, an executive who isn't enthusiastic during the pitch meeting and throughout the development process may find it difficult to garner the required support for that all-important next job.

But how honest, or ethical, is the enthusiasm a buyer expresses about any given project? A buyer of programs can't intentionally mislead the creative team by giving every indication that the project being pitched is going to be a go and then surprise everyone by passing on it a few days later. Is it ethically wrong for a buyer to jump up and down in favor of a project during the pitch meeting, forcing higher-ups to be the bad guys who say no? Such shenanigans might allow buyers to be perceived as advocates to the creative team, but it certainly won't endear them to bosses.

Most programmers and creative executives entertain multiple story ideas on a daily basis, so how many times can a pitch genuinely excite them? How many original ideas and narrative voices are there anyway? Thus, many programmers assume a false posture as they seek to convey excitement about run-of-the-mill properties, particularly if a significant player brings in a project, one who commands being treated with respect.

How excited can a programmer be about a program like ABC's *Are You Hot?* (2003) (Figure 5-6). The show, which failed with audiences and critics alike, was a variation of a mean TV program where contestants were judged solely on their physical attributes, with a flashlight at the ready to zoom in on any physical

FIGURE 5-6
Shows that simply require contestants to look good without demonstrating skills, talent, or effort, like *Are You Hot?*, are examples of what many call "mean TV." (iStockphoto.com # 2243912, Jacom Stephens.)

imperfections. Or how excited can executives be about Adam Sandler's *Click* (2006), about a man with a magic remote control, even if the film has the earmarks of a moneymaker. Yet if a large number of people up the line had not expressed enthusiasm about these projects, they would not have seen the light of day.

Often, bored programmers who have experienced any number of repetitive pitches assume a kind of faux enthusiasm for projects they don't really care about, the feeling being that a person can't reject absolutely everything. Of course, a few programmers have climbed the corporate ladder by doing the reverse, by—falsely—finding every project not quite right, just not good enough. One programming executive once told me proudly that he passed on everything to establish himself as one tough customer with very high standards. If one of the projects he passed on ended up as a success elsewhere, he was ready with the justification that when the project was pitched to him, it was totally, and he meant totally, different.

Some feel that the prevalence of faux enthusiasm has severely tainted the entertainment business. After all, whom can you trust if everyone is simply assuming a pose? If one had a dollar every time a writer or producer left a pitch meeting convinced that the meeting went well and that an offer was a done deal, one would be very rich indeed.

107

MEDIATING AND ETHICS

Rick Jones, with the long title of director of entertainment postproduction and scheduling administration at ABC, has a unique programming position, one that requires him to mediate between parties that often have conflicting interests. Jones's primary job is to supervise the editing of theatrical films for air on television.

Directors of films purchased for air on television are always given the opportunity to execute the edits requested by the network's Broadcast Standards and Practices (BS&P) departments. It is Jones's responsibility to mediate between the studio and the BS&P editor responsible for making sure that the film meets standards for acceptability. Jones must also make sure that the film complies with additional network requirements, such as running time and scheduling.

As a mediator, Jones needs to be an advocate for both the network and the studio that made the film. Sometimes the network and the studio (the licensee) are at odds, and it may appear as if no mediated solution is in the offing. If no agreement is reached, then the buyer (the network) goes in and makes the changes it wants. It's stipulated in the contracts that networks have the right to do this, unless, of course, the contract specifies that no changes or edits can be made. But stepping in to make the edits is a last resort, one that Jones seeks to avoid.

Here are some representative situations that could test ethical boundaries in the mediating process:

- The studio does not want to make a certain edit. To expedite matters, should the mediator tell the BS&P editor that the director refuses to make the edit, even if the mediator knows that the refusal is not coming from the director herself and that the director, in fact, has no idea she is being used in this ploy?
- Can the mediator tell the network that a requested edit cannot be made, even if this is untrue? This situation illustrates how difficult being an advocate of the studio can be. It can also apply to our E*T*H*I*C*S rubric. In terms of *E,* one can question whether the mediator has considered and evaluated all the options before saying the edit cannot be made seamlessly. This situation does not meet the *T* test, because it's untrue that the edit can't be made. The matter of *H,* potential harm, is tricky, depending on the quality of the film in question. If the film is a potboiler, it's unlikely that any great *H*arm would be done if the edit were made; if the film is truly a work of art, however, making the edit could potentially butcher the film. Does it then depend on the situation, the *S.* Is a *C,* code of ethics, being violated in saying an edit cannot be made?
- The network does not have to honor any deal that a producer makes for product placement in a film. Thus, if a producer says that a sequence featuring a particular product must stay in the film to honor the producer's agreement, the network does not have to comply. Should a mediator allow the deletion, or wiping, of the products the producer agreed to include in order to substitute other products that could financially benefit the network? The technology for this exists, but would there be anything ethically off-base in taking advantage of this technology?
- If the mediator feels that the BS&P requested edits are excessive, can the mediator justify telling the BS&P editor that the changes have been made, even if they haven't, because the requested changes were arbitrary and there's a chance the BS&P editor might not notice, and if he did notice, it might be too late to do anything about them without moving heaven and earth?

- If the mediator feels that the editor assigned to execute the edits on a film does not make clean edits, does the mediator let a poorly executed edit stand out of fear that if he requested that more work be done, the editor might make it worse?

Jones must ensure that all projects submitted to ABC meet the network's requirements for broadcast. Sometimes a project will come in long for the time allotted. Say the running time for a two hour movie is 89 minutes, but it's delivered at 91 minutes instead. The producer doesn't want to take out the two minutes and the network, understandably perhaps, depending on one's perspective, does not want to lose two minutes of ads or promo time.

One solution at Jones's disposal is vari-speeding, a process that speeds up the film. If vari-speeding is not done properly, some sequences will appear jerky. If done correctly (i.e., running the film no more than 3% faster), few people, if any, will be aware that the vari-speeding has taken place, particularly if the audio is also corrected to run at a faster pace. According to Jones, if the audio is vari-sped without pitch correction, the sound ends up as if a 45 record were played at 78 speed. A film can also be slowed down if it comes in short, using a reverse vari-speed procedure.

So here's the ethical dilemma: If the producer steadfastly refuses to trim the troublesome two minutes, how about vari-speeding without informing the studio. Okay? Not okay?

FLIGHT 93

In the previous chapter, we looked at a controversial topic, a bird flu pandemic, from the point of view of the producers behind *Fatal Contact*. In this chapter, we examine a controversial topic from the point of view of the network programmer.

When it comes to defining controversy, the events surrounding the terrorist attacks of September 11, 2001, definitely apply. Many sensitive issues are attached to the occurrences of that day, including patriotism, national security, intelligence gathering, the feelings of surviving family members and friends, as well as factual accuracy. Also, many inherently dramatic stories are associated with that day, none perhaps more than the events that took place aboard United Flight 93, where passengers and crew prevented the plane from hitting its target, either the White House or the U.S. Capitol.

David Craig, formerly an A&E programming executive and the supervising producer of the Emmy-nominated *Flight 93* television movie, said four factors

109

controlled the telling of the story of Flight 93: (1) the dramatic focus would be on the personal stories; (2) the film would not be political in nature; (3) the film would be authentic, done as accurately as possible by using the extensive public record, including the report of the 9/11 Commission and having the writer, Nevin Schreiner, meet with family members; and (4) restraint in all matters would be of the essence.

According to Craig, the development and production of the film raised a number of complex ethical questions, including the following:

- When is it too soon or too late to revisit the events of 9/11? Is five years the right amount of time for audiences to be willing to revisit the events of that day?
- If you go forward, when do you air the program and how do you publicize it without being guilty of exploiting a tragedy?
- During the development of the script, how do you balance what is happening on the plane with what is happening on the ground?
- What should you show of the passengers and crew entering the cockpit to thwart the terrorists' plans? How far past existing documentation can you, as a programmer, authorize to maximize the drama while adhering to the need for authenticity, particularly as there is so much debate about whether or not the passengers and crew commandeered the cockpit?
- "Let's roll." This now-famous phrase uttered before passengers and crew confronted the terrorists is mired in controversy. For example, who said it? Who owns the copyright for it? Are there legal concerns in using the phrase? As a programmer, how do you want the phrase handled? Should you leave it out? Have someone on the plane say it? Have President Bush repeat the phrase in the film to show that it has become part of our culture?
- Are the terrorists portrayed in the script as too sympathetic, too religious, too committed to their cause, or too polite, perhaps, as they board the plane? Are they cast as too good looking?
- How do you want religion handled to avoid making the film ideological? For example, in the script one terrorist tells another, "God be with you," and Verizon operator Lisa Jefferson, played by Monnai Michaell, recites the Lord's Prayer with one of the passengers. How many people do you want shown reciting this prayer without crossing the line into ideology?

- Do you include the names of the people who perished on the flight in the crawl? If you decide to do so, do you also include the names of the terrorists who also perished?
- If you include a crawl, what should the crawl contain?
- Should the film include actual news footage of the World Trade Center being hit and falling apart? If so, how many times, and how long should the shots be? As a programmer, do you leave these decisions to the director, producer, or editor?
- If you want the film to show the passage of time, a passage that would suggest healing, how do you want this done? Visually? In dialogue? In the crawl? Would a healing message offend people who have not yet experienced healing?
- In keeping with the stated desire to avoid politics in the film, during script meetings what do you say you want included to enable viewers to understand what the administration was doing at the time? Do you instruct the filmmakers to include a scene with Vice President Cheney? Should the film include the White House response to the attacks? How should the film handle discussions about having U.S. planes "engage" (i.e., shoot down, Flight 93)?
- As a programmer, how do you convince advertisers to sponsor a film about 9/11?
- Do you dedicate the film to anyone? If so, to whom and how do you do it?
- Do you include the United logo, with or without permission from the airline?

As you can see, the development of the film raised a number of difficult, complex ethical questions.

Let's answer a few of these questions. There are no visuals in the film of United, because United would not authorize their inclusion. "Let's roll" is said off-camera. The crawl does not include the names of the terrorists. The crawl reads, "With great courage and resolve, the passengers and crew of Flight 93 prevented their plane from reaching its target, the White House or the Capitol Building." The film is dedicated "to the passengers and crew of Flight 93 and to their families." Though the script at one time included a scene with Vice President Dick Cheney, there is no such scene in the final cut of the film. If you want to see how some of the other questions were handled, check out the DVD of the film.

DIFFERENT KINDS OF ETHICAL QUESTIONS FACING PROGRAMMERS

Programming ethics cover a wide range of topics. To illustrate this range, let's take a look at the ethical issues facing the Outdoor Channel, a niche cable channel that according to its website, www.outdoorchannel.com, seeks to educate and entertain sportsmen. As a conservation organization, the Outdoor Channel is dedicated to portraying outdoor activities in a responsible light. It is not a preservation organization, which, according to the Outdoor Channel, would seek to eliminate access to the outdoors. Rather, the Outdoor Channel seeks a responsible stewardship, which it does by creating a set of ethical guidelines that differ markedly from what most people associate with ethics and the media.

According to Wade Sherman, former senior vice president of programming for the Outdoor Channel, these guidelines are based on the channel's ethical standards as well as viewer feedback. The guidelines, which are revised yearly, are distributed to contributing producers and advertisers. They include the following:

- To preserve the concept of a fair chase, animals cannot be hunted in a fenced or contained area. Animals cannot be trapped while being hunted.
- Even if the practice is legal in the area where filming is taking place, there should be no hunting or spotting from the air.
- If a group of hunters flies into an area, it is recommended that the party stay the night before starting the hunt.
- Bedded animals should not be hunted. Though some hunters might feel that landing a bedded animal reveals a high level of skill in that the hunter has avoided disturbing the animal by making noise or allowing the animal to track a scent, the Outdoor Channel prohibits this practice because outdoor enthusiasts find the practice objectionable.
- Bird dogs are acceptable, but the use of dogs in hunting bears is not allowed. If a dog chases a bear up a tree and the hunter shoots the bear, where is the sport or skill?
- Life vests as flotation devices are encouraged.
- Shooting near water is cautioned against as a safety issue, because bullets can skid in the water, hitting unintended targets.
- Because the "harvest" is seen as the culmination of a hunt, there can be no replays of the kill, and slow motion is also prohibited.

To ensure that producers of shows for the Outdoor Channel adhere to ethical practices, they are referred to a number of organizations, including the following:

- The Mission Statement of the Safari Club International (www.safariclub.org)
- The standards of the International Hunters Association (www.ihea.com)
- The National Safe Boating Council (www.safeboatingcouncil.org)
- The National Marine Manufacturing Association (www.nmma.org)
- The National Off-Highway Vehicle Conservation Council (www.nohvcc.org)

An interesting programming situation arose in early 2007 when outdoorsman and hunter Jim Zumbo, who had a show on the Outdoor Channel, *Jim Zumbo Outdoors*, posted a controversial entry on his blog. In the blog, Zumbo condemned the use of AR and AK rifles to hunt prairie dogs, calling them assault weapons and terrorist rifles. He wrote, "Sorry folks, in my humble opinion, these things have no place in hunting. We don't need to be lumped into the group of people who terrorize the world with them." He added that game departments should ban assault rifles.

The outcry was swift. The use of the term "ban" is like a red flag in front of a bull to gun enthusiasts and members of the National Rifle Association (NRA). Zumbo was accused of calling anyone who owns or uses an assault weapon a terrorist. E-mails and Internet postings condemned Zumbo.

Even though he took back his words and apologized, calling his words "ill-conceived," particularly his uses of "ban" and "terrorist," Zumbo was severely chastised by the NRA; he lost his sponsorship; he lost his blog; he lost his column in the magazine *Outdoor Life*; and he lost his program on the Outdoor Channel.

The Outdoor Channel took down Zumbo billboards and canceled his show as sponsors pulled out. After the fracas, the Outdoor Channel website simply said, "This program is not airing on the Outdoor Channel at this time." Subsequent visits to the Outdoor Channel website revealed that Jim Zumbo's show was not included in the program listings. The Outdoor Channel's response is a clear indication of the fragile relationship that exists between programming decisions and public opinion as expressed on the Internet as well as the relationship between programming and advertisers.

113

REALITY AND ETHICS

Programmers who want success (and what television programmer doesn't want
to pick the next *Joe Millionaire* or *American Idol*?) have to pay close attention to
reality programming. Perhaps engaging in wishful thinking, people have been
predicting the demise of reality programming for years, but reality doesn't seem
to be going away. In fact, reality shows seem to be on a steady ascent, morphing
when needed to catch a trend or otherwise capture audience interest. Reality
shows such as *The Osbournes* about Ozzy Osbourne, the former rock star, and
his family (2002–2005) or Anna Nicole Smith's *The Anna Nicole Show* (2002–
2003) may be train wrecks, but they're wrecks the audience wants to witness.

114

Reality is cheap to produce, and the coveted younger demographic tunes in.
Any programmer who doesn't take reality seriously risks losing a paycheck,
much in the way that NBC risked losing viewers and advertisers when it moved
too slowly and developed too little reality programming. This is a situation that
NBC has since rectified; the network announced that NBC would regularly
program reality in the 8 p.m. time period as part of its so-called 2.0 strategy to
save money and to improve ratings.

Besides finding reality programs that will connect with audiences—say a *Dancing
With the Stars*, which has lasted six seasons as opposed to *Are You Hot?*, which
barely made it though five episodes in 2003—programmers face a number of
ethical issues when they seek to ride the reality gravy train. Consider these
examples:

- Is there any rationale for reality programming besides its cost effectiveness
  and its appeal to the younger demographic?
- In green-lighting reality programming, are programmers appealing to the
  lowest possible denominator, to use the phrase coined by NBC programming executive Paul Klein?

- Are unsophisticated contestants being exploited by the reality shows they hope will give them a shot at 15 minutes of fame?
- Are the 20+ page contracts many reality contestants are asked to sign (i.e., forced to sign if they want to participate) unfair and a violation of the rights of the candidates?
- In a quest for ratings, does it become increasingly tempting for a programmer to encourage the making fun of contestants, as judge Simon Cowell did on *American Idol*, season 6, when he called a contestant a "bush baby" because of his large eyes, which Cowell said made him look like a creature who lived in the jungle (at press time the incident was available on YouTube as "American Idol/Bush Baby Remix"). Audiences seem to like having some contestants ridiculed and insulted, as the strong ratings for *American Idol*, season 6, revealed. An ambitious programmer might request that more and more insults be levied at ever-eager contestants, despite any ethical considerations.
- Does a programmer intentionally mislead viewers by controlling what happens (or is seen on air) in a reality program?
- How far does a programmer go to achieve ratings? For example, would scheduling a kind of most dangerous game, where losing costs a contestant his life, be going too far?
- Does a programmer cancel a reality show because of pressure or protests from advertisers or advocacy groups, as may have been the case in early 2006 when ABC canceled prior to air the reality show *Welcome to the Neighborhood*, where contestants competed to win a house and the contest was won by a gay couple?
- If one of the reality shows a programmer has developed turns out to be a hit, should the programmer find ways to stretch the contest to make the show last longer, for example, by starting the competition earlier and taking detours such as going behind the competitions themselves to get close and personal with key contestants, as *American Idol* seems to have done? Interestingly enough, China's State Administration of Radio, Film and Television limited the duration of extended reality competitions along the lines of *American Idol* because it felt that the competitions were taking too long so that the stations could capitalize on strong ratings. The Chinese authorities were also concerned about Western influence on Chinese culture.[11]

---

[11]"China Limits 'Idol' Worship," in "Arts, Briefly," complied by Lawrence Van Gelder, *The New York Times*, March 5, 2007, B-2.

And then there are questions about the editing that takes place in reality shows. It should come as no surprise to anyone that reality shows are heavily edited, causing some to question how much reality actually exists in reality shows. That old reality stand-by and innovator, *The Real World*, for example, shoots on a ratio of 300 to 1 (i.e., five hours of tape for every one minute on screen).

The editing process can manipulate what viewers see. Anyone who has done some editing knows that an editor can do almost anything, much like a magician who can make things appear and disappear. In fact, reality story arcs are most often determined after the existing footage has been viewed. The stories are thus shaped by the editing, most often with the tacit approval of programming executives. Sometimes this approval isn't so tacit; in fact, programmers often encourage the manipulation of reality through editing to "juice it up," referring back to the term that producer Ken Kaufman used in Chapter 3.

Reality editing raises all sorts of ethical questions about what's real and what isn't, what contestants are favored and which ones are not, and what outcomes are fixed and which ones are not. Some people believe that television programming is cyclical, that it repeats itself; what was popular a few years back will be popular again. The similarities between the quiz show scandals of the 1950s and current reality shows support this contention. Just as it was hard to tell what was fixed in the quiz shows of the past, it's just as hard to know what's real in today's so-called reality programs. Letting viewers think they are determining with their votes the outcome of a reality contest when decisions are actually made in editing bays or in programming suites similarly muddies the reality landscape.

You Decide

- What do you think are the ethical responsibilities of programmers in charge of reality?
- What kinds of reality programs do you feel cross ethical boundaries?
- If you do, how do you distinguish between a responsible reality show and an irresponsible one?
- Why do you think viewers enjoy train wreck reality shows?
- Why do you think viewers like contestants on reality shows to be insulted or mistreated?
- Do you think that if a programmer directs the creative team on a reality show to make sure that the editing process delivers something sexy or controversial to connect with viewers, and if the programmer goes on to say that a larger shooting ratio is needed, is that programmer manipulating reality to such an extreme that no reality remains?
- Or does everyone assume or know that reality shows are already heavily edited? If that is the case, is the programmer who asks that more and more editing be done in no risk of crossing ethical lines or violating our E*T*H*I*C*S rubric?

SHORT TAKES

Animal Ethics

Creative executives do not want to be involved in projects where animals are mistreated. The American Humane Society's Film and Television Unit closely monitors the treatment of animals on sets, including the humane treatment of cockroaches, as Susan Orlean wrote in *The New Yorker*.[12] Protecting cockroaches may seem a bit extreme to some, but programmers simply do not want to risk not getting a seal of approval from the American Humane Society. No one, after all, wants to be accused of allowing animals to be unethically treated.

If a theatrical film being submitted for airing on television raises Humane Society concerns, troubles ensue, as was the case years ago when ABC decided to air the Academy Award–winning film *Patton* (1970) and it was discovered that wires had been used to trip horses during filming.

When Current Events Impact Programming Decisions

When actual events hit too close to home, programmers and news directors alike have to make quick decisions about what is and what is not appropriate for dissemination. When a current event looms, as Greg Braxton wrote in *The Los Angeles Times*, entertainment executives "scramble to scrutinize their prime-time schedules to ensure that scheduled movies, comedies and dramas are appropriate in tone."[13]

Following 9/11, numerous programming changes were made to avoid insensitive portrayals on television, a topic we will discuss in another context in Chapter 10. No jokes about long lines at airport checkpoints were allowed after 9/11, for example. During sweeps programming, the four times during the year when ratings are used to determine advertising rates, however, the pressure to get ratings or make noise can cause ethical lines to be crossed, even when dealing with sensitive current events. This was the case in 2003 when *48 Hours* showed clips of videotapes that convicted rapist Andrew Lester made of his drugged victims, in the process adding fuel to the debate about ethics and increasingly coarse prime-time TV programming.[14]

[12]Susan Orlean, "Animal Action," *The New Yorker*, November 17, 2003, p. 92.
[13]Greg Braxton, "When Crises Make TV All Too Real," *The Los Angeles Times*, February 10, 2003, E-1, 16.
[14]Tracy Wilson, Brian Lowry, and Elizabeth Jensen, "CBS Draws Fire for Airing Clips of Rapist's Videos," *The Los Angeles Times*, February 20, 2003, A-1, 19.

Host Actions

Sometimes the public actions as well as the private actions of entertainers lead to programming changes. For example, when Paul Reubens, aka Pee-Wee Herman, was arrested at an X-rated theater for alleged indecent behavior, his show *Pee-Wee's Playhouse* was canceled by CBS in 1991. Reubens was not doing his show at the time of the arrest, but CBS determined that his off-camera activities warranted the cancellation of his program.

Michael Savage's show on MSNBC, *Savage Nation*, was canceled in 2003 after Savage, while on air, told a caller to "get AIDS and die."[15] And in 2006, Melanie Martinez, the host of the PBS Kids Sprout network, was fired after she revealed she had appeared in a video called *Technical Virgin*, a spoof about how women can keep their virginity.[16]

Borrowing, Copying, or Outright Stealing

In Chapter 3, we looked at getting started or acquiring material from the point of view of the creative team, specifically producers, writers, actors, and directors. In this chapter, let's discuss how programmers decide to embrace a particular concept and to nurture it to production, focusing on borrowing, copying, ripping-off, or outright stealing.

If one accepts that imitation is the way 90% of movies and television shows are developed, it then becomes difficult to say with any certainty that a particular project was a true original. For example, if a western succeeds one television season and there are westerns galore in the ensuing seasons, as happened after the success of *Gunsmoke* in 1955, did those subsequent westerns borrow, copy, or steal from that groundbreaking show?

In movies, where there are sequels of successful films leading to series such as *The Matrix* trilogy, *The Pirates of the Caribbean* trilogy, or the *Mission Impossible* series, it's possibly even more difficult to tell if one film is a rip-off of another or if the cultural climate is such that a number of like-themed films are coming out at one time. This was the case when a number of films dealing with adults becoming kids and kids becoming adults came out at approximately the same time. Was *Big* (1988), a major success starring Tom Hanks, a rip-off of Kirk Cameron's *Like Father, Like Son* (1987), a forgotten failure on the same theme? Was another little-known film with the same setup, *14 Going on 30* (1988), the

[15]Brian Lowry, "Savage Gets the Boot after On-Air Anti-Gay Outburst," *The Los Angeles Times*, July 8, 2003, E-1, 12.
[16]"PBS Removes Preschool Show Host over Video," *The Los Angeles Times*, July 25, 2006 E-10.

inspiration for the 2004 film with Jennifer Garner, *13 Going on 30*? Or is the age-switch story simply an established storytelling convention that can be executed in a number of ways?

Then also ask yourself if the big theatrical films made from successful television shows such as *The Dukes of Hazard* (2005) or *Miami Vice* (2006) are rip-offs of classic television shows that reveal the limited imagination of studio heads or if they are homages or reinterpretations of the classic programs that defined our culture at particular points in our history.

Many American films, as well as many successful American television programs, have their origins in different parts of the world. Entrepreneurial producer Roy Lee has tapped into the Asian market to strike gold in America with such films as *The Ring* (2002), *The Grudge* (2004), and *The Departed* (2006), among others, and television producer and now NBC programming head Ben Silverman, for one, has succeeded in adapting programs from abroad, such as *Coupling* (2003), *The Office* (2006), and *Ugly Betty* (2006). But what about all the other imitations from abroad that aren't legitimately optioned? Are they simply borrowed, copied, or stolen?

And what about the television shows made from successful movies? Are they rip-offs of originals? Most fail (e.g., *Dirty Dancing*, 1988), but, a few, like *M*A*S*H* (1972) or *Buffy, the Vampire Slayer* (1997), succeed in their own right. And what about the countless "behind the scenes" television movies about classic television shows, like *Behind the Camera: The Unauthorized Story of "Charlie's Angels"* (2004) or *Behind the Camera: The Unauthorized Story of "Three's Company"* (2003)? Are these rip-offs?

As noted in Chapter 3, the execution of an idea is what makes the difference. But when it comes to reality television, the borrowing, copying, or stealing of ideas becomes increasingly intense. Part of the problem is that if one reality show succeeds, it's possible to get a near duplication on the air quickly and relatively cheaply.

Mike Darnell at Fox has become the poster boy for taking concepts that have worked on other networks and transforming them into similar shows on Fox. As Bill Carter observed in *Desperate Networks*, "Darnell learned quickly a lesson he would apply again and again: Ideas in reality television were almost completely uncopyrightable. A little twist on the notion, and, presto, you have a new reality. Such tweakings became a Darnell specialty."[17]

---

[17]Bill Carter, *Desperate Networks* (New York: Doubleday, 2006), p. 107.

Can the twist or the tweak cross ethical lines? As noted in Chapter 1, Steve McPherson at ABC clearly thinks so, particularly since Fox's *Trading Spouses*, the show McPherson labeled as a rip-off, beat ABC's *Wife Swap* to air. *Trading Spouses* premiered July 27, 2004; *Wife Swap* had to wait until September 29, 2004, for its debut.

Similarly, is Fox's *So You Think You Can Dance* (2005) stolen from ABC's surprise hit *Dancing with the Stars* (2004), or was the time simply right for reality television shows about dancing? Was Darnell simply observing a trend or was he crossing ethical lines without having to worry about any copyright or legal ramifications?

You Decide

Watch DVDs of the shows discussed using our E*T*H*I*C*S rubric, and make your own evaluations about what's original and what's not, what is ethical and what is not. Again, be prepared to back up your observations.

MTV AND THE PROGRAMMING OF SEX

Having premiered in 1992, MTV's *The Real World* has succeeded in remaining popular with its target audience. To maintain its hold on viewers, some people wonder if the show has crossed ethical guidelines by focusing too much on sex and controversy.

In an article titled "Sex with Acquaintances Is MTV Focus," Renee Graham focused on season 15 of *The Real World*, set in Philadelphia. Graham feels that since the 12th season, set in Las Vegas, the show's emphasis has consistently been on sex. Graham wondered if the show should be retitled *Real Sex*.[18] Kate Aurthur wrote in *The New York Times* that the casting of a bulimic who shocked her housemates by her anorexic appearance in the 17th season, set in Key West, caused the show and MTV to enter "murky ethical waters."[19] Paula Meronek,

[18]Renee Graham, "Sex with Acquaintances Is MTV Focus," *The Ann Arbor News*, September 26, 2004, C-8.

[19]Kate Aurthur, "On MTV 'Real' Star's Grim Reality," *The New York Times*, May 2, 2006, B-1, 8.

the bulimic in question, may have been self-aware,[20] which was the justification provided for her inclusion in the show by Jonathan Murray who created the show with his deceased partner, Mary-Ellis Bunin, but was Meronek's inclusion an exploitation of her condition for the benefit of the show?

Programmers need to make adjustments to keep existing shows fresh and appealing to an audience that has greater and greater entertainment options, but if the way to keep a show alive is to emphasize sex or to shock audiences with unsavory details, some media observers contend that ethical lines have been crossed.

In the next chapter, let's take a look at fact-based projects.

[20]Patrick Goldstein, "Perfect Teammates: Bonds, Reality TV," *The Los Angeles Times,* May 9, 2006, B-6.

CHAPTER 6
Ethics and Fact-Based Stories

A number of ethical issues arise in connection with works based on fact. In this chapter, we are going to look at some hot-button areas associated with factual works and the ethical quandaries that result. As participants noted at the 1979 landmark docudrama symposium held in Ojai, California, fact-based programs have to be responsibly handled and they need to be fair.[1] If this is not the case, problems arise. But determining what constitutes responsible handling and what's fair is not always easy.

Works that are touted as based on fact, or inspired by actual events, or based on a true story should, in fact, have a sound factual basis, should they not? As Mike Piller, then CBS director of dramas based on fact, noted at the docudrama symposium, "when you use a disclaimer—whether you want to call it 'based on truth,' 'inspired by truth,' 'historical drama'—you are still giving the viewer the impression that it is true."[2] This "impression" can at times be intentionally misleading.

WHAT'S REAL AND WHAT ISN'T

In truth, the based-on-fact label is often meaningless, reduced to what legal departments consider acceptable risks, regardless of the factual basis. The reasoning goes something like this: If it's not a legal problem, then it's not a

---

[1] Lee Margulies, editor, "Academy of Television Arts & Sciences Docu-drama Symposium 1979," *Emmy Magazine*, Summer 1979, D-15, 16.

[2] Ibid., D-25.

problem. Often, facts are abandoned in favor of what somebody considers a good story, as director Barry Levinson said when asked about the factual basis of the 1996 film *Sleepers*, based on the book by Lorenzo Carcaterra. Though the film carried a number of disclaimers, Carcaterra maintained that the story is true. He changed some names, making finding court records impossible, but Carcaterra has insisted that the story—about four boys who were abused at a home for boys and how they got revenge—is true. For Levinson, whether or not the events actually occurred is "irrelevant."[3] What matters is that the story, which concludes with a priest perjuring himself to save the lives of two of the boys, is a good story. As the saying goes, truth may be stranger than fiction, but fiction often wins out over truth.

But some works contain more fiction than others, even in projects that tout a factual pedigree. For example, many feel that theatrical films claiming to be based on fact are much freer with the *T*ruth than fact-based television projects. Ilene Amy Berg, who produced the fact-based television movie *Baby M* (1988), about a fierce custody battle between a surrogate mother and the couple who engaged her services, feels it's ethically wrong to hold fact-based projects on television to a higher standard of truth than theatrical true stories, which often play fast and loose with the truth. Berg feels that if the same standard were applied, more films than *The Hurricane* (2000) or *Munich* (2005), discussed later in this chapter, would be victims of a vigilant fact police.

A 2006 film directed by the legendary Sidney Lumet, *Find Me Guilty*, tells the story of mobster "Jackie Dee" who chose to defend himself when he was tried under the Rico Act, which was designed to go after organized crime. Possibly as a result of Jackie Dee's defending himself, the trial became the longest mob trial in the United States. The film carried a disclaimer saying that "most" of the exchanges in the courtroom were based on court testimony. There is no way for the viewer to tell which parts are from the trial transcript and which parts aren't. This kind of loose language is what causes media observers, like Berg, to question the fact-based claims of theatrical films.

Interestingly enough, the Internet Movie Data Base (www.imdb.com) said in its description of the Robert De Niro directed and Eric Roth scripted 2006 film *The Good Shepherd* that the film was "the true story of the birth of the CIA through the eyes of a man who never existed."[4] Whoa. The true story told from

---

[3]Ann Oldenburg and Elizabeth Snead, "Unrest over *Sleepers*," *USA Today*, hellskitchen.net/issues/sleepers/lef428.html, accessed January 8, 2007.

[4]www.imdb.com, accessed December 27, 2006.

the point of view of a man who never existed! Let me read that again. Is this a joke? Probably not, just a further example of how difficult it is to tell what's fact and what's fiction.

Daily Variety, in a 2006 VPlus supplement, addressed the issue of factual accuracy in theatrical films in a section titled "Just the Facts." The subheading read, "*Daily Variety* explores how the truth behind this year's crop of pics gets massaged into Hollywood's own brand of cinematic veracity."[5] The article then looked at 10 films, including *The Queen*, the Helen Mirren vehicle about how Queen Elizabeth of England handled the death of Princess Diana with an assist from Prime Minister Tony Blair. The article then broke down the films into three sections, the genesis, the liberties taken, and the spin. The spin served as a justification for the films' factual errors. Though the liberties taken (i.e., the factual inaccuracies noted) were not substantial ones, it is nevertheless noteworthy that an entertainment trade industry publication focused on factual errors in theatrical films, proving that more attention is being given to factual errors.

If one wanted to disagree with Berg, in a sense accepting the seeming double standard that it's in a way more acceptable to distort the truth in theatrical films than it is in television works, the justification would be that because broadcast television uses the public airwaves, there is a greater need for responsibility (i.e., fact-checking) in programming for television.

If you want to accept the seeming double standard, people choose to pay to go to a movie theater to see a film, whereas broadcast television viewers simply turn on the set, often stumbling upon a fact-based project. People have made a decision to accept the version the theatrical film portrays, which is not the case with broadcast television. These arguments may not convince Berg or others who object to the restrictions placed on broadcast fact-based projects, but they do explain why the differences exist.

In the 1950s, the quiz show scandals exploded after it was discovered that, contrary to all claims of secrecy and the use of isolation booths, favored contestants like Charles Van Doren on *21*, for example, were given answers. Some justified this practice by claiming that the quiz shows were simply entertainment and that everyone knew that fakery was involved. Similarly, previously setup sequences in today's reality shows are tailored for maximum hype, distorting the very reality the shows are ostensibly promoting. It's thus increasingly difficult to know what's real or false, what's fact or fiction.

---

[5]"Just the Facts," compiled by Peter Debruge, Steven Gaydos, and Carole Horst, *VPlus*, *Daily Variety*, December 21, 2006, B-2.

The question becomes how ethical, responsible, or fair is it to emphasize the legend or the shortened, easy-to-digest version instead of the facts in order to make a statement, ignoring some facts while reinforcing a legend (a legend here defined as the popular or accepted version of events, the fantasy, or the easy-to-digest version). Is a Department of Factual Verification in order, in keeping with the position held by the protagonist at a magazine much like *The New Yorker* in Jay McInerney's landmark book, *Bright Lights, Big City* (1984)?

How ethical, responsible, or fair is it to pass off fiction as truth in *any* project? For example, reality television operates on the basis that reality dictates what happens on reality shows, as discussed in Chapter 5. Reality programs are presumably executed without scripts, with the camera simply recording what happens. Never mind that writers and editors can create any story that the producers or networks desire, creating a false reality designed to trick a gullible public.

Let's examine some specific issues that arise in connection with fact-based works.

DOCUMENTARIES AND ETHICS

Documentaries are factual, right? Not so fast. Let's pause for a moment. Maybe they aren't.

As California State University Fullerton Professor Larry Ward notes at the start of his documentary class, the term "documentary" itself is misunderstood and abused, applied to everything from newsreels to instructional films to travelogues and television specials. Indeed, different definitions of the terms abound. Dictionary definitions don't offer much clarification—for example, defining documentaries as "consisting of, concerning or based on documents" or "presenting facts objectively without editorializing or inserting fictional matter, as in a book, newspaper account, or film."[6]

Though many do see documentaries as objective, in truth they aren't. Most documentaries have a distinct point of view and possibly more of an agenda than the more maligned docudramas, works that mix fact with dramatic license while using actors. In his seminal book on documentaries, Erik Barnouw noted that from early times, "documentary film was infected with increasing fakery."[7]

---

[6]William Morris, editor, *The American Heritage Dictionary of the English Language* (Boston: Houghton Mifflin, 1976) pp. 387.

[7]Erik Barnouw, *Documentary* (New York: Oxford University Press, 1993), p. 24.

Nevertheless, many continue to define documentaries as truer than other works that claim a factual pedigree. If that is indeed the case, what ethical responsibilities does a documentarian face?

For John Fox, an Emmy Award–winning series producer of *Heritage: Civilization and the Jews* (1984), documentary filmmakers have to find the truth that they want to tell; for Fox, this is a truth that benefits the public. According to Fox, every choice the filmmaker makes involves a moral judgment, including where to place the camera, and he feels strongly that a documentary should engage an audience's moral compass.

To accomplish this, he believes the following:

- That words cannot be taken out of context
- That visual editing tricks should not be used
- That events should not be presented out of sequence
- That any reenactments should be carefully researched and labeled, as he questions if completely accurate reenactments are even possible

Fox adds that opposing points of view should be included in documentaries, even if the documentarians have decided what truth they want to tell, because ignoring the opposition makes for a failed documentary, one that does not benefit the public because the public has not been given enough information to make a sound *E*valuation.

You Decide

Can a reenactment, even one that is clearly labeled, be *T*ruthful? Do you think that labeled or unlabeled reenactments are potentially confusing? When it comes to reenactments, what do you think is responsible? What do you think is fair? What do you think is ethical?

OLIVER STONE

Several works have suffered significantly as a result of perceived factual inaccuracies, inaccuracies that are increasingly disseminated by blogs and websites dedicated to uncovering untruths. Though Oliver Stone's 2006 film about 9/11, *World Trade Center*, generally escaped the fact-checking police, Stone previously did not get away unscathed. In fact, Stone's *JFK* (1991) is seen as the poster child of irresponsible filmmaking (i.e., a work that mixes fact and fiction in an attempt to validate a conspiracy theory). Hotly debated, the film does have some defenders as well as numerous detractors.

In a controversial 1992 essay, "Footfalls in the Crypt," Norman Mailer strongly defended the film, for example, saying, "Even when one knows the history of the Garrison investigation and the considerable liberties that Stone has taken with the material, it truly does not matter, one soon decides, for no film could ever be made of the Kennedy assassination that would be accurate."[8] Mailer added that if the film were successful and widely seen, it would be criticized as a "monstrous act" because it would then "be accepted as fact by a new genera-tion of moviegoers. One can only shrug. Several generations have already grown up with the mind-stultifying myth of the lone assassin. Let cinematic hyperbole war then with the Establishment's skewed reality. At times, bullshit can only be countered with superior bullshit. Stone's version has, at least, the virtue of its thoroughgoing metaphor."[9]

FIGURE 6-1
The fact-based police are not your ordinary police; the fact-based police do not go after criminals; they go after real or per-ceived factual errors. (iStockphoto.com #2709890, Frances Twitty.)

Many, however, find the presentation of conspiracy theories unethical because of the potential for uncertainty and confusion. One can argue that everyone is entitled to a particular point of view, but if a conspiracy theory is given credence, if it is believably and powerfully portrayed, it then becomes *the* accepted version, in a sense "the only book on the shelf," a term that fact-checkers use to explain their vigilance. Not everyone experiencing a conspiracy will know the other side or the complete picture, creating concern that the conspiracy theory will become the embraced version of events.

THE FACT POLICE ON THE ATTACK

Sometimes critics and pundits find it easier to cite factual errors than to cite more fundamental objections about a given work. Saying a work is "filled with errors" is a lot easier than systemati-cally describing and analyzing factual errors. To do thorough fact-checking requires a great deal of work, but the fact-based police (Figure 6-1)

[8]Norman Mailer, "Footfall in the Crypt," in *JFK: The Book of the Film: The Documented Screenplay* (New York: Applause Books, 1992), p. 446.
[9]Mailer, "Footfall in the Crypt," p. 447.

are nevertheless at the ready to insist that errors in a film or television program abound. Sometimes the fact police attack the accuracy of work that hasn't been seen. This tactic often achieves quick results and garners immediate attention. Often the public will more readily accept that a work is "filled with lies" than it will accept objections that appear *too* detailed or pedantic. It is easier for people to grasp the statement that something is "full of distortions and lies" than it is to examine itemized objections about the theory or philosophical premise behind a work. If a critic does not like what a work is attempting to do, the easiest response is to attack its factual accuracy. (See the accompanying box about how the fact-based police often attack early, even before a work has been seen.)

THE FACT-BASED POLICE ATTACK EARLY

The fact-based police don't have to wait to actually see a movie or a television program to mount an attack. In fact, it often seems as if proponents of factual accuracy feel they can present a stronger case precisely because they haven't seen a given work. Timing is also everything. It is better to identify errors and to skewer quickly because outrage after the fact dissipates very quickly. Some of the strongest, earliest attacks over errors and misinterpretations in *The Reagans* (2003), *The Passion of the Christ* (2004), or Robert Greenwald's documentary *Uncovered: The Whole Truth about the Iraq War* (2003), among others, were launched by people who admitted they had not personally seen the works in question. As *The New York Times* critic Alessandra Stanley wrote in connection with *The Passion of the Christ*, "sometimes you don't have to see a film to know you aren't going to like it."[10] Similarly, sometimes you don't have to see a film to know it's inaccurate.

People who pounce on factual inaccuracies before actually seeing a work might be taking their lead from former *The Los Angeles Times* television critic Howard Rosenberg, who never missed an opportunity to attack the mixing of fact and fiction in fact-based programming, ever fearful that a public he underestimated would be irrevocably confused and tormented by such a mix. (See, for example, Rosenberg's commentary in a "You Decide" box presented in Chapter 3.) For Rosenberg, dramatizing a factual story meant that the work by necessity had to be inaccurate. In one of his final columns in 2003, he predicted the factual inaccuracies that were bound to take place in the future.[11]

[10]Alessandra Stanley, "The TV Watch: Hollywood Stumbles at Doorstep of Politics," *The New York Times*, November 6, 2003, B-5.
[11]Howard Rosenberg, "History Rewritten to Make Us Feel Good," *The Los Angeles Times*, June 6, 2003, E-1, 14.

Critics of former President Jimmy Carter's 2006 book about the situation in the Middle East, *Palestine: Peace Not Apartheid*, initially attacked the book over its factual inaccuracies and uncredited sources,[12] though Carter himself claimed he sought to describe the situation between Israel and Palestine "accurately."[13] Rather than attacking the book for its premise that Israel may be responsible for mistreating Palestinians, critics primarily focused on the errors in the book. Regardless of how one feels about the volatile situation in the Middle East, wouldn't it be fairer, wouldn't it be more ethical, to say upfront that one objects to the thesis of a work instead of framing one's objections behind a ready list of factual distortions or inaccuracies? But facts are easy to attack, and a ready audience exists to embrace the charges of factual inaccuracy that members of the fact police happily provide.

If the listing of real or perceived factual errors takes center stage, trouble ensues, and when millions of dollars and reputations are at stake, the troubles escalate at an alarming pace. In 2000, a high-profile film with Denzel Washington, *The Hurricane*, about boxer Rubin "Hurricane" Carter, lost prestige and chances at Academy Award consideration because of factual inaccuracies about Carter's

FIGURE 6-2
Boxers like the one depicted here have many things to think about in the ring, but reported factual inaccuracies in the 2000 film *The Hurricane* about boxer Rubin "Hurricane" Carter hurt the film's performance as well as limiting the film's chances for award recognition. (iStockphoto.com #3444137, Somin23.)

130

legal battles as well as his matches (Figure 6-2) that were published on the Internet and in the press. Simply put, the emphasis on the inaccuracies significantly hurt the film. The studio's legal department might have cleared the film, but, as discussed previously, what's legal is not necessarily what's true.

Sometimes, publicized factual inaccuracies do not hurt a film if, and this is a big if, the studio responds quickly and convincingly to the charges. In contrast to the slow way it handled *The Hurricane*, Universal responded quickly when questions started to be raised about factual errors or liberties in the film *A Beautiful Mind* (2001). Errors about the film's handling of the life of uberscientist John Nash were posted on the Web and written up in the press. Charges that the film omitted Nash's alleged homosexual interludes and incorrectly portrayed his relationship with his wife quickly disappeared because Universal promptly dismissed the

[12]Josh Getlin, "Maps in Carter's Book Are Questioned," *The Los Angeles Times*, December 8, 2006, A-44.

[13]Jimmy Carter, "How I See Palestine," editorial, *The Los Angeles Times*, December 8, 2006, A-43.

charges as insignificant to the emotional and powerful human story of the film.[14] The film went on to win an Academy Award as Best Picture, as opposed to the slighting *The Hurricane* received.

Steven Spielberg got some unexpected flak from Jewish groups that complained about factual errors in *Munich* (2005), his film about Israel's retaliation for the killing of Israeli athletes at the 1972 Olympics. Generally unspecified errors were cited, though the vitriolic attacks on the film's accuracy may have more to do with the film's approach, which included humanizing Arabs.

Spielberg may have hired top spin handlers, including the person who steered *A Beautiful Mind* away from charges of factual inaccuracies,[15] but he was not able to overcome the bad press against the film. *Munich* did not break any box office records, certainly not in light of some of Spielberg's megasuccesses such as *E.T.: The Extra-Terrestrial* (1982), *Jurassic Park* (1993), or *War of the Worlds* (2005), nor did it win significant critical praise. In a very real sense, *Munich* simply disappeared, having alienated its target audience. *Munich* suffered, much in the way that Spielberg's 1997 film *Amistad* did against allegations of plagiarism.

THE PATH TO 9/11

In 2006, to coincide with the fifth anniversary of 9/11, ABC aired a docudrama miniseries called *The Path to 9/11* on September 10 and 11. Touted by ABC as a public service, it aired without commercial interruptions. The film carried a lengthy disclaimer/advisory, which was repeated a number of times during the broadcast. It said, "Due to the subject matter, viewer discretion is advised. The following movie is a dramatization drawn from a variety of sources, including the *9/11 Commission Report* and other published materials, and from personal interviews. The movie is not a documentary. For dramatic and narrative purposes, the movie contains fictionalized scenes, composite and representative characters, and dialogue, as well as time compression."

Despite ABC's insistence that the film was a docudrama and not a documentary, the film was heavily criticized as being inaccurate. A DVD of the film had been announced, but at press time no DVD is available, causing some to speculate that the controversies associated with the film halted DVD distribution. Criticisms included the following:

---

[14]Patrick Goldstein, "The Big Picture: Playing 'Mind' Games," *The Los Angeles Times*, January 22, 2002, F-1–10.
[15]Rachel Abrahamowitz, "Munich?" *The Los Angeles Times*, January 23, 2006, E-4.

- The film was charged with presenting a confusing juxtaposition of news footage and dramatized scenes, blurring the lines between news and entertainment. The complaint that docudramas blur fact and fiction is not a new one. To cite one example among many, similar complaints were raised in articles and editorials about *The Atlanta Child Murders* in 1985. Commenting that *The Atlanta Child Murders* was a particularly bad example of the docudrama form, a *USA Today* editorial proclaimed that docudramas falsify history and mangle truth. The editorial said, "In 'docudrama,' TV moviemakers create scenes that never occurred. They invent statements that were never made. They shrink events that took months to evolve into scenes minutes long. Worst of all, they contrive sensational situations to grab an unsuspecting audience. So what is seen is not history. It often isn't much fact."[16] Vociferous criticism of fact/fiction blurring in docudramas is clearly not new, and the charges against *The Path to 9/11* vividly revitalized the debate.

- The film was accused of depicting President Bill Clinton as too preoccupied with the Monica Lewinsky scandal to pay attention to the threat posed by Bin Laden and Al-Qaeda, with Eric Alterman in *The Nation* saying that the entire film was based on lies and that Clinton's depiction as totally focused on Lewinsky was just one of the lies.[17]

- Critics claimed that the film had real people who were being portrayed by actors saying or doing things the real people say aren't true. Or as a *The New York Times* editorial about the film put it, "You do not show real people doing things they never did."[18] It is admittedly hard to agree about what is and what is not legitimate dramatic license when it comes to putting words in the mouths of characters who are portraying actual individuals, and this particular film added more fuel to this debate.

Moreover, an FBI consultant walked off the set during filming and quit because of the film's inaccuracies, saying that scenes were "misleading or just false."[19] Also, key scenes were omitted, such as President Bush's response to the attacks while in a Florida classroom.

Most of the attacks on inaccuracies in *The Path to 9/11* came from the left, from so-called Clintonistas, some of whom saw the film as a right-wing conspiracy.

[16]Editorial, *USA Today*, February 8, 1985, A-12.
[17]Eric Alterman, "Lying about 9/11? Easy as ABC," *The Nation*, October 2, 2006, p. 10.
[18]Editorial, *The New York Times*, September 12, 2006, A-24.
[19]Edward Wyatt, "More Questions of Accuracy Raised about ABC Mini-Series of 9/11 Prelude," *The New York Times*, September 12, 2006, B-1, 7.

Some wanted the miniseries canceled because of the inaccuracies. Some questioned if ABC's licenses should be revoked if ABC insisted on airing the miniseries.

A few years earlier, it was the right that objected to inaccuracies in a miniseries. The project under attack was *The Reagans* (2003). The right wing pressured CBS to cancel airing the series. This pressure was successful, unlike the call to cancel *The Path to 9/11*, and CBS funneled the miniseries to Showtime, its sister company.

Nevertheless, months after it aired, *The Path to 9/11* continued to make news based on its handling of the *T*ruth. The debate about what was true and what was fiction and why changes in the film were made at the last minute got another hearing.

On January 28, 2007, while appearing on *Hannity's America* on Fox News, the writer and producer of *The Path to 9/11*, Cyrus Nowrasteh, and former CIA terrorism expert and the person who created a unit to track Osama Bin Laden, Michael Scheuer, both proclaimed that the edited scenes in the film were based on fact. Nowrasteh maintained that what was in the script was true and that edits, made under pressure from Clinton supporters, were "an attempt to suppress his story." Scheuer said on the show that there had been many opportunities during Clinton's time to capture Bin Laden.

The scene that *Hannity's America* focused on was the one in which national security advisor Sandy Berger refuses to give the order to kill Bin Laden, thus, according to Scheuer, aborting one of the missions against Bin Laden. *Hannity's America* showed the scene before and after the edits were made, carefully using kyrons at the bottom of the screen to label the parts that were cut in the editing process. Hannity's point was that the pressure to make the edits prevented the public from seeing what he termed the real path to 9/11, specifically that the Clinton administration could have done more to capture Bin Laden and that the edited version distorted the truth. For him, the edited version watered down Nowrasteh's carefully researched truth under pressure from the left. Hannity did not lambaste docudramas for blending fact and fiction. Instead, he felt that the truth had suffered when edits were made in the film at the last minute.

Attacks on factual accuracy are often based on definitions of *T*ruth as determined by the politics of the right or the left. The *T*ruth is thus used as a pawn to push a particular political agenda. Inaccuracies can range from the trivial ("the dress she wore in real life was red; in the movie, it was green") to the significant (having the wrong person commit a crime, contradicting the official record), but if inaccuracies are used to bolster a partisan position, has an ethical line been crossed?

With the current emphasis on finding inaccuracies in all sorts of media outlets, it's important to question both the significance of the errors and whether or not there is a partisan or political agenda behind the charges. Often, it's not just about what is true and what isn't. Some people simply grandstand when they say such and such is "grossly inaccurate" or that people are going to be presented with totally false data when they watch a docudrama. Granted, it can be difficult to distinguish between a docudrama and a documentary, but are the inaccuracies in one or the other going to cause the sky to fall and licenses to be revoked?

Some feel the fact police are trying to curry favor, for example, by attempting to switch the focus from a real problem in society to an easy target, namely, entertainment programming that dares to mix fact and fiction. When this is the case, the charge that a piece is inaccurate lacks a solid ethical basis requires careful *I*nvestigating and *E*valuating. Uncovering the *T*ruth is never easy, particularly when so many documents are readily available to be used one way or the other.

134

Let's take a look now at what happened when a fact-based book turned out to be fiction and see what ethical issues arose.

You Decide

Determine how much factual information is needed for a work to be truthful. If you have six verifiable facts and four made-up incidents in a program, can you still claim that you have a truthful piece? Is it a question of 60% fact and 40% fiction? Does it depend on the importance of the sources or the topic, necessitating *S*ituational ethics? Unless something is done quickly to get beyond perceived errors, as was the case with *A Beautiful Mind*, will factual errors ignite fires, as occurred with *The Path to 9/11* and *The Reagans*? Here are other questions to consider:

■ Do you think it's up to spin specialists and media consultants to determine what is a significant error and what isn't?

■ What ethical issues might be involved in criticizing the factual basis of a work you haven't seen? Suppose you have not seen the work, but you've heard a lot about the errors, and the people who told you about the errors seem knowledgeable, even if they haven't seen it themselves. How would you be able to *E*valuate the situation to determine what's *T*rue and what isn't?

■ What in your opinion is more important in a factual work, emotional truth or factual truth? If a work touches you emotionally, is that more important than its adherence to the facts? Is a good story more important than a factual one?

The bottom line is, what is responsible? What is fair in dealing with fact-based projects?

A MILLION LITTLE PIECES BY JAMES FREY

The question that took center stage in early 2006 around Frey's book, *A Million Little Pieces*, published in 2003, involved responsibility. Specifically, if an author lies and fabricates the truth in a work of nonfiction, should book publishers and editors be held responsible?

James Frey's memoir *A Million Little Pieces* became a best-seller after Oprah Winfrey selected it to be one of her book club selections. Frey appeared on her program to discuss his descent into despair and his eventual recovery. In the book, Frey describes in great detail his run-ins with the law, the time he spent in jail (Figure 6-3), and the suicide of his girlfriend. Winfrey pronounced herself touched by his account, lavishing praise on Frey and thus catapulting the book to bestseller status.

Though questions existed about the book's authenticity and its negative depiction of a recovery center, widely assumed to be the Hazelden Rehabilitation Center in Center City, Minnesota, it was only after the Smoking Gun website, owned by Court TV, challenged Frey's factual accuracy on June 8, 2006, that the controversy exploded as a cause célèbre. Some insisted that a memoir has to be true to the facts, whereas others claimed that a memoir by its very nature is the writer's interpretation or vision, thus not subject to rigorous factual checking.

FIGURE 6-3

James Frey, author of *A Million Little Pieces*, exaggerated the time he spent in jail in his memoir, causing an outcry about the book's factual basis. (iStockphoto.com #2065110, Naphtalina.)

135

It should be noted here that the original publication of *A Million Little Pieces* did not include a disclaimer indicating that certain parts of the book had been fictionalized, though Frey at one point had considered labeling the book as fiction. A fictionalized account of one's rehabilitation would not have had the same cachet, which may be why Doubleday decided to publish the book as nonfiction.[20]

When the controversy first broke, Frey maintained that the book was essentially factual and that he had reams of collaborating documentation that he had provided to his publisher. He wrote on his website, "This is the latest investigation into my past and the latest attempt to dis-

---

[20]Edward Wyatt, "Best-Selling Memoir Draws Scrutiny," *The New York Times,* January 10, 2006, B-7.

credit me. . . . So let the haters hate, let the doubters doubt, I stand by my book, and my life, and I won't dignify this bullshit with any sort of further response."[21]

With his mother by his side, Frey went on *Larry King Live* to defend himself. During the show, Winfrey called in to voice her support of Frey, saying that the book's message of redemption resonated with her.

In spite of Frey's assertions and Winfrey's support, the debates about the book's factual basis continued, as more people questioned the book's fabrications. Meanwhile, Frey's publisher indicated that the factual accuracy of the book didn't really matter, issuing a statement that included "Recent accusations against him not withstanding, the power of the overall reading experience is such that the book remains a deeply inspiring and redemptive story for millions of readers."[22]

Key ethical issues involved in the Frey controversy include the following:

- How truthful does a writer have to be when writing a work of nonfiction, the *T* in our rubric?
- What is the responsibility of the editor and publisher to fact-check a work of nonfiction, the *E* in our rubric?
- What's the potential *H*arm resulting from a falsification of the facts, specifically the treatment Frey received in rehab, the *H* in our rubric? In the book, Frey describes being physically abused by residents, having a root canal without anesthesia because the facility didn't allow the use of Novocain, routinely vomiting blood, and receiving poor medical attention. Carol Collerman, who worked for many years at Hazelden said, "I have had young people say to me that if they had a child who was having problems, they would never send them to treatment after reading that book."[23] If Collerman's evaluation is correct, the falsification could potentially result in significant *H*arm.

The questions about *A Million Little Pieces* went directly against Winfrey's vision of the book as inspirational. Winfrey relied on the publisher to do the necessary fact-checking, but as the evidence of falsification mounted, she withdrew her

---

[21]Steven Zeitchik, "Standing by Her Man," *Daily Variety*, January 12, p. 47.
[22]Edward Wyatt, "When a Memoir and Facts Collide," *The New York Times*, January 11, 2006, B-1, 9.
[23]Edward Wyatt, "Treatment Description in Memoir Is Disputed" *The New York Times*, January 24, 2006, B-1, 8.

support and in what media observers described as "remarkable" television,[24] she did a live *Oprah Winfrey Show*. On the program, she told Frey she felt duped and that he had betrayed millions of readers.

Frey confessed that a tough guy image (Figure 6-4) of himself caused him to, in essence, lie.

Winfrey said she had made a mistake calling Larry King, saying, "I left the impression that the truth does not matter, and am deeply sorry about that, because that is not what I believe." She added, "To everyone who has challenged me on this issue of truth, you are absolutely right." As discussed previously, what's legal may not be ethical, as the lack of truth in Frey's book demonstrated, causing Winfrey and others to demand a new set of principles or guidelines for publishers of nonfiction books, the *C* in our rubric, requiring a great deal more investigation than previously undertaken, the *I* in our rubric.

FIGURE 6-4
James Frey, author of *A Million Little Pieces*, also sought to portray himself as much more of a tough guy than he actually was. (iStockphoto.com #3169860, Sean Locke.)

137

Also appearing on the *Oprah Winfrey Show* was Nan A. Talese under whose imprint the book was published. Talese said that the Doubleday lawyers reviewed the book for legal issues, not for factual accuracy, something Winfrey said would need to change. Eighteen months later, on July 28, 2007, at the widely covered Mayborn Literary Nonfiction Writers Conference of the Southwest in Grapevine, Texas, Talese went on the attack, an attack that aired on C-Span, accusing Oprah Winfrey of bad manners and of ambushing Frey.

Talese may not have justified or defended herself on the January 2006 *Oprah Winfrey Show*, but months later she supported Frey and her decision to publish his book. After a keynote address by prolific writer Joyce Carol Oates who spoke about the ethics of nonfiction writing and whether or not truth was the highest value in nonfiction writing, Talese said that Winfrey should be the one apologizing for her rude behavior, not Frey for his memoir.

A related question becomes: Should book reviewers be obligated to check the facts behind the books they are examining? In a compelling article in the now-defunct magazine *Brill's Content*, which examined the media, Steven Brill asserted

---

[24]Paul Brownfield, "Critic's Notebook: Humiliation—But on the Last Page Absolution," *The Los Angeles Times,* January 27, A-22; "On Oprah's Couch," editorial, *The New York Times,* January 27, 2006, A-22.

that reviewers should bear some responsibility for investigating the factual basis of works labeled as nonfiction.[25] Of course, *A Million Little Pieces* was not the first work to fudge the facts and fool the public. Brill referred to several nonfiction books that duped the public. He referenced Henry Abbott's *In the Belly of the Beast: Letters from Prison* (1981), Abbott's highly fictionalized account of his time in prison that fooled people such as literary giant Norman Mailer, who wrote the introduction to the book and believed Abbott's assertion that he was innocent of the charges that landed him in jail. Brill also referred to Joseph Jett's *Black and White on Wall Street: The Untold Story of the Man Wrongly Accused of Bringing Down Kidder Peabody* (1999), Jett's fictionalized account of the racism he experienced on Wall Street.[26]

In his article, Brill quoted Johanna Berkman, *The New York Times* reviewer of Jett's book. In a comment that supports the general lack of fact-checking that is done, Berkman said, "I typically expect that when a book is published that people don't lie."[27] Similarly, Charles McGrath, in 1999 the editor of *The New York Times Book Review*, is quoted by Brill as saying, "Publishers don't check at all. They just rely on the authors,"[28] which apparently was part of the problem with *A Million Little Pieces*.

Brill wonders if readers who purchased Jett's book should get a refund.[29] Interestingly, as discussions about *A Million Little Pieces* continued throughout 2006, plans were made to refund customers for the cost of Frey's book if they can claim that they would not have bought the book if they had known that facts had been fudged.[30]

FREELANCE BOOK EDITORS AND FACT-BASED PROJECTS

What about freelance editors who proofread and polish manuscripts before publication? Don't they fact-check?

[25]Steven Brill, "Reward: What Book Reviews Don't Review," *Brill's Content*, July/August 1999, pp. 35–36.
[26]Ibid., p. 36.
[27]Ibid.
[28]Ibid.
[29]Ibid.
[30]Motoko Rich, "Publisher and Author Settle Suit over Lies," *The New York Times*, September 7, 2006, B-1.

Before we explore the ethical issues faced by freelance editors, let's take a look at what these editors do. According to freelance editor John Morrone, a freelance editor edits punctuation and strives to make the manuscript clear and consistent. It's the editor's responsibility to ensure the integrity of a book and to ensure that it's consistently clear.

As noted by journalists Scott Collins and Matea Gold in connection with the controversy over Frey's *A Million Little Pieces*, "Veterans agree that few nonfiction books will ever be vigorously fact-checked, because publishers' profit margins are too meager to justify the cost."[31]

Similarly, Frey's Doubleday editor, Nan A. Talese, has said, "The trouble with book publishers is that they don't have the staff or they don't want to have the staff to ensure the veracity of a writer."[32] Freelancers like Morrone who are paid by the hour are thus often asked to do "light" review.

Sometimes, however, a freelancer is asked to "check everything." When this request is made, the freelancer's job is to query everything. This sometimes causes authors to feel threatened or insulted by having to "prove" the truth of what they have written. For example, Morrone recalled one author who got angry when a number of errors in the manuscript were found. This author wrote in the manuscript's margin, "Go write your own op-ed piece and go fuck yourself."

A freelancer thus has to ask himself or herself if the text should simply be accepted or if facts need to be verified, even if the publisher has not requested a thorough review. A freelancer has to question whether or not he or she can trust the narrator of a manuscript. If the narrator can be trusted, the editing process is a lot smoother, because the freelancer can focus on seeking clarity. If the narrator cannot be trusted for whatever reason (conflicting versions of events, secrecy, falsification), the freelance editor has to devote energy and time to create a consistent voice for the book.

According to Morrone, ethical questions that a freelance editor faces on a regular basis include the following:

- Accepting or declining an assignment if the subject matter does not fall into an area of interest or expertise.

[31]Scott Collins and Matea Gold, "Winfrey Throws Book at Frey," *The Los Angeles Times*, January 27, 2006, A-22.
[32]Edward Wyatt, "Writer Says He Made Up Some Details," *The New York Times*, January 12, 2006, A-19.

139

- Accepting or rejecting an assignment because the subject matter contradicts one's personal beliefs.
- Letting something go (i.e., "biting one's tongue") because the freelancer's function has been curtailed as a result of cost cutting or a directive not to investigate too deeply.
- Avoiding inserting one's own politics into a manuscript.
- Facing the temptation of turning a manuscript into the freelancer's vision and not the vision of the author. Some authors are very malleable, making the temptation that much greater.
- Considering showing off or grandstanding on trivial matters to establish one's superiority over the writer.
- Praising a manuscript when it contains gibberish in order to keep getting freelance assignments needed to pay the rent.
- Navigating a conflict between the book's author and the book's editor.
- Claiming a manuscript has been fully vetted in a responsible and fair manner when it hasn't.

The issues that freelance editors face figure prominently in any discussion about the role of factual accuracy, in terms of James Frey's *A Million Little Pieces* as well as all works based on factual accounts.

RIGHTS AND ETHICS

Beginning filmmakers are often stumped when deciding what rights are needed when they are developing a fact-based story. Securing the rights of key individuals involved in the story becomes a primary concern. It's not an easy process. Here are some of the issues filmmakers need to consider:

- Are rights indeed needed?
- Is the public record adequate so that rights are not needed?
- Are necessary rights available?
- If more that one set of rights is available, how many should the filmmaker go after?
- How should the rights holder be approached? By whom? When?
- What promises or guarantees should be made to the rights holder?
- If a lawyer controls the rights, how does this impact on the nature of the negotiation?
- What should be included in a contract with the rights holder?
- How long should the rights option last?
- What is a fair amount to pay for the rights?

You Decide

Clearly, many of the questions about rights and ethics presented in this chapter raise a number of ethical considerations. For example, is it ethical or unethical to interview a participant in a true story while doing research and then not secure that person's rights because you or your legal team have determined that the public record is adequate and that no rights are needed?

Or if you know the rights are available, is it ethical or unethical to claim you have optioned the rights as you try to set up the project, working on the assumption that if a buyer bites, you will be able to get the rights? This way, if there is not a sale, you haven't had to put up any money for an option. Doing this has caused many a producer to engage in a frantic quest after being given the go-ahead, only to find that the rights are no longer available or that the option price has gone way up.

What if you suspect or know that the option dollars you are providing are going to be used illegally? Many of the popular true crime stories involve some unsavory characters whose lives, though fodder for good drama, are not squeaky clean. The Son of Sam law was established so that criminals could not profit from their crimes. Thus, a criminal whose story is being told ostensibly cannot sell his or her rights for profit. One way around this, however, is to give the money to a surrogate, a middle person, who keeps a writer/producer "clean" while nevertheless having key access to the person whose story is being told. Ethical? Unethical? Reasonable? Fair?

Another rights situation arises when a decision has been made not to secure rights. A decision is made to proceed because the public record is strong. Court transcripts exist, the story has been widely covered, and so on. There is, however, a key scene that the public record does not support, a scene that might invade someone's privacy. You don't want to cut the scene. Revising the scene to skirt the potential legal problem can raise ethical concerns. Can you meet the challenge legally while failing the test ethically? If skirting the problem fails and you still want the scene, do you quickly hire a research specialist with clear instructions to find enough sources to justify the scene legally, if not ethically?

SECURING APPROVALS CAN RAISE ETHICAL CONCERNS

If you do secure the life rights of a key player in a fact-based story, what you want is for that individual to be available to you to help flesh out story points and provide the necessary documentation. What you don't want is for that individual to contradict what you want to do in your project and for him or her to demand story approval. Most producers, in fact, are careful to structure deals that do not include granting anything resembling story approval to the rights holder, because approvals often make it impossible for a project to reach completion.

Many a project has been halted at the gate because a producer made the "mistake" of granting a rights holder story approval. Similarly, having the rights holder read a script can lead to suggestions that can impede a project's initial vision or lead to long delays as revisions are considered and then implemented, often resulting in bad feelings all around. Some, of course, might say that these revisions could improve the authenticity of the film and that it is unethical to secure someone's rights only to ignore that person's input. But many practitioners of the true-story genre have found that embracing the version of events provided by the person whose rights have been secured leads to a glorification of that individual in the project.

This may have been the case with Richard LaGravenese's fact-based film *Freedom Writers* (2007) about the efforts of a dedicated teacher, Erin Gruwell, to reach out to students (Figure 6-5) who had been dismissed by the system in Long Beach's gang-infested Wilson High School. Gruwell, who is portrayed by Hillary Swank in the film, was an active collaborator on the film and she comes off as super heroic, even while Long Beach residents insist that even back in 1993 to 1998 when the film takes place, things were not as grim as the film portrays. Gruwell and LaGravenese stand by the accuracy of the film, although critics maintain that there was more of a racial mix in Gruwell's class than portrayed in the film and that Gruwell was helped by many other teachers at the school.[33] The film, however, has her standing alone fighting the system, the latest in a long line of super-dedicated movie and television teachers who are totally committed to their students, much like the teachers in *Room 222* (on television from 1969 to 1974), *Stand and Deliver* (1988), with Edward James Olmos, and *Dangerous Minds* (1995) with Michelle Pfeiffer.

FIGURE 6-5
Exaggerating a teacher's contributions can lead to ethical violations in fact-based projects. This was the charge made by Long Beach, California, residents about the 2007 film *Freedom Writers*, about teacher Erin Gruwell. (iStockphoto.com #3106127, Brian Wilke.)

Many of the television projects I developed while at ABC glorified the rights holders participating in the telefilm. For example, the fireman (Figure 6-6) whose rights were secured often ended up being the only hero in a movie, even if his participation was minor and his rights were secured as protection to bolster a project's authenticity.

Also, Michael Mann's 1999 film *The Insider*, about whistle blowing in the tobacco industry,

---

[33]Gina Piccalo, "Did 'Writers' Get It Wrong?" *The Los Angeles Times*, January 9, 2007, E-1.

had *60 Minutes* producer Lowell Bergman as a consultant on the project. The film told events from Bergman's perspective, causing Mike Wallace of *60 Minutes* as well as other critics to question the film's veracity.

FIGURE 6-6
A fireman whose rights are secured for a project will sometimes be portrayed as much more of a hero than he actually may have been. (iStockphoto.com #1978679, Danny Bailey.)

You Decide

When you watch a TV program or a theatrical film based on a fact-based story, try to spot whose rights were secured, based on how the characters are developed and presented.

HOW TO INTERACT WITH RIGHTS HOLDERS ETHICALLY

Experienced producer Phillip M. Krupp, who was mentioned in Chapter 4 in connection with the film *Edges of the Lord*, navigates the rights waters very carefully. He has successfully produced a number of fact-based projects including *Menendez: A Killing in Beverly Hills* (1994) about two sons who murdered their parents, *Amber Frey: Witness for the Prosecution* (2005) about the notorious Scott Peterson case, and *A Girl Like Me* (2006) about a boy who feels he should be a woman.

For Krupp, the key to securing a person's rights is to get that person's complete trust. When approaching a rights holder, he describes in detail what he envisions for the project, avoiding misrepresenting his intentions. Up front, he does not offer to let the rights holder read the script nor does he give the rights holder approvals. He feels a significant responsibility to the rights holder and feels that if he is forthcoming and detailed about his vision of a project, the rights holder will not feel insecure or dubious, leading to a request to monitor the script or, worse, a refusal to grant the rights. In this way, Krupp is able to feel he is treating the rights holder ethically while not granting story approvals.

You Decide

How would you go about securing rights for a fact-based story? Would you let the rights holder read your script or book? How would you handle the various ethical questions entailed while—and this is a very big "while"—making sure that your project goes forward?

Having examined some ethical issues involving fact-based projects, let's in the next chapter take a look at issues associated with how works are rated and how audience measurement is conducted.

CHAPTER 7

Ethics and Ratings

The entertainment industry lives or dies based on ratings, box office tallies, and units sold. If people aren't listening to shock-jocks on radio (no matter how outrageous or controversial they are), if no one is going to a celebrity blog, if no one is going to see a film on the opening weekend, if no one is watching a television program, the prospect of a long and prosperous run is greatly diminished. In addition, labels, or ratings, on movies, television shows, records, or video games can influence how many people are going to be buying tickets, watching, or playing. A restrictive label can severely limit potential audience reach, producing weak audience totals and causing advertisers to look elsewhere for sponsorship opportunities. How movies, television shows, records, and video games are rated thus becomes of primary importance.

In this chapter, we will look at two different kinds of ratings. First, we will look at the ratings that are placed on entertainment products, and then we will examine audience measurements as calculated by Nielsen Media for television and Arbitron for radio. Our mission in the first part of the chapter is to examine what kinds of ethical issues arise when assigning ratings to movies, television shows, records, and video games. In the second part of the chapter, we will explore the ethical issues that come up in the reporting of ratings.

PG, PG-13, TV-MA

Why do labels for entertainment programs exist? To warn consumers about content? To enable parents to gauge what might and might not be right for their children? To enable politicians running for reelection to grandstand about the need to stop the coarsening of the culture? Or do they exist because entertainment has a strong moral obligation to the public, as the Motion Picture Code of 1930 claimed?

Labels or ratings exit for a number of reasons, some of them valid, some of them perhaps less so. One prevailing reason stands out. Ratings exist to prevent the government from gaining the power to legislate oversight, thus challenging the entertainment industry's desire to self-regulate. The *Daily Variety* obituary for the legendary president of CBS, Frank Stanton, who passed away at the age of 98, lauded his work in staving off government intrusion "as television grew into an entertainment and news powerhouse."[1] Stanton was able to act quickly during the quiz show scandals of the l950s.

By acting quickly, Stanton helped keep the government from intervening to address the quiz show crisis, a crisis that some equated with America's loss of innocence, the feeling being that if you couldn't trust the television in your own living room, who could you trust? Stanton's ability to keep the government from stepping in cemented his reputation as television's savior and helped make CBS the powerhouse Tiffany network.

Whenever a politician begins to question the effectiveness of ratings and to suggest that more action is needed (meaning that the government needs to step in), industry lobbyists such as Dan Glickman, president of the Motion Picture Association of America (MPAA), who replaced Jack Valenti, himself a strong proponent of industry self-regulation, tell concerned legislators that existing ratings systems are effective,[2] that existing ratings help keep parents duly informed, and that no governmental oversight is needed or desired: The industry can and will monitor itself.

After radio personality Don Imus referred to the Rutgers' women's basketball team as "nappy-headed hos," MSNBC fired him, prompting an editorial in *Television Week* that said, "Note to the Federal Communications Commission: Media companies can make judgment calls without your help . . . we have been strong supporters of media outlets deciding for themselves what kind of speech they want to put on their airwaves, without government mandate or threat."[3]

---

[1]Ted Johnson, "Stanton Was Tiffany Titan," *Daily Variety*, December 27, 2006, p. 1.
[2]Jules Shiver Jr., "Senator Blasts Film, TV Ratings," *The Los Angeles Times*, September 29, 2004, C-1, 5.
[3]"In Imus Flap, TV Execs Show Good Judgment," editorial, *Television Week*, April 14, 2007, p. 12.

The Imus situation is discussed further in Chapter 9, but it's important in this chapter to note that the distaste for government action is so strong that if a media outlet responds aggressively, as was the case with Imus, the industry as a whole responds by saying that government involvement is not needed, even if some people feel that there was a rush to judgment to get rid of Imus.

If the movie industry self-regulates, if television programs carry their own ratings, if record companies place warnings on songs that might be objectionable, and if the video game industry similarly self-regulates, proponents of governmental controls are kept at bay. Clearly, self-service is a major part of self-regulation, causing some to interpret the stated altruistic motive of entertainment giants as motivated by greed and not by a sincere desire to keep the public informed. Others, however, vociferously point out that governmental involvement truly is unwarranted, and, contrary to what some grandstanding politicians might want the country to believe, not a step in the right direction. The marketplace can monitor itself, avoiding the intrusion of "big government." These individuals point out that having the government involved does not necessarily make things better.

147

MOVIE RATINGS

In 1968, the Motion Picture Association of America (MPAA), in partnership with the National Association of Theatre Owners (NATO), created a ratings system for movies that was intended to enable parents to monitor their children's movie going. The initial ratings were G for general audiences; M for mature audiences; R for restricted audiences, applying to movies where anyone under 16 was not admitted without a parent; and X, meaning that no one under 17 was admitted. Over the years, the ratings have been modified (Figure 7-1).

A film that is rated NC-17 faces a number of roadblocks, as many outlets will not permit ads for NC-17 movies and many theater chains will not run NC-17 movies. Producers whose films are to be distributed by major studios are contractually obligated to deliver a film that has an R rating. A film that receives an NC-17 thus has to be recut until it receives the necessary R rating.

Producer Bill Unger, for example, details the difficult process he went through to get an R rating for *True Romance* (1993), based on a script by Quentin Tarantino and directed by Tony Scott. The process was a difficult one with many

A G-rated motion picture contains nothing in theme, language, nudity, sex, violence or other matters that, in the view of the Rating Board, would offend parents whose younger children view the motion picture. The G rating is not a "certificate of approval," nor does it signify a "children's" motion picture. Some snippets of language may go beyond polite conversation but they are common everyday expressions. No stronger words are present in G-rated motion pictures. Depictions of violence are minimal. No nudity, sex scenes or drug use are present in the motion picture.

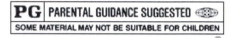

A PG-rated motion picture should be investigated by parents before they let their younger children attend. The PG rating indicates, in the view of the Rating Board, that parents may consider some material unsuitable for their children, and parents should make that decision.

The more mature themes in some PG-rated motion pictures may call for parental guidance. There may be some profanity and some depictions of violence or brief nudity. But these elements are not deemed so intense as to require that parents be strongly cautioned beyond the suggestion of parental guidance. There is no drug use content in a PG-rated motion picture.

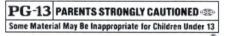

A PG-13 rating is a sterner warning by the Rating Board to parents to determine whether their children under age 13 should view the motion picture, as some material might not be suited for them. A PG-13 motion picture may go beyond the PG rating in theme, violence, nudity, sensuality, language, adult activities or other elements, but does not reach the restricted R category. The theme of the motion picture by itself will not result in a rating greater than PG-13, although depictions of activities related to a mature theme may result in a restricted rating for the motion picture. Any drug use will initially require at least a PG-13 rating. More than brief nudity will require at least a PG-13 rating, but such nudity in a PG-13 rated motion picture generally will not be sexually oriented. There may be depictions of violence in a PG-13 movie, but generally not both realistic and extreme or persistent violence. A motion picture's single use of one of the harsher sexually-derived words, though only as an expletive, initially requires at least a PG-13 rating. More than one such expletive requires an R rating, as must even one of those words used in a sexual context. The Rating Board nevertheless may rate such a motion picture PG-13 if, based on a special vote by a two-thirds majority, the Raters feel that most American parents would believe that a PG-13 rating is appropriate because of the context or manner in which the words are used or because the use of those words in the motion picture is inconspicuous.

An R-rated motion picture, in the view of the Rating Board, contains some adult material. An R-rated motion picture may include adult themes, adult activity, hard language, intense or persistent violence, sexually-oriented nudity, drug abuse or other elements, so that parents are counseled to take this rating very seriously. Children under 17 are not allowed to attend R-rated motion pictures unaccompanied by a parent or adult guardian. Parents are strongly urged to find out more about R-rated motion pictures in determining their suitability for their children. Generally, it is not appropriate for parents to bring their young children with them to R-rated motion pictures.

An NC-17 rated motion picture is one that, in the view of the Rating Board, most parents would consider patently too adult for their children 17 and under. No children will be admitted. NC-17 does not mean "obscene" or "pornographic" in the common or legal meaning of those words, and should not be construed as a negative judgment in any sense. The rating simply signals that the content is appropriate only for an adult audience. An NC-17 rating can be based on violence, sex, aberrational behavior, drug abuse or any other element that most parents would consider too strong and therefore off-limits for viewing by their children.

FIGURE 7-1
(Courtesy of the MPAA.)

back and forth decisions involving possibly switching to black and white from color to minimize the violence. Getting an R rating for the film was a two-week process that involved counting the number of times Patricia Arquette shot James Gandolfini and making both minor and major adjustments. Troubling for the MPAA was Arquette's seeming euphoria or rage after she vanquishes Gandolfini.

The movie ratings system is voluntary. A producer who selects not to submit his or her film for a rating greatly limits the chances that the film will be widely seen, though, in recent years, some producers, mostly the producers of low-budget independent films, have opted to release their films as unrated. The DVD market has also chosen to offer both the rated and unrated versions of some films. Interestingly enough, unrated DVDs tend to outsell rated ones 3 to 1, according to Judith McCourt of *Video Store Magazine*.[4] Producers or distributors can thus decide if they want their film to be rated. See the box on the 2007 film *Captivity* to learn how both the distributor and the MPAA handled this controversial film.

BILLBOARDS AND A FILM'S RATING

In 2007, After Dark Films submitted its film *Captivity*, starring Elisha Cuthbert and Daniel Gillies and directed by Roland Joffe (*The Mission*, 1986), to obtain a rating. In the film, a fashion model and a chauffeur find themselves in the basement of a serial killer. As part of the ratings process, the MPAA reviewed billboards for the film. These ads contained graphic images of a woman being tortured. (At press time, a number of sites on Google showed the billboards, including www.movieweb.com.)

The MPAA rejected the ads, but After Dark Films posted them anyway in Los Angeles and New York. Many complaints followed, and the billboards were eventually removed. But as William Triplett and Ian Mohr reported in *Daily Variety*, "After Dark Films was slapped with an unprecedented sanction by the Motion Picture Assn. of America."[5] The sanction resulted because the MPAA had ruled the billboards unacceptable, but After Dark Films put them up anyway.

Had After Dark not submitted *Captivity* for a rating, the MPAA would have had no authority over the billboards. Because the ratings process had started, After Dark Films received this unique sanction.

[4]Mike Snider, "DVDs Rate a Closer Look," *USA Today*, August 14, 2003, D-1–2.
[5]William Triplett and Ian Mohr, "Pic Shackled by MPAA," *Daily Variety*, March 26, 2007, pp. 1, 41.

The MPAA's website states, "The movie rating system is a voluntary system operated by the MPAA and the National Association of Theatre Owners (NATO). The ratings are given by a board of parents who comprise the Classification and Rating Administration (CARA)."[6] The website also states that "the Rating Board has always conducted itself at the highest level of integrity."[7] Nevertheless, some have complained that the qualifications of the people doing the ratings are suspect, that violence gets an easier pass than sex, that the ratings system lacks transparency, and that studio films get more lenient treatment than do independent films.

A 2006 film by Kirby Dick and Eddie Schmidt, *This Film Is Not Yet Rated*, available on DVD, seriously questions MPAA policies. In the film, private investigators are dispatched to unmask the identities of board members. The film includes interviews with filmmakers such as Kimberly Peirce (*Boys Don't Cry*, 1999), John Waters (*Pink Flamingos*, 1972), Mary Harron (*American Psycho*, 2000), Kevin Smith (*Clerks*, 1994), Matt Stone (*Southpark*, starting in 1997), and Atom Egoyan (*The Sweet Hereafter*, 1997) that question the ratings process administered by the MPAA, in particular the board's willingness to give violence a pass while coming down hard on sex, especially gay sex. *This Film Is Not Yet Rated*, in fact, juxtaposes similar heterosexual scenes and gay scenes; the heterosexual scenes get an R rating, whereas the gay scenes get an NC-17. How fair or ethical is that, the filmmakers ask? If the theater owners (NATO) who help bankroll the MPAA have a vested interest in the rating a film is assigned, how fair or ethical is *that*, the filmmakers ask? The filmmakers also question how raters are selected and why they are anonymous. The MPAA has claimed that the raters need to be anonymous so that they will be free from outside influences, but editorials like the one in *The New York Times*, September 8, 2006, call for "greater transparency in the ratings process."[8]

This Film is Not Yet Rated created results. Not only did it alert people to an ongoing situation that frustrated filmmakers, it caused change when the MPAA announced modifications in the ratings process in January 2007. It's not often

150

---

[6]www.mpaa.org/FilmRatings.asp, accessed October 29, 2006.

[7]www.mpaa.org, accessed October 29, 2006.

[8]"Rated R, for Obscure Reasons," editorial, *The New York Times*, September 8, 2006, A-26.

that a film, television show, or book can claim to have prompted a change of course, but as David M. Halbfinger wrote in *The New York Times*, "Stung by a low-budget documentary that assailed the movie rating system last year, motion picture industry officials are vowing to make the system more transparent to filmmakers and more accessible to parents."[9]

While keeping the G, PG, PG-13, R, and NC-17 classifications, the MPAA will make the process more transparent, including, for example, making the following changes:

- Filmmakers will now be allowed to cite scenes from other movies when they are appealing a rating. Up until now, they had not been allowed to do this, something filmmakers such as Dick and others strenuously objected to.
- No longer will the appeals panel be composed of just people from studios and theater owners. This could allow independent filmmakers to have a voice.
- Rating rules will be posted on the MPAA website to demystify the process, making it more public.
- Attempts will be made to give parents more information about R-rated films, letting them understand that some R-rated films may not be appropriate for younger viewers, even if those viewers are accompanied by adults.
- Film raters will be replaced when their children are grown. That some raters no longer had children was a major complaint.
- Training for raters will be formalized.
- Parents will be discouraged from taking children to R-rated films. R-rated films will carry a new advisory, "Generally, it is not appropriate for parents to bring their young children with them to R-rated motion pictures."
- A liaison will be appointed to answer filmmakers' questions about the ratings process.
- Lastly, a May 10, 2007, release from the MPAA indicated a new area that the organization will address, namely smoking in movies. According to the release, "The Motion Picture Association of American (MPAA) today

[9]David M. Halbfinger, "Hollywood Rethinks Its Ratings Process," *The New York Times*, January 18, 2007, B-1.

announced that the rating system is enhancing the amount of information provided to parents on the issue of smoking in films. In the past, illegal teen smoking has been a factor in the rating of films, alongside other parental concerns such as sex, violence and adult language. Now, all smoking will be considered and depictions that glamorize smoking or movies that feature pervasive smoking outside of an historic or other mitigating context may receive a higher rating."[10]

These changes are definitely steps in the right direction, according to editorials in both *The New York Times* and *The Los Angeles Times*.[11] The changes probably won't please everyone, but *This Film Is Not Yet Rated* and the changes that resulted reveal how much importance is attached to ratings and how they are conducted.

You Decide

Conduct your own research about the MPAA. Using our rubric, *E*valuate and *I*nvestigate the MPAA from an ethical perspective. What do you think about NATO being a part of the MPAA, helping to bankroll it? What do you see as the *T*ruth as to how and why the MPAA exists and why it made changes in the ratings process? What

*H*arm, if any, can come from the MPAA's rating process? Go to the MPAA's website, www.mpaa.org, to *I*nvestigate the organization's *C*ode of ethics, and then using the *S* for *S*ituational ethics, determine if you feel that different movies do, in fact, call for different approaches.

152

TELEVISION RATINGS

In addition to requiring V-Chip technology for sets 13 inches and over to enable parents to block programs they feel are inappropriate for their children, part of the Telecommunications Act of 1996 included the creation of a voluntary ratings system for television programs. This system, known as the TV Parental Guidelines, includes age-appropriate labels as well as content indicators: D for dialogue, L for language, S for sexual content, V for violence, and FV for fantasy violence. The networks adopted this voluntary ratings system, though NBC resisted and only included the content indicators sometimes also called content descriptors, in 2005.

[10]"Film Rating Board to Consider Smoking as a Factor," MPAA Press Release, May 10, 2007, p. 1.
[11]"Reforms for Movie Ratings," editorial, *The New York Times*, January 19, 2007, A-26; G—for Good Ideas," editorial, *The Los Angeles Times*, January 19, 2007, A-27.

TV PARENTAL GUIDELINES

The *TV Parental Guidelines* are designed so that "category and program-specific content indicators will provide parents with information that will help them make informed decisions about what their children should watch on television." The *TV Parental Guidelines* describe a voluntary rating system consisting of six descriptive labels designed to indicate the appropriateness of television programming to children according to age and/or maturity; content indicators concerning sexual situations, violence, language or dialogue; agreement to transmit on Line 21 of the vertical blanking interval; display of on-screen rating icons and indicators; and the establishment of an Oversight Monitoring Board.

The *TV Parental Guidelines* will apply to all television programming except for news, sports, and unedited MPAA rated movies on premium cable channels. The *TV Parental Guidelines* (labels and content indicators, and respective meanings) are:

For programs designed solely for children:

TV-Y (All Children—*This program is designed to be appropriate for all children.*) Whether animated or live-action, the themes and elements in this program are specifically designed for a very young audience, including children from ages 2–6. This program is not expected to frighten younger children.

TV-Y7 (Directed to Older Children—*This program is designed for children age 7 and above.*) It may be more appropriate for children who have acquired the developmental skills needed to distinguish between make-believe and reality. Themes and elements in this program may include mild fantasy or comedic violence, or may frighten children under the age of 7. Therefore, parents may wish to consider the suitability of this program for their very young children. Note: For those programs where fantasy violence may be more intense or more combative than other programs in this category, such programs will be designated **TV-Y7-FV**.

For programs designed for the entire audience, the general categories are:

TV-G (General Audience—*Most parents would find this program suitable for all ages.*) Although this rating does not signify a program designed specifically for children, most parents may let younger children watch this program unattended. It contains little or no violence, no strong language and little or no sexual dialogue or situations.

TV-PG (Parental Guidance Suggested—*This program contains material that parents may find unsuitable for younger children.*) Many parents may want to watch it with their younger children. The theme itself may call for parental guidance and/or the program contains one or more of the following: moderate violence (V), some sexual situations (S), infrequent coarse language (L), or some suggestive dialogue (D).

TV-14 (Parents Strongly Cautioned—*This program contains some material that many parents would find unsuitable for children under 14 years of age.*) Parents are strongly urged to exercise greater care in monitoring this program and are cautioned against letting children under the age of 14 watch unattended. This program contains one or more of the following: intense violence (V), intense sexual situations (S), strong coarse language (L), or intensely suggestive dialogue (D).

153

> **TV-MA** (Mature Audience Only—*This program is specifically designed to be viewed by adults and therefore may be unsuitable for children under 17.*) This program contains one or more of the following: graphic violence (V), explicit sexual activity (S), or crude indecent language (L).
>
> The rating icons and associated content symbols will appear for 15 seconds at the beginning of all rated programming. Under the *TV Parental Guidelines*, the rating guidelines will typically be applied to television programs by broadcast and cable networks and producers, while television stations retain the right to substitute the rating they deem appropriate for their audience. Participants agree to transmit program rating information on Line 21 of the Vertical Blanking Interval. The Industry notes that cable networks and television stations will provide rating information to newspapers and publishers of printed and electronic program guides, and will request that these publishers include the appropriate information in their guides.
>
> The FCC Report No. GN 98-3, March 12, 1998.

The networks themselves rate the shows, causing some to question how the ratings are determined. The networks want to use the ratings to avoid further governmental intervention, and an Oversight Monitoring Board exists to make certain that the ratings are properly applied and to handle viewer complaints and questions, but questions remain about the accuracy of the self-imposed ratings. Each episode of a series is rated individually, but can the concerns of advertisers cause a network to soft-peddle a rating to avoid giving a show a rating that is too harsh, which might therefore alarm advertisers and cause them to pull their advertising spots?

Advertisers are likely to stay clear of anything that is rated TV-MA, which may explain why so few programs on broadcast television carry this label. The 1993 Steven Spielberg–directed holocaust film *Schindler's List* received the first TV-MA network rating when it aired unedited and uncensored on NBC in 1997. Generally speaking, however, the TV-MA designation is reserved for edgy cable programs like FX's *Nip/Tuck* or HBO's *Da Ali G. Show* or *The Sopranos*.

In addition to the TV Parental Guidelines ratings, networks can also place advisories on shows to warn viewers about strong content. *NYPD Blue*, for example, always carried an advisory in addition to its TV-14 rating. In contrast, to date in its record-breaking run, *The Simpsons* carried an advisory only once, that being on the infamous gay marriage episode of 2005 where Homer decides to promote tourism in Springfield by performing gay marriage ceremonies.

If an episode carries an advisory, affiliates have to receive advance notice. Cautious advertisers are likely to stay away, making the network decision to include an advisory a Solomon-like dilemma. On the one hand, broadcast ethics clamor for the need to inform viewers. On the other hand, the marketplace is very worried about advisories. Advertisers are generally fearful of a backlash from viewers when programs carry advisories, and networks are aware that advertisers fret about shows that carry advisories.

Many thus feel that the use of advisories is arbitrary, as they are often used to appease critics and politicians rather than to alert viewers. Ellen DeGeneres, for example, was extremely angry that ABC placed an advisory on the 1997 "coming out" episode of *Ellen*, the one where she announced that the character she played was gay. She argued publicly and forcefully that there was no need for that episode, which had Oprah Winfrey playing her therapist, to carry an advisory.

The controversy over television ratings is, in fact, worldwide. For example, in the summer of 2007, a major controversy erupted in Thailand when a proposal was made to revise an existing, reportedly successful, TV rating system with one that was much more restrictive and cumbersome. The proposed system would require the imposition of mandatory time slots for programs, according to the ratings assigned.

The objections to the proposal were so strong with charges that censors were guilty of insulting the intelligence of viewers and programmers alike with a "dumbing down" process that the Thai government put the new proposals on hold, subject to further review.

155

You Decide

*E*valuate the ratings placed on some of the shows that you watch. Do you think the ratings and the content indicators/descriptors are accurate? Also, think about a show that has an advisory. Why do you think an advisory was used? What do you think of the wording of the advisory? Do you think the advisory was warranted? Think about a show that did not carry an advisory but that you feel might have had one. Why do you think no advisory was included?

As discussed in Chapter 10, during November 2006 sweeps, NBC aired *Madonna's Confessions Tour* as a special starting at 8 p.m. with a TV-14 rating. The special had caused some controversy before airtime because during one number from the show, Madonna wore a crown of thorns while on a giant cross. Pope Benedict XVI reportedly declared this number blasphemous.[12] The visuals of Madonna on the cross were edited—Madonna initially said she would pull the special if this number was censored, but she ultimately

[12]Tom Dorsey, "Madonna's 'Confessions' Spices Up NBC's Thanksgiving Eve," www.courier-journal.com/apps/pbcs.dll/article?Date=20061122&Category=COLU, accessed November 24, 2006.

reluctantly agreed to the edit. She did, however, continue to wear a crown of thorns for the television special. A number of words were bleeped from the show, and shots of Madonna's middle finger were digitally blurred. Suggestive dancing was also blurred, and there was gender blurring as well, but the program did not carry an advisory, though it aired at 8 p.m. Do you think it should have carried an advisory? What criteria would you use to determine whether or not this special needed an advisory or possibly a TV-MA rating?

MUSIC AND VIDEO GAMES

The push to label a product is strong; it's powerful and it possesses a wide reach. In 1895, the Parents Music Resource Center, with the backing of Tipper Gore, wife of then-Senator, later Vice President, and then presidential candidate and environment activist Al Gore, sought to curtail music defined as indecent or violent by including labels on records (Figure 7-2) that contained explicit lyrics. The labels, which the trade group Recording Industry Association of America (RIAA) agreed to, read "Parental Guidance: Explicit Lyrics."

FIGURE 7-2
Putting warning labels on records was seen by some as a way to combat indecent or violent music. (iStockphoto.com #2715040, Joey Nelson.)

The Entertainment Software Rating Board (ESRB), established in l994, successfully assigns ratings to provide information about the content in computer and video games so parents can make informed purchase decisions. ESRB ratings have two equal parts: Ratings symbols suggest age appropriateness for the game, and content descriptors indicate elements in a game that may have triggered a particular rating or may be of interest or concern (Figure 7-3).

The Cellular Telecommunications and Internet Association (CTIA) has also adopted "a content rating system for video, music, pictures and games that they sell to cell phone users,"[13] a further indication of the emphasis placed on ratings.

The Advisory Committee to the Congressional Internet Caucus held a conference in September 2006 to discuss the pros and cons of using government warning labels about sexually explicit material carried online.[14] Here again, the question becomes what can the industry do to prevent such governmental intervention.

[13]Matt Richtel, "Carriers Adopt Content Rating for Cell Phones," *The New York Times*, November 9, 2005, C-5.
[14]www.netcaucus.org/events/2006/label, accessed November 8, 2006.

ESRB Rating Symbols

EARLY CHILDHOOD
Titles rated **EC (Early Childhood)** have content that may be suitable for ages 3 and older. Contains no material that parents would find inappropriate.

EVERYONE
Titles rated **E (Everyone)** have content that may be suitable for ages 6 and older. Titles in this category may contain minimal cartoon, fantasy or mild violence and/or infrequent use of mild language.

EVERYONE 10+
Titles rated **E10+ (Everyone 10 and older)** have content that may be suitable for ages 10 and older. Titles in this category may contain more cartoon, fantasy or mild violence, mild language and/or minimal suggestive themes.

TEEN
Titles rated **T (Teen)** have content that may be suitable for ages 13 and older. Titles in this category may contain violence, suggestive themes, crude humor, minimal blood, simulated gambling, and/or infrequent use of strong language.

MATURE
Titles rated **M (Mature)** have content that may be suitable for persons ages 17 and older. Titles in this category may contain intense violence, blood and gore, sexual content and/or strong language.

ADULTS ONLY
Titles rated **AO (Adults Only)** have content that should only be played by persons 18 years and older. Titles in this category may include prolonged scenes of intense violence and/or graphic sexual content and nudity.

RATING PENDING
Titles listed as **RP (Rating Pending)** have been submitted to the ESRB and are awaiting final rating. (This symbol appears only in advertising prior to a game's release.)

FIGURE 7-3
ESRB Rating Symbols and Content Descriptors. (Reprinted courtesy of ESRB.)

FIGURE 7-3
(Continued)

ESRB Content Descriptors

Alcohol Reference - Reference to and/or images of alcoholic beverages

Animated Blood - Discolored and/or unrealistic depictions of blood

Blood - Depictions of blood

Blood and Gore - Depictions of blood or the mutilation of body parts

Cartoon Violence - Violent actions involving cartoon-like situations and characters. May include violence where a character is unharmed after the action has been inflicted

Comic Mischief - Depictions or dialogue involving slapstick or suggestive humor

Crude Humor - Depictions or dialogue involving vulgar antics, including "bathroom" humor

Drug Reference - Reference to and/or images of illegal drugs

Edutainment - Content of product provides user with specific skills development or reinforcement learning within an entertainment setting. Skill development is an integral part of product

Fantasy Violence - Violent actions of a fantasy nature, involving human or non-human characters in situations easily distinguishable from real life

Informational - Overall content of product contains data, facts, resource information, reference materials or instructional text

Intense Violence - Graphic and realistic-looking depictions of physical conflict. May involve extreme and/or realistic blood, gore, weapons and depictions of human injury and death

Language - Mild to moderate use of profanity

Lyrics - Mild references to profanity, sexuality, violence, alcohol or drug use in music

Mature Humor - Depictions or dialogue involving "adult" humor, including sexual references

Mild Violence - Mild scenes depicting characters in unsafe and/or violent situations

Nudity - Graphic or prolonged depictions of nudity

Partial Nudity - Brief and/or mild depictions of nudity

Real Gambling - Player can gamble, including betting or wagering real cash or currency

Sexual Themes - Mild to moderate sexual references and/or depictions. May include partial nudity

Sexual Violence - Depictions of rape or other violent sexual acts

Simulated Gambling - Player can gamble without betting or wagering real cash or currency

Some Adult Assistance May Be Needed - Intended for very young ages

Strong Language - Explicit and/or frequent use of profanity

Strong Lyrics - Explicit and/or frequent references to profanity, sex, violence, alcohol or drug use in music

Strong Sexual Content - Graphic references to and/or depictions of sexual behavior, possibly including nudity

Suggestive Themes - Mild provocative references or materials

Tobacco Reference - Reference to and/or images of tobacco products

Use of Drugs - The consumption or use of illegal drugs

Use of Alcohol - The consumption of alcoholic beverages

Use of Tobacco - The consumption of tobacco products

Violence - Scenes involving aggressive conflict

An organization like Child's Play, created by gamers Mike Krahulik and Jerry Holkins, donates video games provided by gamers and video game makers to sick children seeking to offset the negative reputation of video games, as reported in an article in *The New York Times*, December 27, 2006.[15]

[15]J. Peter Freire, "From Far and Wide, Video Gamers Join in a Child Charity," *The New York Times*, December 27, 2006, A-19.

But not all industry self-regulation receives pats on the back or whole-hearted seals of approval. For example, a Federal Trade Commission (FTC) 2007 study expressed concern that material not suitable for children is being marketed to minors. Though the FTC continues to support industry self-regulation, it found a general lack of care in making sure that children are not subjected to inappropriate marketing. Specifically, the FTC study found that "entertainment industries continue to market some R-rated movies, M-rated video games and explicit-content recordings on television shows and other sites with substantial teen audiences."[16]

AUDIENCE MEASUREMENT: TELEVISION AND RADIO

After examining key reasons why the media employs ratings labels, let's now look at ratings in terms of audience measurement from an E*T*H*I*C*S perspective. In television, radio, and, increasingly, the Internet, audience measurement is the currency that determines success or failure, survival or oblivion. If audiences aren't there, the end is near. Nielsen Media Research measures television audiences, and Arbitron measures radio audiences. Ratings determine advertising rates, and billions of dollars per year are at stake; ratings dictate who has a job and who doesn't; and ratings are the reason programming executives get up at the crack of dawn to get the numbers and start spinning the good or bad news.

Though competitors come and go, and there is always a company ready to take over, Nielsen Media has had a virtual monopoly on television ratings. Nielsen consistently seeks to stay ahead of the curve and to squelch competition by providing subscribers who have seen an expansion from 3 channels to more than 500 with increasingly sophisticated and specialized data that go way beyond household viewership and demographics. These include measuring via digital video recorders (DVRs) and VCR playbacks, viewing while students are away at college, and viewing of commercials, to name a few of the areas that Nielsen Media has developed or is exploring.

No longer content to gauge audience awareness of shows as a means of determining what shows are likely to succeed, programming executives want to know how engaged viewers are in the shows that they watch. Viewer engagement is the new buzz phrase used by programmers. Undoubtedly, Nielsen and others are seeking to find a quantitative means of measuring audiences' engagement in a show.

[16]William Triplett, "FTV Tells Biz to Curb Blurbs," *Daily Variety*, April 13, 2007, pp. 1, 30.

FIGURES 7-4 and 7-5
Bad weather can affect ratings. Weather, good or bad, is one of many variables that make quantifying ratings difficult. For example, when the country switched to daylight savings time earlier than usual in 2007, ratings were down as people spent time outdoors instead of being in front of the television set. A local sporting event can preempt regular programming, similarly impacting ratings. (iStockphoto.com # 2901630, Nick Tzolov; iStockphoto.com #2354688, Bill Grove.)

Providing ratings information to subscribers has enabled Nielsen to charge subscribers hefty amounts. For example, in 2003, "both NBC and Viacom signed long-term deals worth between $400 and 500 million,"[17] enabling Nielsen to post approximately $600 million in revenue.[18] These dollar figures explain why contenders are always at the ready to challenge Nielsen, even if it costs massive amounts to assemble the resources to conduct audience measurements.

Interpreting television ratings is no easy task. For example, if research staffs are cut because of belt tightening or consolidation, the analysis of the ratings information may be compromised, necessitating the use of software products such as Strata Cable (www.strata.com) to assist in quantifying the ratings. With so many variables, tabulation becomes exceedingly difficult. According to research specialists, there can be more than a hundred variables to analyze, including weather (Figures 7-4 and 7-5), local preemptions for sporting or special events,

[17]Steve McClellan, "Nielsen's Whiting Stands Firm," www.broadcastingcable.com/index. asp?layout=articlePrint&articleID=CA422024, accessed November 13, 2006.
[18]Ibid.

technological breakdowns, or program-related variables such as seasonal specials that compete with one another.

With so much at stake and so much money dependent on ratings, it's no wonder that friction often exists. For example, advertisers might want ratings for commercials in order to know who is and who is not watching commercials, whereas fearful broadcasters might not want this, because their ad rates might go down if the ratings indicate that people are not sticking around to watch the commercials. It's bad enough that the remote made it easy for couch potatoes to change channels and that viewership is suffering, but if ratings document that people are not watching commercials, broadcasters might be facing another heavy hit.

In the 1960s, the Media Rating Council (MRC) was established with the following mission:

> The Council seeks to improve the quality of audience measurement by
> rating services and to provide a better understanding of the applications
> (and limitations) of rating information. The Mission Statement of the
> MRC is as follows: (1) to secure for the media industry and related users
> audience measurement services that are valid, reliable and effective; (2)
> to evolve and determine minimum disclosure and ethical criteria for
> media audience measurement services; (3) to provide and administer an
> audit system designed to inform users as to whether such audience
> measurements are conducted in conformance with the criteria and
> procedures developed.[19]

161

Again designed as a self-regulating body, the MRC is funded by the industry. Its accreditation process is voluntary, though both Nielsen and Arbitron submit to the MRC's accreditation process. For our purposes, the MRC joins a long line of media organizations that maintain that self-regulation is the right way to go. Interestingly enough, the MRC seeks to expand its role beyond radio and television to the Internet and beyond, according to Toni Fitzgerald's 2005 *Media Life Magazine* interview with George Ivie, MRC's executive director.[20]

Because so much is at stake in regard to ratings, finding the good news in weak ratings has become a much-needed skill, particularly as the expanded universe

---

[19]www.mrc.htsp.com/history.jsp, accessed June 28, 2006.
[20]Toni Fitzgerald, "MRC On Its Mission as Media Overseer," www.medialifemagazine.
com/News2005/april05/apr25/2_tues/news4tuesday.html, accessed April 27, 2005.

has made good ratings harder to come by. In short, the quest for ratings can lead to some ethical lapses and no small amount of bravado, for example, crowing that a program that came in last in terms of households and last in demographics had a 2% increase in the number of households with incomes of over $50,000 a year. Noted media observer Alan B. Albarran has observed that ratings research can be misused. He wrote, "Inflating or misrepresenting the actual numbers, usually in efforts to secure advertising, is a serious ethical problem as well as grounds for legal action."[21] Indeed, the battle for getting ratings and for spinning ratings can get ugly.

For example, NBC aired only local commercials during its low-rated pregame football show at 7 p.m. on Sundays in 2006 so that Nielsen would not include the show in its national ratings (if no national ads are included in a program, Nielsen does not include that program in its national ratings). This caused network rivals to object that NBC was unfairly inflating its ratings.[22]

THE BATTLE GETS FIERCE

Nielsen introduced its Local People Meters (LPM) in 2002 and announced that it would be switching to LPMs in top markets. Instead of having viewers record what they viewed in diaries, the LPM would keep track of what shows were viewed using an electronic box that tracks data for each member of a household. Rupert Murdock of News Corp. strenuously objected, claiming that the switch was unfair to minorities because LPMs undercounted Latinos and African Americans. An ongoing debate ensued questioning whether or not several Fox and UPN shows targeting African Americans and Latinos suffered ratings hits with the LPM. Some said yes, some said no. The battle continued, with a number of parties weighing in.

Through an organization it funded, "Don't Count Us Out," News Corp. maintained that Nielsen was unfair to minorities, that its sample size for minorities was too small, and that the technicians installing the LPMs were improperly trained. Nielsen countered that its sampling system was constantly being

---

[21]Alan B. Albarran, *Management of Electronic Media*, 3rd ed. (Belmont, CA: Thomson Wadsworth, 2006), pp. 165–166.

[22]John Consoli, "ABC Irked by NBC's Sunday Evening NFL Scheduling Scheme," http:// mediaweek.printthis.clickability.com/pt/cpt?action=cpt&title=ABC+Irked+by+NB, accessed October 16, 2006.

improved and that News Corp. simply didn't want to face the reality that ratings were down. Speaking for Nielsen, Doug Darfield, senior vice president of Nielsen Hispanic Services, said it was difficult to get Spanish-dominant Hispanics to participate in the ratings process; he noted, "a certain percentage of them are, of course, undocumented and especially in this rather toxic climate are [reluctant] to say anything about themselves to anybody. There is also the question of lack of familiarity with the rating process, lack of familiarity with the Nielsen name."[23]

The battle grew fierce and involved the MRC, the National Association for the Advancement of Colored People (NAACP), Congress, and various public figures. Specifically, the MRC denied full accreditation to LPMs in New York City, granting only conditional accreditation. Finally in October 2006, an agreement was reached; Nielsen agreed to spend $50 million to guarantee accurate audience counts, including adding more staff to train households how to use the LPMs.[24]

Ratings battles are not unique to Nielsen and News Corp.—not by a long shot. Ratings battles surfaced in 2006 with charges that individuals who were able to manipulate viewer ratings compromised YouTube. Using www.refresher.com, these individuals made it appear that their posting had a much larger viewership than it had in reality. YouTube senior product manager, Michael Powers, claimed that YouTube technology prevented inflated ratings,[25] but, as discussed in this chapter, when it comes to labels and ratings, someone is likely to try to manipulate, control, or spin the results. After all, ratings can mean the difference between success and failure; ratings can influence thousands or millions or billions of dollars. Would ethical lapses thus be unheard of when it comes to audience measurement?

---

[23]"Nielsen's Darfield: Tracking Hispanic Eyeballs," *Broadcasting & Cable* advertising supplement, October 16, 2006, 16A.

[24]"News Corp., Nielsen Settle Dispute over TV Ratings," www.iht.com/bin/print_ipub. php?file=/articles/ap/2006/10/25/business/NA_FIN_U, accessed October 26, 2006.

[25]Richard Rushfield, "The Web, Etc.: Got Hits? Or Maybe They've Just Got Game," *The Los Angeles Times*, November 12, 2006, E-4.

You Decide

Clearly ratings, as the lifeblood of the entertainment industry, are important, but executives, sometimes or often, depending on your point of view, go to extremes to gain or spin favorable ratings, possibly violating ethical guidelines in the process. Using the E*T*H*I*C*S rubric where applicable, take a look at the following questions and decide what you think. Additional research may be needed, as you delve deeper into the question of ratings.

- Do you think the entertainment industry's use of labels is motivated by a desire to do what's right and ethical to keep the public well informed?
- Do you think the use of labels is motivated by the marketplace, enabling the entertainment industry to maintain its autonomy?
- Do you think governmental oversight of ratings would improve matters or make things worse?
- Does the MRC's mission reflect the ethical position it maintains?

- Why do you think the MRC might want to have a say about Internet ratings?
- Was the sampling system Nielsen used an unfair representation of the African American and Latino communities, as some charged?
- Was Nielsen guilty of rushing the LPM before the technology was adequately tested and before adequate training for the transition was conducted?
- Do you think an organization like Child's Play helps the image of the video game industry?
- Was News Corp. hoping to postpone receiving lower ratings for its shows?
- Was Nielsen guilty of implementing a system that underrepresented minorities?
- Do you trust the number of hits a posting on YouTube receives?

In this chapter, we have looked at ratings from a number of perspectives. In Chapter 8, written by Jeffrey Brody, let's switch our focus to ethical issues associated with journalism.

CHAPTER 8
Journalism and Ethics

By Jeffrey Brody

In this chapter, let's take a look at some of the issues that confront journalists as they grapple with ethics. We can begin on Melrose Place in Los Angeles where the word has gone out that actress Tori Spelling is hosting a party at a popular teahouse. Outside, throngs of photographers, a scruffy lot in jeans and sweats, swarm by the security guard, poised for action. Someone spots an actress—Michele Rodriguez—and the paparazzi (Figure 8-1) surround her, shooting fusillades of photos. It's a feeding frenzy for the paparazzi. Rodriguez takes it in stride. Passing motorists glare at them. They are the same "entertainment journalists" who have contributed to automobile accidents, even death in the case of Princess Diana, and have made a habit of invading the privacy of many in the public light. Yet they routinely sell photos to the entertainment press and can earn more money with a few good pics than a straight news photographer makes in a year.

Footage of paramedics attempting to save the life of Anna Nicole Smith sold for more than $500,000, according to the Splash News & Picture Agency. The video of paramedics working on the former playmate was displayed the day of her death (February 8, 2007) on a German TV channel, RTL, and then posted on the Web.[1] Smith's death became one of the most sought after stories on *The New York Times*'s website and became an obsession with the cable news networks, which treated her death, and the ensuing controversy over her burial and the paternity of her child, like that of a state figure.

---

[1] www.foxnews.com/story/0,2933,251000,00.html, accessed March 5, 2007.

FIGURE 8-1
Paparazzi relentlessly pursue celebrities, causing many to question their journalistic ethics, with some people even wondering if swarming paparazzi can cause a celebrity's death, as in the case of Princess Diana. (iStockphoto.com #2055725, Alex Gumeror.)

Such is the lot of journalistic ethics. The discipline that aspires to be the loftiest of the professions—the public watchdog, the guardian of the public's right to know, the seeker of the truth—often finds itself in the gutter harassing movie stars and obsessing over their demise. This is far from what the founding fathers had in mind when they granted journalists constitutional rights. Journalism is the only profession protected by a constitutional amendment. The First Amendment states that Congress "shall make no law . . . abridging the freedom of speech or of the press."

Government has the regulatory power to license architects, attorneys, nurses, physicians, and teachers. Lawmakers exercise their legal authority over those professions. But they have no power to license the press. Hence, anyone and everyone can consider himself or herself to be a journalist. There is no test, equivalent to the bar exam, required of journalists; there is no training, equivalent to medical school, required of journalists. And there are no regulatory bodies, such as the American Bar Association or the State Board of Medical Examiners, that can fine, discipline, suspend, or eliminate the privileges of a journalist. A lawyer can be disbarred for an ethical infraction. A doctor can lose his license for an ethical infraction. Attorneys and physicians have been stripped of their licenses and barred from practicing forever. At most, a journalist might lose his or her job for an ethical infraction but be free to practice again.

This is even truer in the days of the Internet, as discussed in Chapter 9. With the Internet, a person can blog from his home and reach millions around the world. In the 20th century, one would have to have access to a printing press or a broadcasting studio and be subject to the rules and ethical standards of the publisher or station owner. Matt Drudge proved to the world by breaking the Monica Lewinsky scandal that a blogger operating out of a home office with a cheap Internet connection can influence the world. The First Amendment has a direct influence on journalistic ethics because it allows anyone to practice journalism with or without ethical standards. And it stretches the definition of journalism to include a range of reporters from *The National Inquirer* to *The New York Times; US Magazine* and *Entertainment Tonight* receive the same constitutional protection as *The Atlantic Monthly* and *60 Minutes*. Call it the dilemma of journalism; the Constitution protects both good and bad reporting and writing.

The lesson between what is legal and what is ethical in journalism, which was discussed in Chapter 1, became clear to a college newspaper adviser when two students, attempting to be funny, wrote a scathing review of an off-campus Mexican restaurant (Figure 8-2). The students compared the food the taco stand served to serial killer Jeffrey Dahmer's brains and made crude puns and other offensive remarks about the cuisine.

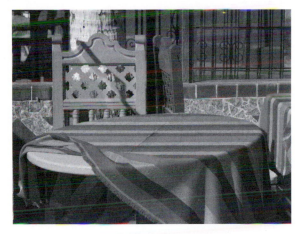

Upon reading the published restaurant review, the adviser became livid. He told the students their writing was offensive and that they should go back and write a professional review. Before the students could do that, a lawyer representing the restaurant sent a letter to the university, threatening a lawsuit. The lawyer's action moved the issue from the ethical to the legal arena, and the university was forced to circle the wagons around the First Amendment. The university's attorney ordered the students to stay put because the Constitution protects the most vicious of commentary. In this case, a restaurant review of questionable ethical judgment turned into a lesson about communications law. The students learned that the First Amendment protected their lapse of judgment and immaturity. The threatened lawsuit never went anywhere, and the students never rewrote the review.

FIGURE 8-2
A scathing review of a Mexican restaurant in a college newspaper raises a number of legal and ethical questions. (iStockphoto.com #2944224, Yang Yin.)

167

If anyone can practice journalism in a free society, it is all the more important for schools to provide ethical training and for media owners to adhere to ethical principles. If there are no external bodies to enforce ethical judgments, the standards have to be internalized to protect the profession. Before discussing ethical problems related to journalism, it is important to examine how journalists can use E*T*H*I*C*S to enhance and improve their profession's credibility and reputation.

To summarize, *E* stands for *E*valuate. Just as journalists need to get both sides of a story, they need to examine all sides of an ethical issue. They have to consider the issue and analyze it from the perspective of the reader and those involved with the story. Just because a journalist has the right to print or broadcast information doesn't mean the journalist has the obligation to do so. For example, it is unethical to reveal troop movements that may get soldiers killed. A decision by the *Cincinnati Enquirer* to publish the names of jurors in a high-publicity murder trial led to editor Tom Callahan issuing a public apology to the judge and jurors. "It was a late-night, deadline decision that simply was wrong," Callahan said. "It was a mistake that could cause harm to those citizens (the jurors). It had the potential to harm the judicial process. There is no doubt that it harmed the trust you have in *The Enquirer*." He added, "All I can say is that we lost our perspective. In being aggressive on a big story, we rushed to a very bad decision."[2]

T stands for *T*ruth. The underlying principle of journalism is to find the truth. Sometimes a journalist can print information that is factually correct but wrong. Leading up to the Iraq War, journalists published stories quoting Bush administration officials saying that there were weapons of mass destruction in Iraq. The Bush administration proved to be wrong. Yet the allegations of weapons of mass destruction disseminated by the press led the American people to support the war. Quoting an official saying something makes the statement factually correct (the official did say it) but not necessarily true. Journalists should aim for the truth and avoid being taken in by politicians, government officials, publicists, and advocacy groups.

H stands for *H*arm. Journalists have the power to ruin lives. They must take into account the tremendous power of the press and their ability to inflict harm. Few people read the corrections that are buried on page 2. The damage done by publishing incorrect information often lives on because of the initial exposure on page 1. The same is true when arrests make page 1 and acquittals are published on B-19—in a single column next to a display ad. Journalists should avoid harming a person's reputation without a compelling reason.

I stands for *I*nvestigating. All good reporting is investigative. Journalists must probe for the truth and confirm information from more than one source. Too often, television commentators speculate without verifying information. They rush into a story without checking the facts. Some reporters are too cozy with sources. In the buildup to the Iraq War, many reporters accepted on face value the inaccuracies the Bush administration said about Saddam Hussein and Iraq. Reporters must be on guard to keep from being manipulated by public officials and public relations executives whose goal is to spin a story and steer journalists away from the truth.

C stands for *C*odes of ethics. All major news organizations have codes of ethics. The Society of Professional Journalists and the Radio-Television News Directors Association have published codes, too. These codes are a good starting point for understanding journalistic ethics. Professionals can refer to them

[2]http://news.enquirer.com/apps/pbcs.dll/article?AID=/20070223/EDIT01/302230056, accessed March 5, 2007.

in the field. They make great training guides for students and beginning reporters.

S stands for *S*ituational ethics. It is important to approach ethical issues on a case-by-case basis. Conflicts often occur when one ethical standard conflicts with another. A news organization may have a policy against using unnamed sources, but a situation may arise when it is necessary not to print the name of a source. The same holds true with printing the names of accusers in sexual-offense cases.

In the Kobe Bryant case, some news organizations chose to print the name of the accuser; others did not. The criminal charges against Bryant were eventually dropped. The case of the Duke University lacrosse team has also raised the question about printing the name of the accuser and her background. Members of the Duke University lacrosse team (Figure 8-3) were vilified by a prosecutor who faced an ethics complaint against him, filed by the North Carolina Bar Association, for his handling of the case. The prosecutor, Michael Nifong, was disbarred as a result of his actions. All charges against the lacrosse players were dropped after the state attorney general intervened and dismissed the case.

FIGURE 8-3
When members of the Duke University lacrosse team were accused of raping a woman, a variety of ethical issues came into play, including the conduct of the prosecutor. (iStockphoto.com #1273980, Strickle).

169

You Decide

Using the E*T*H*I*C*S rubric, come up with possible solutions to the following ethical problems journalists might face:

- What kind of information do you think belongs or doesn't belong in an obituary? Would you include information about a juvenile arrest for a prominent person in your community who has died in his eighties? Would you include that the cause of death was AIDS or syphilis if family members don't want that information revealed? Would you publish that someone has committed suicide if the death occurred in a public place or a private home?
- Do you think the name of the woman who accused the Duke University lacrosse team should have been released? Do you think the name of Kobe Bryant's accuser should have been released?
- When are reporters too cozy with their sources? Do you think that reporters sometimes get too close to the people they are covering? When NBC anchor Brian Williams visited Iraq in March 2007, he mainly reported through the eyes of U.S. sources, saying it was too dangerous to talk to Iraqis. Does only interviewing Americans present a skewed version of the news?

With an understanding of E*T*H*I*C*S, it is now important to examine some of the issues journalists face in their professional lives.

TRIAL BY PRESS

Trial by press has become a major issue. In the United States, two systems of justice have emerged: trial by jury and trial by press. Before a suspect is even arrested, commentators pass judgment on the person's guilt or innocence. The press coverage in some instances borders on libel and invasion of privacy. The damage done to the innocent can never be repaired. The damage done to the public—which gets caught up in the media maelstrom—results in the press losing trust and credibility. Instead of investigating, journalists rely on speculation and unnamed sources, whose credibility can't be challenged because of their anonymity.

The saga of John Mark Karr is a case in point. For a few weeks in August 2006, he dominated the news as the self-confessed killer of JonBenet Ramsey. From the moment of his publicized arrest in Thailand, the pale and histrionic Karr played the press. He told reporters in Thailand that he was present at JonBenet Ramsey's death and that he had a long e-mail correspondence with Michael Tracey, a journalism professor at the University of Colorado who tipped off the police. According to *The New York Times*, "the arrest generated almost as much news media attention as JonBenet's killing at her family home in Boulder on December 26, 1996."[3]

Once the story broke, a slew of experts and former friends, family members, and associates of Karr psychoanalyzed the suspect and speculated on national television about his probable guilt. Some even swore they saw him in Boulder, Colorado, the week of the crime, although the police were never able to prove that.

The upshot of the case was that the district attorney spent tens of thousands of dollars to transport Karr from Thailand to Colorado, the media spent countless hours reporting this new break in the Ramsey case, and the public was whipped up into a frenzy about Karr. But DNA testing proved negative, and the case collapsed like a house of cards.

The media seemed to have forgotten the lessons learned from Richard Jewell and Gary Condit. Jewell, a security guard at the Atlanta Olympics in 1996, found himself the center of media attention after he alerted authorities about

---

[3]Mindy Sink, "Prosecutor Defends Actions after Ramsey Case Falls Apart," *The New York Times*, August 30, 2006, A-16.

a suspicious knapsack that turned out to be a bomb at Centennial Olympic Park. At first Jewell was praised for his alertness, then FBI suspicion turned to him. Several news organizations, including NBC News, mistakenly linked Jewell to the bombing based on information leaked by police sources. Jewell was never charged with the crime, and nine years later Eric Rudolph confessed to the bombing, which killed one person and injured 111 others. The security guard was mistakenly vilified instead of being lauded as a hero.

In the spring of 2001, California Representative Gary Condit found himself in the center of a media whirlwind related to the disappearance and death of Chandra Levy, a former Federal Bureau of Prisons intern. Because the congressman had had an affair with Levy, which at first he had denied, the media pounced on Condit and treated him like a suspect although he was never formally charged or linked to Levy's disappearance and death, which was later declared a homicide and never solved. The affair and subsequent publicity cost Condit his congressional seat. An example of how the press smeared Condit can be found in the slander suit Condit filed against writer Dominick Dunne and *Vanity Fair* magazine. According to Wikipedia:

> In March 2005, a settlement for an undisclosed amount of cash was reached between Condit and *Vanity Fair* writer Dominick Dunne. Condit initiated the suit against Dunne in a New York federal court in late 2002 for $11 million, claiming that statements made by Dunne about Condit slandered him. The comments indicated that Condit ordered the death of missing Modesto intern Chandra Levy in 2001. Condit's attorney said the defamation lawsuit was based on comments Dunne repeated on national radio and television programs in December 2001 where he suggested Condit frequented Middle Eastern embassies for sexual activity with prostitutes, and during those times, he made it clear that he wanted someone to get rid of Chandra Levy. Dunne said he had been "completely hoodwinked" by an unreliable informant.[4]

Yet the damage linking Condit to Middle Eastern embassies, prostitutes, and Levy's death was done. Furthermore, some observers believe the attention the press paid to Condit distracted the nation from the real threat from the Middle East—the terrorists who attacked the World Trade Center and Pentagon on September 11, 2001. Media fascination with sensational sex scandals (the Duke

[4]http://en.wikipedia.org/wiki/Gary_Condit, accessed March 8, 2007.

171

lacrosse team, Gary Condit, John Marc Karr) and celebrity foibles (Brittany Spears, Paris Hilton, Nicole Richie) take precious news time away from examining vital issues. These stories are sideshows that fade in time like the foibles of Madonna, Monica Lewinsky, and Michael Jackson.

INFOTAINMENT

The rise of infotainment, journalism that aims to entertain rather than inform, has damaged the credibility of the press. Instead of focusing on public affairs and social issues and serving as the watchdog of democracy, the press serves as a lapdog for publicists pushing the latest fad, craze, or celebrity. Serious news has been replaced by "news you can use," and editors with tabloid tastes seem to be setting the news agenda. Coverage of city hall has been pushed aside. In its place, newspapers are publishing more "soft news" stories about lifestyles and entertainment. Ellen Humes, an Annenberg fellow, has warned that newspapers copying the tabloids may be losing their most important consumer group—"people who want news as opposed to those simply looking for entertaining background noise." Television news with its emphasis on crime coverage follows the old adage, "If it bleeds, it leads."[5]

The cable news networks turned the deaths of Nicole Brown Simpson and Anna Nicole Smith into running soap operas with shows like *Larry King Live* mixing information with entertainment. The strain of sensationalistic coverage dates to Penny Press of the 1830s and the era of "yellow journalism" at the turn of the 20th century. Joseph Pulitzer and William Randolph Hearst were known for developing a journalism that spread "death, dishonor, and disaster" over page one and proffered a news mix of sex, murder, and sensationalism along with self-promotion. Both Pulitzer and Hearst established floating newsrooms in ships at sea to cover the Spanish American War.[6]

Many of today's television talk show hosts have revived this formula. James Fallows, in *Breaking the News*, criticized the weekend news shows for reducing commentary to shouting matches. Even Jon Stewart, the host of Comedy Central's *The Daily Show*, said that enough was enough when he chastised CNN for trivializing the news. In many instances, serious discussion has been reduced

---

[5]Robert G. Picard and Jeffrey Brody, *The Newspaper Publishing Industry* (Boston: Allyn & Bacon, 1997), p. 139.

[6]Joseph R. Dominick, *The Dynamics of Mass Communications* (New York: McGraw-Hill, 2007), p. 84.

to shtick. Instead of cogent analysis, Bernard Goldberg, author of *Bias*, and Eric Alterman, author of *What Liberal Media?*, resort to rhetorical flourishes and hyperbole when attacking each other's views. Referring to Goldberg and Ann Coulter, whom he described as a "blonde, bombshell pundit," Alterman said in the introduction to *What Liberal Media?*: "It's amazing neither one thought to accuse 'liberals' of using the blood of conservative children for extra flavor in their soy milk decaf lattes."[7] Goldberg compared his treatment at CBS to being whacked by a Mafia don (or Dan Rather in this case). Coulter and others like her have built their reputations by being outrageous rather than ethical.

This shtick dominates contemporary American discourse, both on the right and on the left as personified by Coulter and Al Franken, Dennis Miller and Michael Moore, Michelle Malkin, and Alterman. It personifies itself in hyperbole, sarcasm, and personal attacks. It thrives on satire and irony. The goal is to be glib and attract attention to the writer's cleverness rather than argument. Shtick is the opposite of ethical communication and an anathema to a journalism that seeks truth and understanding. Shtick does little to engage people in deeper meaning. It is mostly gimmick bereft of content.

MAKING UP STORIES

The credibility of journalists has also been damaged by several prominent cases of plagiarism, which is when writers either copy or make up stories that are outright lies or ones that stretch the facts. Journalism students from Columbia University exposed a phony story about "monkey fishing" in the Florida Keys that was published by *Slate Magazine*. The fictitious yarn was about how fishermen cast for monkeys on one of the Keys. The story, written by Jay Forman and published in 2001, was retracted in February 2007, after Forman confessed that the entire story was untrue.[8]

The most egregious example of making up a story occurred in 1980 when Janet Cooke of *The Washington Post* published a story about "Jimmy," an eight-year-old heroin addict. The story was so compelling that readers wanted to help Jimmy, and the judges of the Pulitzer Prize awarded Cooke journalism's highest honor for her gripping and poignant story about the child addict. The paper was forced to return the prize after Cooke was unable to locate Jimmy for her editors. She later admitted that she had made up the story, and that Jimmy did not exist.

[7]www.whatliberalmedia.com/intro.pdf, accessed May 27, 2007.
[8]www.slate.com/id/109707, accessed March 9, 2007.

The list of journalists caught fabricating stories and columns includes Jason Blair of *The New York Times*, Stephen Glass of *The New Republic*, Jack Kelley of *USA Today*, and Patricia Smith and Mike Barnicle of *The Boston Globe*. These journalists held positions at prestigious publications and coveted spots as national correspondents, foreign correspondents, and columnists.

Blair disgraced journalism by using material from other reporters, making up facts, pretending to be covering stories outside New York, and misquoting sources. Blair's misdeeds contributed to the resignation of the two top editors at *The New York Times*—editor Howell Raines and managing editor Gerald Boyd—and damaged the news organization's reputation as the country's paper of record. *The New York Times* launched an in-depth investigation into Blair's work and published a lengthy report about his plagiarism and fabrications of at least three dozen articles, including the following example:

> In this article about black comic book heroes, Mr. Blair appears to have used material from an article published several weeks earlier in *Metro Times*, an alternative weekly newspaper in Detroit. For example, in *The Metro Times*, Sarah Klein, a staff writer, quoted Kenjji, an African-American creator of comic books, as saying, "I collected comics as a kid, but I was consistently disappointed, because I didn't find myself represented." Mr. Blair wrote that Kenjji said, "I collected comics as a kid, but I was constantly disappointed by the fact that I did not find myself represented."
>
> Mr. Blair includes quotations and paraphrases from Kenjji throughout the article. Kenjji's manager and partner, Kito S. Jumanne, said in a telephone interview that Mr. Blair did not interview Kenjji.[9]

Glass made up six stories and fabricated parts of 21 others.[10] Glass received notoriety and became the subject of a film, *Shattered Glass*, which documented his deceptions. They often bordered on the fanciful. A story about a teenage hacker shaking down a Silicon Valley firm led to his downfall when a reporter for *Forbes Digital Tool* found no evidence of the hacker's existence or the firm he supposedly worked for. Glass tried to cover his lies by forging documents, building a phony website, and printing phony press releases.[11]

[9]Query.nytimes.com/gst/fullpage.html?res=9806E3D71F39F932A25755C0A9659C8B, accessed May 27, 2007.
[10]Robert Neuwirth, "Through a Glass Darkly: Magazine Pays Piper for Stories Lax on Facts, Chock Full of Fiction," *Editor & Publisher*, New York, June 20, 1998, p. 4.
[11]Ibid.

Kelley, who was *USA Today*'s star correspondent, fabricated and plagiarized at least 20 articles for more than a decade, including interviews with Elian Gonzalez's father in Cuba (Elian Gonzalez is the little boy whose mother brought him from Cuba to the United States in 1999, causing an international furor when his father in Cuba wanted him returned to Cuba) and a visit to Osama bin Laden's terrorist camps in Afghanistan. The newspaper launched an investigation into his activities and determined that Kelley had lifted more than 100 passages from other articles without credit.[12]

Both Smith and Barnicle, two accomplished writers, could not account for characters and items published in their columns. Smith was "forced to quit after admitting she had fabricated characters in four of her columns."[13] Barnicle published unattributed jokes from George Carlin and resigned after questions arose about whether he had fabricated characters in a column.[14] That these prominent journalists at established news organizations crossed ethical lines and carried on their deceptions for years, in some cases more than a decade, raises serious questions about the credibility of the press. The first principle of journalism is accuracy. Every story should be factual and factually correct. There is no place for plagiarism and no place for fiction in a news story. These scandals damaged the reputations of the writers' respective news organizations and cost some editors their jobs. With each revelation, the public loses confidence in journalism, and the critics who aim to stifle the press and smear news organizations gain credence.

CBS news anchor Dan Rather lost his job after he broadcast a story about President Bush's service in the National Guard during the Vietnam War. The story was based on fake documents that turned out to be forgeries. Rather rose to prominence reporting about President Kennedy's assassination in 1963 and fell from grace for a mistake uncovered by conservative bloggers. He resigned as anchor of the *CBS Evening News*, and four other employees were terminated after an independent panel found they "had failed to follow basic journalistic principles in the preparation and reporting of the piece."[15] Embarrassed CBS chairman Leslie Moonves said, "We deeply regret the disservice this flawed *60*

[12]Jacques Steinberg, "Panel Says Poor Standards Allowed Deception at *USA Today*," *The New York Times*, April 23, 2004, A-16.
[13]www.cnn.com/US/9808/19/barnicle, accessed March 10, 2007.
[14]Ibid.
[15]www.cbsnews.com/stories/2005/01/10/national/main665727.shtml, accessed March 18, 2007.

Minutes Wednesday report did to the American public, which has a right to count on CBS News for fairness and accuracy."[16] This illustrates not only how Net journalists can serve as a check on the mainstream press but also the power of the Internet and its impact on reporting.

You Decide

The Internet also has raised questions about how ethical journalists should handle graphic and lurid images that can be posted for dissemination around the world. As an exercise, analyze the following from an ethical point of view:

- What are the standards for printing images of the dead?
- What are the standards for printing images of injured civilians and soldiers?

- Are terrorists who display pictures of beheadings on the Internet using the media?
- Should the media have shown the complete footage of Saddam Hussein's execution?
- Should the media have shown the complete footage of Daniel Pearl's execution?
- Do news photographers take advantage of people's suffering during times of disaster and tragedy?
- Should news organizations display pictures of grief?

176

The world has become a trickier place for professional journalists. Journalists working for the mainstream media face increasing pressure from citizen journalists and bloggers on the Net as well as from organizations willing to publish images and information once considered taboo. Easy access to information from around the world has placed pressure on traditional media gatekeepers who often have to make instantaneous decisions in a 24/7 news cycle. The time for reflection has been cut down in an age where the cable news networks and news websites compete to be first with a scoop. Furthermore, some organizations for political purposes exploit the easy accessibility of publishing on the Internet and put out propaganda that can be viewed with a simple mouse click.

On September 11, 2001, the cameras of the world's media focused on the Pentagon and World Trade Center. Instantaneous footage of the collapse of the towers and the attack on the Pentagon appeared live on television. As the trade towers burned, some of the trapped either jumped or fell to their deaths on the

[16]Ibid.

sidewalks below. Journalists covering the scene saw the bodies on the ground, but they kept them out of the viewer's site. They followed the principle that pictures of the dead should not be broadcast live for fear of traumatizing their friends and family. Journalists also avoid publishing gruesome photographs for shock value and to show respect for the decedent's family. When a Pennsylvania state official called a news conference, then stuck a handgun in his mouth and committed suicide before an audience of photojournalists, newspapers avoided printing the most gruesome photographs, although the complete death sequence moved on the wires. Journalists must ask themselves if there is a compelling reason for the public to see such images. For a discussion about visual ethics, please refer to Paul Lester's analysis of the topic in the text's website.

Such is the case with a December 8, 2006, story in *The New York Times* about medical students learning about how medicine is practiced in Cuba. *The Times* published a picture of students peering at a cadaver whose flesh looked like it had been peeled off and whose chest had been split open. In a story about medical training, where a variety of photographic opportunities were available, displaying a picture of a cadaver borders on the gratuitous and the sensational.

FIGURE 8-4
Images of war and the war dead are often controlled by governments seeking to emphasize primarily positive news. (iStockphoto.com #981928, Curtis J. Morley.)

Showing pictures of the dead and wounded in war is more debatable. How far should journalists go in witnessing historic events? Battlefield photographers accompanied troops during the American Civil War. The awesome destruction that occurs in war demands coverage. Yet there is always a tension between reporting the truth and sanitizing the images of war. Governments attempt to control the type of images released to the public for fear that the utter brutality of war (Figure 8-4) would undermine morale at the home front and be overwhelming to civilians. In World War II, the Roosevelt administration at first censored pictures of American war dead. The first picture of fallen American soldiers was published in *Life Magazine* in 1943. It was a photograph of three soldiers lying face down on a New Guinea beach. No blood or open wounds were visible, and the tide had washed away their footprints and all other vestiges of the battle.

Iconic images of the Vietnam War include the point-blank execution of a Viet Cong suspect by a South Vietnamese general, a naked girl running in agony after being injured in a Napalm bomb attack (Figure 8-5), and the burning of villages by American soldiers. It has been argued that these images helped turn American public opinion against the war.

FIGURE 8-5
Many feel that this iconic, Pulitzer Prize photo taken in 1972 by Nick Ut of a girl, Kim Phuc, struck by napalm during the Vietnam War caused the nation to turn against the war. (Nick Ut, AP/World Wide Photos.)

In the Persian Gulf War and the Iraq War, the government attempted to control the movement of journalists and was quite successful by isolating them in the Persian Gulf War and embedding them in the Iraq War. Both strategies played into the government's public relations hand. Later, critics argued that the Bush administration was sanitizing the Iraq War by not even allowing photographs of flag-draped coffins. As the Iraq War continued, the press became more assertive and images of American soldiers in combat and victims of suicide bombings appeared on the front pages of newspapers and on newscasts.

These images sometimes raised the ire of the military. When *The New York Times* published a picture of a dying soldier on January 29, 2007, Lieutenant General Raymond T. Odierno, the commander of coalition troops, wrote to the newspapers and complained that the news organization had violated an agreement against publishing casualty photos without the prior written consent of the service member. Furthermore Odierno expressed concern about the impact of the picture on the soldier's family:

> What is disturbing to me personally and, more important, to the family of the soldier depicted in the photograph and the video, is that the young man who so valiantly gave his life in the service of others was displayed for the entire world to see in the gravest condition and in such a fashion as to elicit horror at its sight.
>
> This photograph will be the last of this man that his family will ever see. Further, it will cause unnecessary worry among the families of other soldiers who fear that the last they see of their loved ones will be in a *New York Times* photograph lying grievously wounded and dying.[17]

Images of Americans injured or killed in combat, as well as hostages beheaded, have been posted on the World Wide Web for propaganda purposes. The beheading of American journalist Daniel Pearl and American hostage Nicholas Berg by Islamic terrorists posed a problem for mainstream journalists.

---

[17]Raymond T. Odierno, "Letter to the Editor," *The New York Times*, February 3, 2007, A-26.

Once the video of the barbaric execution was posted on the Internet, media outlets throughout the world had the choice of broadcasting the footage in its entirety or selectively editing it. Editors had to decide how much of the material they should use. Most chose to report about the event but to delete the most gruesome aspects of the footage. However, the images were available to anyone with access to the Internet. There is no question that these images were posted to instill fear and gain a propaganda victory for terrorists.

The same problem arose with the execution of Saddam Hussein (Figure 8-6). There was an official video and a second video shot apparently by a cell phone camera that showed the entire hanging. American networks stopped short of showing Hussein's body dropping—but some websites posted the complete cell phone coverage of the execution.[18] In the Internet era, journalists have to be vigilant about maintaining ethical standards even if they face competition from news sources that don't share the same principles.

The Dart Center for Journalism and Trauma (www.dartcenter.org), based at the University of Washington, provides a number of services for journalists, students, and educators to address the various issues and responsibilities that impact journalists who are covering a hot-button story or tragedy. Included in the resources that the Dart Center offers are booklets such as "Covering Children and Trauma: A Guide for Journalism Professionals," "Child Clinicians & the Media: A Guide for Therapists," and "Tragedies and Journalists: A Guide for More Effective Coverage."

A key section of "Tragedies and Journalists" makes this observation:

> Journalists face unusual challenges when covering violent or mass tragedies. They face the possibility of being a first responder to a violent event. They interact with victims dealing with extraordinary grief. Journalists who cover any "blood-and-guts" beat often build a needed and appropriate wall between themselves and the survivors and other witnesses they interview. But after reporters

FIGURE 8-6

Many media observers felt that the media exercised poor judgment in showing graphic images of the execution of Saddam Hussein, shown here not at his execution but on Iraqi currency. (iStockphoto.com #1217445, Nicholas Belton.)

---

[18]topics.nytimes.com/top/reference/timestopic/people/c/bill_carter/index.html?offset=60& 48k, accessed May 27, 2007.

talk with people who have suffered great loss, the same wall may impede the need of journalists to react to their own exposure to tragedy.[19]

Later in the booklet, the authors, Joe Hight, who covered victims of the Oklahoma City bombing for *The Oklahoman* in 1995, and Frank Smyth, the Washington representative of the Committee to Protect Journalists, add, "Ethical issues include the question of whether to provide aid to injured victims or help in the evacuation before emergency responders arrive. Simply doing your job and ignoring the victim's plight might be considered morally wrong by the public."[20] Indeed, many observers have wondered why a news photographer would take a picture of a person in distress rather than helping, but others would disagree, saying the picture had to be taken to let the public know what was going on.

How a local, national, or global tragedy is reported weighs heavily on the consciences of journalists, and organizations such as the Dart Center exist to provide guidance and support as well as to raise important questions about journalistic integrity.

CODE OF ETHICS

In summary, let's look at the principles that have been adopted by the Society of Professional Journalists. The SPJ Code of Ethics offers guidance for journalists confronted with ethical problems:

> **Preamble** Members of the Society of Professional Journalists believe that public enlightenment is the forerunner of justice and the foundation of democracy. The duty of the journalist is to further those ends by seeking truth and providing a fair and comprehensive account of events and issues. Conscientious journalists from all media and specialties strive to serve the public with thoroughness and honesty. Professional integrity is the cornerstone of a journalist's credibility. Members of the Society share a dedication to ethical behavior and adopt this code to declare the Society's principles and standards of practice.

[19]Joe Hight and Frank Smyth, "Tragedies & Journalists," The Dart Center, Department of Communication, The University of Washington, 2004, pp. 3–4.
[20]Ibid., p. 31.

Seek Truth and Report It Journalists should be honest, fair and courageous in gathering, reporting and interpreting information. Journalists should:
- —Test the accuracy of information from all sources and exercise care to avoid inadvertent error. Deliberate distortion is never permissible.
- —Diligently seek out subjects of news stories to give them the opportunity to respond to allegations of wrongdoing.
- —Identify sources whenever feasible. The public is entitled to as much information as possible on sources' reliability.
- —Always question sources' motives before promising anonymity. Clarify conditions attached to any promise made in exchange for information. Keep promises.
- —Make certain that headlines, news teases and promotional material, photos, video, audio, graphics, sound bites and quotations do not misrepresent. They should not oversimplify or highlight incidents out of context.
- —Never distort the content of news photos or video. Image enhancement for technical clarity is always permissible. Label montages and photo illustrations.
- —Avoid misleading reenactments or staged news events. If reenactment is necessary to tell a story, label it.
- —Avoid undercover or other surreptitious methods of gathering information except when traditional open methods will not yield information vital to the public. Use of such methods should be explained as part of the story.
- —Never plagiarize.
- —Tell the story of the diversity and magnitude of the human experience boldly, even when it is unpopular to do so.
- —Examine their own cultural values and avoid imposing those values on others.
- —Avoid stereotyping by race, gender, age, religion, ethnicity, geography, sexual orientation, disability, physical appearance or social status.
- —Support the open exchange of views, even views they find repugnant.
- —Give voice to the voiceless; official and unofficial sources of information can be equally valid.
- —Distinguish between advocacy and news reporting. Analysis and commentary should be labeled and not misrepresent fact or context.
- —Distinguish news from advertising and shun hybrids that blur the lines between the two.

—Recognize a special obligation to ensure that the public's business is conducted in the open and that government records are open to inspection.

Minimize Harm Ethical journalists treat sources, subjects and colleagues as human beings deserving of respect. Journalists should:

—Show compassion for those who may be affected adversely by news coverage. Use special sensitivity when dealing with children and inexperienced sources or subjects.

—Be sensitive when seeking or using interviews or photographs of those affected by tragedy or grief.

—Recognize that gathering and reporting information may cause harm or discomfort. Pursuit of the news is not a license for arrogance.

—Recognize that private people have a greater right to control information about themselves than do public officials and others who seek power, influence or attention. Only an overriding public need can justify intrusion into anyone's privacy.

—Show good taste. Avoid pandering to lurid curiosity.

—Be cautious about identifying juvenile suspects or victims of sex crimes.

—Be judicious about naming criminal suspects before the formal filing of charges.

—Balance a criminal suspect's fair trial rights with the public's right to be informed.

Act Independently Journalists should be free of obligation to any interest other than the public's right to know. Journalists should:

—Avoid conflicts of interest, real or perceived.

—Remain free of associations and activities that may compromise integrity or damage credibility.

—Refuse gifts, favors, fees, free travel and special treatment, and shun secondary employment, political involvement, public office and service in community organizations if they compromise journalistic integrity.

—Disclose unavoidable conflicts.

—Be vigilant and courageous about holding those with power accountable.

—Deny favored treatment to advertisers and special interests and resist their pressure to influence news coverage.

—Be wary of sources offering information for favors or money; avoid bidding for news.

Be Accountable Journalists are accountable to their readers, listeners, viewers and each other. Journalists should:

—Clarify and explain news coverage and invite dialogue with the public over journalistic conduct.

—Encourage the public to voice grievances against the news media.

—Admit mistakes and correct them promptly.

—Expose unethical practices of journalists and the news media.

—Abide by the same high standards to which they hold others.

Reprinted by permission from the Society of Professional Journalists, www.spj. org. Copyright © 1996–2007 by the Society of Professional Journalists.

In the next chapter, written by Brian Gross, we will be taking a look at new media from an ethical perspective. Some of the lessons learned from journalism will apply because much of the content used by new media outlets is derived from journalistic sources or journalistic methods.

CHAPTER 9
Ethics and New Media

By Brian Gross

In 2006, it was estimated that around 1 billion unique individuals the world over used the Internet.[1] They had the option to visit, create, or contribute to what is estimated to be more than 200 billion web pages,[2] not to mention the option to participate in untold real-time text, audio, and video chats. On top of that are the billions upon billions of e-mails sent and received day in and day out. This revolution in information and communication has taken a scant decade to reach from its entry into the consumer market to this level of penetration and has the potential for ever-greater integration into whatever corners of and activities in the world that it hasn't yet reached.

Before we look into the numerous ethical conundrums swirling in the Internet, it's important to look at how and why the Internet developed, and what perceptions have since formed about it. J. C. R. Licklider of MIT is credited with giving the first description of what would become the Internet in August 1962 while discussing his "Galactic Network" concept. He described a globally interconnected set of computers through which each computer could quickly access data and programs from any other computer.[3] The Internet itself, therefore, was intended from the beginning as a neutral mechanism—a medium, not a message. It's like ink and paper. Any person can take up the pen and write

---

[1] "How Big Is the Internet?" About.com, March 4, 2007, http://netforbeginners.about.com/cs/technoglossary/f/FAQ3.htm.

[2] "What Is the Invisible Web?" About.com, March 4, 2007, http://netforbeginners.about.com/cs/secondaryweb1/a/secondaryweb.htm.

[3] Internet Society, www.isoc.org/Internet/history/brief.shtml, accessed March 18, 2007.

186

FIGURE 9-1
The invention of the printing press in 1450 began the media explosion that has now expanded to new media all over the world. (iStockphoto. com #3116620, Anna Pustovaya.)

whatever he or she wants on the paper. But although the Internet medium is, like ink and paper, neutral, it is also potentially universal and instantaneous, which can't exactly be said about the ink and paper.

When Johannes Gutenberg invented the printing press (Figure 9-1) in 1450, ink and paper, of course, took on a more universal tone, so much so that the king of England enacted the Licensing Act of 1662, which allowed for the seizure of printed materials considered to be hostile to the church or government.[4] But the paradigm shift from the written word to the printed word, though extremely significant, will probably take a back seat in the history books to the shift that we are still now traversing between the printed word and the digitized word (a shift that is happening much more quickly than did the shift from the written to printed word).

The Internet not only allows ideas to be communicated much more widely and cheaply than does the printing press, but it allows for them be disseminated almost instantaneously. Take, as an example, the 74-second "Hillary 1984" video posted on YouTube.com on March 5, 2007. The video, an altered version of the Apple ad run during the 1984 Super Bowl (and never again, because George Orwell's estate sent a "cease and desist" letter to Apple for infringing on the author's book *1984*[5]) to introduce the Macintosh computer, was watched more that 100,000 times in just 2 days.[6] In no time it was the lead political story of the week across the United States.

[4]"A History of Copyright," www.intellectual-property.gov.uk/resources/copyright/history .htm, accessed April 1, 2007.

[5]Peter Cohen, "Obama Video Not Funny, Says '1984' Owner," www.pcworld.com/article/ id,130222-c,copyright/article.html, accessed April 1, 2007.

[6]Carla Marinucci, "Intrigue Grows over 'Hillary' Video," *The San Francisco Chronicle*, March 20, 2007, http://sfgate.com/cgi-bin/article.cgi?f=/c/a/2007/03/20/MNG0UOOA1Q1.DTL, accessed April 1, 2007.

The video's creator, Phillip de Vellis (who initially posted his creation anonymously as ParkRidge47), claims he didn't expect the video to gain such a mass audience: "I'm really stunned by the attention it got. I thought it was pretty cool when I did it and that it would get passed around on some progressive blogs. But I had no idea it would be shown on TV."[7] Be that as it may, the fact is that while most of what is posted openly on the Web does remain obscured among the hundreds of billions of other pages, it has the potential to "go viral." And what are the consequences? Phillip de Vellis says, "I'll leave that to other people to decide."[8]

The difference between a sheet of paper and the Internet can be seen, in some ways, like the difference between a knife and a gun—with all the intrinsic ethical controversies intact. Both can cause *H*arm, but, depending on the *S*ituation, one is capable of much more damage, much more quickly than the other. I could write something defamatory or inaccurate on a piece of paper and drop the paper in a busy pedestrian thoroughfare, or I could post the same defamatory or inaccurate bit of information on a website. There is the potential for both to cause great and irrevocable damage, but which medium is more powerful—the knife or the gun? Or, like the National Rifle Association says, is it as simple as "guns don't kill people, people kill people"? Therefore, should no greater efforts to regulate the Internet be made than there are efforts to regulate paper and ink? And are there specific ethical concerns that apply to the Internet that don't apply elsewhere, simply because of the nature of the medium?

This is where we step from the neutral reality of the Internet to the question of how the Internet is perceived. When the Internet first entered the mainstream, in the late 1990s, it was seen as a great leveler, allowing individuals or minority dissenting opinions the possibility to reach the kind of audience that had hitherto been reserved for mass media alone. A great number of books and scholarly articles have been written about the free Internet commons, where all ideas can mix equally—and how they should be protected from being controlled or altered by the interests of big business and government.

---

[7] Chris Cillizza, "Creator of Hillary Attack Ad Speaks," http://blog.washingtonpost.com/thefix/2007/03/author_of_hillary_attack_ad_sp.html, accessed April 1, 2007.
[8] Ibid.

When Licklider's "Galactic Network" concept took its first steps in 1965 (with the telephone line connection of a computer in Massachusetts with a computer in California) and as it developed more and more connections through the 1970s and 1980s, the first incarnations of the Internet were, by necessity, used mostly to convey scholarly information between academic institutions. Big universities were, by and large, the only entities to possess the computers, skilled personnel, and facilities capable of providing Internet service. And the Internet could have stayed within this rarefied milieu—with essentially only computer specialists using it for their own purposes. But then, in stepped the long arm of the law. In 1985, the U.S. National Science Foundation offered funding of Internet projects on university campuses, but with the explicit caveat that "the connection must be made available to *all* qualified users on campus." In other words, social science departments had to have the same access as computer science . . . and physical education, for that matter.[9]

Of course, this move by the U.S. federal government didn't *require* that this nascent Internet be freely available. Those who wanted access to government money, however, had to provide free access. In this way, although the Internet can function as a mass media reaching a mass audience, like radio and television, it has not developed with the same commercial content model or public perception as did radio and television. Its development is perceived to be more like that of the telephone, where the use of and content passing through the medium is, for the most part, determined by the medium's users, not by the corporations that provide the service.

Certainly many would take issue if telephone service providers arbitrarily—or even systematically—interfered with their customers' ability to call whomever they wished whenever they wished. Even greater would be the outcry if the telephone company somehow put a filter on the words or ideas that could be uttered over the phone. Yet this is exactly, as you will see, what has happened and what continues to happen in many instances on the Internet.

Similarly, television and radio stations would be deluged with complaints and lawsuits if everyone who wanted to were allowed to speak their piece on the air; yet this kind of thing happens all the time on the Internet. Take, for example, the April 2007 flap that occurred when New York shock jock Don Imus (Figure 9-2) called the Rutgers women's basketball team "nappy-headed hos," as discussed in a different context in Chapter 7. The outcry was immediate and

[9]www.isoc.org/Internet/history/brief.shtml, Internet Society, accessed March 18, 2007.

deafening, resulting in the end of the decades-long CBS career of the radio veteran. Yet the Internet is chockfull of content far more abrasive, including, for example, an 11-inch tall, plush, white-furred teddy bear, sold by cafepress.com, wearing a T-shirt emblazoned boldly with the phrase that proved to be Imus' death knell. The product description innocuously reads: "Our plush bear is a cutie in his own message-bearing t-shirt and festive red ribbon. He's a great gift for Valentine's Day, baby showers, birthdays, get well-wishes, a pair of wedding bears, or any reason you dream up. Put a smile on someone's face. Just grin and bear it!"[10]

FIGURE 9-2

That radio personality Don Imus called the Rutgers' women's basketball team "nappy-headed hos" resulted in an Internet media frenzy that almost ended Imus's broadcasting career. (Globe Photos, Inc.)

189

You Decide

Because content on the Internet can reach a mass audience, should decisions about what to put up or allow on the Internet be based on the same ethical standards as those used for traditional mass media, such as radio and television? Should the same standards be applied to all sites on the Internet? If not, on what basis should these choices be made?

What do you think the result would be if a brick-and-mortar gift store in your town were to stock a white bear wearing a T-shirt emblazoned with the quote, "Nappy-Headed Ho"? Why do you think there has been no reaction to the bear when placed on a website? What does this say about ethical concerns on the Internet versus face-to-face encounters?

[10]"Nappy Headed Ho Clothing," www.cafepress.com/NappyHeadedHo.123453717, accessed May 1, 2007.

ETHICS OF THE INTERNET SERVICE PROVIDER (ISP)

Consumer Internet services morphed, for the most part, out of the private bulletin board system (BBS). BBSs came into being in the late 1970s and had their heyday in the early 1990s. They were privately run networks that allowed registered users (often for a fee) to sign their computers on through a phone line to download and upload files, send messages, and have real-time, text-based chats with other users. Unlike the Internet of today, BBSs were primarily a local phenomenon, since the connection phone numbers were local, and most users were not willing to incur long-distance telephone charges to connect with a distant service. Still, some BBSs, along with providing local services, also had a gateway to the Internet, through which users could send messages (electronic mail, or "e-mail") to users of other BBSs that were similarly connected to the Internet.

BBSs were mostly the result of computer hobbyists setting up these networks for no other reason than because they could (though in France, a service called Minitel, started by Telecom, the then-government-owned telephone company, came into being nationwide in 1983, and still survives today). Fees, if there were any, were typically only collected to actually cover the costs that the system operator (SysOp) incurred, such as the cost of phone lines and computer maintenance. The software used to run most BBSs was freely available, if not incredibly flexible or user-friendly. And oversight of what happened on these networks was negligible—limited to the capacity of the SysOp to respond to complaints directed by users to him or her, if any.

America Online (AOL) came into the BBS fray in 1991 (after earlier incarnations as Gameline and Quantum-Link). Essentially AOL started out as a mega-BBS that, instead of only having access numbers in one localized area, had local access numbers throughout the United States. It also provided more than the usual general fare of BBS functions, adding online games and a proprietary graphical user interface (GUI) that was much more user-friendly than typical BBS software. Instead of having to memorize or consult a list of various command codes in order to navigate through the connection, users could click intuitive graphical representations of buttons and menus.

AOL's proprietary (meaning that only paid subscribers to AOL's service could use it) GUI was a first step away from the open concept for the Internet, even though when it was introduced, AOL was essentially not yet connected to the Internet. But mainstream consumers flocked to the new GUI because of the relatively moderate learning curve required to get started.

Though many consumers were already using computers at work for word processing and spreadsheets, AOL became *the* reason for many to get a computer at home as well. Other similar services existed, such as CompuServe and Prodigy, but they didn't set entry-level users in their sights as squarely as did AOL CEO Steve Case. The result was that AOL attracted the majority of new, nontechie users, quickly becoming the leading figure in mainstream online interactions.

Having started in 1991, AOL claimed 1 million users by 1994. In November 1997, it passed 10 million members. One year later, in November 1998, AOL had reached 14 million members, and then surpassed 15 million before the end of same year. At the same time, its closest competitor, CompuServe, registered a mere 2 million users.[11]

CompuServe's service was more in line with the kind of Internet service that we are familiar with today—without a lot of proprietary content. But the Internet at the time was not nearly as robust, user-friendly, or varied as it is today. With flashing text and annoying and erratic page design elements that were there just because they could be—not, in most cases, to serve any useful or even aesthetic purpose—it's little wonder many people gravitated to the highly controlled and consistent experience that AOL created with its exclusive content. Had web developers not learned lessons from AOL about addressing the user experience, the Internet would have probably remained a chaotic, lost wasteland (and AOL would not have so precipitously lost its corner on the market as an ISP in the first few years of the new millennium). But AOL set some other precedents that raise ethical questions about the power of the Internet service provider.

POWER OF THE ISP

By the time the Internet had developed enough promise for BBSs to take the next step—from e-mail to web browsing—and become Internet service providers rather than closed networks, AOL was at the forefront and, if not calling the shots on how the Internet operated, it called its own shots and thus could single-handedly affect the nascent Internet experience for mainstream users.

[11]Internet Access: AOL Surpasses 15 Million Members; Christmas Day Makes AOL History with Record Number of New Members Signing Up: Company Business and Marketing, "Edge: Work-Group Computing Report, January 4, 1999, www.findarticles.com/p/articles/mi_m0WUB/is_1999_Jan_4/ai_53513666," accessed March 25, 2007.

AOL CEO Steve Case underlined at the time his intent to mold not just AOL's service, but also the "medium" of the Internet:

> We are gratified that so many people are embracing the Internet and choosing to go online with AOL. This record-setting growth—fueled by AOL's strong brand, unmatched content and AOL 4.0's convenience and ease-of-use—continues to accelerate the global momentum of our service and the medium.

Case added:

> We believe that an ever growing online community makes AOL even more valuable to our members. We are committed to working day and night to continue to improve the service and make it more and more essential to our members' everyday lives. For us, this is all about building a medium that we can be proud of.[12]

But many argued, and had evidence to back it up, that when Case said he was building "a medium that we can be proud of," the "we" he was referring to was AOL, not the members of the Internet commons. As an example, when AOL allowed its users access to Usenet newsgroups (Internet-based public forums arranged by topics on which users can post messages and responses) in 1994, it removed at least one newsgroup from the standard list view: "alt.aol-sucks." The newsgroup was available in the alternative description view, but was renamed "Flames and complaints about America Online."[13] AOL also blocked several "riot girl" feminist discussion forums because, as a spokeswoman said, they were afraid, with the word "girl" in the title of the forum, some girls might "go in there looking for information about their Barbies."[14]

These two examples highlight two very different ethical issues, but the same fundamental question. The "alt.aol-sucks" instance was obviously and most directly designed to protect the interests of the ISP, whereas the "riot girls" blocking could be said to be protecting the interests of an unsuspecting public. But in either case, is it right for an ISP to block or change content that is not

[12]Ibid.

[13]http://en.allexperts.com/e/a/ao/aol.htm, "AOL at AllExperts," accessed March 18, 2007.

[14]"Business Technology; No More 'Anything Goes': Cyberspace Gets Censors," http://query.nytimes.com/gst/fullpage.html?res=9C02E1DB143CF93AA15755C0A962958260, accessed April 1, 2007.

illegal? And if it does, does it have the ethical obligation to inform those who run up against these blocks or encounter this editing that the content has been blocked or edited? Or are ISPs like restaurants with a set menu? You wouldn't go to an Italian restaurant for sushi. But, rightly or wrongly, there is the impression that Internet service should be not an Italian restaurant or a Japanese restaurant. It should just be a "restaurant," where every dish, from Philippine pig's blood soup (*dinuguan*) to country biscuits and gravy, is served.

You won't find CBS airing commercials for NBC programming, nor will you find either of them running sultry dating commercials featuring cooing buxom blondes in the middle of their evening news broadcasts. Should we expect otherwise from ISPs?

As another, less direct, example—ostensibly to save on bandwidth, AOL also had the practice of recompressing many image files before they were viewed on computers that were using AOL as an ISP. The result was not only that the quality of many images was degraded, but the new image file format (.ART) was unreadable by most non-AOL applications and image software.[15]

As these examples alone illustrate, whether they take advantage of their power or not, ISPs have the capacity to dramatically alter the user's experience of the Internet—often in ways that are not readily apparent. Unless a user has another point of reference, how is he or she to know what is missing, what has been altered or added?

193

You Decide

In the case of AOL in the mid-1990s, when it controlled a huge share of the Internet market, do you think AOL had an increased ethical responsibility either to maintain an unbiased view of the contents of the Internet for its subscribers or to clearly highlight its tampering with the content?

[15]"Configuring the AOL Browser—Open Air Studios," www.openairstudios.net/aol.shtml, accessed March 18, 2007.

"FREE" INTERNET SERVICE PROVIDERS

Some ISPs have offered free Internet access, though the field has narrowed markedly, so that the only major remaining player is United Online's NetZero. Of course, there is never a free lunch—the service, like broadcast television and radio, is supported by advertising that is displayed in the toolbar or browser. When the service was first introduced in 1998, it promised unlimited dialup access. In 2001, it capped access at 40 hours per month.[16] At this writing, the service has been reduced to "up to 10 hours" of free access per household, per month.[17] But what if this "free" Internet access model were to be changed from providing unrestricted access to the Internet (with an advertisement bar and a time limit) to providing only selective Internet access? What if, when searching the Internet for a good deal on a bicycle, only sites, products, and prices from stores that had paid a fee were displayed?

Fundamentally, limiting listings to a select few is no different than what any other mass media currently does. Free local papers feature paid ads and inserts that certainly don't mention the prices that nonadvertising competitors charge for the same products. Why shouldn't free Internet access do the same?

Similarly, some city, state, and provincial governments are now gearing up to, or already do, provide free wireless Internet access in their jurisdictions. The deal that the city of San Francisco made with Earthlink (and, by extension, Google) to provide wireless Internet access throughout the city stipulates that the service must allow "users to access the lawful Internet content of their choice."[18] On the other hand, in the city of Saskatoon's plan to provide wireless Internet access, the government admits it will block adult content, gambling sites, and pages that promote hate or racism, according to Andrew Thompson, the minister responsible for information technology in the Canadian province of Saskatchewan.[19]

[16]Gwendolyn Mariano, "United Online Cuts off Some Paying Customers," cnetNews.com, http://news.com.com/United+Online+cuts+off+some+paying+customers/2100-1023_3-276540.html, accessed March 18, 2007.

[17]"Free Internet Access," http://account.netzero.net/s/landing?action=viewProduct&productId=free, accessed March 18, 2007.

[18]"Wireless Broadband Internet Access Network Agreement Between the City and County of San Francisco and Earthlink, Inc." http://www.sfgov.org/site/uploadedfiles/dtis/tech_connect/process/SanFrancisco.Wireless.Network.Areement.Final.pdf, Accessed March 18, 2007.

[19]Janet French, "Free Internet Access to Be Offered in City," www.canada.com/saskatoon starphoenix/news/story.html?id=0ecf5a1d-de77-42b2-aa59-389cc1ece9b1, accessed March 18, 2007.

Another high-visibility "free" Internet service provider in many countries is the public library system (Figures 9-3 and 9-4), where, in many cases, filtering software is used in an attempt to block objectionable content. In the United States, the Children's Internet Protection Act (CIPA), which was passed in 2000,

FIGURES 9-3 and 9-4
Libraries around the world have had to adjust to the growing demand for Internet service, by taking steps such as filtering and removing material from the Internet and book shelves that might offend certain segments of a particular community. (iStockphoto.com #100118, Kenneth C. Zirkel; iStockphoto.com #29919, Kenneth C. Zirkel.)

mandated filtering software in libraries and schools that receive government funding. The law was challenged, but in 2003 the U.S. Supreme Court upheld the provision, even though critics charged that filtering software can't possibly catch all targeted material and will likely inadvertently block nonobjectionable material. The common refrain of the opposition was that library patrons might be blocked from finding information about "breast cancer" because of possible software blocking of all pages containing the word "breast."[20]

In Canada, filtering software was added to all public library computers in the province of Ottawa in 2003, though after a different progression of events. Library workers filed a grievance asserting that their library's no-filter Internet use policy would result in staff being exposed to pornography in the workplace, making it a "hostile environment."[21]

No doubt the debate will continue and gain new nuance, limited only by the limitless human capacity to, at one end, push the limits and, at the other, pull them back.

196

You Decide

Should entities that provide Internet service for free (or those that provide it for a fee as well) spell out to users any limitations they have placed on the free flow of content from the Internet? In how much detail and in what manner? Should Saskatoon detail how, for example, it defines hate sites and how it will go about blocking them? Would a lengthy written disclaimer or explanation that users have to agree to before using the service really do anything to ameliorate this situation, especially since people usually don't read these agreements? Do you think efforts to limit sites that might offend library patrons or certain city dwellers are motivated by ethical concerns, or do you think they are motivated by other considerations, for example, a positive public image?

[20]Lisa M. Bowman, "Supreme Court Backs Library Net Filters," CNET News.com, June 23, 2003, http://news.com.com/2100-1028_3-1019952.html, accessed April 6, 2007.

[21]"Overview: The Filtering Debate in Public Libraries," www.cippic.ca/en/faqs-resources/Internet-censorship-public-libraries/#faq_filter-prevents-access, accessed April 6, 2007.

ETHICS OF GOVERNMENT INTERFERENCE

As the examples of public libraries and San Francisco's and Saskatoon's "free" Internet services illustrate, the government has the power to curtail (or at least to try to curtail) the breadth of Internet service, but it is arguably an imprecise art. Moreover, local concerns vary from locality to locality, from country to country. San Francisco's deal with Earthlink states that users should be able to access all legal content. That sounds tame enough, but in the United States, where illegal obscenity is defined locally, how do you rein in a global medium like the Internet? Will Earthlink have to block different content in the Castro, as opposed to Chinatown?

And while Minister Thompson of Saskatchewan can let it easily roll off his tongue that his government will block adult content, gambling sites, and pages promoting hate or racism, that really is quite a mouthful of fuzzy flavors. Will he block sites with information about sexually transmitted diseases, sites that offer gambling where real money is not at stake, religious sites that call homosexuality a sin? How much of an Internet will be left if the full implications of these limits are carried through?

In April of 2007, the government of Thailand blocked access to all content on the popular video site YouTube.com because it discovered a 44-second video where photos of Thailand's king were defaced. YouTube's head of global communications, Julie Supan, said: "We are disappointed that YouTube has been blocked in Thailand, and we are currently looking into the matter." She went on to state that "the Internet is an international phenomenon and while technology can bring great opportunity and access to information globally, it can also present new and unique cultural challenges."

In this instance, the challenge runs deep, as a man was jailed for 10 years in Thailand for being found guilty of defacing photos of the king in December of 2006.[22] *Not* blocking the YouTube site would not only pose cultural challenges, but it could arguably spark a dramatic legal crisis in Thailand. What is a government to do in a case like this? Request that the site remove the material? Undoubtedly similar or even more severely "illegal" material exists elsewhere among the 200 billion and growing pages on the Internet. Should the government shut down the entire Internet?

---

[22]"Thailand Blocks Access to YouTube," http://news.bbc.co.uk/2/hi/asia-pacific/6528303. stm, accessed April 6, 2007.

Should Google (the owner of YouTube) have taken down the video immediately after the Thai government asked the company to do so? There are numerous documented cases of YouTube removing other "illegal" material that, for example, violates U.S. copyright laws,[23] and in no case is copyright infringement punishable by imprisonment in the United States. So what makes Google less ready to cave to Thailand's laws against what is, to its government, a much more serious crime?

Given the fact that Google (along with Yahoo and other Internet search engines) has also agreed to create a special version of its popular search engine for China, which excludes sites that the Chinese government deems as harmful to Chinese viewers, the troubling parallels and contradictions on Google's part in this situation with the Thai government are thrown into even deeper relief. Of course, it's as easy as shooting fish in a barrel to harp on Google's record of contradictions and conundrums. As today's behemoth player on the Internet (like AOL was in the 1990s, when cyberspace wasn't nearly as sprawling as it is today), it's hard to find a cauldron of controversy in which Google isn't boiling.

In a way, Google's position with China mirrors the position Western governments find themselves in with China. And Google's rationale for continuing to interact with China, despite China's many policies that run counter to its own, also runs parallel to the rationales of Western governments. Robert B. Zoellick, the U.S. deputy secretary of state in charge of the National Committee on U.S–China Relations, stated on September 21, 2005, that "We can cooperate with the emerging China of today, even as we work for the democratic China of tomorrow."[24] It's not a stretch to compare this attitude to the kind of "appeasement" that led to the ceding of Czechoslovakia to Germany in 1938 as a result of the Munich Agreement.[25] "Don't be evil" is Google's informal corporate motto, and many question if it is living up to this motto. Jimmy Wales, chairman emeritus of the nonprofit Wikimedia Foundation and co-founder of the sprawling collaborative Internet encyclopedia project Wikipedia (which is blocked in China), said on March 8, 2007 (at a dinner at the Foreign Correspondents' Club of Japan in Tokyo), that collaborating with the Chinese government in the way Google does is "something I would never do. I think access to

---

[23]"YouTube Removing Comedy Central Clips," http://money.cnn.com/2006/10/30/technology/youtube_comedycentral, accessed April 6, 2007.

[24]"United States Urges China to Be Responsible World Citizen," http://usinfo.state.gov/eap/Archive/2005/Sep/22-290478.html, accessed April 7, 2007.

[25]"Agreement Concluded at Munich, September 29, 1938, between Germany, Great Britain, France and Italy," www.yale.edu/lawweb/avalon/imt/munich1.htm, accessed April 7, 2007.

information is a fundamental human right." But striking a conciliatory note, Wales said, "We all need to keep our eyes on" activities of major Internet players in China, to check whether they are trying to improve the environment in the country by lobbying for changes of the laws.[26]

Obviously a discussion of government interference on the Internet would be woefully incomplete without mentioning the world's most populous country, China, which indisputably has the most complicated Internet filtering systems on the Web. A majority of the filtering occurs at a lower level than the ISP—with the backbone of the Internet in China, from which ISPs make their connections to the Internet. The filtering/censoring that goes on in China at various levels is so complex, changeable, and covert that exhaustive studies done by such institutions as the Harvard Law School and the University of Toronto have found that, although there are many obvious across-the-board roadblocks, the closer they looked at the filtering, the more detailed it seemed to be. And it often changed from day-to-day.[27] It would have to change constantly in order to put and keep the kind of cap that the Chinese government appears to want to put on Internet content. Still, plenty gets through, especially to those who can exercise a little know-how and persistence to circumnavigate the filters.

China is not, by any means, the only country to put so many resources into this filtering of sexual, political, religious, and social content. The University of Toronto's Open Net Initiative lists China, Vietnam, Myanmar, Uzbekistan, Iran, Syria, and Tunisia as having "pervasive" filtering. It labels the filtering in Saudi Arabia, Yemen, and South Korea as "substantial" and places 13 other countries on its watch list, including Germany and France, who attempt to block neo-Nazi content, and the United Kingdom and Norway, for their efforts to block child pornography.[28]

With the resources and effort that must be poured into controlling the Internet (on an ongoing and escalating basis) and the decidedly mixed results of these efforts, it begs the question, why do some of these more cautious countries even allow their citizens access to the Internet at all. Undoubtedly some of these regimes would rather see themselves wake up from the nightmare. But it is a testament to the power of the concept of the Internet that they do allow the

199

[26]"Google, Yahoo Accused of Aiding China Censorship," www.linuxinsider.com/story/g8bY2sBPhOZWrG/Google-Yahoo-Accused-of-Aiding-China-Censorship.xhtml, accessed April 7, 2007.

[27]"Empirical Analysis of Internet Filtering in China," http://cyber.law.harvard.edu/filtering/china, accessed April 6, 2007.

[28]"Internet Filtering Map," www.opennet.net/map/index2.html, accessed April 6, 2007.

Internet to persist, however hobbled. It's hard to know which is the chicken and which is the egg: the Internet or the global economy. But in either case, the two have become intimately intertwined and only North Korea remains off the grid (though it maintains a limited closed network, similar to a BBS, mentioned earlier in this chapter).[29]

You Decide

Do you think the Open Net Initiative should have put Germany, France, and the United Kingdom on its watch list for blocking neo-Nazi material and child pornography? Under what circumstances do you think blocking of content is just common sense, rather than a corruption of the free flow of information? Do you think that persons in other cultures would have the same views as you do? What role do you think ethics should play in a government's decision to block certain Internet content?

BUILD IT AND THEY WILL (ALL) COME

That a ballet dancer in China can go into a chat room from an Internet café in Beijing and practice English with a cheerleader from Topeka, Kansas, in real time and with little expense is a startling development. Equally startling is that a Canadian pedophile in St. Thomas, Ontario, can find an audience on the Internet for the live video stream of his molestation of a child. In this case, which occurred in November of 2006, a police officer happened to be surreptitiously viewing the act, and the perpetrator was tracked down within two hours to face charges.[30]

As Bugsy Siegel famously said about opening a casino in the middle of a wind-swept desert, "build it and they will come." Many will argue that Las Vegas now brings out the worst in the innumerable people who end up clearing out their bank accounts at the automatic teller machines, which are always just a few steps away from the slots or card tables that have just swallowed up their last infusion of cash. The same people will argue that placing a sign that says "Know your limit, play within it," does little to counter the potential *H*arm.

[29]Tom Zeller, "The Internet Black Hole That Is North Korea," www.nytimes.com/2006/10/23/technology/23link.html?ex=1319256000&en=ddfb36d2f8248b7a&ei=5088&partner=rssnyt&emc=rss, accessed April 6, 2007.

[30]"Internet Cops Arrest Man after Witnessing Child Abuse Live Online," www.cbc.ca/canada/toronto/story/2006/11/02/child-abuse.html, accessed April 6, 2007.

It could as easily be argued that before the Internet, pedophiles, hate mongers, and terrorists subsisted in a windswept desert of their own—cut off, for the most part, from others who shared their ideals or predilections and therefore less able to be goaded on or supported in their plans and actions.

In Western society, where privacy is codified into law and persons are innocent until proven guilty, there is the tendency to allow individuals to make their own choices and for the government to do little to curtail the amount of rope that individuals can draw with which to hang themselves—or others. For pedophiles, neo-Nazis, and extremists, allowing information to flow freely over the neutral medium of the Internet is akin to leaving a wad of cash on an unmade hotel bed (Figure 9-5) when the maid is due to come in to clean things up.

Like pedophiles, neo-Nazis, and extremists, other arguably less-reviled social minorities have also found community on the Internet. Homosexually inclined persons have been able to make contact with others who have similar orientations with much less fear of exposure or the trouble that exposure might cause them (in some countries, laws against homosexuality carry the penalty of death). Whether

FIGURE 9-5
For individuals seeking to exploit the service, allowing information to flow freely on the Internet may be akin to leaving cash on an unmade hotel bed. (iStockphoto.com #2363691, M. B. Cheatham.)

this change has fundamentally altered the fate of members of this group is not clear, even though much has been made of the change, especially as it may apply to homosexual youth (see the accompanying box). But it is clear that the Internet has made opportunities for forming cyber communities among minorities that had great difficulty forming communities in the past. The Falun Gong movement, which was first introduced in China in 1992 and was banned by the Chinese government in 1999, keeps an active Internet presence, even if blocking any sites referencing the movement is a top priority in China's Internet filtering efforts.[31]

CHILDREN AND THE INTERNET—TO MONITOR OR NOT TO MONITOR?
The Story of Robbie Kirkland

Leslie Kirkland of Cleveland, Ohio, whose 14-year-old son Robbie committed suicide in 1997, wrote about her son and the Internet: "Because he was so closeted with our family and his friends, [the Internet] provided him a safe place to be out and meet others like him. What a heart-warming feeling it must have been for him to connect with other teens that were gay. Due to being closeted, he did not know that there were other teens experiencing the same range of emotions as him."

Despite these elements of the Internet that Ms. Kirkland found positive, she also saw negative aspects, in that the Internet "exposes gay youth to hard-core pornography and unhealthy views of the gay community." She feels that the Internet "gives the impression that being gay is all about sex," noting that "adolescence is a time of raging hormones so gay youth can't help but be curious and gravitate to on line pornography." Especially disturbing to her were the sexual advances she discovered her son had encountered on the Internet. After Robbie's death, she found that an adult man had sent her son a pornographic videotape of himself, requesting that Robbie respond in kind. With some investigation, it was found that the man was a high school guidance counselor.

She concluded that "obviously, parents should closely monitor and supervise their children on line (Figure 9-6) and put a block on pornography sites" but noted that "monitoring a gay youth that is not out to his/her family will inhibit him/her from going to gay websites, for fear of discovery by his/her family," which, of course, presents a bit of a catch-22.[32]

[31]"Falun Dafa Clearwisdom.net," www.clearwisdom.net/emh/index.html, accessed April 7, 2007.

[32]"The Robbie Kirkland Story," www.times10.org/kirkland22001.htm, accessed April 6, 2007.

FIGURE 9-6
Protecting children who use the Internet has become a primary concern; some feel that children should never be exposed to pornography or violence on the Internet, whereas others feel children should have totally free access to the Internet and should discuss what they don't understand or find confusing with a parent or guardian. (iStockphoto.com #312786, Greg Nicholas.)

203

DOES NET NEUTRALITY EQUAL WORLD CHAOS?

A great number of ethicists, governments, and organizations share Wikipedia co-founder Jimmy Wales's view that free and equal "access to information is a fundamental human right." It's not unlike some of the reasoning that went into the decision of the United States's "coalition of the willing" to go to war in Iraq in 2003. Among many other complaints that the United States had with the Iraqi regime of Saddam Hussein was that there "is no political debate nor are there even articles in Iraqi newspapers that question the government. Those who have tried are now in exile or dead."[33]

The Falun Gong's website keeps a running tally of the alleged disappearances and other persecutions visited upon its members in China who persist in prac-

[33]"Iraq: A Population Silenced," www.state.gov/g/drl/rls/15996.htm, accessed April 7, 2007.

ticing and spreading information about the principles of the movement. The group's leader, Li Hongzhi (who has said that part of the reason for the world's chaos today is that "aliens have introduced modern machinery like computers" into the world[34]) is in exile in the United States. If conditions are similar in China and Iraq, why are responses from the global community, including the cyberworld, different?

If access to information is a fundamental human right, then how far are we willing to go to protect it? And who will take responsibility for any *H*arm that could potentially come from the access to this information? Who will pay for the funerals of Thai citizens if riots were to break out in prisons where persons have been jailed for defacing the image of the king—a definite possibility if the government metes out 10-year terms for local transgressors but then allows everyone else to watch the same actions (and cause them to replay over and over again) with the click of a mouse?

Who will pull the global economy out of a nosedive if chaos ensued because China's government was unable—at least partly because of net neutrality, were it enacted—to control the growth of what many call the dangerous cult of Falun Gong? And while Iraqi citizens may now have the right to blog freely without government interference, many would argue that there is no government interference because, after the departure of Saddam Hussein, there is no longer an effective Iraqi government—despite U.S. President George Bush's assertion on January 16, 2007, that "some of my decisions actually have worked, like getting rid of Saddam Hussein and helping the Iraqi government form a unity government."[35]

This is to say that there are many different sides and conflicting ideals to every argument, and that ideals (like democracy or net neutrality; see the accompanying box) are just that—perfect ideas that can only be a target, never a reality. Considering ethics means attempting to balance on the razor's edge between appeasement and blind idealism, with endless and vociferous rhetoric from either side vying to throw you off balance.

[34]"Falun Gong: An Evil Cult?" www.bbc.co.uk/dna/h2g2/A2922644, accessed April 7, 2007.

[35]"President Bush Defends Decision to Send Additional Troops to Iraq," www.pbs.org/newshour/bb/white_house/jan-june07/bush_01-16.html, accessed April 7, 2007.

NET NEUTRALITY: A PERFECT SOLUTION IN AN IMPERFECT WORLD?

Various concerns about maintaining the free, equal, and unbiased nature of the Internet have led many to call for what has come to be dubbed "net neutrality." Net neutrality isn't a completely new concept. The U.S. government was concerned with a similar issue as far back as 1860 when it was subsidizing telegraph lines and equipment for sending messages from one coast of the United States to the other. An act from June 16, 1860, states that "messages received from any individual, company, or corporation, or from any telegraph lines connecting with this line at either of its termini, shall be impartially transmitted in the order of their reception, excepting that the dispatches of the government shall have priority."[36]

As with the subsidization of the early Internet in universities, this telegraph law only covers impartiality in those services that are funded by the government. Anyone else with the funds to string a line across the country without intersecting with the government-funded one could ostensibly discriminate however they liked. Nonetheless, net neutrality supporters cite both of these U.S. laws in their arguments for imposing net neutrality on all ISPs.

The fact is that net neutrality, like democracy, is an ideal that has never been fully realized—and possibly can never be, simply because the protocols, structure, and hardware of which the Internet is comprised are so varied. Ease of access to sites is not always equal, depending on traffic levels, the quality and speed of equipment and connections, and so on. Additionally, different Web interactions require different levels of service. A website containing only text can easily be transmitted, even if service is erratic. On the other hand, real-time voiceover Internet applications require a steady stream of bandwidth in order to function properly. At the extreme, ISPs could be called upon to upgrade computer networks and equipment in Guyana so that content served from this severely technologically disadvantaged country can be on an equal footing with the net offerings of apple.com. But, as with all ethical issues, the impossibility of reaching or verifying the ideal does not absolve those involved from grappling with the issues.

Of course, ISPs already offer tiered service or charge extra for heavy Internet users. In the case of cable companies that offer Internet service, the bandwidth required to transmit the television signal always takes precedence over Internet bandwidth. And if the cable service also provides a telephone service, that bandwidth is also usually given priority, where it wouldn't be if the ISP subscriber contracted with a third-party

---

[36]Rodrigue Tremblay, "Commercialization and Future Access to the Internet Highway," Global Research, February 18, 2007, www.globalresearch.ca/index.php?context=viewArticle&code=TRE20070218&articleId=4843, accessed March 25, 2007.

phone service provider that is simply using the ISP's bandwidth without providing any remuneration to the ISP. In fact, in 2004, Madison River Communications, a North Carolina ISP, blocked its customers from using the Vonage VoIP service. The Federal Communications Commission (FCC) entered into a consent decree with Madison River that required the company to pay a fine and restore service. But in other countries, such as the United Arab Emirates, VoIP providers, such as Skype, have been universally blocked (although users constantly find new ways around the block and post their successful solutions in Skype forums, only be shut down again with updated blocking software).[37] Many ISPs the world over block or curtail bandwidth to some peer-to-peer (P2P) file-sharing software, such as BitTorrent, or to high-traffic users generally (sometimes depending on the time of day).[38]

You Decide

Using our rubric, *I*nvestigate ISP blocking or throttling instances. *E*valuate the stated (if any) and possible motives behind each instance. What do you see as the *T*ruth behind the action? Is the Web activity being curtailed really putting undue pressure on the ISP's system, if that is the stated reason? Is there any way to know? Does the ISP provide evidence to back up its claims? Or is the ISP trying to push out a competitor to one of its own pay services or those of its affiliates or parent company? Is the blocking political? Is the ISP responding to future threats or the problems it could face if this specified action grew? Is the blocking *S*ituational—blocking some instances of one activity but not another—or blocking in one location but not another, as in the case of the United Arab Emirates (UAE) ISPs blocking VoIP? If you were in charge of improving the financial success of an ISP, when and under what conditions, if any, would it be ethically appropriate to intentionally adjust user service levels, either selectively or uniformly?

206

THE ETHICS OF "GOTCHA" POLITICAL BLOGGING

The rise of the use of YouTube and websites in political campaigns in the United States is just one example of the endless chatter, spin, and gotcha tactics that the Internet has enabled. In the 2006 midterm elections, Virginia Republican Senator George Allen's unsuccessful reelection bid was derailed by controversy when he made a quip about a volunteer for his rival's campaign who had been

[37]"Skype Forums," http://forum.skype.com/index.php?showtopic=70441&hl=dubai, accessed March 25, 2007.

[38]"Bad ISPs," www.azureuswiki.com/index.php/Bad_ISPs, accessed March 25, 2007.

shadowing his every move with a digital video camera, apparently in an attempt to catch any slip of the tongue or moment of bad humor that might prove useful to unseating the senator. The senator referred to the volunteer, S. R. Sidarth, as "Macaca, or whatever his name is." Later, possibly after "Googling" the word, it was pointed out that in some European cultures, "Macaca" is a racial slur used against African immigrants. Allen, reached after the political firestorm erupted, explained that he didn't know what the word meant, but that maybe it had been derived from the nickname his campaign had for Sidarth, "Mohawk," because of his hairstyle. In response to that comment, Sidarth pointed out that he didn't have a Mohawk, but a mullet, adding, "I was annoyed he would use my race in a political context."[39] Mullet, Mohawk, or Macaca—the video clip went up on the Internet and in no time it was the hot topic on political and news programs and articles. Whatever Allen's legislative accomplishments, if he gets a footnote in history, his "Macaca" comment will likely be it.

Bruno Giussani, a Swiss political commentator, when asked his opinion on the impact of blogs on the upcoming 2008 U.S. presidential election, said, "It will be huge, and lead to chaos." He later extrapolated on his comment in the political blog, *The Huffington Post*, saying that although many expect the Internet to be a place "where true conversations may start on real issues towards real solutions," instead he expects that the 2008 campaign "will be a campaign dominated by information chaos. Where it will become impossible to tell candidates apart; to say clearly who stands for what; to figure out who's behind what message—and particularly behind personal attacks; to detect where truth is and believe anyone." He went on to say, "Historically we had spin doctors; now everybody has the tools to be a spin doctor, which means that the political ball will spin in every possible direction, faster than ever."[40]

Some, like absurdist playwright Eugene Ionesco (Figure 9-7), might not be overly distressed with such a dire-sounding prediction. In fact, they might conclude that not being able to "detect where truth is and believe anyone" might actually bring us closer to recognizing and acknowledging the *real* truth; as Ionesco wrote, "[he] could take almost any work of art, any play, and guarantee

[39]Tim Craig and Michael D. Shear, "Allen Quip Provokes Outrage, Apology," www.washingtonpost.com/wp-dyn/content/article/2006/08/14/AR2006081400589.html, accessed April 7, 2007.

[40]Bruno Giussani, "The 2008 Chaos Election Theory, or: the Year of User-Generated Swiftboating," www.huffingtonpost.com/bruno-giussani/the-2008-chaos-election-t_b_45205.html, accessed April 7, 2007.

FIGURE 9-7
Absurdist playwright Eugene Ionesco would have found the chaos resulting from political blogging to
his liking, as the truth behind the chaos might eventually be found, much in the way that theater-goers
go to the theater to find truth. (iStockphoto.com #2274243, Joshua Blake.)

to give it in turn a Marxist, a Buddhist, a Christian, an Existentialist, psychoana-
lytical interpretation and 'prove' that the work subjected to each interpretation
is a perfect and exclusive illustration of the creed, that it confirms this or that
ideology beyond all doubt."[41]

INDIVIDUALS AND THE INTERNET

Up to now we've been taking the wide-angle view on the Internet, considering
the ethical issues that have and will continue to affect the trajectory of its development and its scope. But because the Internet both provides content to and
invites content from the individuals who use it, users face numerous ethical
issues every time they open their browsers.

[41]Henry Adler, "To Hell with Society" *The Tulane Drama Review*, 1960, vol. 4, no. 4, p. 58.

Were it not for an individual posting a video of the king of Thailand's picture being defaced on YouTube, the Thai government would have never blocked the site, and more than 649 news articles wouldn't have been written about the incident within two days.[42] Thai YouTube visitors who may have been using the service to post their own creations and ruminations wouldn't be blocked from doing so because someone in the United States (according to the profile of the poster) was flouting Thai law. Even when YouTube took down the first video, additional individuals created and posted new and, some might say, worse videos, with the king's face superimposed over a monkey and with profanities sprawled across it.[43]

But it's not only countries that have to do damage control to protect their image and values from individuals on the Internet. Anyone with a product to sell can be "flamed" on the Internet, often without knowing it until it's too late. When this book goes to print and is put up for sale on Amazon.com, for example, it will be fair game for anyone to click here, enter some information there, and then post a review of the book—whether they've read it or not. Competing authors could criticize it in an attempt to squash their competition. I could get my friends to sign on and praise it. There are even so-called power reviewers on Amazon who I could pay to post a review of it.

Don Mitchell, a Boston management consultant, and Amazon.com's number three product reviewer (the number one reviewer, Harriet Klausner, a former librarian from Georgia, has posted more than 13,500 reviews since 1995, or more than three a day), charges $750 to review products that he wouldn't otherwise review. He donates the money to Habitat for Humanity, but accepting money for a review (whether donated to charity or not) would be a big ethical no-no for most journalists. Mitchell says he's not bound by the ethics of professional reviewers.

Amazon.com, for its part, is also unconcerned. Sean Sundwall, a company spokesman, says, "At the end of the day, whether you're paid or not, people want an accurate review. Just because you're paid doesn't mean you're inherently biased, because everything is a matter of opinion."[44]

[42]"Google News," http://news.google.ca/nwshp?ie=UTF-8&oe=UTF-8&hl=en&tab=wn&q=thailand%20youtube, accessed April 8, 2007.

[43]Ambika Ahuja, "YouTube Seeks to End Ban in Thailand," www.usatoday.com/tech/news/2007-04-08-youtube-thailand_N.htm, accessed April 8, 2007.

[44]"Amazon Critics Bask in Spotlight," www.fortwayne.com/mld/journalgazette/living/17047549.htm, accessed April 8, 2007.

Another place where "nonprofessional" commentators abound is in the "blogo-sphere," a word that was coined in 1999 (as a joke[45]) and represents the social network of Internet-based journals, or web logs, that have become popular and intricately interwoven. Sites such as MySpace, Bebo, and Facebook have hun-dreds of thousands of regular users and log millions of visits per day. Users post their thoughts, videos, pictures, pretty much anything that can be conveyed through the Internet, and others comment, link, and interact. Of course, with so much content posted each day, it's unlikely that anything will go viral, but anything that does can do a whole lot of good or bad for the individual who posted it or any person, place, or thing at which the post might be directed. Gloria Knowles Kim, the manager of International Migration Services, a Van-couver, Canada-based immigration consulting firm, says that blogging and Internet forums have great power to affect her industry because there are so many horror stories of unscrupulous consultants disappearing in the night with their client's money. "Trust is everything in this business," she says, "and people look to the Internet to find any stories, good or bad, about a consultant they may be considering contracting with." As discussed in Chapter 1 in connection with industry standards, trust again becomes key.

RateMyProfessors.com allows students to anonymously comment on university professors in such areas as clarity, easiness, helpfulness, and even hotness. The site, owned by Viacom, obviously has its adherents and detractors—as well as its very broad user agreement, which in part says that postings should not "affect us adversely or reflect negatively on us, the Site, our goodwill, name or reputa-tion or cause duress, distress or discomfort to us or anyone else, or discourage any person, firm or enterprise from using all or any portion, features or func-tions of the Site, or from advertising, linking or becoming a supplier to us in connection with the Site."[46] With postings like "i learned more by not listening to this guy . . . thats how awesome it was"[47] for a California Institute of the Arts music professor, it's hard to see how such comments wouldn't generate at least some discomfort for someone.

[45]"Blogosphere," http://en.wikipedia.org/wiki/Blogosphere, accessed April 10, 2007.
[46]"Terms of Use Agreement," www.ratemyprofessors.com/TermsOfUse_us.jsp, accessed April 10, 2007.
[47]"Mark Bobak—California Institute of the Arts—Music," www.ratemyprofessors.com/ShowRatings.jsp?tid=679999, accessed April 10, 2007.

Though there is no RateMyBoss.com site, plenty of bloggers write about their work—and get in trouble for it. Catherine Sanderson, a former secretary for the U.K. accountancy firm Dixon Wilson, was dismissed for "gross misconduct" because a lawyer for Dixon Wilson claimed her blog "risked bringing the company into disrepute." In fact, Sanderson neither mentioned the name of the company in her blog, nor her own name. Her picture, however, was posted on the site. A Paris tribunal ruled in March 2007 that she had been dismissed "without real and serious causes" and ordered her former employer to pay compensation and legal fees.[48]

But bloggers don't just get themselves fired, they often get others fired by bringing to light information or comments sent in e-mails or that otherwise flew under the radar—a function that used to be primarily reserved for so-called legitimate journalism. Colorado Democratic state representative Michael Merrifield stepped down as chairman of the House Education Committee when an e-mail he had written, which said charter school supporters should have a "special place in hell," was posted on a Republican activist's blog.[49] And a regional sales director for the drug company AstraZeneca, Michael Zubillaga, was fired in April 2007 when a blogger posted part of an article he had written for an internal company publication, the Oncology Newsletter. His advice to his sales team for calling on doctors included "There is a big bucket of money sitting in every office. Every time you go in, you reach your hand in the bucket and grab a handful. The more times you are in, the more money goes in your pocket."[50]

More and more public figures are blogging as well, and they can get into trouble easily. Whereas it wouldn't be news if a normal citizen opined in a blog that a neighboring city was mired in crime, when West Ranch town council president Dave Bossert blogged that neighboring Canyon Country, California, was a "cornucopia of crime," it was cause for many apologies, meetings, and spins. In a subsequent blog entry, Bossert wrote, "Yes, I apologize for offending the many good folks in Canyon Country by making such insensitive, broad

[48]"Employee Wins Compensation after Being Fired Because of Blog," www.workplacelaw.net/display.php?resource_id=8423, accessed April 10, 2007.

[49]"State Senator Said Investigators Have Leads on Threatening E-Mail," www.summitdaily.com/article/20070410/NEWS/104100077, accessed April 10, 2007.

[50]"Sales Manager Fired over Net Comments," www.phillyburbs.com/pb-dyn/news/147-04082007-1327046.html, accessed April 10, 2007.

statements about their community."[51] No doubt, with the difficulty of gaining information about tone from the written word on the Internet, this statement could have been perceived as cavalier.

Bloggers in some countries face far direr consequences for their blogging. The first blogger to go for jail was journalist Sina Matlabi, jailed in Iran in 2003.[52] Others have gone to jail in Egypt and Bahrain. But while some governments crack down on bloggers, they have obviously seen the power in the blogosphere too, as Iran's President Mahmoud Ahmadinejad started his own blog.[53]

Although blogs may seem to give outsiders an inside track to what others are thinking, many also argue that they can be used to manipulate public opinion. In a March 29, 2007, speech, U.S. President George W. Bush quoted two Iraqi bloggers, who he says wrote that "Displaced families are returning home, marketplaces are seeing more activity, stores that were long shuttered are now reopening. We feel safer about moving in the city now. Our people want to see this effort succeed. We hope the governments in Baghdad and America do not lose their resolve."[54] It was later disclosed that Mr. Bush had met with the bloggers, Omar and Mohammed Fadhil, in the Oval Office three years prior, in 2004,[55] causing many to question the veracity of the picture that the brothers painted of the situation on the ground in Iraq.

212

A U.S. nonprofit organization, Spirit of America, helped to fund the creation of an Arabic-language blog service that "gives voices to those working for freedom and democracy in the Arab world." They stated that "everyone who creates a blog is promoting moderate and progressive information and viewpoints in the Arab world,"[56] which suggests, at least, that those who choose to espouse other views or goals would not be welcome. This despite the fact that their motto is

[51]Katherine Geyer, "Council Member Sorry for Blog," www.the-signal.com/?module=displaystory&story_id=47496&format=html, accessed April 10, 2007.

[52]"Blogging in the Middle East Is a Tough Choice," http://rawstory.com/news/2006/Blogging_in_the_Middle_East_is_a_to_09142006.html, accessed April 10, 2007.

[53]"Iran's President Launches Weblog," http://news.bbc.co.uk/2/hi/middle_east/4790005.stm, accessed April 11, 2007.

[54]Bob Cesca, "The President's Bloggers vs. The Body Count," www.huffingtonpost.com/bob-cesca/the-presidents-bloggers-_b_44572.html, accessed April 10, 2007.

[55]"Name That Blogger," www.todaysthv.com/news/news.aspx?storyid=43722, accessed April 10, 2007.

[56]"Arabic Blogging Tool: Viral Freedom," www.spiritofamerica.net, accessed April 11, 2007.

"Support independent new media and free expression in Iraq and the Arab world." This policy, if that is what it is, is not fundamentally unlike RateMy-Professor's policy of disallowing postings that will make anyone "uncomfort-able," but Spirit of America's policies could result in creating a skewed view of the reality of public opinion in the Arab world, especially if, as in President Bush's blogging reference, the fact that the comments came from a "blogger" is seen as lending street credibility or veracity to the content.

You Decide

Do you think RateMyProfessor.com is violating its guidelines to make no one uncomfortable by allowing a review like "i learned more by not listening to this guy . . . thats how awesome it was" to remain on the site? If so, why do you think the site allows it to stay? What would happen to the site if it removed all such comments? If you think a comment like this violates RateMyProfessor.com's policy, why do you think it created these policies if it doesn't enforce them? Is it just to guard against legal liability should any *H*arm come to anyone as a result of anything posted on the site?

Do you think that product reviewers on websites like Amazon.com really are nonprofessionals and therefore should be allowed to charge for their reviews? If not, how could Amazon.com stop these instances? Do you think paid reviewers should state in their reviews that they were paid? Again, how could this be enforced?

213

In this chapter, we have examined ethical issues associated with new media. In the next chapter, let's take a look at ethical issues involved with censorship and celebrity reporting.

CHAPTER 10
Censorship and Celebrity

The Broadcast Standards and Practices (BS&P) departments at the networks were created in the 1950s as a result of the quiz show scandals. The mission of the BS&P censors was to protect the networks from embarrassing displays of poor judgment on the part of advertisers and producers.

Over time, the BS&P departments became the guardians of morality by monitoring sexual content, controversial issues, and medical information, among other duties. At different times, BS&P departments were reduced in size as a result of budget constraints, but since Janet Jackson's "wardrobe malfunction" at the 2004 Super Bowl and the raising of FCC fines tenfold to $325,000 per incident, per station, it is unlikely that BS&P departments will be eliminated or be cut back anytime soon.

There is, in fact, speculation, if not concrete evidence, that BS&P departments may soon have some kind of oversight responsibility over news. Overseeing news would be a new development because in the past BS&P departments had no control over news because news departments were separate from the entertainment divisions. But with the recent missteps by news departments rushing to file a story before all the facts have been checked (e.g., CBS's Dan Rather and President George W. Bush's military service), there is a strong perception that television news requires ombudsmen.

A BROADCAST STANDARDS AND PRACTICES QUESTIONNAIRE

When I started my 8-year tenure as a network censor, working on editing theatrical films for television and fact-checking true stories, I refused to label what I did as censorship. Yes, I made requests for changes, but I wasn't censoring. I called myself a Broadcast Standards and Practices editor, not a censor. It was only after a few years that I was able to call a spade a spade and to call myself what I was, a censor.

Before we proceed, here's a questionnaire I'd liked you to take. It's designed to gauge your views on censorship matters. The reason I would like you to take the questionnaire at the start of this chapter is because censorship is such a complicated topic involving so many ethical issues that a great deal of confusion can exist if one doesn't first take the time to determine one's starting position. If one doesn't have a clear starting position about censorship issues, confusion follows. If one doesn't know what the issues might be, it can be difficult to understand how Broadcast Standards and Practices executives function.

Please answer the questions in order; do not go back to change answers and do not skip any of the questions.

1. Do you believe in freedom of speech? Yes No
2. Do you believe that censorship destroys creativity? Yes No
3. Do you believe in censorship of any kind? Yes No
4. Do you believe that children should be allowed to view or listen to anything they want to? Yes No
5. Do you believe that the government should regulate the content of entertainment programming? Yes No
6. Do you believe seeing an act of violence on television or in the movies can cause a viewer to engage in aggressive behavior? Yes No
7. Do you believe that children should be protected from indecent or obscene material? Yes No
8. If you go to see a movie based on a true story, do you expect that the movie will be a factual account? Yes No
9. Do you think using the Lord's name in vain is acceptable on radio or television? Yes No
10. Do you think using the Lord's name in vain is acceptable on radio or television when children are likely to be in the audience? Yes No
11. Does a radio chain have the right to ban or censor a song that does not coincide with its programming philosophy? Yes No

12. Do you feel that criticism of the president is okay during times of national emergency? Yes No
13. Do you think that certain explicit books should be banned from publicly funded libraries? Yes No
14. Do you think that pornographic websites should be allowed in public libraries? Yes No
15. Do you believe nudity is acceptable in television commercials? Yes No
16. Do you believe that sexual intercourse should be shown in feature films? Yes No
17. Do you feel that there is a glorification of so-called alternative lifestyles on television? Yes No
18. Do you believe that claims made on television commercials are accurate? Yes No
19. Do you think racial stereotypes are acceptable on television? Yes No
20. Do you believe many broadcast censorship decisions about sex and violence are made on an arbitrary basis? Yes No
21. Do you believe that the V-chip is a good idea to enable parents to monitor what their children are watching? Yes No
22. Do you know anyone who uses the V-chip? Yes No
23. Please circle A or B, whichever comes closest to what you think:
    A. I believe that the media is on the left.
    B. I believe that the media is on the right.

After you have finished the questionnaire, go back and see if you spot any contradictions or inconsistencies in your answers. For example, if you answered in question 3 that you do not believe in censorship of any kind and later state that children should be protected from offensive material, you may find yourself confronting the fact that censorship issues are not always clear-cut, often causing people to feel caught between a rock and a hard place. For example, you may feel that the government should not be involved in regulating entertainment content (question 5) yet you may feel that public libraries should not carry pornographic websites (question 14).

Similarly, if you think in question 21 the V-chip is a good idea, but in question 22 admit that you know few people or no one who uses the V-chip, does it remain a good idea? Question 23 about the media essentially on the left or the right has always produced surprising results in the classes I teach.

I often ask my students in the Censorship and Regulation classes if their opinions about censorship have changed over the course of a semester. Every day there's something going on that touches on censorship issues. One day, as discussed in Chapter 7, it's Madonna saying she refuses to edit the scene from her "Confessions" tour where she hangs from a cross while singing "Live to Tell"; another day it's Madonna reluctantly accepting NBC's proposed edit. *E*valuating the incidents that occur almost daily leads to a more informed perspective about censorship.

I find the best way to use the questionnaire in the classroom is to tabulate all the answers to gauge how the class as a whole initially approaches censorship issues and how these issues relate to ethics. After all, television is the most powerful communications device of the 20th century, and as such, many feel it should be controlled or monitored, whereas others vehemently disagree.

Contrary to what many people think, BS&P departments do not have rigid guidelines that systemically rule on what's acceptable and what is not. Though media practitioners and pundits alike will insist that censorship decisions are made arbitrarily (question 20), this is very much an oversimplification. BS&P departments make value judgments on a case-by-case basis, judgments that are dependent on ethical considerations. In this chapter, we examine the role ethics play in the way BS&P departments make their decisions.

VIOLENCE

Many studies assert that violence (Figures 10-1 and 10-2) on television leads to violent behavior on the part of people, mostly children, who consume a diet of violent television. Industry practitioners and others routinely challenge these studies as generally flawed (e.g., the sample size was too small, the methodology was faulty and imprecise, the scope of the study was too limited, and so on). Nevertheless these studies and the news stories that periodically link violent behavior to television viewing cannot and should not be ignored.

Here are a few sample, representative headlines focusing on violence and the media. You can check the footnotes if you want additional information about these studies. I am simply using the headlines to indicate the range and number of studies that have been undertaken regarding violence and the media:

- "Broadcast Violence Gets New Scrutiny"[1]
- "Video Games and Childhood Violence"[2]

[1] Jube Shiver Jr., "Broadcast Violence Gets New Scrutiny," *The Los Angeles Times*, May 30, 2005, C-1.
[2] Internet-week@update.internetweek.com, accessed August 22, 2005.

FIGURES 10-1 and 10-2
Many studies maintain that seeing violence on television leads to aggressive behavior. Thus, the youth seeing the gun on television in the first picture could become prone to violent actions, possibly even turning the gun against himself, as in the second picture. (iStockphoto.com #1098849, Nicholas Burke; iStockphoto.com #3275229, Joan Vincent Canto.)

- "Police: 'Sopranos' Inspired Disembodiment"[3]
- "Youth Says He Got Idea for Sexual Abuse from Springer Show"[4]
- "Kids' Aggression, Entertainment Violence Correlated"[5]
- "Study: Teens Who Watch Much TV Prone to Violence"[6]
- "Vicious Videos"[7]

[3]Story.news.yahoo.com/news?, accessed January 28, 2003.
[4]Mireya Navarro, "Youth Says He Got Idea for Sexual Abuse from Springer Show," *The New York Times*, January 8, 1999, A-10.
[5]Lisa Mascaro, "Kids' Aggression, Entertainment Violence Correlated," *The Ann Arbor News*, November 5, 2001, 1.
[6]"Study: Teens Who Watch Much TV Prone to Violence," www.usatoday.com/news/nation/2002/03/28/tv-violence.htm, accessed July 27, 2006.
[7]Diane Swanbrow, "Vicious Videos," *Michigan Today*, Summer 2006, p. 8.

Aware of the studies that link violence and television entertainment, network censors must evaluate how much or how little violence is acceptable:

- To a public that seemingly craves action (read violence) in its entertainments while at the same time publicly condemning any glorification of violence
- To advertisers who, save for a few heat-seeking advertisers who want controversy, are an essentially conservative group, particularly if they want to be known as family friendly.
- To the network's own standards

How many bullet hits are too many? When will a depiction of a vigilante-style payback tempt a viewer to take the same action? Should the execution of a terrorist be allowed to be more detailed/graphic than the killing of an innocent child? BS&P departments confront these and many other ethical questions on a daily basis.

IMITABLE ACTIONS

Ask Broadcast Standards and Practices executives what's the worst thing that can happen on their watch, and you may get a variety of answers. Many will say that it's their job to make sure that there are no surprises in the shows they cover. Al Schneider, who was head of Standards and Practices at ABC for many years, almost made "no surprises" a mantra during his tenure. Almost all, however, will say that imitable actions are what they fear the most. By this they mean an action in a program causes a viewer to imitate that action, causing *H*arm to himself or others.

This is why BS&P editors handle suicide so carefully, lest a viewer follow all the steps of a suicide. I once asked Tom Kersey, a legendary Standards executive, what his most difficult call had been in his long and illustrious career. He paused and said he regretted approving the rape of an inmate in *Born Innocent* (1974). The rape was accomplished with a broom. The film starred Linda Blair of *The Exorcist* (1973) fame, and after the film aired, copycat rapes with brooms occurred. For Kersey, this was his most difficult decision, a decision he made at the last minute when an appeal was made for realism, and it became the decision he most regretted because of the imitable actions that followed.

BALANCE, ERRORS, AND VALUE JUDGMENTS

Olivia Cohen-Cutler, the senior vice president of Broadcast Standards and Practices at ABC, defines her job in terms of making ethical decision on a daily basis.

One of her primary functions is ensuing that balance is maintained, avoiding advocacy programming that proselytizes one point of view while ignoring other sides.

Cohen-Cutler notes that ABC/Disney has 221 affiliates. She is very much aware that the 221 affiliates are made up of different markets, each with a different level of community acceptance. Cohen-Cutler and her staff seek to protect these affiliates; in other words, she strives to ascertain that the programming ABC distributes is acceptable to the various communities served by the affiliates. If it isn't acceptable, the risk of fines by the Federal Communications Commission (FCC) looms large, as does the threat of government regulation.

For Cohen-Cutler, BS&P departments like hers exist to make certain that the government does not step in and take control away from the networks. Refer to Chapter 7 on the topic of governmental control. To maintain standards, among other things, her department creates rules for reality programs, determines what is and is not acceptable in times of crisis, negotiates with executives inside and outside the company, and every year creates the ABC Television Network Advertising Standards and Guidelines to define rules in a number of key areas. These guidelines have 60+ categories, including scheduling restrictions, endorsements, challenges, gambling, and hypnotism.

It's Cohen-Cutler's department that determines what ratings programs carry (again, see Chapter 7). ABC has, in fact, only assigned a TV MA rating once, that being to *Saving Private Ryan* (1998), directed by Steven Spielberg, which has aired on ABC several times to commemorate Veteran's Day. The film contains strong language and violence, but Spielberg's contract prevented any editing of the film, prompting the TV MA rating.

Thanks to YouTube and various Internet sites, viewers readily spot real or perceived errors and are quick to post their findings of flaws or errors on the Web. Cohen-Cutler, for example, feels that *Seinfeld* alum Michael Richards's tirade against blacks at the Laugh Factory in 2006 would not have become watercooler news around the country were it not for immediate postings on YouTube.

Because errors are subject to immediate searchlight scrutiny, BS&P executives have to be super diligent. Some might even say that all the attention to errors provides a kind of job security for Standards executives. In the past, only a few people might have noticed that someone in the background was mouthing obscenities (as was rumored to have been the case in an early Bette Midler television special), whereas today Internet postings immediately alert an increasingly large audience.

You Decide

What errors have you spotted in the television shows you watch? Be as specific as you can. Were they really errors, or do you think a Broadcast Standards and Practices executive decided to let something pass?

SEX

Does the media influence people's sexual attitudes? Specifically, do people get their ideas about sex from the media? Genetics and environment clearly play a role in a person's sexual development, but many point to the kinds of studies discussed at the top of this chapter to support the theory that sex in the media leads to sexual promiscuity in real life. Network censors thus feel a responsibility to monitor the level of sexual activity. In other parts of the globe, there is greater tolerance for sexuality than there is in the United States. Conversely, the United States tolerates more violence than other parts of the world.

You Decide

You are a Broadcast Standards and Practices editor making decisions about sexuality. Using the E*T*H*I*C*S rubric, how would you handle the following situations involving sexual matters? What kinds of information would you need to know to make an informed decision that supports strong ethical values?

- How much on-camera sexual activity do you accept at different times of the day?
- How long do you allow an onscreen kiss to last, and how much tongue activity, if any, do you accept?
- Do you accept a shot of a naked side-breast or partial naked butt (male or female) at different times of the day?
- Full-frontal male nudity in *Shameless*, a popular Channel 4 show in England, is acceptable, whereas full-frontal male or female nudity cannot pass muster in the United States, even on basic cable. Censors need to be aware of the cultural differences, as many programs have a profitable life abroad. There seems to be a cultural difference between what one country will accept or tolerate in terms of sexual content versus what another country finds objectionable. How do you handle this matter?
- Advisories warn potential viewers that a program contains violence or sexual content. Most advertisers and affiliates don't like advisories. Also, stations have to be advised well in advance if a program is to carry an advisory, and this requirement makes scheduling difficult. When do you think you should advocate putting an advisory on a program? Think of a particular program when you answer this question.

- Television seeks younger viewers who are reported to seek edgier (sexier) fare. As a censor, do you allow greater sexual activity to please potential viewers, or do you keep a lid on sexual content to appease wary advertisers?
- A producer is planning to film a love scene between two men, precisely the kind of scene that creates terror in the minds of advertisers and affiliates. This was the situation I faced when I was a network censor at ABC and the network was airing the miniseries *The Richest Man in the World: The Aristotle Onassis Story* (1988). What would you do in such a situation?
- Many a producer has complained to network censors that she has seen more sex on television in the afternoon than she is being allowed to include in her prime-time show. Do you think a network censor can justify greater sexual activity in an afternoon soap opera than in a prime-time program? Do you think that viewers (mostly women) who watch alone in the afternoons without their families present are more tolerant of sexual activity?
- Can the intensity of a love (sex) scene be reduced by lessening the sound effects? Or, conversely, can the suggestion of sexual activity that is taking place off-camera be intensified with sound effects, as was reportedly the case when off-camera sound effects suggested that oral sex was taking place in Fox's hit *Joe Millionaire* in 2003?
- In a television movie about a woman who remembers that her father sexually abused her when she was a child, would you allow dialogue that indicates that part of the woman's guilt is that she felt some pleasure while she was being abused? Censors faced this quandary in 1993 with the television movie *Not in My Family*.

A number of variables can determine how these questions are answered. Daytime programs tend to be more tolerant of sexuality, because it is assumed, rightly or wrongly, that families will not be watching together, thus the individual watching alone will be more accepting of sexuality than if the entire family were present.

Sometimes, however, an unexpected variable turns up. In the case of *The Richest Man in the World: The Aristotle Onassis Story*, one of the actors refused to lie in bed with another man after the scene had been carefully choreographed to be acceptable to Broadcast Standards and Practices. The actor simply felt that it would hurt his career were he to appear in bed with another man.

Often, sound effects can be used to edit a scene. Producers seeking extra leeway in a scene's visuals will frequently offer to trim sound effects. This can be an effective way to soften the intensity of a sequence, but there are also times when sound effects are used to up the intensity, as was, I believe, the case with the sound effects that simulated oral sex in *Joe Millionaire*.

Not in My Family, the 1993 telefilm about sexual abuse, created one of the most intense battles I experienced in my tenure at ABC. The director, Linda Otto, a passionate advocate of women and children's right, fought hard to include the dialogue about the sexual pleasure the woman experienced while her father abused her. She felt the dialogue reflected the terrible conflict that the woman faced, a conflict that caused her to keep the abuse secret for most of her life. Otto provided research to bolster her case, but the Broadcast Standards and Practices executives refused to allow the dialogue, fearing that it would *H*arm victims of sexual abuse by inappropriately focusing on sexual pleasure instead of the trauma of sexual abuse. The Standards executives did not budge in their belief that the line would prevent victims of abuse from coming forward. The line was thus never included.

223

A DIFFERENT BS&P APPROACH

Sometimes a BS&P editor will use a different approach to let a producer or executive know that an ethical line has been crossed. Included here is an excerpt from a letter a BS&P editor prepared for a producer who was felt to have crossed the line by creating films that exploited women's lives. The producer specialized in allegedly true stories that featured women whose trials and tribulations in a world dominated by abusive men and an uncaring social system had all the makings of a soapy soap opera. In the letter, the BS&P editor pretended to be a woman pitching her story to the producer; the letter was sent unofficially, but the message to the producer was clear:

> My name is Gloria. I live at the California State Correctional Institute for Women in Oxnard. My story contains that combination of elements you consider essential to a successful movie for television.
>
> Mine is a simple and sad story—poignant and eloquent—but one which will speak to every woman viewer.
>
> The nightmare began in Baton Rouge, Louisiana, in 1949. I was seventeen. It was then my sadistic, alcoholic stepfather committed me to the county institution to keep me quiet about the sexual advances he was heaping on my paralyzed little brother, Gabriel.
>
> This isn't simply the story of my own internment in a cesspool world of MALE brutality funded by the STATE in that county home. While Gabe was being sexually brutalized at home by his demented stepfather, my little sister Charlene—my beloved "Charlie"—escaped that house of horror one rainy night. Sadly, she escaped to the streets where brutal and uncaring MEN paid her and beat her for the sexual pleasure she could give them. Escape it was, but escape to what? What could an under-educated, one-eyed redhead expect in the back alleys of Baton Rouge. She ran from pain and ran to heartbreak and diseases (aren't there promos here?) and died riddled with pus-oozing sores 5 years ago.
>
> Perhaps if we look with the right angle of vision we can locate good even in tragedy, because her death did serve as an inspiration and as a result I managed to escape my hell as well—escaped the nightly raped by male nurses and, well, you get the picture—more budget cuts, more male exploitation.
>
> Of course, as you might imagine, both my complexion and hair were a wreck from the years of shock treatments, so I was never able to offer any potential employer an attractive, sexy applicant façade, and as a result I was homeless for many years living with filth and degradation and facing heartless insults each day because of budget cuts for adequate low-cost housing.

224

Finally I was able to make my living for three years as a surrogate mother and made enough money to buy a trailer home (Figure 10-3) outside of Tulsa where I met the perfect man—Buck. It was bliss for the first six months. He made me feel like a real woman, if you know what I mean. (I see this as a tastefully done softcore sex scene—the kind you are so well known for.) We had our own child—a lovely daughter, flaxon-haired Samantha. What I did not suspect, he started molesting our daughter when she was two months and three days old.

What could I do? I moved out of the trailer and took him to court. But the venal, vile MALE judge only scoffed and intended to return the child to him. I was forced to flee my beautiful Tulsa with my daughter and disappear into soothing FEMALE hands and into the underground system that protects all of us hideously wronged mothers on the run.

I was captured and put here in Oxnard, but Samantha is safe now, hidden away. And I will stay here forever if necessary to protect her. But

FIGURE 10-3
In the fictitious story a Broadcast Standards editor created to encourage a producer to exercise restraint and avoid making telefilms that exploited women, the main character "Gloria" bought herself a trailer home, such as the one in this picture, before things went from bad to worse. (iStockphoto.com #2134221, David Edwards.)

late at night I sometimes wonder about the wisdom of having placed her in that lesbian commune in Salt Lake City.

Don't you agree that the impact of "our" film can be enhanced by letting thousands of exploited women know there's an 800# they can call for help.

Yours in exploitation, Gloria.

You Decide

What is your opinion of the unofficial BS&P approach? Do you think that this memo touches on some real ethical issues, or do you think it crosses the line?

Would you handle some of the questions in the previous "You Decide" section using a similar approach?

PRESSURE GROUPS

Pressure groups seek to impose their views on as many people as possible. Though often associated with the right, pressure groups also exist to promote leftist causes. In a society that increasingly thrives on media visibility and exposure as well as on political correctness, pressure groups have really come into their own. Indeed, well-organized pressure groups have a great deal of power.

Our focus in this chapter is on BS&P departments and their charge to uphold high moral and ethical standards, so we will examine how BS&P executives respond to pressure groups. Simply put, when should pressure groups be catered to and when should they be ignored?

Let's take the Parents Television Council (PTC), for example. According to its publication, *Because Our Children Are Watching*, the PTC seeks "to restore responsibility and decency to the entertainment industry."[8] An influential group

---

[8]"Because Our Children Are Watching," Parents Television Council 2004 Annual Report, inside cover.

that publishes a list of the top 10 best and worst shows for family viewing and prides itself on causing advertisers to drop out of controversial shows like FX's *Nip/Tuck*, the PTC is sometimes hard to predict. Sometimes the PTC's approval or disapproval surprises, such as the organization's support of ABC's airing of *Saving Private Ryan* when ABC affiliates were fearful of being fined if they ran it in 2004, though it had aired previously.

The PTC provides an Internet FCC complaint form that facilitates sending complaints to the FCC. To obtain a complaint form, go to www.parentstv.org and click "Take Action," then "File an FCC complaint." The complaint can be sent directly to the FCC after it is completed. Couldn't be easier, but how ethical is it for someone who has not seen an entire program to file a complaint?

To file a complaint to the FCC, it is not necessary to have seen the program in question. An editorial in the June 19, 2006, issue of *Broadcasting & Cable* requests that the FCC require complainants to state in an affidavit stating that they saw the offensive program when it aired on TV, as opposed to accepting complaints from those who were responding to "Web-mob pressure" and may not even have seen the program.[9] Like the PTC, Commercial Alert, an organization dedicated to preventing commercials from taking over broadcasting, encourages people to take action about rampant product placement with a complaint form that can be accessed by going to www.commercialalert.org and clicking the take action link, then clicking Product Placement for the "Tell the FCC: Stop Covert Commercials on TV!" form. See the accompanying box.

TELL THE FCC: STOP COVERT COMMERCIALS ON TV!

In May 2005, Federal Communications Commissioner Jonathan Adelstein gave a rousing speech about the "most pernicious symptoms" of "increasing commercialization of American media." In particular, he singled out product placement and corporate shills in "news" programming. "The use of covert commercial pitches is penetrating deeper and deeper into our media," Adelstein said.

Tell all FCC commissioners today to require TV stations to make "clear and prominent" disclosure of all covert commercials, including product placement and corporate shills.

[9] "The Big Chill Becomes Law," editorial, *Broadcasting & Cable*, June 19, 2006, p. 42.

This form reprinted courtesy of Commercial Alert.

There are variations in the requests made by different pressure groups, necessitating a case-by-case response, as in the "S*" of our rubric. Different groups, even groups one might not at first see as pressure groups, from different countries request different things. For example, in 2006, the Indian government requested that MTV and several other music channels run on-air apologies for showing what it considers to be indecent music videos that feature sexuality, smoking, and drinking.[10] The apologies ran, seemingly making the Indian government a powerful pressure group indeed.

---

[10]Lawrence Van Gelder, compiled by, "Arts Briefly," *The New York Times*, June 12, 2006, B-2.

FROM THE PERSPECTIVE OF A BS&P VETERAN

Roland McFarland, vice president, Broadcast Standards, Fox, has been a censor for some 35 years. Having been the executive on *The Brady Bunch* (1969–1974) at a time when married people on television slept in twin beds, he has witnessed many changes over the years. He now sees a greater willingness on the part of creative teams to listen to BS&P concerns at the start of the negotiations, as opposed to an earlier time when every note had to be debated ad infinitum. With the threat of FCC fines looking, creative teams are more cautious, as no one wants to put affiliate stations at risk of fines and censure.

McFarland feels great care has been taken by BS&P departments to promote public health and medical accuracy. He finds audiences are increasingly sophisticated about spotting inaccuracies, but he also feels that viewers themselves have to become media literate. Audiences need to know how to become responsible, attentive viewers who know how to voice their objections when there is something on air that they don't like.

In terms of reality, McFarland has seen a BS&P switch in emphasis away from protecting the audience to protecting contestants. Vetting of participants has significantly increased to avoid surprises, such as the revelation uncovered by the Internet site, The Smoking Gun, that John Rockwell on *Who Wants to Marry a Multi-Millionaire?* (2000) had been accused of abusing a former girlfriend.

HEIGHTENED SENSITIVITY, OR POLITICAL CORRECTNESS RUN AMUCK?

In times of national crisis, BS&P executives, working in concert with other divisions such as sales, programming, and upper management, must decide whether or not certain types of programming are appropriate in light of developments in the news. Standards executives must quickly *E*valuate the mood of the country as well as the significance of the current event. What *H*arm will result if something inappropriate is broadcast? Often, Standards executives have the luxury of time to *I*nvestigate a particular claim or a medical supposition, but in times of national crisis, important decisions need to be made quickly. Does a program need to be pulled? Does a line of dialogue need to be adjusted? As NBC's network group president Randy Falco has said, "We need to determine what's right for the viewer, based on the level of the disaster and the impact on the nation."[11]

[11]Greg Braxton, "When Crises Make TV All Too Real," *The Los Angeles Times*, February 10, 2003, www.takebackthemedia.Org/newspro/arc87.html, accessed October 21, 2006.

Adding to the difficulty of making theses decisions is the fact that a great deal of money can be involved. Pulling a show and substituting something else is easy enough to talk about in theory, but it's not that easy to execute and the execution can be extremely costly. In truth, a great deal of money is involved in pulling a program. Ethical decisions about what is the best thing to do in a crisis can run into a mountain of financial realities. Editing a line of dialogue at the last minute may only cost a few thousand dollars, but the cost of canceling an entire program can run into hundred of thousands of dollars.

As indicated earlier, Standards executives have no set rules to guide them regarding every issue that could possibly come up, so decisions in times of crisis need to be executed quickly and the decisions need to be the right ones. I once worked for a Standards executive who told producers that if they wanted a quick answer, the answer was no. In times of crisis, however, the decisions have to be made quickly and the answer perhaps shouldn't always be no.

You Decide

You are the Standards executive facing the following situations. Using our E*T*H*I*C*S rubric, see how you would handle the following scenarios:

- After the *Columbia* shuttle disaster of 2003, do you postpone the airing of a television movie, *NTSB: The Crash of Flight 323*, about a commuter plane crash in Colorado?
- Again, after the *Columbia* shuttle accident, do you pull an airing of the film *Armageddon*?
- Do you pull an episode of the reality series *Meet My Folks*, where prospective suitors are accepted or rejected by parents, because it's inappropriate following the *Columbia* crash?
- Do you postpone the airing of the show *John Doe*, about an astronaut who was killed, because of the Columbia crash?
- After 9/11, do you cut a scene from the pilot of *24* where a terrorist blows up a commercial airliner?
- Three weeks after 9/11, do you allow *The West Wing* to do an episode about the events of that day?
- Do you allow the show *Third Watch* to incorporate what happened on 9/11 in two episodes?

- Do you switch the airing of the pilot of *The Agency* with another episode after 9/11 because the pilot included terrorist bombings and a reference to Osama bin Laden?
- Do you cut a line from *Friends* about waiting a long time in line at airport security following 9/11?
- Do you delete a reference to "hunky firemen" in *Will & Grace* after 9/11?

The West Wing and *Third Watch* did do 9/11 episodes; also, all of the above other adjustments/changes were made, according to Michael Freeman in *Electronic Media*[12] and Greg Braxton in *The Los Angeles Times*.[13]

NTSB: The Crash of Flight 323 had already been pulled after 9/11, so it's being pulled after the *Columbia* crash was its second time. There were some complaints that too many line edits were made to comedies following 9/11, causing some to question how politically correct shows needed to be, but because television is so very powerful and because it comes into people's homes, executives like Cohen-Cutler and McFarland continue to use ethics to *E*valuate what adjustments need to be made in times of crisis.

[12]Michael Freeman, "Setting Standards for a New Era," *Electronic Media*, October 8, 2001, p. 20.

[13]Braxton, "When Crises Make TV All Too Real."

CELEBRITY

When sports fans (Figure 10-4) call in to talk radio programs, they refer to themselves as members of the team they favor, referring to what *we* must do or not do to help the team, whom *we* should trade or not trade, and what *we* must do to keep or start winning. Clearly, fan participation and identification are integral parts of the contemporary media landscape. What would broadcasting or call-in shows do without them?

More and more, audience participation must be sought, as reality shows and tabloid publications clamor for audience participation and feedback. *You're the One That I Want*, which premiered on NBC at the start of 2007, where the audience selected the stars of a Broadway production of the classic musical *Grease*, is one notable example, if not a ratings getter. Vote, vote, and vote and be sure to let the media know who looks better in identical dresses or if you prefer a star's hair long or short.

FIGURE 10-4
When sports fans have an opinion about a player who has or has not been playing well, they want their opinions heard. Fan involvement and fan participation have become crucial to media celebrity reporting. (iStockphoto.com #1606316, Rob Friedman.)

Your opinion matters. That is the media message. Your opinion matters about everything! Our media culture empowers audiences to feel entitled to have an opinion about everything, and, most important, to know everything about celebrities. Jon Stewart on *The Daily Show* on December 20, 2006, referred to God as a celebrity along the lines of a Paris Hilton—a celebrity who is a celebrity because she is a celebrity—because, as his show makes clear, in American culture, celebrity is everything.

The information sweep about celebrity raises numerous questions about privacy boundaries and ethics. Specifically, what about celebrities is and is not of legitimate concern to the public? And if it isn't of legitimate concern, should the public still have full and ready access?

FIGURE 10-5
For biographer Patricia Bosworth, including or not including actor Montgomery Clift's experiences in gay bars was a difficult decision (Clift is shown here in a still from *From Here to Eternity*). (Globe Photos, Inc.)

THE TOTAL PICTURE REVEALED

When Patricia Bosworth wrote her 1978 landmark biography of the actor Montgomery Clift, star of *Red River* (1948), *A Place in the Sun* (1951), *From Here to Eternity* (1953), and *The Misfits* (1961), she was not planning to

include accounts of his experiences with sadomasochism at gay bars (Figure 10-5). As a serious biographer interested in gathering all available information about her subject, she discovered this aspect of his life while conducting her research. At first, she saw this information simply as part of that research, not something she would include in her book. The details of his sex life were too graphic, she felt. Her editor, however, convinced her that this part of Clift's life provided valuable insights about him that illuminated his life and art.

Neil Baldwin, a distinguished visiting professor of history at Montclair State University as well as a biographer and historian whose most recent book is *The American Revelation* (2005), had an experience similar to Bosworth's. When he was a graduate student at SUNY Buffalo, he worked with Williams's literary executor, the renowned publisher of New Directions, James Laughlin, to catalog the papers the poet William Carlos Williams had donated to the school. In doing their work, Baldwin and Laughlin found a number of personal letters that Williams had written about his numerous extramarital affairs. Laughlin classified many of the documents, love letters mostly, as restricted, using different kinds of restrictions, some documents only available to researchers, some restricted to a certain year (presumably well after Williams's wife had passed away).

Some 10 years later, when Baldwin was writing his critical biography of Williams, *To All Gentleness* (1984), he originally did not feel he could or should write about Williams's infidelities. He wondered if revealing these private details was ethically correct. In fact, in Baldwin's original manuscript, he omitted the information.

As with Bosworth, Baldwin was encouraged to include reference to the affairs by his editor, who felt that not revealing them would constitute a serious omission when writing about the poet who influenced a generation with signature works like the poem, "Patterson." For Baldwin, providing the total picture became paramount. See the accompanying box to examine what Bosworth and Baldwin wrote.

TWO BIOGRAPHICAL SKETCHES

Describing the rough sex bars Clift frequented, Bosworth wrote about a time when producer Frank Taylor found Clift in the backroom, frequented by rough trade, of a bar called Dirty Dick's, where the passed-out, fully clothed Clift was stretched out on a table "while butch dykes, drag queens, transvestites, guys in leather jackets crawled over him humming like insects."[14] Taylor recalled that "Some were kissing his neck, others were fondling his crotch. I thought I was going to vomit. It was the most debauched scene I've ever witnessed."[15]

Baldwin described Williams's infidelities to his wife, Flossie, on page 181 of his book. He wrote, "He was overcome with guilt about his false steps as a husband. Reciting names, dates, and places to Flossie he told his wife he had been with many other women during their forty married years. He could not help himself. Women—all women—fascinated Williams, beyond words. . . . Williams had taken advantage of Flossie's quietness and faith, turning to other women, in New York City and elsewhere."[16]

[14]Patricia Bosworth, *Montgomery Clift: A Biography* (New York: Harcourt Brace Jovanovich, 1978), p. 386.
[15]Bosworth, *Montgomery Clift*.
[16]Neil Baldwin, *To All Gentleness: William Carlos Williams: The Doctor Poet* (New York: Atheneum, 1984), p. 181.

You Decide

In light of what is currently reported about celebrities, do you feel that Bosworth and Baldwin were ethically correct to include details about their subject's private sex lives? Do you feel the initial concerns of Bosworth and Baldwin were valid? Do you think they should have included the details without the encouragement of their editors?

LUNCHING ETHICALLY IN HOLLYWOOD

If everyone has the potential to be a celebrity for a moment in time, real and would-be power players, producers, directors, writers, actors, and other media players frequently feel a strong need to position themselves as celebrities and to demand that they be treated as such. One way to establish a claim to celebrity involves where one dines and, most important, whom one dines with.

People are convinced that a lot of Hollywood business takes place over meals, with real power players like Jeffrey Katzenberg reportedly doing two power breakfasts a day, one right after the other. These food fests take place at various restaurants, called watering holes, deemed industry worthy by the power elite.

Julia Phillips's book *You'll Never Eat Lunch in This Town Again* (1991) reinforced the canon that lunching is an important conduit to business, a lot weightier activity than the one described by Stephen Sondheim in the song "The Ladies Who Lunch" from the musical *Company* where indolent women with nothing important to do arrange their lives around meaningless time-filling lunches.

Indeed, lunching in Hollywood is an important expense account activity (Figure 10-6). Even a low-rent company hanging on by threads will not cut expense account meals because of their perceived importance in maintaining and nurturing relationships. Less actual business, however, may take place at these meals than the company accountants might think when they review the receipts.

Two television producers had a very bad lunch reputation (as well as a fair number of canceled lunches) because they would pull out a long list of projects to pitch over lunch, thus spending the entire lunch pitching their wares. Bad form. Better to simply say you'd like to send over a script and then report back to your team that the exec seemed really excited about the reading the script. The truth? Maybe not exactly, but Hollywood players readily engage in this kind of acceptable puffery.

Who you lunch with says a lot about your status in the business. One junior executive seeking to establish his credentials in a new job boldly invited the head of a department to lunch. Put in his place, he was told he was not "ready" for such a lunch, that he should come in for an in-office meeting instead and that he might be ready for a lunch in a few years.

Hollywood is a town built on relationships, and the lunch ritual is part of building relationships. It is possible to spot ethical lapses in the lunch routine, particularly when expenses can reach astronomical heights. But breaking bread is not likely to go away, even as budgets tighten. So here we have a real-world situation juxtaposed with possible ethical infractions. Some might say the line is crossed only when one lunches with an enemy or a Hitler to further one's career.

FIGURE 10-6
Being seen at the right red carpet events is a big part of being a media celebrity. Celebrities, real and imagined, see fancy meals and red carpet events as extremely important. (iStockphoto. com #2848893, Baldur Tryggvasom.)

RIGHT TO KNOW?

The following may illustrate some of the complexities involved in seeking to determine what private details the media should reveal about celebrities. In 2000, the venerable *The Plain Dealer* in Cleveland printed a story citing unnamed sources who claimed that a local talk show host, Joel Rose, was being investigated for "mailing packages containing underwear and pornography to several area women."[17]

The day the story was published, Rose committed suicide, proclaiming his innocence in a suicide note, thus raising difficult questions about the reveal. Should the paper have held the information until it could be confirmed beyond anonymous sources? Was the paper in some way responsible for the suicide? Several years later, Rose appeared to be exonerated, though still the primary suspect, when it was found that "the DNA in the saliva on the packages did not match Rose's."[18]

Clearly, the published details about Rose, which resulted in his suicide, caused great *H*arm. Was the information about the investigation off limits until confirmed on the record? If Rose was indeed a public figure, was this private information of concern to the public at this early stage? Or is an information-hungry audience entitled to know all, no matter at what stage of an investigation?

REVEALING ALL

Important questions persist when dealing with celebrities in the media. What to include? What to exclude? How do you *E*valuate? What is the *T*ruth? What *H*arm might be caused by the reveal?

Media entrepreneur Jeff Sagansky, the former president of CBS Entertainment and president and CEO of Pax TV, is currently on the board of American Media, publishers of *The National Inquirer* and *Star*, among others. He is adamant that

---

[17]Kimberly Conniff, "Overkill," *Brill's Content*, November, 2000, p. 126.
[18]Ted Gup, "Gotcha: You May or May Not Be a Suspect, but You Will Be All over the News," August 18, 2002, www.washingtonpost.com, accessed August 21, 2006.

the culture is coarsening and that violence in the media is a major concern, particularly if the violence depicted can cause *H*arm.

For Sagansky, the many studies that indicate a correlation between violence in the media and subsequent aggressive behavior in exposed individuals are conclusive. He sees a direct link between the two, but in terms of celebrity, he feels strongly that people who court the public, people whose careers depend on publicity and the attention of the media, are fair game; for him, all details about these individuals can be revealed: if your career and livelihood depend on being in the public eye and courting the press, you can't select what can and what cannot be revealed about you.

Of course, determining who is and who is not a celebrity and who is or is not seeking press coverage can prove difficult. It's almost a chicken or the egg situation: which comes first, a person's courting of the media or the media's courting of the person they have defined as a celebrity? Is a CEO a celebrity, for example? Donald Trump clearly seeks press coverage, but some CEOs don't seek the limelight. Are they celebrities all the same as a result of their positions and influence? Nevertheless, the definition of a celebrity as someone who seeks public recognition and publicity greatly clarifies the issue.

FIGURE 10-7
A celebrity with a secret gay lifestyle needs to be careful, as many in the media would eagerly reveal his hidden life if they could. Some reporters, however, would not expose him, unless he had widely proclaimed the lie that he was heterosexual. (iStockphoto.com #1367590, Joe Augustine.)

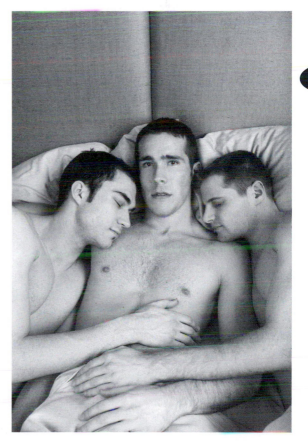

For Roberta Plutzik, a former entertainment and celebrity author who conducted hundreds of celebrity interviews, it's fair game to reveal a celebrity's private activities *when* the celebrity contradicts himself. For example, if a celebrity sought fan approval by perpetuating a lie, exposing that lie became part of Plutzik's job as an entertainment journalist. Thus, if a celebrity involved in a DUI proclaimed never to drive when drinking, exposing the lie or contradiction would have been legitimate, according to Plutzik's code of ethics. However, if a male celebrity who never insisted he was heterosexual was seen on a date with another man, for Plutzik and some others, the celebrity's privacy would have been respected (Figure 10-7).

You Decide

As an exercise, see if you would draw the line anywhere in the following list of celebrity denials that prove to be lies. Is there anything you feel should not be revealed from an ethical point of view, even if the celebrity has previously vehemently denied the truth:

- A terrorist past
- A previous marriage
- A previous heterosexual affair
- A history of alcoholism
- A passion for cross-dressing
- A promiscuous present or past

- An ongoing homosexual/lesbian relationship
- A fake birthday that makes the celebrity younger
- Use of steroids
- An addiction to prescription drugs
- A child out of wedlock
- An abusive past with charges filed
- A prison record
- AIDS
- A parent with Alzheimer's disease

Using our E*T*H*I*C*S* rubric, where appropriate, determine the reasoning behind your opinions.

CELEBRITY GOSSIP

Indonesia may be considering banning celebrity gossip shows because they are "sinful" and exploit "people's shameful secrets,"[19] but in many ways it seems as if everything about celebrities is fair game. Celebrities who crave attention realize that, in a crowded field, one has to be more outrageous than the next to command coverage. But even mundane, predictable details can get media attention. Many celebrity journalists appear to be on automatic pilot, matter-of-factly reporting celebrity trivia as if it merited significant media attention. Also, as commentator Katie Roiphe charges in *Brill's Content*,[20] many entertainment commentators are raising the bar by speaking as if they themselves had intimate, personal knowledge about a celebrity's actions. It's not enough to report the details; the celebrity journalist has to be personally connected, a celebrity confidant.

[19]"Quick Takes," *The Los Angeles Times*, August 17, 2006, E-5.
[20]Katie Roiphe, "Profiles Encouraged," *Brill's Content*, December 2000/January 2001, pp. 57, 58, 60.

It follows that fans themselves feel they too can comment about the celebrity's actions, both private (do you think that breast augmentation surgery is successful or unsuccessful?) and public. Not only can fans know everything about a celebrity, but they feel fully entitled to provide detailed commentary that is often mean-spirited, much in the way that longtime *New York* magazine critic John Simon felt free to make negative comments about how women looked on stage.

First, the media provide the public with every private detail on or off the record about a celebrity. Second, the public is invited, encouraged, to provide commentary, which assumes the kind of personal involvement that sports fans have when they feel they are part of the teams they support. Popular sites like www.pinkisthenewblog.com, www.popsugar.com, www.televisionwithoutpity.com, www.perezhilton.com, or www.gossiprules.com thrive on this kind of interactive involvement. Traditional print publications like *The Los Angeles Times* invite "street corner critics" to review films that have not been made available to movie critics.[21] Everyone, it seems, has become a "citizen journalist," fully empowered to offer opinions about every imaginable topic.

MEL GIBSON

In the summer of 2006, uber actor Mel Gibson (Figure 10-8) was arrested for drunk driving in Malibu after a reported night of partying at Moonshadows, a Malibu eatery. When stopped, Gilson ranted that "The Jews are responsible for all the wars in the world." As the son of a Holocaust denier, Gibson has long been suspected of having an anti-Semitic agenda in the making of the film *The Passion of the Christ* (2004), a charge Gibson has repeatedly denied.

239

The news of Gibson's arrest and comments became instant fodder for the media. The website TMZ.com published the sheriff's report of the arrest, and the media pursued Gibson's fellow revelers, making them the 15-minute celebrities they might secretly have longed to be all of their lives. The hunt was on. Gibson's co-stars were sought out; both pro- and anti-Gibson voices were given ample space to comment, and comment again. As *Daily Variety*'s chief television critic, Brian Lowry, commented, "The sudden demand for talking heads to discuss all things Mel Gibson provided another reminder that there are no greater contributors to coarsening the national debate than those willing to spout off on every topic unburdened by research or facts."[22]

[21]Melissa Pamer and Kelly-Anne Suarez, "It's Up to You, the Reviewer," *The Los Angeles Times*, August 21, 2006, E1, 3.
[22]Brian Lowry, "Tuning In," *Daily Variety*, August 2, 2006, p. 4.

FIGURE 10-8
When uber actor Mel Gibson was arrested for drunk driving in Malibu, California, he said, "The Jews
are responsible for all the wars in the world," causing a media frenzy. (iStockphoto.com #3222493,
Wayne Howard.)

The trade publication *Broadcasting & Cable* asked the question, "Who do YOU
think will score the big interview with Mel Gibson," encouraging readers to cast
their votes at the publication's website, www.broadcastingandcable.com. The
magazine provided a detailed list with reasons why certain interviewers such as
Oprah Winfrey, Barbara Walters, Diane Sawyer, Larry King (the list goes on)
might or might not land what *Broadcasting & Cable* termed the "post-rehab
sit-down."[23]

Was the Mel Gibson arrest of legitimate concern to the public? Was it possibly
good gossip about a major star that reinforces the comforting realization that
famous people have flaws like the rest of us? Was it an opportunity for a ready-
to-respond public to chastise a famous person for messing up when he should
have every reason to enjoy his fame and fortune? Was it simply good gossip
that provided a needed distraction from the war in Iraq and the escalating situation in the Middle East? Or did the comments generate attention because
Gibson had long denied being anti-Semitic?

[23]"Getting Gibson: The Post-Rehab Sit-Down," *Broadcasting & Cable*, August 7, 2006, p. 5.

The widely covered Mel Gibson incident did, in fact, become a big story. Shortly after Gibson's outburst, ABC dropped its miniseries with Gibson about the Holocaust, issuing a statement that the project was being abandoned because no script had been delivered, not because of Gibson's remarks. Everyone had an opinion, everyone except most studio executives who were reluctant to go against one of Hollywood's most powerful players, though actor Rob Schneider denounced Gibson in a full-page ad in *Daily Variety*, an open letter in which he said, "I, Rob Schneider, a ½ Jew, pledge from this day forth to never work with Mel Gibson-actor-director-producer and anti-Semite."[24]

After the inciting incident itself, commentary about Gibson's apology followed: Would his apology and offer to meet with Jewish leaders enable him to overcome the stigma of the outburst? How sincere was he when he claimed that in his heart he was not an anti-Semite? Like Henry Ford before him, who apologized for the anti-Semitic articles he published in the *Dearborn Independent* but nevertheless continued his tirades against the Jews, would Gibson reveal his true feelings about Jews when the furor died down?

TOM CRUISE

Tom Cruise, for many years the number 1 box office star in the world, has long been the subject of tabloid celebrity interest (Figure 10-9). All of his actions were duly reported and photographed and the rumors never stopped, in spite of the tight controls his public relations people insisted on. Rumors about his sexuality, rumors about the influence of Scientology, or rumors about the restrictions placed on what he could and could not be asked in an interview always hovered in the background. But when Cruise jumped up and down on Oprah Winfrey's couch while proclaiming his love for *Dawson's Creek* star Katie Holmes and when he

FIGURE 10-9
Tom Cruise's extreme, eccentric behavior may have cost him his lucrative producing deal with Paramount. (Globe Photos, Inc.)

241

[24]"An Open Letter to the Hollywood Community," *Daily Variety*, August 3, 2006, p. 7.

challenged Matt Lauer on the *Today* show about prescription drugs, the rumors took a sharp turn and his celebrity took a direct hit.

The hit was so hard that Sumner Redstone, the cantankerous chairman of Viacom, felt justified terminating Cruise's production company's contract with Paramount, a division of Viacom, on the grounds that Cruises off-screen behavior was too much of a risk and claiming that Cruise was, in fact, "out of control."[25] Cruise, the celebrity, was no longer worth the money, and the man with the power and money, Redstone, unceremoniously challenged Cruise's celebrity status and fired him, proving that a celebrity is only as valuable as his last box office tally. For Redstone, Cruise's recent films had not performed up to expectations, and Cruise's previous deal gave him too large of a take. Thus, Redstone decided that Cruise's deal with Paramount was not a good one for the studio.

Many felt that Redstone treated Cruise badly, possibly even unethically, but the power that celebrities possess, even if it is carefully guarded and nurtured, is transient. Today's celebrity is tomorrow's old news, causing many to feel that the media regularly exploit celebrities and then toss them aside like rag dolls when the next celebrity appears on the horizon. This exploitation presently includes exposing anything and everything about the celebrity and inviting consumers to weigh in with their own interpretations and comments. When one sees a current celebrity being photographed by seemingly countless paparazzi, one can speculate how long the limelight will last and if the celebrity will still be photographed a year later. When one thinks this way, it's easy to feel sorry for celebrities and to question if they are, in fact, being exploited.

You Decide

Go to a newspaper depot and check out the number of magazines and tabloids. Who are the celebrities on the covers? What are the celebrity stories about? What approaches are being taken? Do you detect any ethical violations? How are the celebrities being treated? Decide for yourself if the media is exploiting the celebrities or if the celebrities are exploiting the media to advance their careers. For example, if, as Sagansky sees it, a performer seeks publicity, is the media crossing ethical guidelines if it invades that person's privacy? Can performers justifiably control what is or is not revealed about them?

[25]Caryn James, "Mission Imperative for a Star: Be Likable," *The New York Times*, August 8, 2006, B-1.

STAR JONES

When the celebrity interviewer becomes the celebrity, trouble usually follows. Most interviewers know to keep themselves in the background, allowing the celebrity to be in the spotlight. Johnny Carson of *The Tonight Show* knew how to do this. He may have been a bigger star than the guests who came on his show to hawk their latest projects, but he knew how to give a star center stage. The spotlight may not last long and the interviewer may outlast the celebrity, but it's an unwritten rule that the interviewer cannot upstage the celebrity.

FIGURE 10-10
Critic Paul Brownfield of *The Los Angeles Times* raises important ethical questions about what it means to go "off-the-record." (Courtesy of Nami Mun.)

When Star Jones of the ABC daytime show *The View* broke this covenant by seeking to become too much of a celebrity herself, she found herself fired. Jones became too hot, too much of a lightning rod because, per *The View* co-host Barbara Walters, the public was doubting Jones's "veracity" as a result of too much self-promotion.[26] Jones apparently made the mistake of defining herself as the celebrity when she *should* have been content to be one of the girlfriends on the show. The ratings for *The View* are up since Jones left and was replaced by Rosie O'Donnell. However, O'Donnell herself risked becoming too much of a celebrity before she left the show, as she engaged in a feud with Donald Trump, accused Kelly Rippa of homophobia, and described Oprah Winfrey's friendship with Gayle King as "very typical of gay relationships."[27]

CELEBRITY VERIFICATION

How does a celebrity interviewer check what a celebrity says or, more generally, how does an interviewer check what a source says, even if the source is not a celebrity? Paul Brownfield (Figure 10-10) of *The Los Angeles Times* assumes that the person he is interviewing is not giving him the

243

[26]Robin Abcarian, "Commentary: The Truth? It's a Point of View," *The Los Angeles Times*, June 30, 2006, E-1, 28.
[27]"Ratings, Conflict Up with O'Donnell," *The Los Angeles Times*, December 23, 2006, E-2.

complete story. He assumes that he is being given the version that the person wants to see in print. Following an interview, he thus goes to what he calls "a trusted source" to verify the information. He calls this doing his due diligence. For Brownfield, a "good source" is someone who is not simply adhering to an agenda, someone who does not stick to a prepared press release.

Brownfield raises interesting ethical questions about going off the record. There are a number of different ways "off the record" can be interpreted. One interpretation is that off the record means "I will not identify you, but I will use the information you give me." A second view is that in means "I will get another source to confirm what you have told me and I will then use the information, but you will not be identified." A third perspective is that it means "I will not use the information you give me. It's simply for research purposes, what is frequently called 'background.'" Most people think that off the record means the third choice, but that is not the way most interviewers use the term. Many people have been burned because they thought off the record meant that what they were saying would not be used, which is not always the case.

Many people like to guess who has been talked to in a celebrity piece, whose version is being spun, and how many people the interviewer spoke to before considering the story finished. It can be fun, for example, to guess whose version of events has been embraced. Oftentimes, it's easy to guess an identity, particularly if a source is named in the piece. If another anecdote is without a source, can one assume that the first source provided the next piece of information? For example, if Joe Smith reveals in a celebrity interview that such-and-such a star is buying a new Beverly Hills home and later in the piece there's an anonymous tip that the star is having an affair with a married man, won't most people assume that Joe Smith provided the details about the affair? Brownfield says one has to protect one's sources by making it impossible to trace a source, but under deadline many a celebrity interviewer has slipped and not protected a source.

You Decide

Do you think an interviewer should explain to his subject which definition of "off the record" is in play? Why? Also, find an example of a piece where you feel the identity of an anonymous source could be deduced, easily or otherwise.

CELEBRITY WORSHIP

It's not just the media that idolize celebrities. *Everyone* loves celebrities, right? Otherwise, why would the media be so committed to figuring out who is hot and who is not, and why else would we so eagerly post our opinions about every action taken or not taken by the celebrity of the moment?

The ongoing changes in the way celebrities are covered in the media continue to raise complex and interesting ethical questions about privacy and the public's right to know. Because so many of us follow the activities of celebrities as if they were members of our immediate families, it's important to analyze exactly how the media cover celebrities—while we are waiting in line at the supermarket reading the tabloids or while we browse the Internet, possibly even as we add a comment or two to the celebrity questions that are posed.

Let's go from celebrities' stories to terminology that is used by media insiders. Celebrity commentators want to be perceived as having inside, personal knowledge, and people who work in the media want to feel that they are insiders who understand all the coded terminology:

HOLLYWOOD INSIDE STORIES AND THE USE OF PHRASES THAT REVEAL HIDDEN ETHICAL IMPLICATIONS: READ ALL ABOUT THE SCANDALOUS PHRASES FOUND ONLY IN THIS BOOK. YOU WILL BE SHOCKED, BUT YOU CANNOT IGNORE THE LANGUAGE USED BY INSIDERS, LANGUAGE THAT IS DECODED HERE FOR THE FIRST TIME. ANYONE WHO WANTS TO WORK IN THE MEDIA MUST READ THE FOLLOWING IN ORDER TO GET HIRED. IF YOU SKIP THIS SECTION, YOU MIGHT AS WELL WEAR A NEON SIGN TO AN INTERVIEW THAT FLASHES ON AND OFF SAYING, "I AM AN OUTSIDER."

This section contains a number of phrases that are frequently used, phrases that suggest a great deal more than the words themselves. These phrases, which reveal a number of ethical positions, function as a kind of shorthand that is readily understood by insiders who know what's up. These phrases include the following:

"He/she takes no prisoners." This phrase, which is most always meant as praise, suggests that the individual is one tough customer who gets the job done. In other words, the ends justify the means. How the means are accomplished is irrelevant.

"I have to make the difficult decisions." This statement usually serves several purposes. One, it establishes that the speaker is the person in charge (George W. Bush, is, after all, "the decider," as he himself made clear, and everyone knows that it's the quarterback who calls the plays, not the armchair quarterback who indulges in second guessing). Two, it also cuts short any follow-up discussion of how or why the difficult decisions were made, leaving people wondering if the "difficult decisions" were made arbitrarily.

"It's on a need-to-know basis, and you don't need to know." This phrase could be used if someone presumes to question the "difficult decisions." Again, the speaker is on the inside, the person in charge, and the person being spoken to is the one who doesn't need to know. In the media, information is power, and this phrase, even if it's spoken softly or jokingly, makes it clear that one person, the speaker, has information that the person being addressed doesn't have.

"Do me a favor." This sugarcoated statement is usually made by a person in power who is "being nice" by phrasing an order in this way rather than by issuing a command.

"You should have a conversation with him." As in sports when the pitching coach goes to the mound to have a "conversation" with the pitcher, as reported by observant commentators, a "conversation" usually means that the recipient is receiving stern advice. When a media executive says she needs to have a "conversation" with someone, it means that someone is in need of a dressing down. As a junior network executive, I was frequently told I needed to engage in "conversation" with wayward producers or writers, and I was also frequently in "conversation" with my superiors over mistakes I had committed.

Phrases like the one made by Colin Callender, the president of HBO Films, "It's a war out there,"[28] or the one made by Sony's Amy Pascal about fired Disney executive Nina Jacobson, "Talent loves her and she knows how to walk the tricky tightrope that all of us in these jobs have to walk, navigating commerce and art"[29] suggest that the world of entertainment is a place

[28]Ken Auletta, "Hollywood Ending," *The New Yorker*, July 24, 2006, p. 41.
[29]Claudia Eller, "Disney Fired Film Production President," *The Los Angeles Times*, July 19, 2006, C-6.

reserved for survivors, individuals who view the media as a battlefield where specialized survival skills are required.

"Welcome to the jungle." This phrase, often used to welcome a new hire, aggrandizes the difficulties associated with the world of entertainment. It also suggests a masculine world filled with jungle-like traps when the reality is most often plush offices with minions to do any heavy lifting. If the person being welcomed to the jungle were to look around and say, "I don't see any jungle here and wasn't that your Mercedes in the parking lot and isn't that Fiji water on your desk," that would be the wrong response. The right response is that you are up to any challenge that the jungle presents and that your off-road vehicle is ready to navigate the rough terrain ahead.

"Be careful what you wish for." A variation of "Welcome to the jungle," this is a phrase that one programming executive used when she bumped into a new hire leaving the parking lot at 11 p.m. a few days after he was hired. The meaning was clear: You wanted this job, and now you aren't so sure, are you?

"We tried to do something that was a little different." This phrase is used by creators of failures to explain a poor performance at the box office, in the ratings, or in sales. The failure may not have been different in any significant way. It may have followed a tried-and-true formula that worked in the past. Saying "I saw it, and what exactly was different about it?" is not the right answer to this excuse. It's much better to commiserate about how difficult it is to try something new.

Saying that someone financed a project with "broken-nose monies" means that mob money was used. It's code, and it's probably best not to ask too many questions here.

"So-and-so is leaving to pursue other interests" or "So-and-so is leaving to spend time with her family." This means the individual in question was fired, pure and simple. Is this a "lie," an untruth by the definition of our E*T*H*I*C*S rubric?

In a politically correct environment where one's sexual preference or age cannot be asked, certain useful buzzwords have come into play that are clearly understood as code. Saying someone is "an experienced performer who has worked on Broadway and in live television," strongly suggests, without actually saying it, that the performer is old, since live television flourished in the 1950s. It's like the line in Edward Albee's 1962 play *Who's Afraid of Virginia Woolf?* when George says there's a daguerreotype of his wife Martha on the mantle, a line designed to reveal how ancient George finds Martha because daguerreotypes were a very early photo process.

Similarly, using a phrase like "She's a perfectionist" to describe a performer immediately suggests to the knowing that this particular performer is difficult to work with.

If a person asked for a recommendation responds, "Oh, he's great. I really like him. He's a great guy, but have you thought about so-and-so," that is immediate code for "Don't hire him!" The candidate has, as the saying goes, been "hosed down" in favor of someone else. No traceable negative comments were ever made, but none was needed. The meaning was clear. Few people offer really direct negative responses when asked for an evaluation of a candidate as the persons vetoed may shortly be in positions of power, but people understand the code.

You Decide

What do these and other phrases suggest to you? What assumptions involving ethics do these types of comments make? When underlings are addressed with representative phrases like "I have to make the difficult decisions," "It's on a need-to-know basis, and you don't need to know," and "Do me a favor," are they being treated ethically?

248

In this chapter, we have looked at ethical issues associated with censorship as well as with celebrity, two very big words beginning with "c." In the next chapter, let's examine some ethical issues involving consolidation, another word starting with "c," and diversity.

CHAPTER 11
Diversity and Consolidation

When people talk about diversity in the media, what exactly are they talking about? Usually the term "diversity" does not refer to the variety of choices available to the consumer—that is, different choices that a consumer can select. Most often, the term "diversity" refers to minority representation, representation in front of and behind the camera, in the front office, among media owners, in newspaper and Internet bylines, and so forth. This is the way we will define diversity in the text.

There are many ethnic minorities around the world, many of which are not fully represented in the media. Diversity advocates want to level the playing field to include many more minorities. These minorities include African Americans, Latinos, Asians, Arabs, and Native Americans, among others.

Most people want to see people like themselves when they go to the movies, turn on a newscast or entertainment program, or venture into the workforce. "Seeing people like me" has become a rallying cry for proponents of diversity. People want to be where they feel comfortable, where they feel they are part of a group, where they are included rather than excluded. A lack of diversity impedes this sense of inclusion.

Changes are on the horizon, however. According to *Noticiero Univision* anchor Jorge Ramos in a 2005 diversity issue of *Emmy*, published by the Academy of Television Arts & Sciences, "The new America has been born. More than half of all newborns in California are Latino, and the rest of the country will follow. In less than fifty years, Hispanics, Asians and African Americans will become the majority of the population. And in 120 years, there will be more Latinos in the U.S. than non-Hispanics and whites."[1]

Ramos added:

> While the network newscasts are continuously losing market share, Spanish-language programming is growing. . . . Spanish-language newscasts are providing their bilingual viewers with something they cannot find in English programming: news about Latinos and Latin America. It is no wonder that some of the most-watched news programs in cities like Miami, Los Angeles, Houston, Chicago and New York are in Spanish. And this trend will not subside in the near future.[2]

As a further indication of the changing media landscape, media companies are changing their focus. Business writer Jennifer Pendleton observed:

> It's no mystery why NBC and other media companies are staking claims on the exploding U.S. Hispanic market. Mainstream broadcast television networks continue to lose audience in the face of exploding channel choices, while Hispanic viewers remain a perennially underserved audience. Cable networks also see the possibilities in targeting an exploding population, particularly since mainstream media players seem so clueless about how to effectively reach them.[3]

Diversity has become a major concern in recent years. In the diversity special of *Emmy*, the editors emphasized that the composition of America is changing quickly and that "By 2050 minority groups will constitute 49.9% of the population."[4] Indeed, television has a very wide reach, one that goes well beyond America's borders. Though countries around the world may not respond to American politics, they do respond to American entertainment, at one point making *Baywatch* the most watched program in the world and making countless American movies international successes. It thus seems very fitting that an organization such as the Academy of Television Arts & Sciences examine television's impact on diversity as the make-up of the population changes.

All four major networks—ABC, CBS, NBC, and Fox—have executives who promote diversity, and stations such as WGBH in Boston have mission state-

---

[1]Jorge Ramos, "The Revolution Has Started," *Emmy*, 2005, vol. XXVII, no. 6, p. 38.
[2]Ibid., p. 40.
[3]Jennifer Pendleton, "Going for Goliath," *Emmy*, 2005, vol. XXVII, no. 6, p. 49.
[4]"Content: Diversity Special," *Emmy*, 2005, vol. XXVII, no. 6, p. 6.

ments that emphasize diversity (see www.WBGH .org). Ron Taylor (Figure 11-1), in his position as vice president of diversity development at Fox, regularly schedules sessions with program show-runners as well as with network executives to encourage them to embrace diversity. For Taylor, some showrunners and executives are stuck in a cultural time warp and thus fail to consider the advantages of a diverse cast; for Taylor, these individuals don't see beyond how things were done in the past.

For example, when I was at ABC in the 1990s, I found it difficult, if not impossible, to promote minority actors. I remember being surprised when I pitched international star and former member of Menudo Ricky Martin right around the time he made a big splash on the Grammys in 1999. Before pitching him, I ascertained that he was getable. I was told that he would need at least $200,000, well below the salaries that stars were receiving on television, but I couldn't gener-ate any excitement, and Martin did not receive an offer.

251

FIGURE 11-1
Diversity specialist Ron Taylor has found that not only is establishing diversity the right thing to do, but it also stimulates good business to have different ethnic groups represented in front of the camera as well as behind the camera. (Courtesy of Ron Taylor.)

Taylor finds that advertisers, often considered to be a conservative, if not seen as a primarily reactionary group, are ahead of the curve when it comes to diver-sity. In his diversity sessions, Taylor shows a three-minute compilation of advertisements that reveal an extensive diversity mix. Taylor finds that advertis-ers are far more willing than some executives to reach out to minorities. He thus discounts the oft-repeated position that a lack of diversity on television is motivated by advertiser concerns.

For Taylor, diversity is simply good business, particularly if one wants to enter the global marketplace (Figure 11-2). He has noted that a few years ago, the primary selling point for diversity was that it was the ethical or right thing to do: diversity needed to be addressed to remedy an all-white cookie-cutter view of the world.

At present, in addition to the ethical considerations, Taylor stresses that diversity is smart business, which may be why Disney is planning to introduce its first

FIGURE 11-2
Competing in the growing global marketplace requires paying close attention to diversity. (iStockphoto.com #3129433, Eva Serrabassa.)

African-American princess in a 2009 feature film, *The Frog Princess*. Disney's collection of princesses generates large amounts of money for the company and it made good business sense to do this, just as Mattel has added dolls of color to its collection of Barbies.

Today's audiences simply demand diversity. Even if they don't always get it. Some shows (Figure 11-3), like *The OC*, which ended its four-year run in 2007, ultimately fail because of a lack of diversity. A program like *The West Wing*, which began in 1999 as all white, quickly adjusted and added an African American actor, Dule Hill, to the mix in 2000.

A program like *Grey's Anatomy*, which began in 2005 and became an instant success, connects with audiences in large part because of its diverse cast. Created by an African-American woman, Shonda Rhimes, it features a diverse cast that enables viewers to find people "who look like me." My students consistently cite the diverse cast in *Grey's Anatomy* as one of the main reasons they like the show.

Many who believe that diversity increases audiences point to the 1997 television production of *Cinderella* as an example of successful colorblind casting. Cinderella was played by an African American, Brandy Norwood, the prince was Asian, Paolo Montalban, and his mother was played by Whoopi Goldberg, an African American. One stepsister was white, Jen Cody, and the other was African American, Janelle Anne Robinson. This kind of colorblind casting succeeded with audiences and critics alike and paved the way forward.

Margaret Cho's *All-American Girl* (1994) didn't work, however. The show's failure made Cho bitter, and her bitterness and disappointment became a key part of her performances as a stand-up comedienne. The show featured Cho as a Korean American struggling to adapt to adapt to an American way of life while living with a family that was clinging to Korean traditions. Some felt that the show failed because it engaged in broad cultural stereotypes, whereas others felt that it failed because it was not adequately supported. Cho would agree with that assessment.

253

HOW TO ACHIEVE DIVERSITY

Given that attaining diversity is both the right ethical thing to do and that, according to Taylor and others, it makes for good business, how should it be achieved? In this section, let's examine a number of tactics employed by proponents of diversity and see how they measure up in terms of our E*T*H*I*C*S rubric.

Over the years, there have been many diversity seminars like the one sponsored by the Diversity Committee of the International Cinematographers Guild and the Diversity Department of the Screen Actors Guild (SAG) on January 21, 2006, featuring Tim Wise, author of *White Like Me*. There have also been numerous studies about minority representation in front of and behind the camera. Most of these studies indicate that minorities are not adequately represented, though some progress is being made.

The question becomes what should be stressed, the lack of representation or the advances that are taking place? If the tactic is to hammer at the lack of minority representation as a way to keep the focus on diversity, does that become a misrepresentation of the *T*ruth? In an article titled "NAACP Should

FIGURE 11-3
If a show lacks diversity, even if it features attractive, likable people in idealized locations such as a beach community, its chances of lasting success are diminished. (iStockphoto.com #728343, Kenneth O'Quinn.)

Acknowledge TV Gains," Brian Lowry chastises the NAACP's tactic of attacking the television industry for poor minority representation at a time, 2006, when progress was being made with programs like *Ugly Betty* and *Grey's Anatomy* on ABC; *Jericho* on CBS; and *My Name Is Earl, Scrubs, The Office, Heroes,* and *30 Rock* on NBC. Lowry feels that pressure on behalf of minority representation should continue, but that "lobbying groups diminish their moral authority . . . when they appear unwilling to acknowledge when real strides are made."[5] Repeating that minorities are underrepresented and that there are "no people like me" can be counterproductive if people disagree with the tactic being used. Others maintain that the pressure has to be kept up until truly significant progress has been obtained.

In the fall of 2006, at the Federal Communications Commission (FCC) hearings about media consolidation in El Segundo, California, producer Moctesuma Esparza, whose extensive body of work includes *Walkout* (2006), *Introducing Dorothy Dandridge* (1999), and *Selena* (1997), spoke about the total lack of Latinos on the air, while fellow panelists talked about the presence of Latinos on radio and television. For example, Jorge Delgado, president and general manager of KMEX-TV and KFTR-TV in Los Angeles, spoke about his commitment to serve Hispanic viewers with quality programming, winning a prestigious Peabody award in the process. As far as Esparza was concerned, however, there are no "people like me" on the air. For a detailed description of the two hearings that were held in the Los Angeles area in October 2006, go to www.fcc/ownership/hearing-california100306.html.

Another tactic involves taking out industry ads that feature your company or organization's commitment to diversity. The Diversity Special issue of *Emmy* magazine contains a large number of such ads. For example, Showtime has a full-page color ad featuring minority actors from its shows with the words "Connected by Our Humanity. United by Our Diversity."[6]

Other ads in *Emmy* proclaiming a commitment to diversity include those by the industry magazine *Television Week* ("We are pleased to support the Academy of Television Arts & Sciences in all of its efforts for diversity in television");[7] BET (Black Entertainment Network) ("It's my culture, my style, my world, my network my choice, BET it's my thing,"[8] which suggests that you will not be an

---

[5] Brian Lowry, "Tuning In: NAACP Should Acknowledge TV Gains," *Daily Variety,* December 6, 2006, p. 2.

[6] *Emmy,* 2005, vol. XXVII, no. 6, p. 5.

[7] Ibid, p. 11.

[8] Ibid, p. 15.

outsider if you make BET your own); and the Writers Guild of America, West ("Committed to success for all").[9]

The Writers Guild ad refers readers to its website, www.wga.org, to check out the 2005 Hollywood Writers Report, which paints a bleak picture for minority writers. There was a small but steady increase in minorities writing for television from 1998 to 2004 with approximately 10% of minority WGA members employed in 2004, but the number of minorities writing for film has been stuck at approximately 6% since 1999.[10]

Another tactic might be to give awards to individuals who have demonstrated a commitment to diversity. In 2003, Lifetime, a cable network designed to reach out to women, took out a full-page ad in *Television Week* in a section that honored the contributions of the Walter Kaitz Foundation on behalf of diversity in the cable industry. The ad said, "Lifetime congratulates honoree Decker Anstrom and salutes the Walter Kaitz Foundation for its dedication and commitment to diversity in the cable industry."[11]

Dick Astin, as chairman and CEO of the Academy of Television Arts & Sciences, created the Televisionary Award to celebrate "individuals who have advanced diversity in our industry: network, studio and production executives who greenlighted shows with diverse creators or hired diverse show runners, producers, directors, writers and performers."[12] The first Televisionary Award went to ABC Entertainment president Stephen McPherson, who championed *Grey's Anatomy*, among other shows with diverse casts.

Are such ads and awards self-serving, merely gestures designed to convince skeptics that something is being done about diversity? Or is something actually being done? Does featuring George Lopez, "the most successful Mexican American in the history of TV,"[13] whenever a diversity figurehead is needed add up to exploitation, fostering false hopes for minorities? Or is Lopez a real inspiration to minorities who are pleased to see one of their own succeeding and opening doors that had previously been closed?

[9]Ibid, p. 27.
[10]"The 2005 Hollywood Writers Report: Catching Up with a Changing America," www.wga.org, accessed January 6, 2007.
[11]*Television Week*, September 15, 2003, p. 21.
[12]Dick Astin, "From the Chairman: Diversity: A Top Priority," *Emmy*, 2005, vol. XXVII, no. 6, p. 4.
[13]Alisa Valdes-Rodriguez, "King George," *Emmy*, 2005, vol. XXVII, no. 6, p. 42.

Simply put, do the ends justify the means? Even if some progress is being made in the hiring of minorities, should the emphasis remain on all that still needs to be done? Many feel that keeping diversity firmly in the picture is the most important thing, not how it's done, even if it means using the race card (i.e., calling individuals who do not reach out to minorities racists, for example, saying, "You are a racist because you didn't hire an Asian in your film.").

Sometimes, diversity outreach uses a hammer and not honey. In the payola settlement of 2007, four major radio broadcasters—Clear Channel Communications, CBS radio, Entercom Communications, and Citadel Broadcasting—did not admit to any wrongdoing but nevertheless agreed to pay a $12.5 million fine and to play records from independent labels and local artists, thereby significantly increasing the diversity representation on radio. With the agreement, airplay is no longer limited to artists on the major music labels, Sony, BMG, Warner Music Group, Universal Music Group, and EMI Group. The settlement was not an easy one to reach, and it necessitated persistence on the part of FCC Commissioner Jonathan Adelstein, but it is designed to increase diversity in the world of radio.

Let's take another look at the creation of "Don't Count Us Out," the organization funded by News Corp., the parent company of Fox, in opposition to Nielsen's Local People Meter, LPM, discussed in Chapter 7. "Don't Count Us Out" can serve as an instrumental way to discuss diversity tactics and to think about the ends justifying the means.

News Corp. felt that Nielsen's developed technology, the LPM, did not accurately reflect what minorities were watching on television. News Corp. was concerned that the initial LPM readings had Fox losing viewership. News Corp. hired a public relations firm to create "Don't Count Us Out," which portrayed Nielsen as an overly powerful monopoly subject to virtually no checks and balances. Nielsen's minority samples were found inadequate, and much was made of Nielsen's hiring the daughter of California Representative Maxine Waters, an African American, to get Waters to speak in support of the LPM at a time when other prominent African Americans opposed it.[14] Some felt it was unethical for News Corp. to fund "Don't Count Us Out," because it had a vested

[14]Chuck Neubauer and Ted Rohrlich, "Capitalizing on Clout," *The Los Angeles Times*, December 19, 2004, A-1.

interest in the ratings. Others disagreed, pointing out that Nielsen was at fault. The end result was that Nielsen was "made to sweat," as one observer put it, and changes were made to improve the measuring service. "Don't Count Us Out" succeeded in postponing the LPM rollout and forcing Nielsen to revise its minority tabulations, at a cost of some $50 million to Nielsen.

A POSSIBLE INDIRECT DIVERSITY CONNECTION

In April 2007, as discussed in Chapter 9, syndicated radio host Don Imus, whose program "Imus in the Morning" was simulcast on MSNBC, called the Rutgers women's basketball team a "bunch of nappy-headed hos." The comment about the mostly African-American team was picked up and distributed by Media Matters for America (www.mediamatters.org), much in the way that YouTube posted *Seinfeld* alum Michael Richards's racial outburst at Hollywood's Laugh Factory in 2006.

Imus's comment about the players did not go unnoticed, unlike some similar remarks made by shock jocks and various pundits. It became a top story on the national news several days in a row, though some might question why Imus was the target and not others.

Initially, Imus was to be suspended for two weeks by CBS Radio and by MSNBC, which is owned by NBC. This suspension was made despite the tremendous amount of revenue Imus brought in. According to *The New York Times*, the program "generates in excess of $20 million in annual revenue for CBS Radio. . . . When advertising revenues for affiliates and MSNBC . . . are included the figure exceeds $50 million."[15]

Quickly, however, key advertisers dropped out. The advertisers were led by Procter & Gamble, considered by many to be a "thought leader" in terms of how and where advertising dollars should be spent. General Motors, American Express, Sprint Nextel, and others flexed their advertising power and followed suit. Suddenly, Imus's bankability evaporated. MSNBC was the first to fire him, followed shortly by CBS Radio.

What's interesting about the Imus dismissal is that it may have been generated by employees, what's sometimes referred to as movement "from the bottom

---

[15]Jacques Steinberg, "Imus Struggling to Retain Sway as a Franchise," *The New York Times*, April 11, 2007, A-1.

up." In other words, employees at NBC and CBS voiced their concerns using e-mail and other means to register their complaints. Technology being what it is, the complaints were quickly assembled, allowing a consensus to be established. Though he apologized, Imus's remarks were deemed too offensive to too many, and he was fired.

If employees at CBS and NBC did, in fact, have a strong say in Imus's firing, it becomes increasingly important for companies to be composed of diverse voices that reject racially insensitive and sexist remarks—in other words, to have employees who can themselves take the lead in objecting to moral and ethical lapses. The more diverse voices that participate in a workplace, the better the chances that remarks that coarsen the culture will diminish.

You Decide

- How do you *E*valuate diversity issues?
- How important is diversity when you decide what you are going to watch or where you are going to spend your entertainment dollars?
- Do you feel diversity progress is being made? How do you define "progress"?
- Do you feel too much emphasis is placed on diversity?
- Do you feel there is potential *H*arm in using certain diversity tactics?
- Were what many would call "Don't Count Us Out's" hardball tactics justified in terms of achieving a desired result?
- Do the ends justify the means when it comes to diversity?

- In terms of the *T*ruth, if I insist that that there are no Latinos in the media, ignoring some key Latinos in movies and television, is it understood that what I really mean is that there are few Latinos in the media and that my exaggeration is thus justified?
- Do you agree or disagree with Brian Lowry that diversity progress should be acknowledged, even if more work needs to be done?
- How do you think the situation with Don Imus could/ should have been handled from a diversity point of view? Are his comments significantly different from the lyrics found in many rap songs? If they are different, how so?

258

CONSOLIDATION AND DIVERSITY

In this section of the chapter, let's look at the relationship between consolidation and diversity. The passage of the 1996 Telecommunications Act drastically changed the broadcasting landscape, paving the way for deregulation and consolidation. The green light for large companies to merge with one another was given after this act was passed.

The abolition of the financial interest and syndications rules (Fin-Syn) in 1995 allowed networks to own the programs they distribute, something that the Fin-Syn rules prohibited. Getting rid of Fin-Syn paved the way for consolidation, and the 1996 Telecommunications Act sealed the deal. At present, the FCC allows a company to own television stations that reach 39% of the nation's viewers. There are no caps on nationwide radio ownership, allowing Clear Channel, for example, to expand dramatically from 40 stations before to more than 1200 stations in 2002. Under deregulation and consolidation, the relaxation of rules has become the norm, a development many businesses applaud.

As a result, fewer owners own/control more and more of the media, as noted in Chapter 2. Specifically, media observer Patrick Goldstein commented that in 2004, "Of the 91 major cable TV networks available in at least 16 million homes, 80% are owned or co-owned by just six media giants."[16]

According to Dan Mitchell, a columnist for *The New York Times*, "Local ownership of radio stations has declined nearly a third since 1975, just 15 formats account for three-quarters of all commercial programming and the top 10 station owners draw nearly two-thirds of all listeners."[17] This concentration of ownership makes it harder for new voices to be heard. As discussed earlier in this chapter, charges of payola against companies such as Clear Channel Communications, CBS Radio, Entercom, and Citadel forced these companies to provide more airtime for independent music.

But it's hard for new voices to be heard. Andrea Wong, formerly ABC's executive vice president of alternative/late night and now president and CEO at Lifetime, complained in 2007 that she was forced to work with fewer suppliers because ideas for reality television are readily stolen. She said, "We're trying to be our own studio more often and develop internally."[18] Consolidation has already made it increasingly difficult for independents, and the fear of ideas being stolen further ups the ante, becoming a further justification for fewer suppliers being allowed in the door.

Many deplore this concentration of media ownership and want it to stop. For example, Maurice Hinchey, a member of the House Appropriations Committee,

---

[16]Patrick Goldstein, "The Zipping Point," *The Los Angeles Times*, March 8, 2004, E-29.

[17]Dan Mitchell, "What's Online: What Can Money Buy?" *The New York Times*, January 27. 2007, B-5.

[18]Josef Adalian, "Wong: Ripoffs Are a Reality," *Daily Variety*, February 2, 2007. p. 5.

has said, "Deregulation has paved the way for a few media companies to dominate the country's information distribution system. Congress must step in to reverse the trend toward media consolidation."[19] Noted columnist and White House Press Corps member Helen Thomas laments the "ever-growing corporate ownership"[20] of the media. The mission statement of the Caucus for Television Producers, Writers & Directors, an organization founded in 1974, includes the following statement: "We are opposed to the growing concentration of ownership of development and television production in fewer and fewer hands. When a small number of mega-corporations control the vast majority of the process, diversity of voice is threatened, and our creative rights and our ability to compete as entrepreneurs are gravely endangered."[21]

FIGURE 11-4
Producer/manager David Craig fears that consolidation will hurt diversity representation, a concern shared by many media practitioners. (Courtesy of David Craig.)

One of the main objections to consolidation is that it hurts diversity, making it increasingly difficult for minorities. At a Peabody seminar held in New York in October 2005, *Flight 93* producer David Craig (Figure 11-4) concluded his remarks with "Some minority groups are already expressing concerns about Big Media's acquisition on the Internet and the potential to reduce their representation."[22]

Students in my classes have expressed similar concerns about the Internet and Big Media as conglomerates feast on acquiring Internet engines, engines that may have been developed by minority entrepreneurs outside the mainstream but are swallowed up by media machines. Cross-media consolidation, where one media entity joins forces with another entity, is one more way consolidation occurs. A giant conglomerate can thus gobble up an organization in a related field to create yet another behemoth.

Proponents of deregulation and a free-market approach insist that diversity does not suffer under deregulation because there are so many more media outlets where diversity can flourish,

[19]Maurice Hinchey, "More Media Owners," *The Nation*, February 6, 2006, p. 15.
[20]Helen Thomas, "Lap Dogs of the Press," *The Nation*, March 27, 2006, p. 18.
[21]"Caucus Mission Statement," *Journal of the Caucus for Television Producers, Writers & Directors*, 2006, vol. XXVI, p. 46.
[22]David Craig, "The Future of U.S. Media," Notes for a Peabody Seminar, New York, 2005, p. 10.

but this argument fails to convince opponents. They maintain that deregulation has a homogenizing effect and that it becomes increasingly difficult for minorities to own outlets that could feature diverse voices.

For example, Makani Themba-Nixon, executive director of the Praxis Project, a media advocacy center, finds that diversity suffers greatly as a result of Big Media "decreasing media ownership by people of color, resulting in loss of industry voice and jobs."[23] Themba-Nixon feels that when conglomerates take away minority businesses (Figure 11-5), these businesses lose their individuality and power as a result of homogenization.

Opponents of deregulation also claim that localism suffers; they contend that fewer local voices are heard as big corporations take over. They also find that fewer local events are covered when Big Media takes over. Jonathan Rintels heads an organization called the Center for Creative Voices, which strongly opposes deregulation. For his organization's take on diversity and localism, see the accompanying box, which contains two items from the Center for Creative Voices.

FIGURE 11-5
Many feel that businesses run by minorities will suffer as conglomerates increase their holdings. Minority business partners, such as the ones in this picture, may find their opportunities limited as conglomerates seize the marketplace. (iStockphoto.com #214466, Nancy Louie.)

[23]Makani Themba-Nixon, *The Nation*, July 3, 2006, p. 18.

THE CENTER FOR CREATIVE VOICES

The Impact of the Two Cs: Consolidation and Concentration

As we reported in our last update, on October 3 in LA, the FCC held a well-attended hearing on media consolidation and concentration, as the Commission considers whether to loosen or entirely toss out its few remaining media ownership limits. The five commissioners of the FCC heard "Rockford Files" producer Stephen Cannell, "Thirtysomething" co-creator Marshall Herskovitz, WGA, west President Patric M. Verrone, R.E.M. bassist Mike Mills, and many other creatives, testify that independent and diverse voices and visions must be restored to today's excessively concentrated, conglomerated, and homogenized broadcast television and radio.

After the tremendous success of the LA hearing, Creative Voices filed two sets of comments with the FCC—one on its own, and one as a member of the Media and Democracy Coalition—urging the Commission to not relax existing limits, and to establish safeguards that allow original, independent, and diverse voices to return to the nation's broadcast airwaves. These comments are available on our website (www.creativevoices.us).

On December 11, the FCC held a second public hearing in Nashville, where many musicians told stories echoing those told to the Commissioners in LA. Country music star Porter Wagoner testified, "If you relax ownership rules more than what they are today, you will not only strip the airwaves away from the American public, but also continue to change the way we will do business in the recording industry which will be bad for not only recording artists, but also for the very companies who seek to ease these ownership restrictions."

George Jones, another legendary Country/Western star, sang the blues to the Commission: "[T]he consolidation of the radio industry has kept me from being played on the radio. It has kept me from earning my full potential as a country artist and has denied my fans and the American public the opportunity to hear my music. Corporate-based decisions in the music industry are nothing more than the opinions and decisions of a few people at the top, but their opinions dictate the operations of thousands of radio stations and that of the American public."

From the Creative Voices Newsletter, January 5, 2007, courtesy of Jonathan Rintels, Center for Creative Voices in Media.

FCC Media Ownership Policies Make Television's "Vast Wasteland" Even Vaster, Creative Voices Tells Commission

WASHINGTON: Misguided FCC media ownership policies harm competition, diversity of viewpoints, and localism—the Commission's key policy goals in regulating media ownership—and prevent the American public from receiving better broadcast television, the Center for Creative Voices in Media told the Commission in comments filed today.

"Former FCC Chairman Newton Minow once famously referred to television as a 'vast wasteland,'" says Jonathan Rintels, Executive Director of Creative Voices. "By harming competition, diversity of viewpoints, and localism, recent ill-considered FCC media ownership policies have had the unintended consequence of making that 'wasteland' vaster. In its current media ownership proceeding, the Commission must reverse these policies and remedy these consequences, so that the public gets what all would agree is truly in the public interest—better television.

"At the FCC's recent public hearing in Los Angeles, the Commissioners heard for themselves from every corner of the creative community, from writers to directors to actors to producers, as well as from their audience, the American public. The opinions were unanimous: action to reverse the consolidation trend in television is pro-creative, and creativity is in the public interest. Network broadcasters have used their control over the public's airwaves to put their competitors—independent producers—out of business. And that is not in the public interest.

"General Electric's recent announcement that it would reduce or eliminate scripted programming on its NBC network in the 8–9 p.m. hour of primetime is particularly illustrative of the unintended harmful consequences of FCC policy changes that have had the practical effect of eliminating independently produced programming from the public's airwaves. Just two years ago, NBC's 8 p.m. hour block was home to *Friends*, a hugely popular hit produced by strong independent producers—one of the few shows still running from the days when FCC policies properly protected the right of independents to access the network airwaves. Prior to that, NBC's 8 p.m. hour block was home to *The Cosby Show*, *Family Ties*, *3rd Rock From the Sun*, *Golden Girls*, *Diff'rent Strokes*—the list could go on and on—all family-friendly shows, all produced by strong independent producers.

"But with GE/NBC taking advantage of FCC rule changes to eliminate independent producers and take over for itself the production of programming, NBC's own in-house studio has developed and produced few successful

8 p.m. scripted shows. Now, admitting failure, NBC will forego scripted programming in the 8 p.m. hour, and replace it with game shows and so-called 'reality' programming—some of the very programming that Newton Minow cited when he described television as a 'vast wasteland.' At the same time, NBC also announced that it would rely even more heavily on programming produced by its own 'in-house' studio—the very studio that has been so markedly unsuccessful in producing scripted programming for the 8 p.m. hour block. Could anything more starkly illustrate how solidly shut the network's doors are to programming from independent sources? And how this is clearly not in the public interest?

"NBC received the right to use the publicly owned airwaves at no cost from the American public in exchange for its promise to serve the public interest. The public—and the Commission—must now ask whether GE/NBC is now using its free ride on those public airwaves to simply serve GE's narrow corporate interest, at the expense of the public interest?

"Tim Winter, Executive Director of the Parents' Television Council, correctly observed at the Los Angeles FCC hearing that families and children benefit as much as anyone from a diverse media environment. Groups like the PTC are not often on the same page as the creators they sometimes criticize. But it has become clear that family-friendly programming has a better chance of reaching audiences in a creative environment where competition, diversity of viewpoints, and localism exist, while crass, lowest common denominator programming is much more likely to proliferate in a consolidated media environment."

From a Center for Creative Voices in Media Press Release, October 23, 2006, courtesy of Jonathan Rintels, Center for Creative Voices in Media.

ADVANCING AN AGENDA

Opponents of deregulation charge that large companies engage in corporate intimidation and partisan politics that limit the free exchange of ideas in the process raising a number of ethical issues. For example, not only do the heads of conglomerates seek to impose their positions via the media, they also can use the media to control their corporate image and interests. Let's look at the following actual incidents and *E*valuate how diversity and individuality might be impacted by corporate interests and consolidation.

- Disney refuses to distribute Michael Moore's *Fahrenheit 9/11* (2004), a documentary produced by Miramax, at that time a part of Disney, that's critical of President Bush. Ari Emmanuel, Moore's agent, is quoted as saying that then Disney head, Michael Eisner, "expressed particular concern that it would anger Gov. Jeb Bush of Florida and endanger tax breaks Disney receives for its theme park, hotels and other ventures there."[24]
- Viacom head Sumner Redstone says, "Senator Kerry is a good man. I've known him for many years. But it happens that I vote for Viacom. Viacom is my life, and I do believe that a Republican administration is better for media companies than a Democratic one."[25]
- Popular Chinese television host Li Yong has to watch what he says on CCTV, the government network, as the Chinese media do not allow for any criticism of Chinese leaders (Figure 11-6).

FIGURE 11-6   265

Shanghai, China, shown in this photo, may be a modern, progressive city architecturally and otherwise, but entertainers in China, such as television personality Li Yong, have to be careful not to criticize the government, as the Chinese media are carefully controlled and monitored. (iStockphoto.com, #2212834, Yun Leung Young.)

[24]Jim Rutenberg, "Disney Is Blocking Distribution of Film That Criticizes Bush," *The New York Times*, May 5, 2004, A-1.

[25]Nikki Finke, "When Might Turns Right: Golly GE, Why Big Media Is Pro-Bush," *LA Weekly*, September 30, 2004, www.laweekly.com, accessed January 6, 2007.

- A Jay Leno or Jon Stewart routine with digs at the administration would not fly in China.[26]
- Warner Brothers decides not to include an antiwar documentary by director David O. Russell as an add-on to the DVD release of Russell's film *Three Kings* (1999) because the documentary might be seen as partisan in an election year.[27]
- In 1998, "Fox scrapped a drama about the sexual harassment charges against Clarence Thomas, reportedly because of objections by Fox's owner, Rupert Murdoch, who is friendly with Justice Thomas."[28]
- Also in 1998, NBC's *Saturday Night Live* deleted a sketch that made fun of networks owned by large corporations.[29]

You Decide

Additional research on your part may be needed to put some of these issues into perspective, but can you see how corporate interests *could* stifle diversity and individuality? A number of positions can be taken about the examples presented. As an exercise, however, explore some situations where you feel diversity has suffered as a result of consolidation. You should also do the opposite by citing some situations where diversity has not suffered as a result of consolidation.

CONSOLIDATION AND JOBS

Wall Street loves it when jobs are slashed. Any announcement that 10% or 20% job cuts will take place to streamline operations is met with approval from the financial community. Consolidation facilitates job cuts, which are said to avoid a duplication of duties and to prop up the bottom line. Lots of jobs are thus

[26]Jim Yardley, "A TV 'King' Pushes the Limits, Flashily but Gently," *The New York Times*, January 21, 2006, A-1, 4.

[27]Sharon Wazman, "Citing Politics, Studio Cancels Documentary," *The New York Times*, September 9, 2004, B-1, 6.

[28]Warren Berger, "Where Have You Gone, Standards & Practices?" *The New York Times*, September 20, 1998, Section 2, 31.

[29]Ibid.

lost as streamlining under deregulation takes place. This makes it increasingly difficult for someone looking to start a career in media. There are a number of ways to look at deregulation and consolidation, as this chapter suggests. In this section, let's examine the ethical implications associated with job cuts.

When the WB and UPN merged in early 2006 to form the CW and thereby stem the losses both networks were experiencing, Wall Street applauded "the move as a refreshingly frank assessment of both network's weaknesses,"[30] even though there would be significant layoffs. The merger also pleased advertisers. The focus was on what programs would stay and which ones would go, not on the staff job cuts or the loss of work for the people involved in the shows that were not picked up for the CW.

Later in 2006, NBC announced cuts to save some $750 million. Most of these cuts were in news; approximately 300 people were eliminated to get rid of "redundancies in news coverage."[31] *Dateline* lost at least 15 full-time employees, approximately 10% of that program's staff, including producers and correspondents.[32]

Many of my broadcast students place job security at the top of their wish lists, but many would argue that under consolidation and deregulation, job security is hard to come by. The reality is that job security and a steady 9–5 schedule are relics of the past, not just in media but in almost every industry save, perhaps, civil service positions. Students committed to careers in the media can thus tell worried parents that their field of choice is no more tenuous than any others.

But do business decisions have to trump people's jobs and disrupt, if not destroy, people's lives? Wall Street may approve of job cuts, but does it even make any real business sense to keep cutting jobs until the people who are left have more to do just to keep their heads above water? Does there not come a point when an individual who still has a job cannot do three jobs at once, even working long hours? We all grew up hearing the phrase "haste makes waste," and at some point the individuals who still have jobs may have to do so much so quickly, in order to keep dancing as fast as they can, that efficiency will suffer. Aren't happy workers likely to be more productive than unhappy ones?

---

[30]Meg James and Matea Gold, "CBS, Warner to Shut Down 2 Networks and Form Hybrid," *The Los Angeles Times*, January 25, 2006, A-17.

[31]Jacques Steinberg, "NBC Lays Off at Least 18 at Three News Programs," *The New York Times*, November 15, 2006, B-2.

[32]Ibid.

Judy Pies, an art consultant in Los Angeles, defines job cuts that ruin people's lives as unethical and immoral. For Pies and many others, the practice of consolidating companies that seek to be in the black by slashing jobs neglects to consider the all-important human element. We live in a time when "quality of life" is stressed, yet, under consolidation, when it comes to cutting jobs, quality of life and human concerns fall by the wayside.

In the world of entertainment, there is a widely held misconception that only the really tough can survive "the jungle." This misconception serves to make job cuts acceptable. If someone loses a job to cuts, it means that person somehow didn't quite measure up. This fallacy tends to blame the person rather than the system, causing people who are not let go to feel like surviving warriors, though some nevertheless feel "survivor guilt" as they wonder why they survived the cuts and others did not. They also wonder if they'll make it through the next round of cuts.

Students have to get beyond the reality of job cuts and refuse to take no for an answer when they seek positions in the media. Networking becomes key. If people with jobs have to work two or three times as hard, job seekers also have to work a lot harder. If you want to be in the game, giving up is simply not an option.

268

CONSOLIDATION AND INCREASED INDECENCY

In the same way that some media observers feel that consolidation has resulted in an increase in conservative talk radio, many feel that there is a direct connection between media consolidation and the spread of indecency. If our culture is indeed coarsening and an increase in indecency exists, consolidation may bear the brunt of the blame.

Though the link between consolidation and indecency may not be readily apparent, FCC commissioner Michael Copps has long felt that such a link exists. Others have also taken up the charge. For example, Patrick Goldstein observed that since the passage of the Telecommunications Act of 1996, "the rise of media consolidation has been closely followed by a steep rise in indecency complaints . . . media conglomerates largely operate at a safe distance from the communities they serve, while locally owned broadcasters have to defend their programming choices at the local grocery store . . . 80% of recent FCC indecency fines have gone to DJs working for two conglomerates, Clear Channel Communications and Infinity Broadcasting."[33]

[33]Goldstein, "The Zipping Point."

Jonathan Rintels of the Center for Creative Voices in Media elaborated on the connection in a study he co-authored with Philip Napoli, associate professor of communications and media management, the graduate school of business Administration at Fordham University, "Ownership Concentration and Indecency in Broadcasting: Is There a Link?" The accompanying box includes key findings from the study.

EXPLORING LINKS BETWEEN CONSOLIDATION AND INDECENCY

The statistical results of the study are striking. Ninety-six percent of all the indecency fines levied by the FCC in radio from 2000 to 2003 (97 out of 101) were levied against four of the nation's largest radio station ownership groups—Clear Channel, Viacom, Entercom and Emmis. The percentage of overall indecency fines incurred by these four companies was nearly double their 48.6 percent share of the total national radio audience.

This report makes clear that when radio station and program ownership is concentrated in fewer owners' hands, as it has been since the passage of the 1996 Telecom Act, the decision by any one owner to broadcast indecent material impacts a substantially larger audience than was possible prior to the lifting of ownership limits. . . .

Although the FCC's definition of indecency focuses more on sexuality and general foul language than on violence, it would seem reasonable to expect a similar pattern, with advertisers' most-coveted demographics gravitating toward programming that is more adult in nature in terms of language and sexuality. Certainly, we see this reflected in the indecency scandal surrounding the 2004 Super Bowl. Janet Jackson's notorious "wardrobe malfunction" has been blamed in large part on Viacom's decision to let its MTV unit design the half-time show, in an effort to take advantage of MTV's well-documented expertise in attracting younger demographics. . . .

Thus it would seem that broadcasters (both television and radio) face powerful economic incentives to provide programming that pushes the indecency envelope, as such programming is likely to attract the audience members that advertisers value most highly. The key question, however, is whether there are reasons to expect that stations that are part of large station groups will be more likely to act on these incentives than stations that are independent or part of smaller station groups.

From "Ownership Concentration and Indecency in Broadcasting: Is There a Link?' courtesy of Jonathan Rintels, Center for Creative Voices in Media.

269

You Decide

Using the E*T*H*I*C*S rubric, where applicable, take a position on the following questions, and back up your views with specifics.

■ What do you think are the ethical implications associated with consolidation?

■ Do you agree or disagree that consolidation encourages indecency?

■ Should a free-market philosophy be the deciding factor in favor of deregulation and consolidation? What other factors might be involved? What role might ethics play here?

■ Do you feel that ethics and consolidation are two separate things that should not be linked together?

■ What ethical considerations might be associated with localism?

■ Is it ethical or unethical to fire people in order to improve the bottom line?

■ Is it ethically okay or not okay to lay people off as a result of consolidation?

■ What ethical considerations, if any, should a manager take into consideration before firing someone?

■ Was Disney correct or not correct in refusing to distribute Michael Moore's *Fahrenheit 9/11*? Approach this question from a business point of view and then from an ethics point of view.

■ Do CEOs have the right to do what they want with their companies?

■ Do you think that individuals who are not fired should avoid feeling "survivor guilt"?

■ Fred Lungren, chairman of radio station KCAA-AM in San Bernadino, California, objected to the firing of radio host Don Imus. He thus planned to run a "Best of Imus" series shortly after Imus was fired. He is quoted as saying, "I'm not going to let networks dictate to me who I run on my station."[34] Do you think that Lungren was making a good business decision? Do you think it was an ethically responsible one?

In this chapter, we have examined diversity and consolidation from an ethical point of view. In the next chapter, written by Carol Ames, let's take a look at the various ethical issues associated with media public relations (PR).

[34]Martin Miller, "San Bernardino Station Will Replay Shows," *The Los Angeles Times*, April 13, 2007, A-21.

CHAPTER 12

The Ethics of Public Relations

By Carol Ames

What is PR? Why do organizations need it? Most people can't answer these questions, but they have an uneasy feeling that PR is something that celebrities need when they're promoting a movie or when they're trying to make the public forget about DUI arrests and unattractive mug shots. In fact, public relations professionals are essential intermediaries between organizations (or clients) and the public. Their most important function is to communicate information back and forth between the two. PR professionals face ethical decisions daily, if not hourly, in this two-way process. Making ethical decisions requires knowledge of the tools available to the PR person, publicist, public information officer, communications executive, or crisis consultant, to list only a few of the titles by which the professional may be known.

Before we can use the E*T*H*I*C*S rubric, some background is necessary on how information professionals execute their responsibilities in both their routine functions and during crisis situations. Public relations and public information officers use many tools and initiatives to communicate information to a variety of publics. Audiences may include employees, stockholders, customers, or the general public. Some PR tools offer control over the message but are expensive. Other tools offer less control but are also less costly. Part of the professional's job is to help clients decide which situations require more control and expense and which can benefit from a well-placed news story—a creative PR stunt that draws news coverage because of its originality or outrageousness, or, these days, an online word-of-mouth campaign. Many of the ethical mistakes that cloud the reputation of public relations occur when PR professionals and their clients do not understand the benefits and the limitations of the various tools, including controlled versus uncontrolled PR materials as well as media relations.

CONTROLLED PR MATERIALS

Costly PR materials such as corporate image advertisements, newsletters, brochures, annual reports, white papers, and speeches are delivered directly to their intended audiences. Direct delivery means that the PR officers and their clients control the content, the message, the medium, and the timing. The client pays for creating the content, for the design and production, and for the distribution or delivery directly to intended readers or other audiences. Controlled public relations materials are therefore similar to paid advertisements in that they are seen, heard, or experienced exactly as the company or client intended. Like paid advertisements, controlled PR materials are costly.

UNCONTROLLED PR AND MEDIA RELATIONS

Less costly are "uncontrolled" public relations tools, such as press releases; stories "pitched" to journalists, editors, and broadcast news outlets; news conferences; special events; and PR stunts, which are now often called "guerrilla marketing." To reach the public using these uncontrolled tools, the PR professional must work with and through news outlets and journalists *without* offering any form of payment or compensation. Reaching the intended public requires persuading news professionals to do stories that they believe will interest their own specific readers, listeners, or viewers.

These activities or tools are known as media relations. Getting a good story—one that is mostly positive—in a major newspaper, trade journal, or broadcast news report often depends on long-standing relationships of trust between an individual PR specialist and an individual journalist. As discussed in Chapter 1, no clear-cut media industry standard exists, but trust is what enables individuals to work together harmoniously.

*E*VALUATE

In media relations work, information officers are the intermediaries between the client organization and the press. They have to evaluate the current situation and balance the needs and wants of both, remembering that the client pays them for providing journalists with story ideas and information. The journalists, however, will only continue to trust PR sources if the information they provide is accurate and timely and if they act as aids rather than barriers to information and interviews most of the time.

PR practitioners and journalists have a similar aim—to provide information or news to the public in the form of a good story. But their agendas—and their very definitions of a good story—are different. PR practitioners want to present their client's story to the public. Journalistic ethics require a balanced story—both the positive and the negative. Journalists, therefore, need to balance the material the PR people present. This means that it is the journalist's job to do independent research and outside interviews to confirm the information presented by the PR representatives; to discover possibly negative information that the PR person has not revealed (because that is contrary to the PR function, unless the question is asked directly); and to provide balancing points of view, perhaps from the PR client's competitors or from known, longtime adversaries.

PR professionals exercise as much indirect control as possible, even in the uncontrolled area of media relations. First of all, this means doing research to know the situation. The PR practitioner also should know the audience of story pitches by reading what journalists write about their client's company and industry. PR also carefully selects which executives will be offered for interviewing, depending on the topic and the circumstances. PR prepares executives by letting them know as many specifics about the proposed article as can be garnered from the journalist. In addition, PR briefs the executives and often also writes a Q&A of potential expected or thorny questions and their possible answers. Finally, the PR representative often sits in on the interview itself, which journalists hate.

Journalists see the PR presence as interfering with the dynamics of the interview. The journalist wants to establish an atmosphere of ease, trust, and common ground to get the interview subject to relax, be herself, and talk candidly. For the journalist, candid and off-the-cuff comments are the essence of good journalism; from a PR point of view, however, they are the essence of PR's lack of control over a story once it is pitched or suggested to a journalist.

The PR person sits in partially to remind the executive that he's in a professional, not a personal, situation. He should remember that everything he says before, during, and after the official interview—on the way to the elevator, for example—can appear in print or on television as the company's point of view. The publicist is also there to clarify casual comments that could be misinterpreted to be a witness about what is said as a precaution against possible misquoting

FIGURE 12-1
Mega-star Angelina Jolie has had her share of PR dilemmas, including when she was quoted referring to her child as "a blob" and when the media were reportedly told that personal questions were off-limits during her 2007 promotional tour for *A Mighty Heart*, a film about murdered journalist Daniel Pearl. On *The Daily Show*, Jolie specified to Jon Stewart that the directives about no personal questions did not come from her. In fact, her lawyer, Robert Offer, said the restrictions were an overzealous "bone-headed" action he himself undertook. (Globe Photos, Inc.)

and finally to remind the journalist about what she claimed was going to be the subject of the interview if she ranges too far a-field or tries to ambush the interviewee with a surprise line of questioning.

One interview danger arises when, for example, a journalist tries to elicit agreement with controversial statements that she herself makes. An example of this journalistic technique made tabloid headlines in early 2007: Angelina Jolie (Figure 12-1) was widely quoted as having said in an interview that her biological newborn was an undefined "blob" in comparison to the foreign babies she had adopted when they were six or more months old, who had definite personalities by the time she met and adopted them. One explanation of the controversial quote was that Jolie had struggled for words to describe her reaction to having her first newborn; the "helpful" journalist may have supplied the word "blob," and Jolie either agreed or didn't explicitly disagree. Different journalists might *E*valuate differently whether it is ethical to use a prompted response as an actual quote.

A savvy publicist would have recognized the ambiguity and interjected to the journalist, "'Blob' was your word, not hers. What would your own description of your baby be, Angelina?" This would have prevented the journalist using the comment as a quote and headed off the media and blogosphere frenzy of calling Jolie a bad mother and a worse person. The journalist would have resented the publicist for ruining a good story and great headlines, but the publicist would have been doing his job—protecting his client by bringing a measure of control to an uncontrolled PR situation.

In Chapter 3, we discussed at what point producers feel they own a story and are free to try to take it to the marketplace. In this chapter we evaluate a totally different concept of owning a story, a concept that raises its own set of ethical questions about ownership.

Journalists happily use PR pitches as ideas for stories and ask for access to interviews and background material. Concurrently, most journalists rail against the ways PR people prepare their clients for the interviews and try to control the story as much as possible. Sometimes, however, the PR representative makes the mistake of thinking of a possible upcoming feature in a major publication as "my cover story" because he or she pitched it and provided client access. It's not. It's the journalist's story. But the journalist couldn't "get the story" without PR cooperation.

Sometimes the journalist-publicist's struggle for control becomes part of the story itself. This happened in 2007 when someone at the high-powered PR firm representing Microsoft accidentally hit "Reply All" and sent Microsoft's internal briefing materials about the upcoming *Wired* story—including an analysis of the writer's personality and possible interview ploys—to the journalist himself. The *Wired* story was to have been about a new openness at Microsoft that had made the company a corporate leader in allowing and supporting employee blogging and even video postings that give unprecedented insider views. The journalist used the e-mail memo as evidence of the old Microsoft's heavy-handedness. This provided journalistic balance to a largely positive story about the company's uses of the new technology.[1] *The New York Times* and other media gleefully followed up on the story of PR stumbling and over-control, explicitly naming the PR firm and also interviewing the journalist.[2]

Usually, the journalist/PR struggle/symbiosis stays in the background. In fact, its intense tug-of-war dynamic often surprises and challenges neophytes in both journalism and public relations.

Clients or senior management also often misunderstand the difference in agendas between PR and journalism and the level of PR control that is possible in a society that values freedom of the press. Misunderstandings lead to irate telephone calls from senior management to the PR representative asking, "Why

[1]Fred Vogelstein, "Gimme a B! Gimme an L!" *Wired*, April 2007, p. 170.
[2]Macropoulos, Angela, "A Misfired Memo Shows Close Tabs on Reporter," *The New York Times*, April 2, 2007, C-4.

the **** is (my archrival) quoted in *my* business section feature in *The New York Times*? Call that writer and make him issue a correction." Experienced public relations executives prepare their clients and companies to expect balancing facts, opinions, and quotations in any story published or broadcast by a legitimate news organization—no matter how much access to exclusive interviews PR people facilitated or how much proprietary research they extracted from operating divisions of their company to "help the writer" with the story.

If a PR pitch results in a story, the public interprets the client's appearance in editorial matter—as opposed to paid advertising—as a kind of endorsement from the news outlet. The news story therefore often carries more weight and influence with the public than a long-running, costly corporate or product advertising campaign. This implied endorsement is both the major advantage of stories resulting from media relations and the major reason that clients and companies are willing to sacrifice control of content, timing, and context to achieve news coverage.

From a company or public relations point of view, the disadvantages of media relations are that the pitching process is time intensive, unpredictable, and uncontrolled. When will the information appear—if at all? What will the news report say? Will the client's top executive be quoted? Will he sound sensible or stupid? Results depend in part on the PR person or the client's relationship of trust with the individual journalist.

Mistakes in the *E*valuate phase of the E*T*H*I*C*S rubric result from: incomplete research leading to a misunderstanding of the dynamics of the situation at hand; trying to exercise complete control over a journalist's story; acting as if PR owns the story once it has been pitched and taken on by a journalist; or trying to require that a journalist provide an advance copy of the story for approval before it is published.

*T*RUTH AND THE "STORY PITCH" BARGAIN

Journalists and editors get many story ideas from public relations representatives, but most members of the media are loath to admit that their story ideas aren't their own. The unspoken bargain between journalists and their public relations sources is that a journalist will mention the PR person's client or organization in any article that results from a PR person's pitch—most likely in a positive or neutral light—but that's never guaranteed.

Sometimes a naive or inexperienced publicist (or one the client keeps in the dark) pitches a story that would have been better left alone. That's fair game for the journalist. The negatives that a journalist already knows from experience or from other sources will appear in the story. Therefore, before pitching a story, it is the publicist's job to know what information a good investigative reporter might uncover. If the possible negative revelations are at all serious, the publicist should advocate that the client take the more expensive approach and pay for corporate advertising to present the company's point of view or improve its public image. The publicist should convince the client or senior management that it's the wrong time to pitch a big story to an investigative journalist. It also behooves clients to be forthright and truthful with their publicity representatives to avoid such blunders.

*T*RUTH OR CONSEQUENCES

Some ethical missteps clients make include telling their PR representatives to lie to the press or manipulating them into inadvertently telling lies by keeping them uninformed or purposely misinforming them. If it turns out the PR person didn't know what he was talking about, credibility and effectiveness as an intermediary with the media are both destroyed.

Also, once a journalist is told a purposeful lie and then discovers the truth—as is inevitable—the relationship of trust between PR person and the media in general is fatally damaged. Probably the PR lie will become part of the news story itself. In any case, the journalist is unlikely to keep a PR lie secret from colleagues, so the information officer's reputation and ability to do the job of trusted intermediary with the media are deeply damaged, even by an inadvertent lie.

The PR professionals need journalists and vice versa. As Kimberly Nordyke, a journalist for the entertainment trade paper, *The Hollywood Reporter*, said, "We couldn't do our job without publicists. They're our best friends and our worst enemies."[3] The view from the other side of the equation holds a similar view. "The PR person and the journalist need each other half the time, and half the time they're out to outwit each other," said Don Spetner (Figure 12-2), senior

[3]Kimberly Nordyke, Q&A, March 21, 2007, California State University, Fullerton.

FIGURE 12-2
PR specialist Don Spetner of Korn/Ferry International sees a love/hate relationship between journalists and PR professionals. (Courtesy of Korn/Ferry.)

vice president of global marketing and communications for Korn/Ferry International, an executive search and consulting firm. "It's love/hate." Spetner sees no problem, however, with being friends with a journalist, who might at some point float a rumor by him to judge his response by saying, "This is what I'm hearing." In this situation, both parties know their professional roles, and both realize they have different agendas. "My objective might be not to have the story run," Spetner said. "Hers would be to make it as interesting and colorful as possible, but I feel comfortable saying, 'I can't answer that' or 'I can't give you that information.'"[4]

[4]Don Spetner, Interview, February 28, 2007, Century City, CA.

To be effective, a public relations practitioner has to tell the *T*ruth. The only ethical alternatives are to say, "No comment" or "I have no comment at this time," which leaves open the possibility of consulting internally with the client or senior management and calling back before deadline with researched *T*ruth—information and facts that disprove or mitigate the reporter's negative take on the client's situation.

You Decide

Here is an example of a real-life situation that raises some ethical issues that can confront information officers as they work on media relations:

You are a recently hired, independent public relations consultant developing a media relations plan for a small public company listed on the NASDAQ stock exchange. The chief financial officer is very interested in getting a boost for the stock by having you pitch an article to the business section of *The New York Times*. In fact, your good relationship with the reporter who covers the industry was probably a strong factor in obtaining this company as a client. As you research the company's business to discover an interesting hook for a story pitch, you discover that the chief financial officer was formerly the CEO of an exchange-listed company that went bankrupt a few years ago. Press archives indicate that there were numerous allegations of backdated stock options and other questionable financial dealings, such as working with a broker who was subsequently accused of pump-and-dump schemes with low-priced stocks. Such schemes cause the stock price to rise quickly through publicity and boiler-room hard-selling to unsophisticated buyers. Then the insiders sell their own shares before the price collapses. Your CFO sold his own sizable stake before the company's stock plummeted, but most of the smaller stockholders lost their entire investments when the company filed for bankruptcy.

- When you ask the CFO about the past situation and what he would say if the reporter asks about it, he responds, "It's irrelevant. It won't come up. It was a different industry. Just pitch the story."
- Would you go ahead and pitch the story to your most important media contact?
- Would you forgo pitching the story, but nevertheless tell the CFO that the writer had turned it down as an idea?
- Would you help the CFO develop plausible answers to potential questions about the company?
- If the CFO asks you to lie to this reporter, would you? Would you lie to another, less familiar reporter? To a less powerful one?
- Are you obliged to pitch this story to this journalist because "that's what we hired you for"?
- When questioned about the CFO's past record, would you ask your reporter friend to "overlook it as a tiny favor, just for me, just this once—it's been years anyway . . . pretty please"?
- Would you take the fact that the CFO has not been forthcoming with you as a warning sign—the cockroach theory that if you see one ethical lapse, there are probably a hundred more?
- Whether or not it means financial hardship for you as a newly independent consultant, what combination of facts and factors might cause you to resign this client and forego your hefty—and much-needed—monthly retainer?

279

*T*RUTH AND CONTROLLED PR MATERIALS

*T*ruth is also an important ethical consideration in controlled PR materials such as brochures, fliers, and mailers. *T*ruth means using no lies or exaggerations in the content. *T*ruth also means maintaining transparency about the origin of the material by clearly identifying the company or organization of origin, as well as a street address, a working telephone number, and, these days, a Web address with other information that clearly identifies the source. Anyone who reads or hears advertisements and other controlled corporate messages knows to take the source into consideration when evaluating whether to "buy" into the message, and the same information should be easily available for evaluating the messages of PR materials.

280

Every local, state, and national election cycle seems to bring ethical breeches in connection with printed political fliers and mailers. *T*ruth of origin is violated when a mailer is attributed to a nonexistent organization with no contact information or with a suite address that is just a rented box at a commercial mailbox storefront. *T*ruth of content is honored in the letter but not in the spirit when a "Democratic Slate" or "Republican Slate" headline implies that the candidates are the political party's official endorsements. Only the fine print identifies the flier as "paid for by those candidates marked with asterisks," who are often precisely the ones who lack their party's endorsement (Figure 12-3).

FIGURE 12-3
Political fliers are often misleading, implying affiliations and endorsements that may not be truthful. (iStockphoto.com #2903258, Judy Foldetta.)

As readers and as consumers, we are always told to "consider the source" of information. Public relations professionals follow the ethics of *T*ruth when they make the source of their controlled material clear, honest, and transparent and when they refrain from lying to journalists under any circumstances while pitching stories, answering press queries, and talking to journalists as part of their ongoing media relations work.

*T*RUTH, WORD OF MOUTH, AND INTERNET PR

For the average person, "considering the source" is extremely complicated in the digital age. E-mail makes it possible to forward ideas, judgments, rants, and blog postings to a couple of friends or to hundreds. Although digital copying and forwarding often prevent the content from becoming as garbled as messages in the childhood game of telephone, the origin often is deleted or obscured. What was the original source anyway? Who cares? If it gives me a laugh, or strikes me as true, or alerts me to a situation that might endanger people, why don't I just forward it to my friends or post it on my MySpace page, where I might have amassed a thousand "friends"? This copy-paste-and-send mentality violates the ethics of *T*ruth of origin.

The Internet blogosphere has complicated the jobs of public relations professionals. Within hours, a single posting in a blog, on a discussion board, or on YouTube can be repeatedly forwarded, viewed, and passed on like a virus at the height of flu season. An Internet rumor—true or untrue—can severely damage the reputation of a company, product, or person. Because the company or client's reputation is the responsibility of the public relations officer, PR must now monitor the Internet rumor mill. PR must quickly and publicly respond to or discredit negative word of mouth, whether it originated as the heartfelt, legitimate complaint of an individual frustrated with the company's automated telephone-answering system; whether it resulted from incomplete information; or whether it was initiated with malicious intent by a prankster or an underhanded competitor. The kind of response and the choice of PR tools require judgment calls and ethical decisions based on experience, a sound evaluation of the situation, an accurate perception of the public mood, and again the PR person's reputation with journalists. For example, would a press conference or an exclusive interview with a national news program quash the untrue rumor or fuel the controversy?

When looked at as a PR tool rather than a problem, on the other hand, the Internet offers multiple opportunities. A company website can provide truth and transparency about an organization and its operations. Posting brochures, newsletters, and annual reports can make controlled PR materials widely available at almost no cost once a flexible website and a responsive company web master are in place. These days, a strong website is an essential part of a company's communications apparatus.

At a bare minimum, ethics requires compliance with the law. Many laws have been passed to specify what are acceptable and unacceptable behaviors

281

in situations where formerly generally agreed-upon norms of behavior and fairness seem to have become confused. For example, the Sarbanes-Oxley Act of 2002 and Securities Exchange Commission (SEC) rules require publicly owned companies to distribute stock market moving news widely and, simultaneously, not "tip" it privately to a favored stockbroker or someone else who will do them a favor in return. To comply, most PR and investor relations executives now post press announcements on the company website while simultaneously distributing them through the Business Wire or the PR Newswire, two paid services that feed press releases directly into newsrooms.

When posted in reverse chronological order on the client's website, press releases serve as a readily accessible history of company news, thus offering the general public transparency when making decisions about buying and selling a company's stock, products, or services. The PR executive can also refer reporters to this resource instead of digging through physical files and copying material to supply background information to a journalist writing a current story about the company. This saves time, but it also cuts out phone conversations that might yield the PR rep some valuable information about the story hook and tone.

Blogs—in particular, ad hoc communities that spring up around brands or companies—have put pressure on companies to be more responsive to customer complaints, comments, and suggestions for improvement. Some companies now have their own blogs written by high-level executives, and a very few even have a CEO blog, where the head of the company responds to posts from consumers and critics.[5] The number here is small because blogging and discussion boards are extremely time intensive, and the public responds badly if they discover that the CEO's "personal blog," is ghostwritten by a PR person.

These days, most people accept that everyone from the president of the United States down to the head of marketing at a small company might have speeches and slide presentations written for them by a ghostwriter, usually a PR person on staff or a specialist hired just for that purpose. Blog readers, however, expect *T*ruth of origin, the *T*ruth about the name of the actual writer, even if the name is a pseudonym or virtual construct, because blogs are "personal commentary," the voice and the opinion of a specific person. Woe to the PR person who tries to trick the public by impersonating an executive or client! Such an action is not only perceived as unethical, but it also frequently backfires, creating a PR nightmare.

[5]Randall Stross, "All the Internet's a Stage: Why Don't C.E.O.'s Use It?" *The New York Times*, July 30, 2006, BU-4.

*E*THICS AND WORD OF MOUTH

Double woe to the PR person and company that try to foist off their marketing points as the view of a real person, an ordinary customer who raves about how good the product is, just because she loves it! For many products and clients—electronic devices, movies, up-and-coming bands, teen idols—there are, of course, enthusiastic and chatty fans who will talk about their love of "X" to any and all who will listen or read. Because the personal endorsement of someone known personally is one of the most effective sales tools of all, marketers and PR professionals are always trying to find these "super fans" and harness their energy and enthusiasm. Thus, the music industry has long recruited "street teams" of young fans (Figure 12-4) and has armed them with fliers and stickers touting their favorite band's upcoming album to pass out in front of concert venues. Seeing kids just like themselves who are also full of enthusiasm builds word-of-mouth momentum for the album's release. In exchange, those super fans get nothing more than a band T-shirt, which they would have bought

FIGURE 12-4
Fans who embrace a music group are often used effectively in word-of-mouth marketing campaigns.
(iStockphoto.com #2053646, Nikada 33.)

anyway, or a ticket to the band's next gig, which is probably far from sold out. Starting with such efforts as Tupperware parties and Avon ladies (your neighbor lady who just loved the lotion), through music street teams, and Internet efforts, an entire industry has now grown up around word-of-mouth and person-to-person marketing.

But don't forget that two other terms for word of mouth are "rumor" and "gossip." The word-of-mouth industry's biggest current issue is disclosure, another way of saying *T*ruth of origin. How does the reader or consumer figure out what is a paid endorsement versus what is "personal," unbiased, word-of-mouth enthusiasm? The public's trust is violated when they can't easily tell by seeing a company logo on the chatty person's shirt, for example, that the recommender is being paid to be out on the streets showing off a new cell phone that takes and transmits photos, or when a writer receives undisclosed compensation in exchange for positive comments or commentary on a blog or MySpace posting or e-mail forwarded to friends.

One technique used by company-compensated bloggers is to include a disclosure button on the home page, which the user must actively click to reach a general disclosure. Because of complaints, however, the Federal Trade Commission (FTC) may be moving toward mandating on-page, on-view disclosure when an entry has been paid for.

As other chapters have shown, many media segments develop codes of ethics and threats of sanctions, partly in an effort to self-regulate ethical issues and avoid government intervention in the form of new regulations and new laws. Like most areas of American business that would prefer less government regulation to more, the Word-of-Mouth Marketing Association (WOMMA) is struggling with this issue and has come out strongly on the side of disclosure—disclosure of relationship and disclosure of compensation—in other words, *T*ruth of origin and possible bias. The preamble to WOMMA's draft professional code cautions: "Remember: Consumers come first, honesty isn't optional, and deception is always exposed."[6] See the box titled "Word-of-Mouth Marketing Association Ethics Assessment Tool: The Ethics 20 Questions."

[6]Word of Mouth Marketing Association, "WOMMA Ethics Assessment Tool: The Ethics 20 Questions," http://womma.org/20questions/read, accessed May 6, 2007.

WORD-OF-MOUTH MARKETING ASSOCIATION ETHICS ASSESSMENT TOOL

The Ethics 20 Questions

Discussion Draft for Public Comment

Ask these questions before launching any word-of-mouth marketing campaign.

Get answers from your agencies and vendors, as well as from their subcontractors.

Think about the risks to your reputation before you cross any ethical lines.

Remember: Consumers come first, honesty isn't optional, and deception is always exposed.

Honesty of Relationship

1. Do we insist that our advocates always disclose their relationship with us—including all forms of compensation, incentives, or samples?

Honesty of Opinion

2. Do we insist that all opinions shared with the public express the honest and authentic opinion of the consumer or advocate without manipulation or falsification?
3. Are those individuals who are speaking for us free to form their own opinions and share all feedback, including negative feedback?
4. Is all of the information provided to advocates, consumers, and the media factual and honest, and are all of our claims accurate?

Honesty of Identity

5. Have we repudiated and forbidden all forms of shill, stealth, and undercover marketing?
6. Does everyone working on our behalf use their true identity and disclose their affiliation with our company and agencies?
7. Do we forbid the blurring of identification in ways that might confuse or mislead consumers as to the true identity of the individuals with whom they are communicating?
8. Do we forbid the use of expressly deceptive practices from our employees/advocates, such as impersonating consumers; concealing their true identities; or lying about factors such as age, gender, race, familiarity with or use of product, or other circumstances intended to enhance the credibility of the advocate while deliberately misleading the public?

285

Taking Responsibility

9. If we use agents or volunteers of any sort, do we actively instruct them in ethical practices and behaviors and insist that all of those working under our instructions similarly comply with this standard?

10. Do we instruct all advocates to repeat these instructions and responsibilities in the downstream conversation?

11. Do we have a plan to monitor any inappropriate word of mouth generated by our advocates?

12. Do we know how we will correct any inappropriate or unethical word of mouth done by volunteers or resulting from actions taken by us?

13. Do we insist that campaign organizers disclose their involvement when asked by consumers or the media and provide contact information upon request?

Respecting the Rules

14. Do we respect and honor the rules of any media we might use, including all such procedures and stipulations as may be deemed appropriate by specific websites, blogs, discussion forums, traditional media, or live events? (Examples of actions that break the rules: violating the terms of service of any online site, spamming, violating privacy rules, or defacing public property.)

15. Do we prohibit all word-of-mouth programs involving children aged 13 and younger?

16. If our campaign involves communicating with or influencing minors aged 14 to 17, do we (a) have mechanisms in place to protect the interests of those teens and (b) have parental notification mechanisms in place, where appropriate?

When Hiring an Agency

17. Does the agency subscribe to the same high standards of ethical behavior and practice, and are they willing to guarantee the ethics of their own work as well as that of all subcontractors?

18. Do they have reporting and operational review procedures in place permitting us to ensure full compliance with all ethical standards?

19. Have they previously engaged in unethical practices?

20. If they have ever engaged in such practices in the past, do they now prohibit them, and will they guarantee that they will not use employees who have engaged in fraudulent practices to work on our behalf?

As an Extra Measure of Assurance, Ask Yourself . . .

■ Would I be uncomfortable if my family or friends were involved in this campaign?

■ Is there anything about this campaign that we would be embarrassed to discuss publicly?

Reprinted by permission of the Word-of-Mouth Marketing Association.

You Decide

You are a college senior excited about your upcoming internship at a record company, a major player in your dream industry, the music business. Because you've had to work all the way through college to pay tuition, it's a major sacrifice for you to work for no pay 16 hours a week at this internship. You are, however, receiving college credit, and you hope to learn about the inner workings of this glamorous company and to make some connections that will help you break into this competitive industry when you graduate in a few months.

Your first day at the internship, after a brief walk around the marketing department, your supervisor, the head of Internet marketing, shows you to a desk bare of everything except a computer. He gives you a couple of unreleased CDs, copies of PR and marketing material, background about the bands and their upcoming tours, and a list of discussion boards and blogs and other Internet sites. He then tells you to use your creativity to tell your friends and post positive comments about these great new albums to help get some buzz going.

You listen to the two CDs. You love the one by a band you yourself discovered before it moved out of a local garage. The other CD, in your judgment, is crap—derivative, clichéd, amateurish, juvenile. Now you have to decide.

- What should you blog, e-mail, and so forth—if anything—about each album and each band?
- What follow-up discussion should you have with your supervisor?
- Is there a way to complete this internship that honors the ethics of *T*ruth?

*H*ARM

Sticks and stones may break my bones, but words can *really* hurt me! This is the universal truth we all knew as kids, even as we bravely chanted back to our tormentors on the playground that "words can never hurt me."

Words do have the power to hurt. Lies always hurt. So do partial truths. Mitigating the damage that words can do is at the basis of public relations and public information, as in the saying, "The truth will set us free." Lies, partial truths, and name calling can harm feelings and reputations . . . even entire brands and companies. The marketing concept of branding is about reputation. Branding is the slow buildup over time of positive associations and experiences, whether we're talking about a particular soft drink, your father and grandfather's choice of pickup truck, or a job-search website.

When established companies are bought or sold, a good portion of the price paid is for "goodwill." Unlike the company's hard assets, such as buildings and machinery, good will includes intangibles, such as reputation, brand equity, public perception, and image that have been built up through years of creative and careful marketing and public relations. PR uses words to accentuate the positive, and if not eliminate the negative, then at least mitigate the negative by offering additional information and alternative points of view.

Remember that our working definition of PR included communication *back and forth* between the client and the public. One of the traditional daily duties of public relations is to monitor the media and compile clips of every article mentioning the organization or product. PR assistants or interns begin the day early by reading the trades and the opinion-maker newspapers and clipping every single mention of the company's brands. These briefs are copied and circulated to all high-level executives in the organization to serve as a daily update on what the media are saying.

Often there are high-level discussions of what options are available to counter a negative tone (or balancing opinion) in press coverage: What news outlet might be receptive to a story pitch? Should the PR person call the paper and ask for a correction (which can and should be done only when there is a clearly factual error)? Should the CEO write a letter to the editor (drafted by the PR person)? Could an op-ed piece under the CEO's byline (but written by the PR person) be placed in a major paper?

The reputations of brands and companies are dynamic and easily damaged. In an age of 24-hour news, viral e-mail rumors, and online posting of amateur video, public relations professionals have to act quickly to address crisis situations such as: customers getting sick after eating at one of a chain's hundreds of franchise locations; a posted video that shows how to disable a company's security device; an explosion at a company facility; employees killed by an enraged ex-employee "going postal"; an accidental shooting of a hunting companion by a high-level official; and numerous other unique or foreseeable contingencies. When such incidents happen, news travels fast and even a seemingly minor incident can escalate into a public relations crisis. Crisis communications specialists all seem to agree that the ethical approach to crisis situations includes telling the *T*ruth and avoiding the *H*arm that can result from members of the public not knowing how to avoid danger.

First, ethical behavior requires that you act fast (ideally before the situation escalates into a crisis). In any crisis, people are likely freeze. Like deer caught in the headlights, they can't get themselves to move and act. That's why ethics demand that organizations have a crisis plan in place.

Ethical companies that have planned what to do in worst-case scenarios spring into action. The CEO shows leadership and ethics by acting immediately to prevent further harm to the public—for example, by pulling an entire product line off the shelves. Because of the harm that can result to the uninformed public, it is unethical "to wait and see" or "give the situation a little time to play itself out."

Simultaneously with executive decisions that prevent harm to the public, the company and its PR representatives access whatever media they can—including expensive full-page, paid corporate advertisements in major newspapers—to announce a product recall or to counter lies and half-truths with information, sound arguments, and rational discourse.

Second, in a crisis the ethical company or organization or individual tells the *T*ruth to the full extent that it is known at the moment (but avoids any speculation about what might have happened or could have been the cause). Disclosing "what is known now" about the current situation is often done via a "company statement" read by a designated spokesperson, with time-dated copies distributed to the media. In an evolving situation, timely and accurate updates should be issued as more is known, so that the company spokesperson comes to be seen as an ally of the media and the public, and so that it's clear that the organization is not trying to hide anything.

289

The public and the press demand to know what happened, where, when, and to whom? In the heat of the crisis, everyone should avoid speculating about why and how, which are best determined later by experts or a special panel of investigators. The press and public also want information on who knew, what did they know, and when did they know it? If the organization's spokesperson seems to be withholding information, the story will become, "Why aren't we being told?"

When information that was purposely suppressed comes out—as it eventually does in a society with a free press—the story is thrust back into the headlines. A new round of media, public, and perhaps investigatory agency recriminations will further damage the company or product's image as the furor crescendos: Why weren't we told? Why did you hide it (the negative results of a drug study, for example)? Then the story quickly becomes "Whom can we sue and for how much?"

Finally and perhaps most importantly, the ethical company and its representatives show human compassion for victims (and avoid language that in any way implies that the victims are to blame). Legal advisors may counsel the company to maintain distance and communicate with careful language. However, not only ethics but also the company's image and brand equity are usually better served by a sleeves-rolled-up company spokesperson (preferably the CEO), by we're-all-in-this-together action, and by repeated expressions of heartfelt sympathy for those who are suffering through no choice or action of their own.

You Decide

Eleven members of an extended family, including a new bride, ended up in three emergency rooms (Figure 12-5) during the night after an elegant Saturday evening, May wedding reception at the most expensive restaurant in the city. The restaurant is your client. The lively party with lots of drinking, dancing, and eating had lasted late, after a huge dinner that included filet, jumbo tiger shrimp imported from Thailand, and a special liqueur supplied by the bride's father from his home village in Lithuania for the last few rounds of toasts.

As the restaurant's public relations representative, what ethical decisions, comments, and actions are possible? What would be unethical? What do you advise the temperamental chef/owner to do today, Mother's Day? What do you or the chef say to the media? If you announce that the restaurant will be closed until the source of the possible food poisoning is determined, won't the bad publicity ruin the restaurant's reputation for fine dining? Should the restaurant go ahead as planned with Mother's Day brunch, one of the restaurant's biggest, moneymaking days of the year? Won't hundreds of people be disappointed if their long-reserved plans are abruptly canceled? What about the mayor who comes every year with his elderly mother?

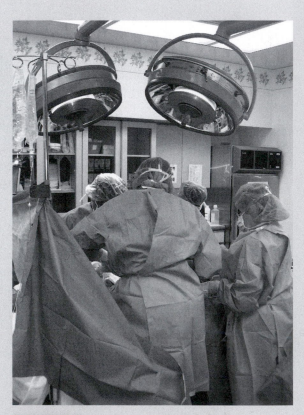

FIGURE 12-5
Having dinner guests end up at a hospital's ER can create a PR nightmare for the restaurant involved. (iStockphoto.com #726174, Scott Fichter.)

*I*NVESTIGATE

As a public relations professional or public information officer, you increase your own and your organization's ability to act ethically through research, research, and more research. Know your client (strengths and weaknesses). Know your product (ditto). Know your executives. Know your competitors and your industry.

Which media cover your industry? For which audiences? Does each have a typical point of view or even a bias? Which specific journalists cover your client? Your client's competitors? What is an individual journalist like as a person? Do you share a love of baseball (Figure 12-6)? Do you have an old friend in common? Did you go to the same college as her brother? Such fundamental human connections imply, "We're similar. We're in this together." This is not about using people, but about keeping the lines of communication open so that the journalist will be amenable at least to listening to your organization's point of view about a controversy or to your PR story pitch.

FIGURE 12-6
Investigating to find out if a journalist has a passion for baseball can help a PR professional establish a valuable line of communication, in the same way that a producer seeks to find common ground with a development executive. (iStockphoto.com #3059041, Rob Friedman.)

Beyond listening, however, don't expect any favors. Listening is what journalists do to get a story. Favors are not part of the equation. Remember that journalistic ethics require balance in the final story.

The more you know, the more sources of information you develop, and the more media contacts you cultivate, the easier it will be for you to recognize when you need to investigate further to understand a specific situation; the faster you will be able to gather necessary information and alternative courses of action; and the better you will become at handling your public relations work in ethical ways. You will be more able to avoid such unethical approaches as lying, trying to lay a guilt trip on a journalist or colleague, or being tempted to divert media attention from your client by revealing negative information about a competitor.

*C*ODES OF ETHICS

Public relations professionals work in a wide range of industries and organizations, but they share common tools—as discussed earlier—and they share ethical concerns. Their professional organizations, including the Public Relations Society of America (PRSA), work to articulate standards of behavior and to provide guidelines for ethical decision making and ethical behavior, whatever the industry. See the accompanying box, which includes the PRSA Member Statement of Professional Values.

PUBLIC RELATIONS SOCIETY OF AMERICA
Member Statement of Professional Values

This statement presents the core values of PRSA members and, more broadly, of the public relations profession. These values provide the foundation for the Member Code of Ethics and set the industry standard for the professional practice of public relations. These values are the fundamental beliefs that guide our behaviors and decision-making process. We believe our professional values are vital to the integrity of the profession as a whole.

Advocacy

We serve the public interest by acting as responsible advocates for those we represent. We provide a voice in the marketplace of ideas, facts, and viewpoints to aid informed public debate.

Honesty

We adhere to the highest standards of accuracy and truth in advancing the interests of those we represent and in communicating with the public.

Expertise

We acquire and responsibly use specialized knowledge and experience. We advance the profession through continued professional development, research, and education. We build mutual understanding, credibility, and relationships among a wide array of institutions and audiences.

Independence

We provide objective counsel to those we represent. We are accountable for our actions.

Loyalty

We are faithful to those we represent, while honoring our obligation to serve the public interest.

Fairness

We deal fairly with clients, employers, competitors, peers, vendors, the media, and the general public. We respect all opinions and support the right of free expression.

Courtesy of the Public Relations Society of America.

From serving the public interest and helping inform the public debate to honesty or *T*ruth and expertise, PRSA's values closely parallel those advocated throughout this book as hallmarks of ethical behavior.

In addition, PRSA asks members to sign a pledge to adhere to their Member Code of Ethics 2000 and to risk being expelled from membership if "sanctioned by a government agency or convicted in a court of law on an action that is in violation of this Code."[7]

[7]Public Relations Society of America, "PRSA Member Code of Ethics Pledge," www.prsa .org/aboutUs/ethics/preamble_en.html, accessed May 6, 2007.

Unlike a state bar exam and a bar association for attorneys, however, there is no licensing requirement for public relations officers, nor is there any necessity to be a member of PRSA to open a PR agency. Nevertheless, the pledge is meant to remind members of the organization's core principles, which include the free flow of information, competition, disclosure of information, safeguarding confidences, avoiding and disclosing conflicts of interest, and acting so as to enhance the profession. For each core principle, the PRSA code elucidates intent and guidelines, and it offers examples of improper conduct.[8]

In ethics, as in other areas, the more you know and the more complete your research is, the more likely you will be to make decisions that you won't regret. Understanding and following professional codes of ethics are additional aids to help you integrate your understanding of the E*T*H*I*C*S rubric into your professional decision-making process.

*S*ITUATION

Public relations, public information, and publicity professionals work for every kind and size of organization, company, and client. They may represent a child actor who has just been cast in a situation comedy and is facing the entertainment press for the first time; or Microsoft in its attempt to stay ahead of Apple in public perception and computer sales; or a government agency trying to explain its rules to the public; or a local tourist bureau trying to put its town's name on tourists' must-see list; or a nonprofit trying to raise money to cure cancer. Because clients and their needs are so disparate, ethical decision making depends on examining each situation in-depth to understand not only its nuances and peculiarities but also its relation to core ethical principles. The excitement of doing public relations work and its main challenges—including ethical challenges—come from the same source: No two situations are exactly alike. So when you face a tough situation that seems to have no precedent in your experience or in your research, what do you do? You follow the steps in the E*T*H*I*C*S rubric, and then you decide.

This chapter has examined ethical issues faced in the work of public relations. The next and final chapter takes a look at the ethical issues faced in advertising and marketing.

[8]Ibid.

CHAPTER 13

Ethical Issues in Advertising and Marketing

In this, the last chapter of the text, let's examine the ethical issues that impact media advertising and marketing. Most people would readily agree that it's unethical to create advertising or marketing campaigns that distribute cigarettes to minors or encourage minors to spend money on items that could cause them *H*arm. Most would agree that there's something morally wrong in doing this, though unscrupulous entrepreneurs might seek to circumvent the various regulations and guidelines designed to protect minors, such as the *C*ode established by the Distilled Spirits Council and Beer Institute, which called for 70% of a radio station's listeners to be 21 or older in order for a liquor ad to be placed on that station.[1]

Not all decisions involving advertising, marketing, and distribution are clear-cut, however, necessitating a close examination of the various issues involved. In a competitive media market, one has to create a buzz or make some noise in order to be noticed, and the tactics employed to do this can violate established ethical norms. Different tactics exist, of course, but let's examine some of the ones most relevant to our course of study.

EXPLOITING CONTROVERSY

One method sometimes employed to garner attention is to exploit controversy. One has to *I*nvestigate and *E*valuate if the controversy is being exploited for commercial gain or if the controversy is simply a timely topic of significant interest to the public.

[1]Claudia Perry, "Radio Alcohol Ads Get New Set of Rules," *The Ann Arbor News*, April 11, 2004, F-2.

Hot button, controversial issues are used in the 2006 General Motors ad for Chevrolet Silverado trucks using John Mellencamp's song "Our Country." In an article titled "The Media Equation: American Tragedies, to Sell Trucks," David Carr criticized the ad for using images of civil rights leaders Rosa Parks and Martin Luther King, for using images of firefighters after the 9/11 disaster, and for using images from Hurricane Katrina to, as he put it, sell trucks by wrapping General Motors in the American flag.[2] The ad, which was available at press time on YouTube, exploits emotional current and past events, again, to sell trucks. One could counter that the "Our Country" ad celebrates America's past and present with images that reveal America's strength in times of adversity, but it's nevertheless hard to escape concluding that the patriotism and tragedy were being exploited to market a product.

In April 2006, Universal Pictures released its trailer for *United 93* about the flight that crashed in a field, thereby avoiding the target that the 9/11 terrorists intended. (Please refer back to Chapter 5 for the discussion of the television film *Flight 93*.) Universal faced a difficult challenge: "how to promote a film about the tragedy without seeming to exploit it,"[3] according to Sharon Waxman in *The New York Times*.

A trailer for a film is different from the film itself. An audience knows what film it has paid to see (unless, of course, the ads are terribly misleading, as discussed later in this chapter), whereas a trailer is simply thrust upon an unsuspecting audience. Several people found the trailer for *United 93* too intense and potentially troubling to the families of the survivors, which added fuel to the debate about exploiting a tragedy to ignite box office returns.

Like other films seeking to garner nominations, *United 93*, had to be positioned so that it did not appear to be promoting a tragedy in order to be considered award worthy. It's noteworthy that Paul Greengrass, the director of *United 93*, succeeded in nabbing an Academy Award for his direction, indicating that the handling of the film managed to avoid charges of exploitation.

If a distributor sells a film about a tragedy too hard, the distributor risks alienating the public as well as the relatives of the individuals who perished in the tragedy; on the other hand, if a distributor doesn't push hard enough, nobody

---

[2]David Carr, "The Media Equation: American Tragedies, to Sell Trucks," *The New York Times*, October 30, 2006, C-1, 5.

[3]Sharon Waxman, "Despite Criticism, Trailer for 9/11 Film Will Run," *The New York Times*, April 4, 2006, B-1, 7.

knows about the project, resulting in box office failure and the evaporation of dreams about award consideration. It's a tricky juggling act, but one that needs to be mastered as the stakes are high.

Harvey Weinstein is a man who knows the importance of awards. Not every Emmy, Golden Globe, Grammy, or Academy Award is an absolute guarantee of a financial boost. In fact, some might argue that the Academy of Motion Picture Arts and Sciences that administers the awards recognizes films that the movie-going public does not care about. Think *Transamerica* in 2006, in which Felicity Huffman played a transsexual. Think also *Half Nelson* in 2007, in which Ryan Gosling played a schoolteacher addicted to drugs. Both Huffman and Gosling received Academy Award nominations in films hardly anyone saw. At the 2005 Academy Awards, host Chris Rock kept referring to the film *White Chicks* starring the Wayans brothers as the kind of film that the movie-going public responds to but that the Academy would never recognize.

Some might even go so far as to say that the Academy of Motion Picture Arts and Sciences increasingly ignores the commercial films that the public pays to see while paying tribute to films that audiences have skipped. Also, some people feel that Emmy Awards do not help a television program succeed. Conventional wisdom has it that *Hill Street Blues* (1981–1987) succeeded because it garnered Emmy Awards, but the cult favorite *Arrested Development* (2003–2006) was not able to capitalize on Emmy Awards.

Nevertheless, it's generally agreed that Academy Award recognition significantly increases box office and DVD sales all over the world. In the same way that a Grammy Award can boost record sales as much as 700%, as was the case after Steely Dan won Album of the Year in 2001 with *Two Against Nature*, an Academy Award can bump box office as much as $20 million to $30 million worldwide, depending on the appeal of the winning film.

If a film has not yet connected with audiences, an Academy Award can help get the word out. Had Felicity Huffman or Ryan Gosling won awards, their films most likely would have seen box office increases. This financial gain is something Weinstein appreciates, and he has become a master at generating interest and controversy for the films his company produces and distributes. In addition to the financial rewards, Academy Awards, as well as other awards, validate finished work and are thus very nice to have.

Sometimes Weinstein wages aggressive, successful campaigns, as he did for *Shakespeare in Love* (1998), and sometimes he fails, notably in the case of *Bobby*, a 2006 star-studded film about the death of Bobby Kennedy conceived and directed by Emilio Estevez. Even though Weinstein reached out to a friendly Hollywood crowd ready embrace a film sympathetic to the Kennedys, the film did not get any Academy Award nominations. On the other hand, Weinstein's *The Queen* (2006) rewarded Helen Mirren with a Best Actress Academy Award on February 25, 2007.

Weinstein is the acknowledged master at capitalizing on censorship. He carefully exploits somebody's not wanting you to see a particular work to create hard-hitting marketing campaigns. This technique can be very successful, unless it backfires, as happened in 1987 when NBC promoted the miniseries *Billionaire Boys Club*, about the illegal activities of Los Angeles–based Joe Hunt and his posse, as the film "Joe Hunt does not want you to see."

Criticism of the *Billionaire Boys Club* promo was swift, particularly since some of the charges against Hunt had not been adjudicated when the film was scheduled to air. Hunt's lawyers tried to get an injunction to block the airing of the film on the grounds that the film could influence potential jurors (Figure 13-1). The promo line made the lawyers' case stronger, but prior restraint injunctions

FIGURE 13-1
Though rarely granted, injunctions to block distribution of works that could influence potential jurors are often sought, as was the case with the trial that involved people depicted in the 1987 television film *Billionaire Boys Club*. (iStockphoto.com #750886, Frances Twitty.)

are hard to get because judges at all levels, including the Supreme Court, don't generally grant them. The First Amendment and the Constitution stand in the way of such injunctions.

Billionaire Boys Club thus aired, though many felt that the promo had crossed ethical lines. Legendary programmer Brandon Tartikoff, who was head of NBC at the time, felt the promo line went too far and it was eventually dropped from the promo rotation. Interestingly enough, some 20 years later the promo is still the subject of heated debate, used to illustrate the total lack of ethics networks sometimes employ to sell a show.

Billionaire Boys Club aside, Weinstein has been quick to exploit any suggestion that his films are being censored or that "the powers that be" are seeking to prevent a work from being seen. When Disney's CEO refused to allow Disney to distribute *Fahrenheit 9/11* (2004), Michael Moore's documentary critical of the way President George W. Bush handled matters after the 9/11 attacks, Weinstein accused Eisner and Disney of trying to silence the film by engaging in prior censorship and corporate self-dealing to protect Disney's theme park franchises (Figure 13-2). By capitalizing on the controversy over Disney's decision, Weinstein was able to generate interest in the film, turning the $6 million film into worldwide box office gold and making it the highest grossing documentary of all time.

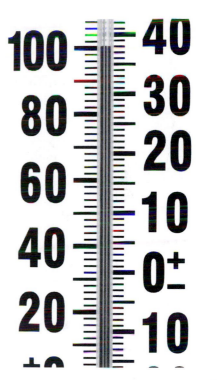

FIGURE 13-2 299
When the Disney corporation decided not to distribute Michael Moore's documentary *Fahrenheit 9/11*, about the aftermath of the terrorist attacks, producer Harvey Weinstein made the censorship a key part of the film's marketing campaign. (iStockphoto.com #2545613, Nick Schlax.)

Similarly, in 2006, when NBC refused to air promotional spots for Barbara Kopple's political documentary about the Dixie Chicks, *Shut Up & Sing*, a Weinstein Company Production about group member Natalie Maine's criticism of President Bush and the backlash of the group that followed, Weinstein again sought to generate interest by means of the boycott of the ads. He said, "It's a sad commentary about the level of fear in our society that a movie about a group of courageous entertainers who were blacklisted for exercising their right of free speech is now itself being blacklisted by corporate America. The idea that anyone should be penalized for criticizing the president is profoundly un-American."[4]

Weinstein also charged that the CW refused the *Shut Up & Sing* ad. He is quoted in *Daily Variety* saying that a CW representative said that the CW didn't have

[4]Pamela McClintock and Joseph Adalian, "Prickly Peacock Nixes Chicks," *Daily Variety*, October 27, 2006, p. 25.

the right kind of programming for the spot. According to the *Daily Variety* report, Weinstein also charged that the CW wouldn't accept such ads, because they were "disparaging to President Bush."[5] Paul McGuire, head of communications at the CW has disputed Weinstein's version. He said that the last communication the CW had with the Weinstein Company was to ask the company in which show it would like to place the ad. For McGuire, Weinstein's claim that the CW rejected the ad was "a naked publicity stunt designed to draw attention to the film."

Similarly, in 2004, when CBS rejected the Moveon.org "Child's Play" ad, Moveon made the most of the rejection. Moveon defines itself as an organization committed to change and improving life in America by criticizing the placing of corporate interests over the interests of everyday Americans. In the ad, which is critical of President Bush, children are shown working at different jobs and at the end, the ad poses the question, "Guess who is going to pay off President Bush's $1 trillion deficit?"

Moveon raised the money to air the ad during the 2004 Super Bowl, but CBS rejected the ad on the grounds that it did not accept advocacy advertising. CBS was inundated with letters and calls from Moveon supporters and others saying that its rejection of the ad was based on bogus reasoning, that advocacy ads appeared on CBS all the time, and that the ad's rejection was clearly a case of corporate censorship of ideas that didn't coincide with CBS's corporate interests.

In the end, Moveon essentially got more mileage out of being censored than it would have if the ad had run. The spot was aired elsewhere and was widely discussed, possibly more so than if CBS had agreed to run the ad. Moveon clearly sought to capitalize on the rejection, causing Jonathan Darman in *Newsweek* to observe, "The Moveon saga shows how in the current polarized political climate, getting censored can be the best publicity there is."[6] Indeed, as the saying goes, getting banned in Boston has real resonance.

Weinstein, like the creators of the General Motors' spot for Silverado trucks, and Moveon.org, has his personal definition of what is and what is not American, and he is very willing to use a marketing soap box to state his case, though he was not as successful with *Shut Up & Sing* as he was with *Fahrenheit 9/11*.

[5]Ibid.
[6]Jonathan Darman, "Behind the Moveon-CBS Ad Battle," *Newsweek*, January 30, 2004, www.msnbc.com/id/4114073/print/1/displaymode/1098, accessed February 11, 2007.

You Decide

- Given that works need to be promoted in order to reach an audience, do you think ethical norms are sometimes crossed when a controversial topic is undertaken? Should controversy take center stage? Should controversy be minimized?
- Do you think time limits need to be imposed before a national tragedy can be turned into a commercial work?
- Can you think of a particular work that exploits patriotism or American values for commercial gain?
- As an exercise, identify as many examples as you can where you feel controversy was exploited to increase revenues. Then list as many examples as you can of

cases in which you feel controversy was responsibly and ethically handled.
- In this section, Harvey Weinstein was presented as a savvy marketer who knows how to exploit controversy. He can, however, also be seen a man who truly believes comments such as the ones quoted in the text about *Shut Up & Sing*. What are your thoughts about his tactics?
- How "*T*ruthful do you think one has to be when it comes to marketing a product?
- How would you "*E*valuate Moveon's capitalizing on CBS's rejection of the "Child's Play" ad?

PRODUCT PLACEMENT AND PRODUCT INTEGRATION

Sometimes it's extremely difficult to tell what's an advertisement and what isn't. This is particularly true in connection with public broadcasting's underwriting statements, which since 1994 have become more like regular ads, even as public broadcasting maintains its noncommercial status.

According to an article in *The New York Times*, "to raise money for noncommercial programming, producers and distributors increasingly allow their corporate underwriters to turn their credits into something resembling regular commercials."[7] No more do viewers simply get something like "This program was brought to you by _____." Instead the underwriting statements resemble regular ads touting a particular product, making it harder to tell what's an ad and what isn't.

In the early days of television, the 1940s and 1950s, it was hard to separate programming content from commercials. Companies such as Lux, Texaco, Philco, Kraft, Schlitz, Goodyear, Ford, General Electric, and US Steel, among others, sponsored shows with their names prominently featured as the hosts presenting the programs. Early television stars like Arthur Godfrey owed their careers, in part, to being superstar salespeople who could sell almost anything

[7]Natives, "On Public TV, Not Quite an Ad but Pretty Close," *The New York Times*, March 28, 2005, C-1.

during a program, people who became closely identified with the products that sponsored them.

The children's *The Howdy Doody Show* encouraged mothers (not fathers, because fathers didn't do the shopping and, except for being the family breadwinner, weren't directly responsible for the care of children) to buy the products Buffalo Bill and his cohorts talked about on the show. If children watching the show couldn't read in order to tell their mothers what products they wanted, colors and other symbols associated with the product were used to make certain that the young audience received the message. Back in the early days, no one worried about host selling, a practice of having the host of a children's television program pitch advertisers' products during the show, which the Federal Communications Commission (FCC) no longer allows. Host selling is now very much a dirty word in the world of children's television, but it wasn't back when television began.

With the current emphasis on product placement and product integration on television, in films, in books, in magazines and on the Internet, we may be making a return to the early days when it was nearly impossible to separate story content from ads.

Let's define the two key terms used in this section. For our purposes, product placement occurs when a product, such as sodas or a car, is displayed in a work. It is no accident that the judges on *American Idol* all have Cokes in front of them. Product integration, on the other hand, occurs when a product becomes part of the story lines, for example, when series episodes revolve around a character's involvement with a product. During the 2004–2005 season of NBC's *American Dreams*, one of the daughters in the show entered an essay contest sponsored by Campbell's Soup, one of the show's advertisers. This product integration story line lasted nine episodes.

In the 2006–2007 season, the underrated, though extremely well-executed Peabody Award–winning NBC show *Friday Night Lights*, the town's high-schoolers gather at Applebee's restaurant, one of the show's sponsors. In a very real sense, then, commercials for Applebee's became part of the program.

Product placement and product integration generate large sums of money at a time when production costs are on the rise and when studios are monitoring all expenditures. It is estimated that in 2003, approximately $3 billion were spent to place products in films and on television programs;[8] $3 billion is a lot

---

[8]Johnnie L. Roberts, "TV's New Brand of Stars," *Newsweek*, November 22, 2004, p. 62.

of money, and agencies and entire departments at studios and networks have been created to facilitate product placement and product integration.

The long list of products receiving prominent placement is constantly growing. It ranges from the aforementioned Coca Cola on *American Idol* to Sears on *Extreme Makeover: Home Edition* to Harley-Davidson in *Blade* on Spike television. And AMC viewers are seeing popup ads at the bottom of their screens for Visine, a Johnson & Johnson product; Johnson & Johnson is an AMC advertiser.

Books are also getting in on the profitable gravy train. In 2001, the high-end jewelry (Figure 13-3) company Bulgari paid popular writer Fay Weldon around 18,000 pounds, roughly $40,000, to refer to Bulgari 12 times in a book called—no surprise here—*The Bulgari Connection*. This arrangement startled a number of people who had been accustomed to the practice in television and films but not in the rarified world of books.

Traditional journalism has also joined the game, reportedly offering watermark ads that superimpose a brand's image, name, or icon directly over editorial content.[9] For example, Target sponsored an entire issue of *The New Yorker*, raising questions about advertisers' influence over editorial content. As Joe Mandese asked in his article, "Ad Infinitum: When Product Placement Goes Too Far," "How far can editorial content go with product placement before it breaches editorial ethics or, just as bad, breeds cynicism among customers?"[10] Product placement and product integration are clearly everywhere, pushing boundaries and testing consumers' levels of tolerance.

FIGURE 13-3
Writer Fay Weldon was paid around 18,000 pounds by Bulgari to refer to Bulgari 12 times in a book called *The Bulgari Connection*. (iStockphoto.com #3521574, Umbar Shakir.)

Many of us can spot the product placement in a television show or theatrical movie. Identifying the products that sometimes overshadow the action becomes part of the fun. The *Mighty Duck* series of theatrical films, for example, filled the

[9]Joe Mandese, "Ad Infinitum: When Product Placement Goes Too Far," *Broadcasting & Cable*, January 2, 2006, p. 12.
[10]Ibid.

screen with product after product. But nothing comes close to Steven Spielberg's science fiction film *Minority Report* (2002), based on a story by Phillip K. Dick and starring Tom Cruise. *Minority Report* wins the prize as the all-time product placement champ.

Minority Report had a reported budget of $102 million, $25 million of which is said to have come from product placement. That's considerably more than the paltry $40,000 for *The Bulgari Connection*. To look at the $25 million from another perspective, it's nearly a quarter of the film's budget, with $5 million said to have come from Lexus alone. If wunderkind, Academy Award–winning Steven Spielberg agrees to place products in his movies in exchange for dollars to help cover productions costs, does that not mean that the practice has achieved a certain level of respectability?

In truth, audiences do not seem to have serious complaints about the trend of branded entertainment, as product placement and product integration are called. Some people are puzzled by this acceptance and wonder why there are so few complaints. My students, for example, tend simply to accept the practice while hoping against hope that branded entertainment will result in fewer commercials and fewer commercial breaks. They don't find the practice particularly intrusive or distracting.

Some even feel that products give a work authenticity, a sense of authenticity having been a justification for fleeting product exposure when I was a network censor in the 1980s; the thinking then was that fleeting images of stores on Rodeo Drive in Beverly Hills, for example, could be included to provide authenticity as long as they did not dominate the screen. Times have changed, however, and products are now prominently featured on network television as part of the financial arrangements involving branded entertainment.

It's as if things have gone full circle, returning to the early days of television when sponsorship was fully integrated into programs. In fact, in 2007, when Ben Silverman was appointed as co-head of NBC, his savvy about branded entertainment added to his strengths. His ability to land in-show sponsorship was a much sought-after skill.

Though there is a general acceptance of the practice, not everyone is in agreement that it's okay. Gary Ruskin, executive director of Commercial Alert, a consumer activist organization (www.commercialalert.org), is a frequent critic. He feels strongly that audiences need to know when payment has been received to feature products. He finds a total lack of transparency when product placement/product integration takes place, and he is calling for strict labels to inform viewers when the practice is used.

Ruskin appealed to the Federal Trade Commission (FTC) and the FCC to insist on better labeling. The FTC rejected his petition, finding that there was inadequate evidence that product placement misled or confused viewers. Therefore, the practice does not constitute deception. As of this writing, Commercial Alert's petition to the FCC claiming that the networks are failing to comply fully with sponsorship requirements is still pending. For a discussion of sponsorship requirements, as defined by the FCC's Section 317, please see the accompanying box, which insists that product placement be clearly labeled.

LABELING PRODUCT PLACEMENT

Section 317 of the Communications Act of 1934, as amended, 47 U.S.C. §317, requires broadcasters to disclose to their listeners or viewers if matter has been aired in exchange for money, services or other valuable consideration. The announcement must be aired when the subject matter is broadcast. The Commission has adopted a rule, 47 C.F.R. §73.1212, which sets forth the broadcasters' responsibilities to make this sponsorship identification.

Section 507 of the Communications Act, 47 U.S.C. §508, requires that, when anyone provides or promises to provide money, services or other consideration to someone to include program matter in a broadcast, that fact must be disclosed in advance of the broadcast, ultimately to the station over which the matter is to be aired. Both the person providing or promising to provide the money, services or other consideration and the recipient are obligated to make this disclosure so that the station may broadcast the sponsorship identification announcement required by Section 317 of the Communications Act. Failure to disclose such payment or the providing of services or other consideration, or promise to provide them, is commonly referred to as "payola" and is punishable by a fine of not more than $10,000 or imprisonment for not more than one year or both. These criminal penalties bring violations within the purview of the Department of Justice.

Thus, for example, if a record company or its agent pays a broadcaster to play records on the air, those payments do not violate these provisions of the law if the required sponsorship identification information is timely aired by the broadcast station. If it is not aired as required by the Communications Act and the Commission's rules, the station and others are subject to enforcement action.

If record companies, or their agents, are paying persons other than the broadcast licensee (such as the station's Music Director or its on-air personality) to have records aired and fail to disclose that fact to the licensee, the person making such payments and the recipient, are also subject to criminal fine, imprisonment or both, for violation of the disclosure requirements contained in Section 507.

Reprinted from the FCC website, www.fcc.gov.

Ruskin of Commercial Alert insists that the networks are not doing enough. He finds the FCC requirement for a single disclosure mention inadequate. As product placement becomes more prevalent, he is seeking disclosure mentions every time a product mention occurs. This is what he is asking the FCC to investigate. Advocates and practitioners of product placement and product integration insist that they would not make the practice intrusive. They insist that when products are introduced, it's done organically, that products are not artificially forced into a work; they say that products are only featured when it's appropriate and when they seamlessly fit into a story arc. Though consumers conditioned not to expect a free ride may express a general acceptance of in-show branding, some might argue that products are not always seamlessly integrated but are, in fact, thrust at viewers whether or not the merchandise fits. Tina Fey's poke at product placement in *30 Rock* where she complains about product placement and then does a plug for Snapple drinks satirizes the insertion of products into story lines. *30 Rock* aside, too much money is involved to permit a great deal of restraint when it comes to product placement and product integration.

MAKING SURE PRODUCTS ARE ON VIEW

Some find product placement and product integration more cumbersome than others. For example, the practice is particularly hard on technical people who have to insert a visual of a product long after a finished film has been locked. Paul Gadd, a producer on *24*, had to do some serious scrambling a day or two before air to insert a visual of Sprint on a cell phone during the 2005–2006 season long after the episode had been delivered. Even if superimposed visuals ease production costs, they can be distracting to viewers, taking them out of the action and breaking up the rhythm of a scene, and, importantly, they can also create extra complications for the crew.

The most vociferous criticism of branded entertainment, however, may come from the various guilds. Both the Writers Guild of America (WGA) and the Screen Actors Guild (SAG) object strenuously, claiming projects are damaged by in-show commercial intrusions, in a sense turning everything into infomercials. The fact that actors are not compensated for having to deliver lines to sell products irks SAG. Similarly, the WGA objects because writers receive no additional compensation for having to write story lines about products.

According to a Writers Guild report, "It used to be that a writer would be asked to weave a love interest into a story. Now that writer is being asked to weave in potato chips, or soft drinks or building supply stores."[11] Writing entails a lot more now than providing a good story as branded entertainment comes to the forefront.

John Furia, a writer and professor, wrote a 2005 opinion piece titled "Plot Line: Drink Pepsi" in which he lamented the branded entertainment trend. He reported that CBS chairman Les Moonves predicted that "up to 75% of all scripted prime time network shows will soon feature products paid for by advertisers and integrated into plot lines."[12]

Like Gary Ruskin of Commercial Alert, Furia found that the rules that require informing consumers when payment has been made to advertise products are not being adhered to. Objecting to what he termed stealth advertising, Furia called for "a notice at the bottom of the screen when an advertising pitch is being made during the content portion of a television program."[13] Advertisers and networks would certainly object to such disclosure, and the $3 billion plus gravy train that branded entertainment provides would surely dry up. Furia's proposal might also seem extreme to individuals conditioned to accept more and more in-show advertising, but it would be one clear way to separate program content from advertisement, and it just might be the ethical thing to do.

News shows are in no way exempt from plugging products. The products in this case are shows that appear on the same channel. Increasingly, television news shows feature stories that are really ads for the other news shows or entertainment programs found on that channel. For example, the stars of shows, the behind-the-scenes stories of the docudrama that just aired, the clothes that were worn, or the parties that took place after the awards shows that just aired, and so on are promoted as if those stories were legitimate news and not ads or plugs, in the process further blurring the lines between news and entertainment.

In an article in the now defunct *Brill's Content*, Eric Effron lamented that NBC news became a "carnival barker"[14] to promote the NBC miniseries *The 70s* (2000). *The 70s*, a sequel to NBC's successful miniseries *The 60s* (1999) touched on key events during that period, possibly justifying NBC's decision to inundate

---

[11]Meg James, "In-Show Product Pushing Chided," *The Los Angeles Times*, November 14, 2005, C-1.

[12]John Furia Jr., "Plot Line: Drink Pepsi," *The Los Angeles Times*, October 23, 2005, M-1.

[13]Furia, "Plot Line," M-6.

[14]Eric Effron, "And This Just In?" *Brill's Content*, July/August 2000, p. 44.

news shows with stories about the 1970s, stories that would, of course, promote the miniseries. The bottom line is that media's emphasis on synergy, cross promotion, and brand building encourage using news as promotion platform, even if ethical considerations are sidelined in the process.

You Decide

- In his article "Ad Infinitum: When Product Placement Goes Too Far," Joe Mandese noted that according to a media study, 66% of magazine readers assume that advertisers pay for the references to brands that appear in consumer magazines.[15] Does this figure seem about right to you? When you note a reference to a product in an article, do you assume that it's a paid mention?

- Do you find branded entertainment a cause for concern in terms of violating ethical norms? If so, why? If not, why? Similarly, do you feel there's anything ethically problematic about blurring the line between entertainment and advertising?

- Do you feel that networks are violating Section 317 of the FCC regulations when they engage in product placement and product integration? How do ethical considerations affect your analysis?

- A producer approaches the director and the writer and says that he can only raise enough money to make a film if he accepts an offer from an advertiser to include a 10-point story line about shoes. Ten points here means five visual references and five dialogue references. The film in question is about teenagers who form a hip-hop group. What would you say if you were the director or the writer? What if the story were about a couple who take an African safari? Do you think financial realities could or should determine the nature of the story based on the sponsor's needs?

- What for you constitutes "selling out" in terms of branded entertainment? What is the *H*arm in selling out?

- Many who are concerned about branded entertainment have called for a *C*ode of ethics that would require clear disclosure. If you were assigned to create such a *C*ode, how would you set it up?

- *E*valuate from an ethical perspective the use of news programs to promote other shows?

- As an exercise, count the number of times a news program, such as the national nightly news, promotes an upcoming segment as if it were news. Does this practice violate journalistic ethics?

308

VIRTUAL ADVERTISING

The technology exists to digitally insert ads just about anywhere. Video insertion technology allows products not originally there to be digitally placed or replaced. Sports broadcasting, for example, has for many years superimposed changing ads behind home plate or on stadium walls, ads that are featured prominently in the broadcasts but that are not actually visible at the games.

[15]Mandese, "Ad Infinitum," p. 12.

Advances in technology have made it possible to substitute a can of Pepsi for a can of Coke if the sponsorship for a program changes, in syndication, for example. Or the next time, 7-Up can be featured if 7-Up sponsors a subsequent airing. This example is from television, but digital insertion applies to films as well.

So the question for us becomes, how ethical is it to place a product in a work when the original contained no such advertising? Doing so might provide needed revenue, particularly if one is able to click on the visual of the inserted product to purchase it, but is it ethical and does it violate an artist's initial intent? Contracts may need to stipulate that no ads will be inserted or that only a small number of insertions will take place. Although with modern technology video insertion is certainly doable, media observers ponder if technology should be used in this way.

In an article titled, "Video Insertion and Virtual Product Placement: A Way to Combat TiVo—or a Fall Over an Ethical Cliff?" media commentator Lawrence A. Wenner observed, "A key ethical concern over video insertion technology mirrors one of its main strengths: It makes insertions look like something that was there all along."[16] Inserting products into program content makes viewers believe that the ads were intended to be there, in a very real sense, tricking viewers into seeing the ads as part of an organic whole.

309

In movies, virtual ads can help cover mounting production costs. The more products placed in a frame, the more money that can be salvaged. In television, the practice makes sure viewers can't skip commercials, as they can with devices like TiVo. Studies indicate that some 40% of consumers who could fast-forward through commercials do not, but the practice of video insertion technology nevertheless raises a number of key ethical concerns, as discussed.

OTHER WAYS TO MARKET

The film *Brokeback Mountain* (2005), the sad love story of two cowboys based on the novella by Annie Proulx, became a cultural phenomenon. Dialogue from the film, such as "I wish I knew how to quit you," became part of the national dialogue; the Internet was flooded with fake ads that parodied (or copied) the film's poster, which featured stars Jake Gyllenhaal and Heath Ledger.

[16]Lawrence A. Wenner, "Video Insertion and Virtual Product Placement: A Way to Combat TiVo—or a Fall Over an Ethical Cliff?" *Media Ethics*, Spring 2003, p. 23.

One of the circulated ads featured President Bush and Vice President Cheney titled *Dumbf*** Mountain*; another had convicted lobbyist Jack Abramoff and disgraced Republican whip Tom DeLay in a movie called *Kickback Mountain*; their friendship often questioned by homophobes, Bert and Ernie from *Sesame Street* also were in an ad simply called *Brokeback Mountain*. These fake ads touched on *Brokeback Mountain's* notoriety, allowing pundits a chance at creativity.

An actual ad, one for *The Ringer* (2005) starring Johnny Knoxville, also parodied the *Brokeback Mountain* ad. *The Ringer* is the story of a man, played by Knoxville, who pretends to have Down syndrome to pay off a debt by winning the Special Olympics. In the ad, Knoxville is in the foreground with a Special Olympics participant in the background, using the same positions Gyllenhaal and Ledger used in the *Brokeback Mountain* ad. *The Ringer* ad was intended to create awareness and boost box office by tapping into a cultural phenomenon, but one can nevertheless question its appropriateness from a moral or ethical point of view.

Some marketers use billboards to promote a project. Driving along Sunset Boulevard in Los Angeles, a street known for its billboards (Figure 13-4) almost as much as the roads that lead to Las Vegas, one is struck by the power of billboards as marketing tools. What should a billboard contain to draw attention? Some are in favor of catchy graphics or slogans; some want beautiful ultrathin people to hawk a product; some favor celebrities; and some, of course, want a sexual component. Sex does not always sell, as numerous studies have shown, but the adage that sex sells is tough to ignore, even if boundaries are crossed in promoting sex to entice commerce.

Sometimes, selling sex causes a billboard to be removed. As a case in point, the billboard for Vincent Gallo's *The Brown Bunny* (2004) was deemed a pollutant on Sunset Boulevard, forcing it to be taken down. The billboard for the adults-only film was a photo of Chloë Sevigny performing oral sex on Gallo, as she does in a graphic, nonsimulated scene in the film. The poster showed the back of Sevigny's head. One did not see Gallo's erect member in her mouth, as in the film, but the billboard clearly indicated that oral sex was taking place.

The billboard company, Regency Outdoor Advertising, made the decision to remove *The Brown Bunny* poster. The removal upset the film's distributor, Wellspring, who sought to turn this act of censorship into a cause célèbre, much in the way that Harvey Weinstein might do, as discussed earlier in this chapter.

FIGURE 13-4
Filling a blank billboard on Sunset Boulevard in Los Angeles, California, with images of beautiful people is a time-tested marketing ploy. (iStockphoto.com #377441, Luis Carlos Torres.)

Another billboard that caused a controversy was the one for *Get Rich or Die Tryin'* (2005), a movie partially based on the life of rapper 50 Cent, also known as Curtis Jackson. The poster showed a man from the back with his arms outstretched; in one hand he held a gun, in the other a microphone, symbolizing the choices 50 Cent faced, a life of crime or a life with music as an escape. People objected to the poster, saying that it glorified crime and that should not be put up near schools where children might see it as promoting gun violence.

That other posters also prominently feature guns, such as the one for the Brad Pitt/Angelina Jolie vehicle, the very popular *Mr. & Mrs. Smith* (2005), didn't seem to be of concern. In the poster for *Mr. & Mrs. Smith*, a film about a married couple who are hired assassins contracted to kill one another, both stars carry guns. Angelina Jolie has her gun in her garter, and Brad Pitt is holding his in this hand pointing it downward.

Though one could say that the *Mr. & Mrs. Smith* glamorized the use of guns as carried by two attractive superstars, making guns appear sexy and fun, there was no outcry over the poster. On the other hand, the poster for *Get Rich or Die Tryin'* was deemed inappropriate. Pitt's gun is pointed downward, whereas 50 Cent's is held up and pointed, ostensibly ready to fire. Does that make the guns in the *Mr. & Mrs. Smith* poster less threatening? If one sees guns as traditional phallic symbols, is Pitt's gun flaccid or at rest while 50 Cent's is not, increasing the threat?

Some saw a racist component to the reaction to the 50 Cent poster. A black man with a gun is somehow more threatening than Caucasians with guns, fostering a kind of double standard in marketing strategies.

You Decide

312

Do you feel guidelines or *C*odes of ethics are needed for virtual advertising? Do you think that the spoof ad for *The Ringer* that parodied the *Brokeback Mountain* ad was appropriate? Would you define that ad as an homage to a popular film? Would you define it as exploiting people with Down syndrome? Was it simply clever marketing and not really offensive to anyone? Was it trying to create controversy? Does your *E*valuation of the ad from an ethical perspective depend on whether or not you have seen the movie? Be prepared to argue a number of different positions. Remember that many successful people in media have debate in their backgrounds, precisely because they are able to think on their feet and to argue different positions. Below are some additional situations for you to *E*valuate.

- How ethically appropriate do you think it was for a poster promoting the film *The Brown Bunny* to depict oral sex?
- What *H*arm, if any, do you see from displaying guns in posters and billboards? Does it make a difference who is holding the gun?
- Observe some posters that are posted in the area where you reside. Do any of them raise questions connected to our E*T*H*I*C*S rubric?
- Do you think that ethical concerns about advertising are less important than the effectiveness of a campaign that generates interest and leads to sales?

CREATING TELEVISION PROMOTIONAL SPOTS AND ETHICS

Howard Schneider (Figure 13-5), senior vice president of on-air promo operations and administration at the CW, has been creating television promotional spots for more than 25 years; these spots inform audiences about current and

FIGURE 13-5
On-air promo specialist Howard Schneider found it difficult early in his career to create a promo for a telefilm about a father who burned his son. (Courtesy of Billy Schneider.)

upcoming shows. For Schneider, every promo raises some kind of ethical dilemma in the creation of a spot that tells an enticing story in 30 seconds or less. Difficult decisions need to be made about what to emphasize in a promo in order to sell a particular show, keeping in mind that promos are designed to attract new viewers, not the ones already watching.

Emphasizing sex or murder may tease viewers who are seeking edgy material into watching a show, though others may find such an emphasis unsavory. If you pander to one constituency, you risk offending another.

Over the years, many members of Congress and the Senate, as well as opponents of violence in the media, have complained about the media's juxtaposition of sex and violence. This technique caused a furor when it was used in the classic television show *Miami Vice* (1984–1989) starring Don Johnson and Philip Michael Thomas. One episode was so egregious in its use of this juxtaposition that NBC decided it could not be rerun on the network. Similarly, any promo seeking to tell its 30-second story by mixing sex with violence encounters stiff opposition.

In Schneider's view, decisions about juxtapositions in promos are up to the individual producers in charge of creating the spots. If he or a Broadcast Standards & Practices executive feels a line has been crossed in a promo, discussions ensue, often resulting in edits or changes. Broadcast Standards & Practices screens all promos at the CW, and at other networks, for approval for air, and some promos are restricted to particular time slots because of adult content.

Schneider adds that because of the Super Bowl wardrobe malfunction in 2004, the FCC fines are so severe that extra scrutiny and diligence are needed to ensure the acceptability of all promos. He adds that a good promo can suggest something that may not be there, that promos often show a lot less than viewers imagine. Nevertheless, a producer of promos has to be cautious. As the CW has a family-friendly brand, Schneider has to be extra careful not to push the envelope too far in seeking to attract viewers.

The most frequent complaint that Schneider hears is about what he calls "misdirection." Another term here would be "misleading." In other words, with misdirection, a promo teases something that is not really in a show. Schneider acknowledges the ethical dilemma involved here, saying it's never his intention to lie; however, promos are designed to sell a show. If an episode is weak and contains no strong dramatic elements, the promo for that episode might have to feature something out of context or to create drama where none existed, in the process possibly misdirecting or misleading some viewers.

Schneider adds that personal doubts or questions often take second place to the demand of the job of making promos. This conflict represents the ongoing tug of war between one's personal ethics and one's job. It's the position of this text that one cannot view ethics in isolation. One has to view ethics in the context of the real world while doing one's best to adhere to a personal *C*ode of ethics.

Asked what was the most difficult promo he ever worked on from an ethical perspective, Schneider didn't hesitate for a moment. Though it was made decades ago, Schneider quickly named the promo he created for the ABC television movie *David* (1988). This promo made him seriously question if he should be in the business of making promos.

David, starring John Glover and Bernadette Peters, directed by John Erman and written by Stephanie Liss, is based on the true story of a man who sets fire to his six-year-old son. This is the story Schneider was asked to promote. At the time, Schneider had a six-month-old son, making the subject of the film particularly troubling as he struggled to create a spot that implied that the son was being set on fire without actually showing it. He had to avoid justifying the father's action while nevertheless creating enough sympathy or empathy to get viewers to tune in for this kind of story. For Schneider, once the decision was made that the film would be produced, it became his job to create the best promo that he could, putting personal conflicts aside. Interestingly enough, *David* was watched by large numbers of viewers, attaining a 30 share and becoming the 11th most watched television movie of the 1988–1989 season.

ARE ETHICS AT PLAY IN ACCEPTING OR REJECTING A PROMOTIONAL SPOT?

A number of factors influence the acceptance or rejection of a television promo. In this section, let's look at a couple of promos that were rejected by the networks and *E*valuate why they were turned down and what part ethics might have played in the rejections. Let's also look at a promotional screening that was canceled.

ABC Television Network's Advertising Standards and Guidelines state that ABC has the right to (1) accept or reject at any time advertising for any product or service submitted for broadcast; (2) require elimination or revisions in advertising copy which violates the company's standards, policies, or guidelines, including federal, state, or local laws or regulations, or is otherwise contrary to the public interest; and (3) reject any advertising that could negatively affect ABC's audience.[17]

As noted previously in a different section of this chapter, networks don't approve of advocacy ads (i.e., ads that promote a particular point of view). This was the reason given in 2004 when NBC and CBS rejected an ad by the United Church of Christ that, depending on one's interpretation, welcomed all worshippers or claimed that other denominations excluded gay men and women. Regarding this rejection, Alan Wurtzel of NBC is quoted in *The Los Angeles Times* saying, "We do not accept commercials that deal with issues of public controversy."[18]

PBS station WNET in New York rejected a spot for the film *Kinsey* (2004) starring Liam Neeson as Alfred Kinsey and Laura Linney as his wife, written and directed by Bill Condon of *Chicago* (2002) and *Dreamgirls* (2006) fame. The

[17]ABC Television Network, Advertising Standards and Guidelines, July 2006, p. 5.

[18]Elizabeth Jensen, "Church Complains About CBS and NBC Rejecting Ad," *The Los Angeles Times*, http://sandiego.indymedia.org/en/2004/12/106908.shtml, accessed February 23, 2007.

FIGURE 13-6
For CBS's David Brownfield, religion is at the top of the list of controversial topics, one possible reason promotions for works that deal with religion at inopportune times are canceled. (Courtesy of David Brownfield.)

fact-based movie told the story of the sex researcher who published *The Kinsey Report* in 1948 revolutionizing the subject of sex. Conservatives such as Judith Reisman, the president of the Institute for Media Education and one of the co-authors of *Kinsey, Sex and Fraud: The Indoctrination of a People* (1990), have demonized Kinsey and his work, accusing him of pedophilia and of using bogus scientific methods in his research. Fear of a conservative backlash as well as viewer complaints appears to have caused the rejection. Plus, sex research remains a volatile topic more than 50 years later.

After Pope John Paul II died in 2005, the cable network Showtime canceled a Boston promotional screening and discussion for *Our Fathers*, its television movie about the church sex scandals in Boston. Religion is clearly a sensitive topic in today's media landscape. In fact, CBS's David Brownfield (Figure 13-6), senior vice president of current programs, says religion is at the top of the list of sensitive or controversial concerns.

Showtime's programming philosophy is to go after controversy and to do shows that receive awards; in electing to make *Our Fathers*, the network wanted to address the timely, controversial topic of the scandals in a film, yet it postponed a promotional screening following Pope John Paul II's death. There are a number of ways to *E*valuate the cancellation. Does it mean that Showtime's commitment to the film was wavering? Why schedule a screening in Boston? Was the locale selected because that's where the story took place and people would be interested, or was it selected to "stick it" to Boston by reminding the town that the scandal had taken place there? Was the cancellation simply the responsible thing to do?

One of my duties as a Broadcast Standards editor was to alert my superiors if any of the upcoming programs featured people who had just died. Back then, programs featuring recently deceased performers were pulled out of sensitivity to the family. It was seen as a matter of taste. Lots of last-minute scrambling took place to replace a program, but it seemed like the ethical thing to do, which may have factored into Showtime's decision to cancel the screening for *Our Fathers*.

MILLION-DOLLAR FRAUD

As we have seen, there are many ways to market or promote a work, necessitating a number of key decisions involving key ethical norms. In this section, let's examine a trailer that left out a major story line, causing some to wonder if it was a case of fooling audiences or if it was simply smart marketing, even if the deletion misled the public.

The ads and trailers for *Million Dollar Baby* (2004)—directed by and starring Clint Eastwood and the film that won Hillary Swank her second Academy Award as Best Actress, following her success with *Boys Don't Cry* (1999)—avoided any mention that the film was about euthanasia. In truth, many saw *Million Dollar Baby* as a justification for the practice, though one would not know this from the trailers and advance publicity.

In the film, Frankie Dunn, played by Eastwood, agrees to help Maggie Fitzgerald, Swank, commit suicide. Instead of focusing on the ethical dilemma that Frankie faced when confronted with Maggie's request for assistance, the promotion of the film focused on the underdog aspects of the story, namely Maggie's persistence to follow her dream of becoming a boxer when everything is stacked against her.

Simply put, was the film an advocacy piece in favor of euthanasia disguised as a feel-good story about an underdog who manages to achieve her dream? One can debate if the film is or is not a defense of euthanasia; however, the promotion of the film clearly avoided any reference to the importance mercy killing played in structuring the story. Was this smart promotion, or was it a trick designed to fool or mislead audiences into buying tickets for one kind of a film but giving them a totally different one?

Granted, marketers had to sell *Million Dollar Baby*, but some might insist that ethical lines were crossed in the way the trailers misdirected audiences. Also granted that the ending of a film shouldn't be given away in a trailer (though some do, essentially telling the entire story so that it becomes pointless to actually go see the movie), but there is such a thing as false advertising, something *Million Dollar Baby* may well be guilty of.

You Decide

- What ethical decisions do you feel should be considered in the creation of television promos or movie trailers? After reading the section about CW's Howard Schneider and his work on *David*, how would you *E*valuate the conflict between ethics and doing one's job?

- In the case of the trailers for *Million Dollar Baby*, do you feel there was or was not something unethical about the misdirection of the promotional trailers? If this is a topic that interests you, do some research on the organizations that protested what they saw as the message of the film, namely that the film promotes mercy killing as a gesture of kindness or humanity. See, for example, what organizations like the National Spinal Cord Injury Association (www.spinalcord.org) or Not Dead Yet (www.notdeadyet.org) had to say.

- Come up with a working definition of the term "advocacy." What role do you think ethics might play in creating parameters for advocacy programming?

- Discuss Showtime's making of a film about the sex abuse scandals involving Catholic priests. Are these scandals suitable material for a telefilm? How much time

do you think has to elapse before tackling a tragedy in a film? Because Showtime decided to make *Our Fathers*, should it have canceled the promotional screening after the death of Pope John Paul II? What role do ethical considerations play in your *E*valuation?

- Do you think a work that features a person who has recently died should be postponed or canceled? After the 2007 Academy Awards, a disgruntled relative took out a full-page ad in *Daily Variety* complaining that his father had not been recognized in the yearly tribute to the industry members who had died the previous year. According to him, the academy responded to his request by saying that not everyone can be recognized. So the questions here become who decides what show should be postponed or canceled and who decides that someone's death is or is not important enough to warrant an industry tribute?

- What do you think constitutes false advertising in television promos or theatrical trailers? In answering this question, do any particular promos or trailers come to mind? Have you, for example, felt that you had been tricked by a misleading sell?

This chapter concludes our journey to examine some of the ethical issues associated with media. It's my sincere hope that this text has been successful in enabling you to use the E*T*H*I*C*S rubric to make sound ethical evaluations that reflect the realities of the marketplace. If ethics are viewed in isolation with no regard for the workplace, unrealistic, ivory-towered pronouncements ensue, which risk making ethics far too other-wordly and of no real assistance to media practitioners. Ethics need to be a vital part of the global marketplace. If the marketplace always wins, there is little chance for ethical considerations to make a dent. On the other hand, if rigid rules about what is and is not ethical are superimposed onto the marketplace with little or no regard for how business is conducted, there again is little chance for ethical considerations to be acknowledged. It's vitally important to keep asking ethical questions and confronting ethical issues as we venture into the global marketplace.

Index

INDEX

INDEX

323

INDEX

325

INDEX